THROUGH STREETS
BROAD AND NARROW

A History of Dublin Trams

Michael Corcoran

Ian Allan
PUBLISHING

I dedicate this book to my family
Nellie, Janet, John, Elaine
and to Michael

First published in hardback 2000
This updated paperback edition 2008

ISBN 978 0 7110 3336 8

Published by Ian Allan Publishing

an imprint of Ian Allan Publishing Ltd,
Hersham, Surrey, KT12 4RG
Printed in England by Ian Allan Printing Ltd,
Hersham, Surrey, KT12 4RG

Designed by
Midland Publishing
and Stephen Thompson Associates

Code: 0804/B1

Visit the Ian Allan Publishing website at
www.ianallanpublishing.com

CONTENTS

Title page picture:
Although only the Dartry, Terenure and Dalkey routes remained in operation when this College Green scene was photographed in 1947, there are no less than nine trams in the picture. Nearest to the camera is Bogie Luxury Saloon No 294, the high-domed car built in 1933 that was one of five originally allocated to the Howth line. It was the last tram from Howth on 29th March 1941, subsequently working the Dalkey route until July 1949.

The advertisements suggest that the Standard Saloon behind No 294 is possibly No 246. The next tram is Luxury Saloon No 57, new in 1935 and the last tram to Terenure on 31st October 1948. Beside No 294 is one of the 220 Leyland Titans that replaced a roughly equal number of trams in 1938-40. The lorries in the picture are a Morris-Commercial and a Ford V8 belonging to CIE. Transport Museum Society of Ireland collection

Picture on opposite page:
Bogie Luxury Saloons Nos 93 and 294 are seen in Castle Street in Dalkey. Both these vehicles were formerly used on the Howth line being transferred to the Dalkey service when route 31 to Howth was closed in March 1941. The two trams lasted until the end of the Dalkey line in July 1949.
F N T Lloyd Jones

INTRODUCTION

TRAMS FASCINATE most visitors to Howth Transport Museum. People want to know all about them: when they were introduced, how the various systems worked and where the trams ran. There is constant puzzlement about their disappearance and much scepticism concerning the reasons. The imminent re-introduction of trams to Dublin has greatly increased the number of enquiries, with frequent expressions of interest in the history of a transport system many people believe should have been retained, improved and extended. There is also much curiosity about the relationship of the former system to the projected new one.

Ireland had three urban electric tramway systems, in Belfast, Cork and Dublin. The Belfast and Cork trams have been the subjects of books but Dublin's haven't. There have been several excellent papers, articles and pamphlets about the Dublin trams and innumerable references to them occur in other contexts. But the lack of readily accessible material has, unfortunately, led to inaccurate information being published and countless historical photographs wrongly captioned.

The absence of a book may be partly due to the Dublin United Tramways Company's early records being lost when the company's head office was destroyed during the Civil War in 1922. This unfortunate loss is exacerbated by the fact that several historically important details were known only to people long since deceased. It is also obvious that many events went unchronicled simply because they were so mundane as to be of little interest when they happened.

This Republic's culture has minimal appreciation of transport and its indispensable role in all our lives. We claim to be interested in history and heritage – but within limits. In film footage showing Dublin in the first half of the twentieth century we see the trams, but always as silent, spectral vehicles forming a mobile backdrop to events that have shaped our lives. Blissfully unaware of their significance, we still manage not to notice them.

A culture which, to the dismay of anyone interested in transport, banishes trams or other vehicles (and the people whose lives were bound up with them) to the background, has a diametric opposite in some transport literature. In this scenario, system histories are presented in a clinical vacuum, leaving readers who have a wider interest in social history wondering about the milieu in which a particular company or fleet operated. And, because elitist attitudes and esoteric jargon can easily alienate an uninitiated person trying to read up about some aspect of transport, a difficult balance must be struck in an effort to satisfy both general and specialist readers. The present volume sets out to do this.

This book is not intended to be a detailed history of the Dublin United Tramways Company but is an effort to explain how one of the top ten tramway systems (the seventh largest) in these islands related to civic and social progress. The Dublin trams, operating as part of a much wider system of public services, cannot be looked at in isolation from the conurbation's development or the lives of its citizens. Neither can the rise and supremacy, the decline and extinction of the Dublin tram be detached from contemporaneous events in broader historical frameworks.

Dublin's tramway system was at its zenith entering the second decade of the twentieth century. It survived the ravages, indigenous and international, of 1913-1918, even beginning a great renewal programme before the First World War ended. Amazingly, this process continued through the upheavals of 1920-1923, which so often affected the system and its staff adversely. During those grim years, the tramway service was one of the few things people could take almost completely for granted – no small tribute to those who operated it.

Still highly regarded in tramway circles during the twenties, the DUTC demonstrated how an obsolete, moribund tramway could be modernised when it took over and rebuilt the Lucan line. The company also became a highly successful bus operator, but unlike many concerns which replaced their trams, the DUTC continued to believe in them. It was the last big commercial company whose commitment to trams resulted in attractive new cars being built into the mid-thirties – a process that might have continued but for a change of management. Indeed, the DUTC system, suitably rationalised, would have formed a significant component of the city transport infrastruc-

Standard Saloon No 46, working the 15 Terenure route is heading towards the Rathmines junction of the Dartry line in CIE days. No 46 was built in 1925 and was scrapped following the abandonment of the Terenure route in October 1948.
F N T Lloyd Jones

ture which will have to be recreated in the future.

An integral and vital part of our past, the Dublin trams deserve better than to have been almost airbrushed from history. Every tramway system is unique in one or more respects, but Dublin's was different in so many ways that it should have engaged the attention of a much wider range of historians than those who devote their research exclusively to transport subjects. Views of this or any other transport network from varying historical perspectives at different times during its existence can be highly rewarding.

To set the tramway system in as wide a context as possible, various related aspects of Dublin's public services are described in three significant years. The earliest is 1872, when the first horse-operated lines opened. Going forward 32 years, 1904 stands out because the by then all-electric system was nearly complete – and is significant for Joycean scholars. Thirty-three years further on, 1937 is important; the last new trams had just entered service and the system was still largely intact, though towards the end of that year modern diesel-engined double-deck buses arrived in Dublin and would, within 12 months, begin to oust the trams.

For this book, having drawn on the work of those who had already written about Dublin's trams, I carried out further research, having noted – and checked – the reminiscences of former tramwaymen. This is essentially a story about ordinary people, passengers or staff, and the vehicles with which they were involved.

'Men who lived and died without a name
Are the chief heroes in the sacred list of fame'.

So wrote Dean Swift, and there are few groups to whom these words apply more appropriately than to Dublin's tramwaymen. They appear fleetingly on film, anonymous to all but their regular passengers who knew them personally and appreciated the excellent service they provided. Outside such close contacts, their vital role in the life of the city and the country has been all but ignored: crews without names on trams without numbers. This omission is made even more regrettable by the sheer grandeur and excellence of the tramway system, and that is not to ignore the DUTC's shortcomings, most particularly its appalling record of industrial relations and its concentration on a middle class clientele.

The trams themselves are of prime importance. They provided clean, efficient and reliable transport, one of the then seedy and ailing city's few positive assets. Most of the Dublin trams were built here and were as characteristic of the city as is its Georgian architecture. To those who knew the fleet, every tram was readily recognisable, even at a distance. The types found on a particular

Sandymount, one of the villages in the Dublin area which has managed to retain much of its identity, was served from 1872 by the Bath Avenue line. It obtained a second and more direct connection with the city, via the Ringsend route, in two stages: to the Grand Canal Dock (Victoria Bridge) in July 1900 and onwards to Nelson Pillar the following March. Shortly after the closure of this line in March 1940, No 263, which dated from 1926, was one of a total of 91 Standard Saloons withdrawn.
Camwell Collection, Tramway Museum Society

service, the slight structural differences or non-standard features of an individual car, a specific blend (or lack) of advertisements - such things unmistakably identified each tram. A source of pride to all involved with them, few people today realise the excellence of Dublin's trams and the distinction they so deservedly earned.

A daunting intricacy of the trams was the apparently haphazard fleet numbering system, which many transport historians have found impossible to fathom, much less record. The reason was simple: there were no numerical gaps, every new tram taking the identity of the one it replaced. In its final composition around the mid-1930s the nominal fleet of 330 passenger cars was of four main types, each represented in both four-wheeled (single truck) and eight-wheeled (bogie) form. However, the designation system resulted in many runs of four or five consecutive fleet numbers producing as many different types of tram. That so complex an enigma was disentangled and the results set out logically is due to a happy train of events.

Luckily, one set of records which survived substantially complete was the DUTC's car building and repair books. These massive and detailed volumes were the keys to deciphering most of the tram numbering mys-

teries. In the 1950s they were thoroughly perused by the late William Birney who already had an encyclopaedic knowledge of the trams as they would have appeared to an observant citizen.

With the information in the tram repair books, his own comprehensive notes and constant study of old photographs, especially those in the National Library collections, Bill Birney put together a formidable record of the cars. This has never been published but is now a central theme of this book. Such information is especially useful from a historian's point of view, because knowing at what period particular vehicles operated can be of tremendous help in dating street scenes, of which in Dublin's case there is, luckily, a cornucopia.

Through Streets Broad and Narrow attempts to make amends to the tramwaymen and their trams. It tries to bring them centre stage from their accustomed, barely perceived, background role, and consciously names people and catalogues vehicles. To maintain a semblance of chronological narrative, certain themes are followed in various chapters, causing some unavoidable overlaps.

Conflicting accounts have made it difficult to be precise about some events, prolonged investigation has failed to throw any light on others. An example concerns the relationship between the track network and the services. Apart from the permanent and well-known services, many of which have survived as extended bus routes, there were several short-lived or recondite workings, some of them now impossible to trace accurately. The result is that there are omissions, but after ten years of research, preparation and verification it is time to publish, even if some details cannot be pinned down dogmatically. So, I apologise for what has been left out and hope that this volume will appeal to Dubliners, students, historians

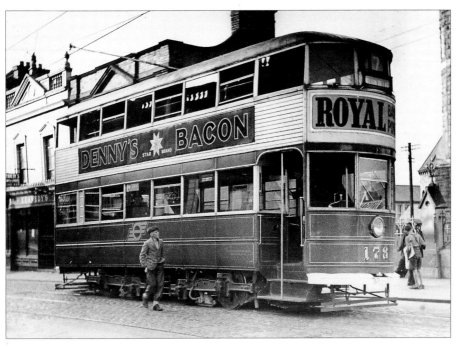

Bogie Luxury Saloon No 178, which was built in 1931, is seen in Dun Laoghaire in 1947, working a service on route No 7. This was one of the trams to have exposed narrow planking along the sides of the upper deck. There were some cars with wider planking but most had exterior cladding in aluminium or steel. No 178 was the last Luxury Saloon to leave the city centre on the night of 9th July 1949, the last time in the twentieth century when the streets of Dublin were graced by the sight of tramcars in public service. A R Spencer

and transport people, or anybody who likes trams. I also look forward to hearing from those people who may, over the years, have uncovered the gems of knowledge I have failed to unearth.

Protocols

Decimal currency and metric measurement were still far in the future throughout the operational life of the Dublin tramways. Trying to write down numbers relating to wages, costs, and fares therefore presented a problem; very few of the imperial units translate exactly into modern equivalents. I hope that my solution of quoting the original figures will be acceptable. The information and examples given below will assist readers in converting from one system to the other.

Money

Up to 1971, our money was in pounds, shillings and pence. There were 240 pennies in a pound, 12 pence in a shilling and 20 shillings in a pound. Amounts were expressed in various ways: £2.67½ could be written as £2.13.6, £2 13s 6d or £2/13/6. 25p could be written as 5s 0d or 5/-. The coins in general use were ½d, 1d, 3d, 6d, 1/, 2/- and 2/6. The 2/- coin was often referred to as a florin, the 2/6 as a half-crown. Slang titles for particular coins included a make (½d), wing (1d), tanner (6d), bob (1/-)

Metric Measurements

Until the changeover to the metric system, imperial units were used to express all dimensions. Exact conversions from one system to the other are extremely difficult and as all dimensions relating to the tramways were imperial, they have been retained throughout the text. There were 12

inches in a foot, 3 feet in a yard; a mile was made up of 5,280 feet or 1,760 yards. In engineering drawings, various scales were used: three quarters of an inch to the foot was expressed in a representative fraction of 1:16, a half-inch to the foot was 1:24. Three different sets of scales were used in various professions: surveying, architecture and mechanical engineering. A dimension of one foot and six inches could be expressed as eighteen inches, 18in or 1ft 6in. A metre contains 39.37 inches, a mile is the equivalent of 1.609 kilometres and a kilometre equals 0.62 of a mile.

In weight measurement, a pound (lb) is equal to 0.454kg, a quarter (28lbs) equals 12.7kg, a hundredweight (112lbs or 4 qrs) is 50.8kg and an imperial ton is 1,016kg. Imperial tare weights were usually quoted on vehicles in terms of tons, hundredweights and quarters, for example 7 tons 15cwt 2qr would appear on a modern vehicle as 7.788kg.

Technical Terms and Nomenclature

When technical terms appear for the first time, their meaning is explained. Where possible, I have refrained from using jargon in favour of simple English.

Names and their presentation have changed a lot in the past hundred years. To place such changes in their proper historical perspective, I have endeavoured to quote the titles in use at the time particular events took place.

Acknowledgements

In the course of my research I have been greatly assisted by many individuals and the staff of a number of institutions to whom I am deeply indebted for their courteous assistance. Staffs of public institutions we

tend to take for granted went out of their way to help. These organisations were; the Central Statistics Office, Coras Iompair Eireann, Dublin Bus, Dublin City Archives, the Garda Museum, the Gilbert Library, the Institution of Civil Engineers in Ireland, the National Archives, the National Library, the Public Record Office, Kew and the Royal College of Surgeons in Ireland.

Among the many newspapers and other publications from which I have quoted, the following are the most prominent: *Evening Herald, Evening Mail, Evening Press, Evening Telegraph, Freeman's Journal, Irish Builder, Irish Independent, Irish Press, Irish Times, Tramway and Railway World* and *Tramway Review.*

Friends and colleagues in the worlds of transport and preservation and in the public services, made great efforts to ensure that this work would be as accurate as possible. The following individuals must therefore be thanked for the help and guidance they have provided in the course of my research: Joe Collins, David Cooke, Ronald Cox, Michael Doyle, Eugene Field, Clifton Flewitt, Brendan Keane, John Kelleher, Jim Kilroy, Geoff Lumb, John Maguire and Cyril McIntyre. I hope I have not left anybody out, if I have it is due to a lapse of memory rather than any intentional discourtesy

It almost goes without saying that any errors or omissions are my responsibility and not those of the generous individuals mentioned above, who tried to keep me on track in the course of my research.

Michael Corcoran
Artane, Dublin
November 2000

Chapter One

THE HORSE TRAM ERA

Mid-Nineteenth Century Dublin

Dublin in the middle of the nineteenth century was a compact and intimate city. It was home to over a quarter of a million people, but the population was falling, dropping from 258,000 in 1851 to 254,000 in 1891. Bounded largely by the Royal and Grand Canals and the Circular Roads, the city had its impressive Georgian squares, majestic public buildings and the splendid thoroughfares laid out in the preceding 90 years by the Wide Streets Commissioners. Although no longer home to a parliament, Dublin had all the other attributes of a capital and was the second city of the British Empire.

Emphasising its imperial status, the city had no less than ten military barracks, with thousands of troops whose colourful uniforms brightened up the streets considerably. There was a large Civil Service, a Chief Secretary in Dublin Castle and the Lord Lieutenant who lived in the Viceregal Lodge in Phoenix Park. The city was also a centre of business and commerce in Ireland and had thriving professional and middle classes.

Much of the grandeur, unfortunately, was illusory, the facade of a city in continuous decline since 1801 when the Act of Union resulted in many people of wealth and influence transferring to London. Furthermore, because the Industrial Revolution had largely bypassed most of Ireland, Dublin did not attract the level of investment that contributed so much to the growth and prosperity of other cities in the United Kingdom. As a result, unemployment was endemic; deprivation and overcrowding were rife.

Formerly elegant Georgian town houses, especially on the north side, were in various stages of degeneration into the profoundly revolting slum status already reached by the many densely populated courts or yards of hovels which should have been long since demolished. Matters were further exacer-

bated by the prevalence of disease and the frightful mortality rate. Life expectancy was little more than half of what it is now. In a society saturated with snobbery and class distinction, social welfare was unheard of, while there was a profusion of workhouses, orphanages and penal institutions.

From about 1850 onwards, the cruel living conditions endured by so many urban dwellers of the period were being made primitively more tolerable with the introduction of the numerous life-enhancing public services taken for granted today. The main streets were lit by gas, manufactured by the Alliance and Dublin Consumers' Gas Company, a monopoly created out of the amalgamation of earlier, smaller undertakings. The previously questionable public water supply was being progressively replaced by the Vartry scheme, which still serves much of Dublin. This in turn enabled the drainage system to be developed and extended, thus improving public health and reducing the chances of contracting some of the many killer diseases then all too common.

Also greatly diminished were the dangers from fire, since the establishment, in 1862, of the municipal Fire Brigade. It had its

headquarters at the White Horse Yard off Winetavern Street, on part of the site now occupied by the Civic Offices, and a second station at Coppinger Row off South William Street. In 1872, the Brigade's then modern equipment included two Shand Mason horse-drawn steam pumps. Escape ladders were stationed at strategic points and could be wheeled or manhandled to where they were needed to effect a rescue. There was as yet no ambulance service, the Fire Brigade simply carried injured people to hospital on one of their equipment carts.

Policing in the city and environs was the responsibility of the Dublin Metropolitan Police, established in 1836. The police divisions were recognisably the forerunners of those in operation today, with the A and B areas south of the river, C and D being on the north side. The E Division covered the area from Irishtown to Kilmainham, taking in Rathmines, the Blackrock, Kingstown and Dalkey townships being in the F Division.

By 1870 the telegraph system, operated by the Post Office, had been in existence for some 18 years. A great boon to business people, who used it increasingly, this service was constantly being extended; a list of the telegraph offices was published in

A view of the tram terminus in College Green dating from around 1885. The single-decker in the centre of the picture was one of those acquired by the DUTC in 1881 from the North Dublin Street Tramways. This company favoured single-deckers, and to reduce costs even further, used only one horse with some of these vehicles.
Lawrence collection, National Library

Thom's Directory, a comprehensive source of information published annually and widely consulted. The telephone was, as yet, in the future.

Until well into the nineteenth century, many Dublin business people resided beside or over their offices and factories. The vast majority of employees lived within walking distance of their workplaces, perpetuating overcrowded living conditions in a city with little scope in its core for desirable residential development. A home in a pleasant suburb would obviously be attractive to anybody who could afford it, if there was a quick and efficient way of getting to and from it.

Railways and Commuters
Kingstown, one of several independent townships strung along the southern shores of Dublin Bay, was an attractive place in which to live. It became even more so when Ireland's first railway, the Dublin & Kingstown, opened from Westland Row in 1834. One of the world's earliest suburban lines, it carried growing numbers of well-to-do commuters from an early date, but at fares beyond the pockets of most people.

By 1860 there were additional railway termini at Kingsbridge, Broadstone, Amiens Street and Harcourt Street. Virtually no suburban traffic originated on the Kingsbridge (Great Southern & Western Railway) or Broadstone (Midland Great Western Railway) lines. However, the Dublin & Drogheda Railway's line into Amiens Street had some commuter traffic from Malahide and Howth. There was also the Harcourt Street line of the Dublin & Wicklow Railway which provided a relatively attractive suburban service, making a major contribution to the development of Bray.

Some country areas not served by rail had horse-drawn mail or other conveyances connecting them with the capital. The wealthiest citizens had their own carriages, while a variety of vehicles plied for hire to those who could afford them. Dublin had an extensive, well-organised system of cabs and sidecars by the middle of the century. The tables of fares or charges were widely known and the hazards or stands well publicised, the entire system being strictly regulated by the Dublin Metropolitan Police who carried out annual inspections.

Between the limited areas served by rail and those accessible only by the relatively expensive cabs, a real need awaited exploitation. Dublin, like most cities, lacked a convenient and comprehensive public transport system to move large numbers of people cheaply and efficiently into and out of the the city centre. The solution came from two sources.

Early Public Transport: Horse Buses
Blaise Pascal was a pioneer of urban public transport introducing a regular service of horse-drawn cars in Paris in 1662. Although these disappeared within a short time, the principle was revived more than 150 years later. In 1823 Stanislas Baudry was running vehicles in Nantes with the Latin fleetname 'Omnibus', literally, 'for all'. When George Shillibeer introduced a similar service to London in 1829, he adopted the same name, which soon became a generic vehicle description.

The success of this venture prompted some Dublin businessmen to start their own services in the city. In 1834 a new system of routes was announced but successfully opposed by the private hire vehicle operators, the jarveys, whose legal advisers were able to show that omnibuses would not comply with existing Dublin carriage laws.

This impasse continued until 1848 when a new Police Act facilitated the entrepre-

neurs and horse buses began operating legally on several routes. The various operators adopted imaginative names like Swift, Shamrock and Favorite. It must, however, be admitted that while the services provided were better than having to walk, horse buses were not the ideal form of public transport.

In the mid-nineteenth century, while the Dublin municipal area was still not nearly developed, even as far out as the North and South Circular Roads, residential areas south of the Grand Canal, which formed much of the city boundary, were expanding. Under the provisions of the Town Improvements Clauses Act of 1847 the Rathmines Township was established in the same year, having as its nucleus the eponymous village.

Over the succeeding half-century, the Rathmines Commissioners built up a highly acceptable level of amenities, including a comprehensive road network with public lighting, water and drainage systems. Boundary extensions brought Rathgar and Ranelagh into the township in 1862, Harold's Cross following in 1866 and Milltown in 1880. As much of the population was professional or middle-class with businesses in Dublin, the main road from Terenure, then still widely known as Roundtown, down through Rathgar and Rathmines and across the Canal into the city was an obvious choice for public transport. Such a facility was indeed provided by John Wilson, a former London omnibus proprietor who worked the route under the fleetname Favorite from the mid-1850s.

The Tram
To ease the burden on draught horses in mining areas, laying rows of heavy timbers end to end under wagon wheels had been practised for many years. The timber baulks were called trams. The word tram is believed to be of Scandinavian origin, meaning 'beam'. It continued to be used after wood gave way to stone and later, iron or steel. In New York in 1832, an Irish coachbuilder named John Stephenson designed and built a horse drawn carriage which ran on rails laid in the street. Compared to the omnibus, this afforded a much improved ride for the passenger and an easier draught

Sackville Street, Dublin, 1880.

A worn postcard showing No 9, one of the original Dublin Tramways Company's 1872 cars about to cross Carlisle Bridge en route for Nelson Pillar. There are no other trams in view, but the double lines diverging to give access to Westmoreland Street and D'Olier Street can be seen clearly. Carlisle Bridge was widened and renamed O'Connell Bridge in 1880 and the statue of Daniel O'Connell was unveiled in 1887. Although the change of name was proposed as early as 1884, Sackville Street did not officially become O'Connell Street until 1924. Lawrence collection, National Library

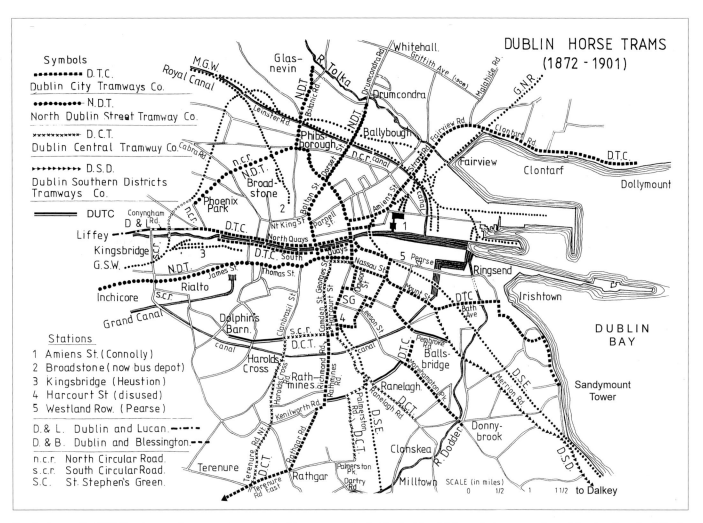

Symbols

●━━━●━━━● D.T.C.
Dublin City Tramways Co.

●●●●●●●● N.D.T.
North Dublin Street Tramway Co.

×××××××××× D.C.T.
Dublin Central Tramway Co.

▶▶▶▶▶▶▶ D.S.D.
Dublin Southern Districts
Tramways Co.

━━━━━ DUTC

Stations

1 Amiens St. (Connolly)
2 Broadstone (now bus depot)
3 Kingsbridge (Heuston)
4 Harcourt St (disused)
5 Westland Row. (Pearse)

D.& L. Dublin and Lucan. ━•━•━
D.& B. Dublin and Blessington. ━━•••
n.c.r. North Circular Road.
s.c.r. South Circular Road.
S.C. St. Stephen's Green.

DUBLIN HORSE TRAMS
(1872 - 1901)

for the horse. In 1859 Stephenson's concept crossed the Atlantic and spread through Britain and the European mainland, the vehicles becoming known as trams.

Legislation

Virtually every detail of tramway promotion, construction and operation was tightly controlled by legislation. There was a succession of statutes, beginning with the Tramways (Ireland) Acts of 1860 and 1861. Both of these enactments, amended in 1876, were more closely geared to the needs of rural light railways than to conventional urban street tramways. Promoters of street tramways preferred to deal with urban local authorities, corporations or town commissioners, rather than the rural Grand Juries, the predecessors of the County Councils.

The Tramways Act of 1870, which did not apply to Ireland, was the most important piece of primary legislation relating to tramways in urban areas. It laid down the method of application for tramway powers in Britain, each company having to promote its own bill. In these, everything from the names of the first directors, capital, exact routes and streets traversed, fares, carriage of goods and many other details had to be set out. The promoters' obligations to every

conceivable group or individual with which they came in contact were also specified. In drafting what they hoped would become Acts, Dublin tramway promoters liberally used or adapted those sections of the 1870 statute appropriate to their needs and circumstances.

In the various Acts, the safety and integrity of all other services in or under the route were protected and sweeping powers were conferred on the local authorities through whose areas the lines ran. Not only had the local surveyor or engineer to be satisfied about every line, its construction and maintenance, but the tramway company was also responsible for the upkeep of the roadway between the rails and for 18 inches on either side.

Orders in Council had to be obtained for the building of any line or group of lines and when these were built they had to be inspected and approved by a government examiner from the Railway Inspectorate, a body composed mainly of officers from the Royal Engineers. A specified time was allowed for the work to be carried out and unless very good reasons were advanced or a further Act obtained, the powers lapsed, usually after two or three years. Finally, when the service opened, bye-laws and reg-

ulations sanctioned by the Board of Trade had to be displayed in the trams and adhered to, and only the type of motive power specified in the empowering Act could be used on the tramway.

The City of Dublin Tramways Company

Under powers derived from the Tramways (Ireland) Act, 1860, the City of Dublin Tramways Company obtained an Order in Council in May 1867. This authorised the construction of a tramway linking the railway termini of Kingsbridge, Westland Row and Harcourt Street. It was to run via the South Quays, D'Olier Street, Great Brunswick (now Pearse) Street, Westland Row, Upper Merrion Street, St. Stephen's Green and Earlsfort Terrace; the proposed route lay entirely inside the Dublin city boundary.

There is some doubt as to whether construction actually began because of objections to the type of rail proposed which might give rise to complaints from other road users. However, the distinguished Dublin tramway official R S Tresilian, writing in *Tramway and Railway World* of 7th July 1910, stated that, 'an experimental piece of tramway was laid down on Aston's Quay, which, owing to the prejudices against, was shortly afterwards removed'.

The Dublin Tramways Company

In 1871, the rights of the City of Dublin Tramways Company, and the Rathmines omnibuses, were acquired by the Dublin Tramways Company, which had a capital of £240,000 and its Dublin office at 31 Lower Sackville Street though its head office was in London. The Board of Directors included George Richardson, John Humphrey and F H Collins, all of London; Dublin members were Frederick Barrington and William Leadbeater Barrington, Managing Director.

The DTC obtained its first Act in 1871, getting two more in 1873 and 1878. Under the 1871 Act, the company received authority for lines from the city centre to Clontarf, Glasnevin, Phoenix Park via North Circular Road, Terenure via Rathmines, Donnybrook, Sandymount via Bath Avenue and along the North Quays from Carlisle (now O'Connell) Bridge to Parkgate Street. The combined routes totalled nearly 17 miles, and work was to be completed within three years. William Barrington claimed that:

'The value of tramways is now genuinely admitted; but as a boon to the poor citizens and their families who live in dark, noisome and often pestilential lanes and alleys, who have now but little chance of refreshing their eyes with the bloom of the country scenery; or invigorating their emaciated frames with the sweet breath of heaven in a pure ozonic atmosphere, tramways could not be too much praised.'

This concern for the less affluent was partially reflected in the DTC Act which made provision for getting them to and from their places of employment at affordable fares. Section 68, repeated in several other Acts, stipulated that the company:

'must run at least two carriages each way every morning and evening in the week (Sundays, Christmas Day and Good Friday always excepted) at such hours, not being later than seven in the morning or earlier than six in the evening respectively, as the Company think most convenient, for artisans, mechanics and daily labourers at fares not exceeding one halfpenny per mile (the Company nevertheless not being required to take any fare less than one penny); provided that in case of any complaint made to the Corporation of the hours appointed for the running of such carriages, the Corporation shall have power to fix and regulate same from time to time.'

Barrington also believed in the ability of trams to impose some much-needed discipline on other traffic. Refuting the charge that Dublin's streets were too narrow to accommodate them, he said:

'Were tramways laid up and down Grafton Street, we should not be witnessing, every day, such a disgraceful confusion as results from the crowding pell mell together of full and empty cabs, chiefly the latter; lumbering omnibuses; Fishbourne's vans; private carriages; and every description of vehicle our city contains…Space would be saved on the roads by the narrower trams, because one tram could do the work of two omnibuses and four horses.'

Fishbourne's was a firm of carriers whose vans were a familiar sight in Barrington's Dublin. Pointing out that there was room in a properly regulated carrying trade for everybody, Barrington also spoke of his concern for the omnibus horses, which were subjected to great physical strain. He criticised the design of the buses and the access to them:

'…the passenger, at great risk if infirm, had two high steps to mount before he could get into the stuffy, close and crowded berth which often awaited him. It is very well and painfully known to most of the residents in the Rathmines township, that especially on wet mornings and evenings, the omnibus accommodation is very far from being adequate to the exigencies of the public.'

The Rathgar Line

Using the unobtrusive and generally acceptable grooved rail that was to become universal in street track, the DTC tackled the Terenure line first. Construction was en-

trusted to Messrs Fisher and Parrish, who had already laid down tramways in Liverpool and London. The work was pushed forward vigorously using box rail weighing 53lbs per yard spiked to longitudinal wooden sleepers and cross tied. Sett paving was laid between the rails and for 18 inches on either side. Apart from complying with the law, this arrangement also benefited the local authorities, Dublin roads having previously been surfaced in macadam. The cost of construction was £3,550 per mile of single line.

The service from College Green, quoted as St Stephen's Green by R S Tresilian, to Rathgar (Garville Avenue) via Dawson Street, St Stephen's Green, Harcourt Street and Rathmines, opened for traffic on 1st February 1872, using four cars; two more were expected imminently. The tramway, laid as was most future track in the Dublin area, to the Irish standard railway gauge of 5ft 3in, was later extended to Nelson Pillar and to Terenure, a total distance of 3½ miles. In Terenure Road, opposite St Joseph's Church, a depot was established; this premises was described in *Thom's Directory* as stables, carhouses and fitting shops.

On the first day, 2,055 passengers are reported to have been carried and two thousand souvenir tickets were issued. Produced by Waller and Company of Suffolk Street, these tickets depicted a double-deck tram pulled by two horses and bore a portrait of Queen Victoria.

The *Daily Express* praised the trams, which took 20 minutes to complete a single journey: 'the insides of the cars are richly cushioned in velvet and fitted all round with fitted plate glass windows and with sliding shutters of Venetian glass....the lamps are placed within ornamental plate glass compartments at the extremities, thus cutting off entirely any unpleasantness which might arise from the combustion of oil'.

More critical was the *Irish Times* which complained that: 'only a pair of horses are provided for each (tram) and these do not appear to be in breeding or stamina up to the mark. The omnibus (sic) was delayed for a considerable time in College Green from the horses being unable to start it. When once put in motion the draught is comparatively easy. A rather high tariff of 3d. for however short a distance is fixed and this may probably lead to opposition. As successors to the badly turned out antediluvian omnibuses hitherto plying on this route the Tramway carriages are an undoubted improvement if only in the desideratum of being properly lighted and properly driven at night.'

The paper went on to allege that most of the employees were Englishmen or foreigners and that this would lead to: 'a large number of hardworking responsible Irishmen being thrown out of employment'.

This was strenuously denied by the company whose service quickly settled down to its daily routine.

The Metropolitan Railway Carriage and Wagon Company of Birmingham built the Dublin Tramways Company's first trams. They had ten windows on each side and were described as 42-seaters, with longitudinal seating for 20 passengers inside and 22 back to back on a knifeboard seat on top. In practice these cars were regarded as 46-seaters, the precise capacity of vehicles with longitudinal seating being a frequent cause of arguments. These disputes centred on the seat space allowed to each passenger. The minimum laid down was 16in, but Dublin Corporation, exercising their supervisory powers at a meeting in January 1873, set the standard at 18in.

Fares

Following complaints, the 3d flat fare was abolished in favour of a system offering 1d stages, which attracted shorter distance travellers. Most of the Acts obtained by the early tramway companies permitted a fare of 2d per mile, with 1½d being allowed for what were called 'inferior carriages'. This often meant seats on the outside of a double-deck tram and would have been intended primarily for those artisans, mechanics and daily labourers who could afford to ride.

Except for a few years after 1944, fare levels were to remain a source of friction between operators and passengers throughout the entire tramway era. The Dublin trams were at all times, up to the formation of CIE, essentially a middle-class mode of transport provided by commercial companies whose principal motive was profit.

Relating the fares charged in 1872, or at any other time during Dublin's first tramway epoch, to a reliable and constant yardstick is difficult. The most widely used base is the consumer price index, with a 1914 benchmark of 100, to which fluctuations before and since can be most readily compared. Figures for the years before 1914 are somewhat haphazard, but the index for 1872 has been calculated at 120 and, with one or two blips, this dropped continuously over the following three decades. Assuming that the consumer price index for 1872 was ⅟₅₆ of that prevailing in February 1999, an 1872 penny fare would be slightly more than 23p at 1999 prices.

Kingsbridge-Earlsfort Terrace

The following notice appeared in the *Irish Times* on 3rd June 1872:

'THE DUBLIN TRAMWAYS COMPANY, New Arrangements. The Public are respectfully informed that on and after this day, June 3rd, the Tramway Cars will run between King's Bridge (near Phoenix Park) and the Exhibition Palace via:- South Quays to Carlisle Bridge, Great Brunswick Street, Westland Row, Merrion Square West, Stephen's Green East and Earlsfort Terrace. Fares will be Two pence in or out between King's Bridge and Carlisle Bridge, Two Pence in or out between Carlisle Bridge and Exhibition Palace and Three Pence for the whole way between King's Bridge and Exhibition Palace, or intermediate distances. The public are also respectfully informed that the Company have in course of adoption a system of voucher's tickets for fare which will not only serve as a check on the correctness of the receipts, but by allowing the public a rebate on the following scale, enlist their aid in the detection of dishonest practices, should they unhappily occur. To any one bringing 16 of these voucher tickets to the office of the Company, the value in money of a ticket of the corresponding amount will be paid thus:

For 16 Voucher Tickets 4d will be paid
For 12 Voucher Tickets 3d will be paid
For 8 Voucher Tickets 2d will be paid
William L Barrington, Managing Director
31 Lower Sackville Street'

A revival of the 1867 proposal, the new route was later known as the 'Three Stations' or Hatch Street Line, connecting the Kingsbridge, Westland Row and Harcourt Street termini. It initially catered for visitors to the Dublin Exhibition of Arts, Industries, and Manufactures at Earlsfort Terrace, and introduced what was arguably the first one-way traffic system in Dublin. Trams going to Earlsfort Terrace, went from Upper Merrion Street through Ely Place and Hume Street to St Stephen's Green, but on the return journey travelled by way of Merrion Row to Upper Merrion Street. The depot for this line was built at Victoria Quay, on the site later occupied by Guinness's transport garage.

Fares Again

On the day the new line opened, the *Irish Times* devoted considerable space to the subject of fares. The 3d fare on the Rathgar line had been raised to 4d on the previous Saturday, 1st June, and three letters of protest appeared in the paper on 4th June. The first writer, AE, was disillusioned: 'Allow me through the medium of your excellent journal to call the attention of the inhabitants of Rathgar to the fact that the Dublin Tramways Company have got the monopoly of the road and thinking themselves safe, advance the fares in place of reducing same. Now, what better off are we than when we had the Wilson omnibus? Many of the inhabitants, impressed with the idea that they would have cheap fares, signed the petition in favour of them, but I now find, on asking many their opinion, that they see their mistake to give the monopoly to any one company of this kind. It is really shameful to see the way the roads are cut up. Many gentlemen had to give up driving themselves into town, so many accidents occur since the establishment of tramway rails.'

A 'Family Man', was resolute: 'Allow me through the medium of your widely circulated journal to protest against the shameful conduct of the Directors or managers of the Rathmines and Rathgar Tramway Company, advancing the fares to four pence to Rathgar. Now, sir, I have been paying since they started, nine shillings a week for myself and six for my two daughters, who go into school every day. Now to our surprise on Saturday last, an extra penny each was demanded, which, in my case, would make twelve shillings a week for one family, so I have given orders that they are not to enter the tram cars again, but to take a cab every wet day only, and I am determined to walk in and out myself, so I will be saving twelve shillings a week. Now I think if many other families would do the same this company would find out that they have made a mistake by not reducing instead of increasing the fares.'

The third correspondent was angry: 'Would anyone inform me through The Irish Times what good we the inhabitants of Rathmines Township have gained by the establishment of this company's line of tramway cars – dear fares, bad roads, cruelty of horses, danger to life and limb – all this and more to accomplish what? The fares we had before, or to enrich an English tramway company? – A Very Old Inhabitant.'

The Sandymount Line

To the southeast of the city, separated from it by the Grand Canal, and bounded on the west by Rathmines, lay the Pembroke Township. It included the three maritime villages of Ringsend, Irishtown and Sandymount. The first two would not have been highly regarded in the 1870s but Sandymount was an attractive centre on which to base suburban development and there were several large houses in the vicinity. Established in 1863 and closely aligned with the Pembroke Estate, the Pembroke Town Commissioners, while not as blatantly commercial as their counterparts in Rathmines, nevertheless encouraged residential development. This further fostered the culture of commuting begun by the Dublin & Kingstown Railway. A tram service passing by or near the front door was more attractive than a walk to the nearest station.

The Sandymount route shared the tracks of the Kingsbridge-Earlsfort Terrace line from D'Olier Street through Great Brunswick (Pearse) Street, Westland Row and Lower Merrion Street. From here, Sandymount trams turned on to newly laid track in Merrion Square North, continuing via Lower Mount Street and across the Grand Canal, the city boundary, into Northumberland Road. Turning left at Haddington Road past Beggar's Bush Barracks and along Bath Avenue and Londonbridge Road, the line then went right, into Tritonville Road and along Sandymount Road. A one-way system brought an outgoing single line through Seafort Avenue on to Beach Road towards the terminus at Sandymount Tower. On the return journey trams left Beach Road at Newgrove Avenue to work the opposite leg of the one-way system, traversing Sandymount Green to resume two-way running at Sandymount Road. The depot was built at Gilford Road.

This DTC service opened officially on 1st October 1872 but there is some evidence that the entire line was not in regular use in its first days. It quickly demonstrated its ability to attract custom, as evidenced by a report in the *Freeman's Journal* on 19th February 1873. At the meeting of the Dublin, Wicklow & Wexford Railway held the previous day, the Chairman lamented the loss of 7,433 passengers from Lansdowne Road and Sydney Parade stations since the opening of the tramway. He also signalled the resolute opposition of his company to any proposals for a tramway serving the Blackrock area.

Litigation

From their earliest days, trams attracted considerable hostility from the drivers of other vehicles, especially cabs and sidecars. Those in charge of other horse-drawn vehicles were often guilty of speeding, officially described as furious driving; such individuals were widely referred to as 'Jehus', a title derived from the Book of Kings. Collisions were often caused by a combination of arrogance on the part of tramwaymen, who knew that their employers would usually prosecute the other driver, and the carelessness or malice of other drivers. On 21st October 1872, when two separate cases were heard before different courts, the magistrate in the Southern Division warned tram drivers and cabmen alike about their behaviour, saying that he would not tolerate further examples of what would today be regarded as road rage.

Just one week later, another of the numerous disputes which ended up in the courts was reported in the *Irish Times* of 28th October 1872, under the heading: 'OBSTRUCTING A TRAM CAR'.

Mr Michael Cauldwell of 14 Wexford street, the owner of cabs, was summoned by the Tramway Company for wilfully obstructing one of their cars at Carlisle Bridge, Westmoreland street and Dawson street, and also for having used insulting language to the driver. As it appeared, however, that it was one of the defendant's drivers committed the offence, and his number had not been given to his employer, his Worship dismissed the case.

Edward Dennis, a dray driver, was also summoned by the same company, and fined 30s for having caused damage to the amount of £2 to one of the cars by allowing his float to come in contact with it on the quays. Mr Ennis prosecuted on behalf of the company.'

While relatively trivial incidents like those just described were regularly decided in favour of the tramway company and its staff, accidents involving personal injury to other road users were treated very differently. In such instances, both driver and conductor were summarily arrested and charged, the decision to exonerate, even if they were clearly not to blame, being left to the courts.

How tramway companies managed their affairs and treated their passengers was always the subject of comment in the media. On 31st March 1873, the *Irish Times* commented: 'We are sure the prosperous Tramway Company will not hesitate to place indiarubber matting on the platforms of their cars in wet weather. The employees would be greatly benefited, and cars would be kept much more free from dust and damp than they are at present in rainy weather. The cost would be trifling, but advantages are not always measured by cost.'

Within a few days, fares were again in the news. Reduced fares for outside passengers, those travelling on the top deck, had been offered during the summer of 1872. Writing to the editor of the *Irish Times* on 31st March 1873, the ubiquitous and timeless Pro Bono Publico noted that the company: 'intend to resume the usual outside fares on the Rathmines line on Tuesday when the winter season will be over.'

He pleaded for the reduction of the inside fare to 2d. until the end of the summer and suggested that the reduced outside fare might be continued with advantage to the company.

Reporting Tramway Development

At the Dublin Tramways Company's half-yearly general meeting held on 20th March 1873 the company's progress was reviewed. The mileage open was 5½ to the end of September 1872, increasing to seven miles by mid-October and nine during the second half of that month. The company, details of whose income was published periodically, quoted the receipts for the week ending 25th January as being £805 3s 8d. By the date of the February meeting, they had 45 tramcars, 13 omnibuses and 412 horses.

The Donnybrook Line

In Pembroke Township, many of the pleasant suburban roads between the Grand Canal and Donnybrook were laid out or planned by 1870. The village itself had more or less lived down the reputation associated with its notorious fair, which ceased in 1855 and there was a likelihood of development continuing southwards towards the River Dodder. The Dublin Tramways Company undertook providing the obvious amenity of a tramway service within the terms of their 1871 Act.

Starting from Sackville Street, the Donnybrook trams shared the Terenure track as far as Dawson Street, then went by way of Nassau Street to Merrion Square North along which they used the Sandymount rails. They branched right along Merrion Square East, went up Lower Fitzwilliam Street, turned left into Baggot Street, and right again into Waterloo Road. Turning left on to Morehampton Road and through Donnybrook village the line terminated just beyond the Dodder at Donnybrook Church.

Opposite the church, a depot was built on part of the site now occupied by the (newer) Donnybrook Garage No 2 of Dublin Bus. Initially, there was no track leading into the building, the trams having to be moved in and out without the benefit of rails, powers to lay them not having been obtained. Other problems were experienced with the building of this line, for which William Barrington assumed responsibility. The DTC directors expected that the Donnybrook service would open by the end of February, and on 14th March 1873, the *Irish Times* carried the following report: 'The tramway system at present at work in Dublin has proved beneficial in even a greater degree than could have been anticipated. Besides the economy of time, labour and expense which it affords individuals, its public benefit includes the merit of inducing and educating popular sentiment towards such agreeable and advantageous locomotion. There are now nearly thirteen miles of tramways radiating from Nelson's Pillar. They have proved of the highest value to the citizens. Their establishment has been an unmixed good inasmuch as there has been no discernible falling off in the ordinary horse cab traffic. On the contrary, it would rather appear to have increased. As for the tramways themselves, it cannot be denied that they are well constructed, well laid and admirably kept. This excellent condition is largely due to the foresight and skill with which they were planned by Mr George Hopkins of London, the eminent tramway engineer and Engineer-in-Chief of the line whose ideas have been carried out in full integrity by Mr Wisdell, acting for the contractors, Messrs. Fisher and Parrish.'

Although the Dublin Tramways Company had powers for further development, the opening of its Donnybrook line effectively completed that company's route system south of the Liffey.

Further DTC Plans

The *Irish Times* report of 14th March 1873 relating to the opening of the Donnybrook line, went on to describe the Dublin Tramways Company's plans for further development of their system: 'The line between Dublin and Dollymount, opening up the extensive districts of the North Strand, Fairview, Clontarf and Dollymount, has been commenced and will be completed by the end of next month, thus providing a May day gift to the inhabitants of this hitherto neglected but promising locality. Immediately that the line is completed that to Glasnevin and the Botanic Gardens with a branch to the Phoenix Park will be in operation by the beginning of summer. Some idea of the scale upon which this revolution of transit to the city and suburbs is being carried out, may be derived from a statement of the extent of stabling and car shedding provided. Mr T Millard, the eminent builder, of Harcourt Street, is the contractor for this branch and his reputation as builder to the Board of Public Works, the Exhibition Building and other public enterprises is a guarantee that nothing but the highest style of excellence is attempted. The building works comprise accommodation of 210 horses and a proportionate number of cars at Kingsbridge; 150 horses at Terenure and extensive stabling at Donnybrook, Sandymount and Glasnevin. The most modern improvements have been introduced and it is a real pleasure for one to walk through these extensive premises and witness the care which has been taken

This drawing of a Metropolitan Railway Carriage and Wagon Company tram supplied to the North Dublin Street Tramways Company, shows clearly the principal features of the first generation of Dublin trams. Noteworthy are the spiral stairs or ladders, platforms with two entrances and knifeboard seats. Author's collection

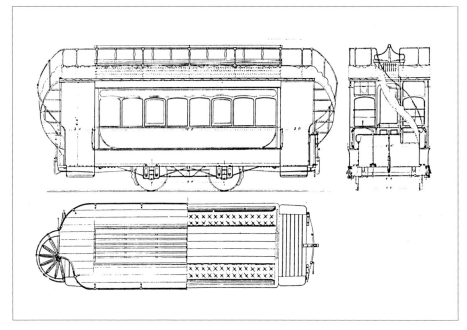

to ensure the health and comfort, and maintain the working capacity of the horses. Of this impressive condition of affairs much is due to the suggestive thoughtfulness of Mr Soutlair CE who has this department in charge.'

The mileage quoted by the *Irish Times* included the Clontarf line, still under construction. There were also apparent discrepancies in the report, which mentioned the Glasnevin line and premises, an area aspired to but never served by the Dublin Tramways Company. A line to Phoenix Park was later laid by the DTC, but not via Phibsboro.

North-East Dublin

While there was considerable development in the southern suburbs and townships, the smaller and less fortunate north side had not fared as well. As we noted earlier, many of the formerly fashionable houses in locations like Dorset Street, Henrietta Street and Gloucester (now Sean McDermott) Street had fallen into a sad state by 1870. Whole terraces of houses in and around Montgomery Street (infamous to Dubliners as 'Monto') had degenerated into brothels, further discouraging settlement by the middle classes. However, to the north-east of this unsavoury enclave there were substantial undeveloped districts where some building, mainly for tradespeople and artisans had taken place from the 1830s onwards, especially around the Ballybough and North Strand areas.

Much of the North Wall and East Wall district was as yet not built up but within it the railway system and the port were expanding. The services associated with these, and some primordial industry, helped the area to develop, but much of whatever traffic might result was not what the tramway company welcomed. In March 1878, Maurice Brooks MP, in a letter to the *Freeman's Journal* criticised the DTC's monopolistic and elitist attitude. He described the DTC as: 'very remunerative, and in some respects a useful institution, making excellent returns to the proprietors, and proving of great convenience to passengers of the genteel and well-to-do classes.'

Construction of the Dublin & Drogheda (later Great Northern) Railway embankment from East Wall Road to Clontarf created tidal

sloblands where Fairview Park is today. Through this and a culvert known as the Middle Arch (or to railwaymen, the Third Arch), under the railway and the present Dublin Area Rapid Transit (DART) depot, flowed the River Tolka, intensively used as a sewer. Litter-strewn and evil smelling, especially at low tide, the sloblands became ever more obnoxious. Local industry made things even worse, a vitriol works at Poplar Row contributing further to the insufferable condition of the sloblands.

Beyond the stone arch railway bridge, what is now Clontarf Road was, in the 1870s, rough and low-lying. This rendered it vulnerable to periodic submersion by the sea, which was immediately over the boundary wall. Particularly severe flooding occurred when there was a combination of high tides, easterly winds and heavy rain.

The village of Clontarf lay at the end of Vernon Avenue. There were some large houses in the area with incipient ribbon development along the main road, but it took some years to overcome popular prejudice to living in such a place. The Clontarf Town Commissioners who were in office by 1870 worked hard to improve both the image and physical environment of the area. They laid out roads and installed a rudimentary drainage system. Gas mains were extended across the city boundary, facilitating the provision of public lighting.

Horse buses had served Clontarf before the advent of the Town Commissioners. The Dublin Tramways Company, convinced that the area had reasonable prospects, obtained powers under their 1871 Act to construct a tramway along the same route. That the line would run beside the sea beyond Annesley Bridge, thus giving it only half a catchment, must have made its chances of reasonable profitability appear somewhat optimistic.

The Clontarf Line

From Sackville Street, Eden Quay and Beresford Place were originally intended to form part of the Clontarf route, going by way of Gardiner Street and Talbot Street to Amiens Street. Their supersession by two alternatives, via North Earl Street or Lower Abbey Street, plunged the scheme into controversy from the moment these routes were proposed. The Abbey Street option offered the advantage of width, serving both business and residential development, while the narrower North Earl Street was lined with shops but trams could put pedestrians at greater risk. Arguments for and against the alternatives were conducted vigorously, causing heated exchanges in the Council Chamber of the Corporation. Much to the disgust of the *Irish Builder* which accused them of selfish commercialism, the North Earl Street shopkeepers won though eventually rails were laid down over both routes.

The terminus was at Dollymount, making this line, at 4.1 miles, the longest of the DTC routes. A depot was established occupying part of the site where Clontarf Bus Garage is today. Contrary to popular belief, the licensed premises known as 'The Sheds' near the corner of Vernon Avenue, owes its name, not to the erstwhile tramway building (tram depots were often referred to as sheds, a term derived from railway usage), but to structures once used for processing shell fish.

Construction of the Clontarf line suffered some delays and before work was complete the local omnibus operators, O'Neills, were forced to relinquish the service because of their manager's ill health. The Dublin Tramways Company assumed responsibility for the omnibus service in March 1873 while they pushed work ahead on the tramway. They were able to arrange for the opening of the line between Amiens Street Station and Clontarf at 5.00pm on Friday 31st May 1873, Abbey Street being reached by September when outstanding work was finished. The fare for the journey was 3d.

As proved by the quickening pace of new building after their introduction, the trams made a major contribution to the development of Clontarf. This can be seen clearly in the way local roads became desirable locations for new residences when an attractive public transport system began to operate. When the tramway opened in 1873, there were some houses on the lower portions of the Malahide and Howth Roads, and on Vernon Avenue and the first houses on St Lawrence's Road were nearing completion. Within a few years, considerable building took place, all of it within convenient walking distance of the tramway.

All of the four tramway lines eventually laid from the northern suburbs into the city crossed the Royal Canal, the bridges over which had very pronounced approach gradients. By the time the Clontarf line was opened, the incline on the city side of Newcomen Bridge had been eased but there was still a considerable rise (which still exists) on the outer side. Human assistance was needed to supplement the horses' efforts to lift their burdens over the bridge and only two days after the service began, an accident occurred.

Patrick Quinn was among a group of men helping to push a tram up the incline at Newcomen Bridge. A wheel of the car unfortunately ran over his foot, causing severe injuries as a result of which tetanus set in and death ensued, an inquest being held at Jervis Street Hospital on 27th June. This tragic incident illustrates the cruelties of life at that time.

Proposed Corporation Workings

Powers granted to local authorities allowed them the use of the tramways in their areas for municipal purposes. Before its completion, there was already such a proposal to use the Clontarf line, and others still at the planning stage, for the benefit of the city.

Shortly after being reformed and reorganised in 1851, Dublin Corporation had appointed its first City Engineer. Parke Neville gave the city outstanding service through more than 30 years in office, tackling one project after another with great energy. Unfortunately, recalcitrant councillors and a lack of investment thwarted several of his progressive ideas. Among the many unpleasant problems he tried to solve was that of refuse collection and disposal, submitting a comprehensive report in March 1873.

Neville proposed setting up six transfer stations throughout the city, three on the north side and three on the south. At these, the refuse carts would, with the aid of special ramps, unload their contents into tramway wagons. These would be moved at night, when normal passenger traffic had ceased, over some as yet unconstructed lines to the Fairview sloblands. The resulting landfill would in time eliminate this increasingly vexatious nuisance. Regrettably, this scheme was not implemented for more than three decades.

Among the statistics quoted in Neville's report was one noting that a contemporary horse tram, fully laden, tipped the scales at 5½ tons. A two horse tram travelled at about 5 miles per hour and a trace horse was necessary for gradients steeper than 1 in 14. Neville envisaged two-horse wagons carrying three to four tons with extra horses as required. He also remarked that the Dublin Tramways Company's Act allowed only for animal haulage, steam being ruled out.

Hours, Wages and the First Strike

Costs and wage negotiations were important aspects of tramway operation right from the start, as evidenced by a letter in the *Irish Times* of 13th May 1872 from the staff. 'We, the drivers and conductors in the employ of the Dublin Tramway Company, respectfully beg, through the medium of your influential journal, to return our sincere and heartful thanks to the company, and especially Mr Barrington, the managing director, for the sympathetic and liberal manner in which they have met our solicitation for an advance of wages and shorter hours. We also cordially return our gratefelt thanks to Mr Kerrigan, the superintendent, for the generous and energetic spirit in which he placed our views before the company. Hoping you will see fit to place this before your numerous readers'.

Despite the foregoing, there was still unrest, a series of dismissals resulting in a strike on Saturday 19th July. Part of the problem lay in the employment of William Barrington's 16-year old son, purportedly to help his father. His mistakes included dealing with the staff in an arrogant and overzealous manner, his father later becoming involved. The company reacted to the strike by putting depot staff and stablemen out to crew the cars, but they were immediately in trouble with the police for not having licences. While this dispute was settled rapidly, discontent over the dismissals continued for a time, some of the tram men taking Barrington to court. Failure to recognise and deal fairly with genuine staff grievances was to bedevil industrial relationships in the tramway companies throughout almost their entire existence.

The 1873 strike was apparently only one of several sources of disagreement among the DTC directorate. There were accusations of waste and extravagance, as well as the purchase of unsuitable horses, which were then allowed to decline further. Profitability was disappointing, with dividends allegedly reduced by lower income than was hoped for on the Sandymount and Donnybrook lines. Barrington was blamed and resigned, being replaced on the board by John Wilson of Rathgar, the former omnibus proprietor. Thomas Vance of Blackrock also became a director, the board then having four members based in London and two in Dublin.

A view of College Green between 1892 and 1898. The foreground is dominated by the statue of King William of Orange whose presence was deemed to be a serious obstacle to the development of the tramway system in the late 1870s. Garden seat tram No 12 on the left, built in October 1889, was electrified and renumbered 186 in December 1899 and can be compared with the knifeboard vehicle approaching from the right. Lawrence collection, National Library

On 1st September, a final settlement of the managerial differences saw William Anderson confirmed in the position of Acting Manager. He reported the continuing success of the passengers' monthly draws, a scheme designed to maximise fare income, and pointed out that operational mileage had reached 14 by August. The following day advertisements inviting applications for the post of veterinary surgeon and seeking harness makers and others to maintain the company's tackle, were published. In the *Evening Mail* of 6th September, Barrington outlined developments since the beginning of tramway operation as he saw them.

Neither the settlement of the July strike nor Barrington's departure solved all the staff problems of the DTC. There were allegations of dishonesty against conductors, the entire staff being blamed for the faults of a few. In the absence of a secure ticketing system, still some years away, statements by what the paper saw as very insensitive management, led the *Freeman's Journal* to deliver an editorial broadside against the company on 18th November 1872.

Two weeks after the opening of the Clontarf line, the Dublin Tramways Company reported receipts for the week ending on 14th June 1873 as £1,512 with 13 miles of tramways in operation. The DTC found the Terenure line to be the most profitable of their system, Donnybrook and Sandymount being less satisfactory. The Sandymount line, however, during its first four months of operation, had abstracted 7,433 valuable passengers from the Dublin, Wicklow & Wexford Railway, drawing the ire of that company's Chairman.

The moderately successful Clontarf line was the first tramway on the north side, an area where the DTC hesitated to open further services. This caution was based on the fact that, beyond the Royal Canal, which less than a mile from Nelson Pillar, little new building was as yet taking place. DTC officials believed that tramway construction should follow rather than precede housing development. There was also reluctance to venture outside urban areas, or beyond the Royal Canal which formed much of the city's northern boundary until 1900.

The North Quays Line

The last line opened by the Dublin Tramways Company under their 1871 Act had its city terminus on Bachelor's Walk beside Carlisle Bridge (widened and renamed O'Connell Bridge in 1880). Known as the North Quays line, it terminated in Parkgate Street at Infirmary Road, virtually duplicating the riverside portion of the Kingsbridge to Hatch Street service on the opposite bank of the Liffey. This line derived much of its revenue from those having business in the Four Courts or the military establishments at The Esplanade (the

Royal, later Collins Barracks), Arbour Hill or Infirmary Road, while leisure time traffic was provided by people going to Phoenix Park or Dublin Zoo.

Opened on Sunday 16th April 1874, the North Quays line was wished well by the *Freeman's Journal* in its announcement of the service the previous day. Noting that the service frequencies would be five minutes on weekdays and four on Sundays, it forecast that this line would be a popular method of escaping the grime of the city and enjoying the fresh air and amenities of the Phoenix Park. The fare would be 2d. Trams on the North Quays line shared the Victoria Quay depot with cars working the Kingsbridge-Hatch Street service.

Until rails were laid across Kingsbridge, trams working the North Quays line had to be moved over a stretch of roadway without track. This situation was similar to that which existed for a time at Donnybrook, where there was no physical connection between the terminus and the rails within the depot. Legislative approval was sometimes necessary to complete a route, as in the case of the Hatch Street section of the line from Kingsbridge. Some further links were also authorised, including the controversial one along Lower Abbey Street and Lower Gardiner Street to connect with the existing route to Dollymount at Talbot Street.

Critical Analysis

Almost as soon as tramway development began, specialist publications began covering the industry. An early analysis of the Dublin Street Tramways Company's performance from 1872 to 1876 by J Kinnear Clarke makes interesting observations, especially about tractive capacity. Finding that expenses for horse power in 1873-4 were excessive because of injudicious purchases, it pointed out the necessity for selling a portion of the stock and replacing it with better animals. This, together with expenditure on forage, were among the reasons for Barrington's departure from the DTC, much of the detail being revealed at the half-yearly meeting on 13th February 1874, when it was reported that the company then had 435 good horses and 70 trams. The number of horses fell far short of the stud of ten per car regarded as the ideal requirement. The best ratio ever achieved in Dublin was slightly better than eight horses per tram.

Clarke noted that on 31st December 1876 the stock consisted of 76 tramcars, 55 omnibuses and 486 horses. In 1874, with some 16 route miles in operation, the DTC had carried 5,269,546 passengers, the gross profit being £14,907 16s. 10d. Six million passengers were carried in 1876, the income of £73,303 representing an average fare of 2.9d.

Some shrewd moves were, however, made by the DTC. As described in Walter McGrath's book, *Tram Tracks Through Cork*, the Cork Tramways Company began operating in 1872 with six double-deck horse cars. These were built by the Starbuck Company, Nos 1-4 being 30-seaters while 5 and 6 were 38-seaters. When the Cork company closed down amid much bitterness in 1875, the rolling stock was purchased by the Dublin Tramways Company and put to work on the Terenure line.

The Act obtained by the Dublin Tramways Company in 1873 authorising some additions to existing lines also covered streets and routes not previously ratified. These included lines from the junction of Haddington Road and Northumberland Road to Ballsbridge, from Donnybrook to Stillorgan and from College Green to Bow Lane (James's Street). None of these new routes was built by the DTC. Trams never reached Stillorgan, and other companies built some of the lines covered in the original 1871 Act. The Dublin Tramways Company did operate in the Inchicore area, however, but with buses, a service being inaugurated from Kingsbridge via Richmond Barracks in January 1877, with a fare of 1d.

Much of the goodwill enjoyed by the Dublin Tramways Company was due to the ability and personality of William Anderson. The frequently conflicting interests and demands of passengers, staff, directors, the Police, Corporation, and Board of Trade all needed his constant attention. Fares, as we have seen, were a sensitive subject about which disputes erupted regularly. Because the trams were well patronised, often overcrowded at peak times, their seating capacity was another frequent source of criticism.

While the minimum seating space of 16 inches per passenger was acceptable to other local authorities, Dublin Corporation decreed this entitlement to be 18 inches in January 1873. At the same meeting, the councillors also discussed the perennial subject of maintaining the 18 inches of roadway on either side of the track for which the company was responsible. In this regard it is noteworthy that throughout their existence, tramway companies were often seen as golden geese. Local authorities benefited greatly from having street surfaces maintained to a much higher standard than previously.

Establishing accurately some details of the pre-1881 Dublin tram companies' operations is thwarted by contradictory facts, some of which appear in the same report. An example occurs in the account of the DTC's General Meeting held on 14th February 1874 when the company was said to have owned 70 cars and 329 horses though later in the same report this number is given as 435. There were also conflicts about the opening dates for certain lines, perhaps

DUTC horse tram No 50 on the Donny-brook line, photographed in Lower Baggot Street. The first No 50 is recorded as being broken up in July 1887, but was probably rebuilt. This picture has been dated to around 1892. There is no further reference to this horse tram, its electric DUTC-built successor appearing in March 1898.
Transport Museum Society of Ireland collection

because the whole line was not ready on the due day, was unacceptable to the Inspecting Officer or was subsequently closed down while repairs or modifications were made.

Another factor, which caused the early companies considerable grief, was control from London, where their head offices and some of their directors were based. Some of these officers are said never to have visited Dublin and charges about absentee directors, the adjective was highly pejorative at that time, were slung about with great abandon whenever the going got difficult.

North Dublin Street Tramways

Because tramways were attractive to company promoters and investors from the early 1870s onwards, competing schemes were sometimes put forward for a particular area. Where successful lines already existed, many such projects seem to have been initiated speculatively, with the intention of obtaining and then selling the authorisation to the existing operator. This situation did not immediately arise in Dublin, however, where the next tramway scheme was intended to serve hitherto tramless and less prosperous areas of the north side.

William Barrington did not remain idle after his departure from the Dublin Tramways Company, whose failure to complete all its authorised lines presented an opportunity for a new enterprise. The convinced pioneer who subscribed to the view that tramways should benefit poorer sections of the community, now promoted the North Dublin Street Tramways Company, in support of which he composed an address to the citizens. 'The prosperity of the North side should march pari passu with the greatness of the Empire itself....there are....living moving streams of humanity, toiling on with more or less fatigue, and only too glad to greet the approach of the smooth but rapid tramcar....That we are not at the moment in the enjoyment of this delightful mode of street locomotion is partly due, I fear I must say, to a want of public spirit on the part of our capitalists'.

In addition to William Barrington, the first directors were Frederick Barrington and John Watson. The Secretary and Manager was R S Tresilian, who was to have a long and distinguished tramway career. The Chairman was William Alexander Carte FRCSI, JP (1829-1899) who was also a shareholder in the Dublin Tramways Company. The NDST started with temporary offices at 41 Dame Street, later moving to 32 Lower Sackville Street where they were by 1877.

The North Dublin Company obtained their first Act in 1875, covering the construction of lines from Sackville Street to Glasnevin and Phoenix Park, and from Capel Street to Drumcondra.

The company's plans were set out comprehensively in an advertisement in *The Nation* of 19th February 1876. This also announced that the NDST would build the Inchicore line, construct tramways at a capital cost of £8,000 per mile (half that of Dublin Tramways Company lines) and introduce American-style one-horse single-deck cars without conductors. Because the NDST had taken over the powers to build some of the lines originally authorised to the Dublin Tram-ways Company, little love was lost between the two concerns. The DTC objected to any advantages being given to the North Dublin or any other tramway company.

From around the middle of the nineteenth century, a considerable swathe of lower middle-class housing was built from Dominick Street north and north westwards. By the early 1870s this was just spreading across the Royal Canal to Drumcondra, which at the time was rural, the village being around the present Richmond Road and Millmount Avenue junction. There were mills on the Tolka adjacent to Millbourne Avenue and some further industry downstream, but the river, as we saw earlier, was effectively a sewer, depositing much foul matter in the sloblands at Fairview.

During the seventies, Drumcondra began to develop as a middle-class suburb. To the west of Drumcondra lay Glasnevin, the village in this case being centred on Washer-woman's Hill. This district contained several big houses and while the owners of such properties were keen to avail of whatever amenities might derive from being in a township, they were not keen on joining with Drumcondra, but were eventually forced to do so, the two districts achieving township status in 1878.

From Annesley Bridge at the western end of East Wall Road, the city boundary ran westwards along the Tolka and Clonliffe Road to Jones's Road, which it tracked to the Royal Canal. It then followed the canal to the sixth lock (Shandon Mills), here turning southwards until it reached the North Circular Road at St Peter's Church. From there it ran along that road as far as the Phoenix Park gate. While the North Circular Road did not have mains drainage until 1884, the developers got in before that, recognising the area's considerable potential.

The Northside Routes

Under the powers conferred by their 1875 Act, the North Dublin Street Tramways Company built the three lines serving the areas just described. From Sackville Street, rails were laid up Rutland (now Parnell) Square, on through Blessington Street and Berkeley Road, where they served the Mater Hospital and Mountjoy Prison. They then followed the North Circular Road to its junction with Phibsborough Road at Doyle's Corner, known at one time as Dunphy's Corner.

Here the tracks diverged, the Glasnevin line turning right into Phibsborough Road, crossing Cross Guns Bridge (officially Westmoreland Bridge) and by way of Botanic Road to its junction with Botanic Avenue. People visiting Glasnevin Cemetery and the Botanic Gardens would have used this service. The tram service to Glasnevin and Phoenix Park commenced on 10th December 1876. Two cars were allocated to the Glasnevin line, the number increasing to four by the time the company held its Annual General Meeting on 23rd February 1877.

From Phibsborough, what was considered to be the main line continued along the North Circular Road, terminating at the Phoenix Park Gate. Apart from the residential clientele, this line derived revenue from Grangegorman Hospital, the cattle market, located at the junction of Prussia Street, Marlborough (now McKee) Barracks, the military hospital on Infirmary Road, the Royal Irish Constabulary Depot in Phoenix Park and from visitors to the Park and Zoo.

A depot was built behind the site of the present shops at the northwest corner of Phibsborough and North Circular Roads. Known as 'Cabra', this adjoined what is now Dalymount Park and explains references in football match reports to 'the Tramway End'. At the company's February 1877 general meeting the cost of the car shed was given as £770, the stables accounting for another £793.

The third NDST line was laid along Capel Street, Bolton Street and Dorset Street, crossing Binn's Bridge into Drumcondra and terminating just short of the junction of Drumcondra Road with Botanic Avenue. The NDST's second Act (1876) authorised the laying of tracks across what was then known as Essex (now Grattan) Bridge, through Parliament Street into Dame Street and a terminus at College Green. Socially, the Bolton Street/Dorset Street section of this route came nearest to achieving William Barrington's goal of providing trams for less affluent citizens, but it is unlikely that they could have afforded to use the service.

Barrington had apparently learned the necessity to economise from his experiences with the Dublin Tramways Company and as a result the Drumcondra, Glasnevin and North Circular Road lines of the North Dublin Street Tramways had lengthy stretches of single track with (mostly) intervisible passing loops. The number of loops was afterwards increased. Later still, when the track was doubled, crossovers were laid at these locations. This explains the large number of crossovers encountered on these lines in later years.

Considerable self-inflicted difficulties were suffered in the construction of the NDST lines, some of the work being condemned as substandard and having to be examined more than once by the Board of Trade Inspector. Later, there were prosecutions against the company arising from the poor condition of the permanent way and its maintenance. William Barrington was the company's contractor. Predictably, several difficulties arose and Barrington was, unfortunately, at the centre of further financial tribulations. There was sharp dissension at board level, leading to his departure from the company.

Despite their difficulties, the NDST managed to effect all-round improvements during the first half of 1877. These were set out in some detail at the half-yearly meeting held on 30th August, when Dr Carte, noted for his ability and professionalism, reported on the stern measures adopted with their

contractors. He also informed the meeting that the company now had 69 horses, 'all in good condition and working order' with ten tramcars in service and five on order.

Inchicore

An important route westward out of the city was by Dame Street, Cork Hill, Castle Street and Christchurch Place, then High Street and Thomas Street. Past St James's Gate and Guinness's Brewery, Mount Brown and Old Kilmainham, on the banks of the Camac River, was an extension of this district, with several mills and other small industries, all capable of generating some tramway traffic. At Kilmainham, the proposed tramway crossed the western boundary of the city which ran along the South Circular Road, the area beyond being the township of New Kilmainham.

Much of New Kilmainham's importance derived from the celebrated Inchicore works, established by the Great Southern & Western Railway in 1852. The works, as it is still known, employed a large staff, with great numbers of skilled craftsmen, many of whom had settled locally. Kilmainham Jail, the long-vanished Richmond Barracks and Goldenbridge Cemetery were also capable of providing some custom for an Inchicore tramway service.

Under its 1873 Act, the Dublin Tramways Company had been authorised to build the Inchicore line as far as Bow Lane (James's Street) but had not done so. The powers to construct this line passed to the North Dublin Company under its 1876 Act, together with authorisation to extend it to Inchicore. At the NDST meeting in February 1877 hopes were expressed that no hole-in-the-corner methods would be used in the construction of this tramway.

At the same meeting a shareholder named William Martin Murphy made some sharp comments about the competence of tramway people. This had been in some doubt when the performance of the locally managed North Dublin was compared with that of the Dublin Tramways Company prior to William Barrington's departure and Dr Carte's assumption of strict control. Murphy claimed that Irishmen were every bit as good as their English counterparts and well able to manage their own affairs. Arrangements for the construction of the line by the same William Martin Murphy, destined to be the giant of the Dublin tramways, were announced by Dr Carte at the NDST meeting on 30th August 1877, a tight timetable and a contract price of £43,000 being agreed.

The line began at College Green, terminating some 2.65 miles away just beyond Goldenbridge. The first section mentioned in the announcement of the Murphy contract took it from College Green to City Hall, the connection to Capel Street being also

covered. The section up Cork Hill and through Castle Street (Lord Edward Street did not exist at that time) caused some concern, but the *Freeman's Journal* was able to report on 22nd November 1877 that, 'Some experiments of a very successful nature were made last night to test the laying of the tramway line on the Cork-hill incline where the gradient is 1 in 14, and presented, it was originally thought, considerable difficulty in the way of tramway engineering. Cars containing 16 persons were run last evening over that portion of the line; first four horses and then two drew the cars and in both cases they ran over the curve without a hitch.'

The North Dublin's General Meeting on 28th February 1878 was informed that since work on the Inchicore line began, building had been encouraged in the area and rents had increased. The line was opened in two sections, the first as far as the Fountain in James's Street. It was capable of being worked through to Inchicore by 13th April 1878 but did not become fully operational until July. A shortage of cars may have contributed to this situation. In February 1878 the company had 15 trams in service and more on order, three of these being expected imminently. The NDST had six and a half miles of tramways open at that time, receipts being 1s 2d per mile as against expenses of 1/-.

The Inchicore route had steep gradients past City Hall and through Castle Street, while further on, Emmet Road outgoing and Mount Brown inbound were yet two more lengthy and exhausting gradients. At the line's outer terminus, a depot suitable for steam trams, should they be introduced, was built on the city side of Goldenbridge at the junction of the present Spa Road. Congestion problems were experienced on the Inchicore line and others terminating at College Green, the main obstruction being the statue of King William III. Mr Begg, a NDST shareholder who expressed nationalist sentiments and spoke regularly at meetings, dubbed this statue 'The Dutchman'. Standing on the site of the present Thomas Davis monument but nearer to the Church Lane junction, King William III was regarded as a badly sited obstacle to the development and operation of the tramway system. His was one of several statues blown up by persons unknown half a century later.

In 1878 James Lombard, who had temporarily replaced Dr Carte as Chairman, recommended that the North Dublin Street Tramways Company should embrace any opportunity for amalgamation with another company. There was general agreement among the shareholders about the desirability of collaboration with the new Dublin Central Company, with whom the North Dublin was to share some track. Later, the close co-operation between these two companies was to provide a significant impetus to the establishment of a unified Dublin tramway system.

One Man Cars: Pay as You Enter

The NDST operated both double and single-deck trams. Their 1876 double-deckers from the Metropolitan Railway Carriage and Wagon Company were described as weighing two and a half tons, built in oak and ash with mahogany panels and costing £194 each. These had eight windows on either side, were 21ft 3in long and 6ft 8in wide with a wheelbase of 6ft 0in. Their interior body length was 14ft 7½in, allowing the ten passengers on each longitudinal bench 17½ inches of seating.

Those 17½ inches represented what could be regarded as a creeping reduction of Dublin Corporation's 1873 allowance per passenger. Over the years, the space allowed for each passenger in trams with longitudinal seats was to remain a controversial subject, leading to many interpretations of capacity and some confusion for vehicle historians.

The 22 passengers seated back-to-back on the upper deck knifeboard were allowed 16½ inches each. The inside seats were filled with, 'best curled horsehair and covered with Utrecht velvet.' All the side windows, except two on each side, were fixed and the cars had sliding curtains on iron rods. Ventilation was by small hinged windows under the upper deck seats in a clerestory arrangement and two oil lamps were fitted inside each car.

According to reports from the NDST's annual general meeting of February 1877, the company had two or three types of car, the last ones delivered being open-sided and much liked by the travelling public. Known as summer trams, these found a special niche on the Phoenix Park line. Gradients of 1 in 28, a shortage of horses and a need for economy made these smaller vehicles attractive to the NDST. As a further step in cost saving, the one-horse single-deck 18-seater cars, six in number, were one man-operated.

Of the one-man trams, William Barrington said, 'On entering, the passengers are requested by notice inside to deposit their fares in an ingeniously contrived box at the upper end of the car, placed obliquely behind the driver. This box is a Shawson's Patent Fare Receiving Box and is thus placed in order that the driver, without trouble to himself, can ascertain if all the fares are paid, and if not, who is the delinquent.'

Barrington also pointed out that the fare collection box, apart from saving the wages of a conductor, would additionally preserve the driver from temptation, 'not himself receiving fares, which, although visible to him through a transparent front, fall into an inaccessible safe at the bottom of the farebox'. Drivers carried change for passengers who did not have the exact fare.

Dublin Central Tramways Company

An act of 1878 incorporated a third concern, the Dublin Central Tramways Company, with offices at 19 St Andrew's Street. William Barrington was the original promoter, but appears to have departed following allegations of financial irregularities. The Chairman was James F Lombard, a director of the Hibernian Bank, and the DCT also brought centre stage the powerful personality of William Martin Murphy.

Born in 1845, the son of a Bantry (Co Cork) building contractor, Murphy was educated at Belvedere College from where he went on to study architecture. At the age of 19, he had to go home to take over the family business on the death of his father. This he did successfully, returning to Dublin in 1875 and developing widespread interests in tramways and railways. Murphy acted as a contractor for the North Dublin Tramways in the construction of its Inchicore line, taking shares in the company.

On 3rd September 1878 William Martin Murphy entered into a contract to build and equip the lines of the Central company. Originally opposed by the North Dublin, the Central later entered into co-operation with the NDST, the intention being to offer transfer facilities between the two systems. Murphy was to receive payment in shares, which he sold at a premium on completion of the work, and became a director of the Dublin Central Tramways Company.

The North Dublin shared its College Green terminus with the Dublin Central Tramways. The Central, operating three routes with a total length of six and a half miles, ran from College Green over North Dublin tracks in Dame Street. Central trams went on to their own tracks on turning into South Great George's Street. They continued southwards through Aungier Street and Camden Street, where the line for Ranelagh diverged through Charlotte Street, now built over. From Charlemont Street, the line crossed the Grand Canal, beyond which Ranelagh Road had to be raised to ease the gradient for trams approaching the canal bridge.

At the Ranelagh Triangle, also known as The Angle, the Clonskea branch, worked by single-deckers, headed for the terminus and depot at Vergemount, just beyond Milltown Road. The opening of this section on 17th March 1879 was covered in the *Irish Times* on the following day when it was reported that, owing to bad weather on the preceding days, people were discouraged from travelling, tramway traffic being down on St Patrick's Day. However, this did not interfere with the opening of the new service.

'The new line that was opened to Clonskea by the Central Tramways Company inaugurated the opening under most favourable circumstances. The district has hitherto been accessible only by tortuous and embarrassing modes, although the residents include a large body of commercial gentlemen, but now a ready approach to the great business portion of the city is afforded. The citizens on the other hand are placed in the enjoyment of an additional 'lung' by the facility afforded of visiting a most salubrious and picturesque locality. The cars of the company have been built in Birkenhead and are designed to carry eighteen and twenty passengers inside and four – two each side of the driver – outside. The fittings are well designed and the seats are divided by brass rails to prevent any disputes between querulous passengers as to the accommodation for each.'

Past the Triangle, the main line ran along Charleston Road, turning into Belgrave Square and up Palmerston Road to its terminus at the junction of Palmerston Park. Public services began on 3rd May 1879. The Starbuck cars for this service were painted vermillion and claimed to exceed the minimum 16 inches of seating per passenger stipulated in the Stage Carriage Act. Their stairs also earned praise on two counts: easy accessibility for women and improved safety compared with earlier vehicles. In fact, a few weeks later, on 4th June, an unfortunate passenger, Thomas Cunningham of North Strand, was killed when thrown from the ladder of a Dublin Tramways Company Clontarf car at the junction of North Earl Street and Sackville Street.

From Camden Street, the Central's longest route swung westwards into Harrington Street at Kelly's Corner. It followed the South Circular Road to Leonard's Corner, where it turned left into Upper Clanbrassil Street. After crossing Harold's Cross Bridge, it continued along what is now Terenure Road North, serving the western portion of Rathmines Township. From Terenure (then also known as Roundtown) which, although just outside the Township, was an important neighbouring village, it continued to Rathfarnham, terminating at Church Lane.

The service was opened as far as Terenure on Whit Monday, 22nd June 1879. On that day, the company's 22 cars are reported to have carried 8,053 passengers. In a prospectus issued by the contractor later in June 1879 it was announced that the entire system was in operation. A depot, made redundant by subsequent events, was built on the site now occupied by the more northerly houses of Cormac Terrace at Terenure.

Three Into One: the DUTC

All of the three tramway companies operating in Dublin City were quite small. The largest, the Dublin Tramways Company, worked about 16½ route miles. Four of its six lines, those to Sandymount, Donnybrook, Terenure and Clontarf, shared a city centre terminus at or near Nelson Pillar. O'Connell Bridge, formerly Carlisle Bridge, renamed when widened and reopened on 6th August 1880, was the connecting point for the other two routes serving either line of quays. One of these was the North Quays line from Bachelor's Walk to Parkgate Street. The second, the South Quays line, ran from Kingsbridge via Westland Row to

Earlsfort Terrace. Its extension to Hatch Street was opened on 23rd June 1879, at which time extra cars were on order. The company had five depots, at Sandymount, Donnybrook, Terenure, Victoria Quay and Clontarf.

The DTC had a rather haughty image, although it was very open in its dealings, especially in publishing regular reports about its performance. It had obtained powers for several more routes than it actually constructed and was widely seen as a monopoly. It steadfastly refrained from constructing lines that might be unprofitable, but objected to their being built by a competitor.

Disdain for the less fashionable areas was displayed at the DTC's half-yearly meeting in August 1877. The Chairman refused to identify the proposers of a branch from Harrington Street to Kingsbridge via the Coombe. Their suggestion that this would be, 'a well-paying branch to the prosperous Rathmines tramway system', was greeted with laughter. 'You know this locality', said the Chairman, 'I have been introduced to it lately and I know what it is' … 'Who are the writers?' interrupted one shareholder, '…They ought to be in a lunatic asylum'.

The North Dublin Street Tramways Company operated about eight route miles from Sackville Street to Glasnevin and Phoenix Park via North Circular Road and from College Green to Drumcondra and Inchicore. The North Dublin had depots at Phibsboro (Cabra) and Inchicore.

Smallest of the three companies, the Dublin Central Tramways Company had about six and a half route miles. Its main line ran from College Green to Rathfarnham via Harold's Cross. A second went from College Green to Palmerston Park and there was also the Ranelagh to Clonskea route, regarded as a branch. Clonskea and Terenure (Rathfarnham Road) were the locations of this company's depots. There was considerable co-operation between the North Dublin and the Central, reinforced by an Act of 1880.

While all of the companies were profitable, some of the lines had, at times, rather sparse traffic with infrequent headways during certain periods of the day. A merger was an attractive option, offering integrated services and the probability of increased passenger numbers. The possibility of mergers had been mooted several times and it had been argued as far back as 1877 that there was unnecessary competition between the three companies. Failure to build authorised lines, the powers for which had passed successively from one company to another, was put down to commercial timidity. This situation was partly attributed to the presence on the Dublin boards of London-based directors who had no knowledge of Dublin or its potential for tramway development.

At a general meeting in February 1879, Dr Carte, Chairman of the North Dublin Street Tramways Company, referred to the likely benefits accruing from co-operation and amalgamation. His company was already sharing tracks and collaborating with the Central, whose half-yearly meeting (its first), took place in 39 Dame Street on the same day as that of the longer-established NDST.

The tramway companies held two general meetings each year at which the results for the previous six months were presented. The February 1880 meetings of the North Dublin (on the 19th) and Dublin Tramways (27th) were upbeat, the most interesting item being perhaps the acquisition of a gas engine by the NDST to crush corn. A few weeks later, on 13th March, a merger was announced. Guided by their Dublin-based directors, the three concerns, reached agreement on 13th July and so was born the Dublin United Tramways Company.

Sanctioned by the Dublin United Tramways (Amalgamation of Companies) Act, the combined enterprises became a legal entity on 1st July 1881. The new undertaking had seven directors on its prospectus, only one of whom, John Humphries, had a London address. The other six, James Fitzgerald Lombard, Thomas Vance, David Drimmie, William Carte, William Martin Murphy and John Richardson Wigham all lived in the Dublin area. Humphries subsequently resigned, Alderman W F Cotton JP later becoming a director. Directors' fees, fixed at £1,500 per annum, worried one shareholder, the redoubtable Mr Begg of North Dublin fame. Over the next few years, he periodically argued that the fees were excessive and thought the company could be managed more economically by three directors.

William Anderson, formerly Manager of the Dublin Tramways Company, became Secretary and Manager of the Dublin United Tramways Company, his assistant being R S Tresilian from the North Dublin concern. The combined capital of the three constituents, Dublin Tramways £328,000, North Dublin £105,000 and Central £80,000, was increased to £560,170 by the DUTC.

The new company, which had offices at 31 Lower Sackville Street, took charge of 32 miles of track and 137 tramcars, mostly 46-seater double-deckers. Of these, 82 came from the Dublin Tramways Company, 25 from the North Dublin and 30 from the Central. Some sources quote the number of cars at 132, this figure highlighting a type of discrepancy frequently encountered in the histories of transport companies. These were usually due to an accountant listing as assets rolling stock regarded as unserviceable by the Engineer or not available to the Traffic Manager. During the first six months of the

DUTC's existence, four and three quarter million passengers were carried, a million car miles were run and £48,000 was earned. On 31st December 1882, the company had 136 trams, three omnibuses and 963 horses.

Improvements and Extensions

Right through the horse tram era, the DUTC consolidated and improved its system. By February 1883, the city terminus for trams coming from Harold's Cross and Palmerston Park had been moved from College Green to Nelson Pillar, thus introducing what the company regarded as cross-town services. Connections were made northwards past Nelson Pillar, physically joining the former DTC and NDST systems.

Here it should be explained that the entrance to the Pillar faced southwards towards O'Connell Bridge. Trams terminating south of Nelson Pillar, opposite the GPO, were often referred to as stopping in front of the Pillar, while those on the north side were said to be at its back or behind it.

Utilising the new north-south connections, the Phoenix Park service coming in through Phibsboro was extended past the Pillar to a new terminus in College Green. To cope with the increased traffic, the number of lines over O'Connell Bridge was increased from two to four, establishing a layout that would remain a feature of the tramway system for over half a century. Tracks had also been laid in College Street by 1885, enabling Inchicore cars to work through to Westland Row.

Other connections were made from Harrington Street to Harcourt Road and Camden Street to South Richmond Street, integrating the former DTC and Central systems. A siding was also built from Westland Row into Lombard Street East, thus reducing the congestion formerly caused by trams waiting at Westland Row railway station. With the opening of Lord Edward Street on 27th July 1886, the Inchicore line was diverted from its original Castle Street route to operate along the new thoroughfare. Three trams, including No 9, formed part of a civic procession to mark the occasion.

The original track laid by the pre-1881 companies consisted mainly of box rails fixed to wooden sleepers, the oldest dating from 1872. In February 1883, it was announced that the DUTC had examined improvements in permanent way technology since the first horse trams had run eleven years previously. They had decided to adopt the more modern and durable girder rail, laid on concrete and gauge-spaced with metal ties. Starting with a section of the Kingsbridge line in 1884, this type of rail was henceforth used for all new work and renewals of existing track, the task being completed by 1896.

The only new suburban horse tram route opened by the DUTC was that to Dolphin's

Barn. This village lay about three-quarters of a mile westwards along the South Circular Road from its junction with Clanbrassil Street at Leonard's Corner on the Rathfarnham line. The area began to develop during the 1880s but for some years it was not sufficiently populated to persuade the DUTC that a tramway would be profitable. Horse trams eventually reached Dolphin's Barn in February 1896, having a short but chequered career of less than three years.

Beginning in the Rathmines area, a parcels service was inaugurated in 1883. From modest beginnings, this was destined to become a highly profitable enterprise for the DUTC. Parcels could be handed to company officials or agents and collected or deposited at specified points, the depots or offices of the company or its agents. In its first accounting period, the service cost £334 to operate, but the receipts were £359, leaving a profit of £25.

Advertising on tramcars became a further lucrative source of income the company canvassed actively. In horse tram days, the advertisements were of two types: either paper posters or painted boards which were supplied by the advertiser for attachment to the trams, the actual signwriting being frequently contracted out.

At the half-yearly meeting held on 2nd February 1886, Dr Carte reminded those present that the date was the 14th anniversary of the first DTC tram on the Rathmines line. He contrasted the position prior to the arrival of the trams when buses ran to Rathmines every 13 minutes carrying 31 passengers with that in 1886 when trams were running every three minutes on the same route and capable of carrying 41 passengers.

DUTC meetings, held twice a year, were usually well-ordered affairs, receiving excellent press coverage. An exception was that of 4th August 1885 which began quietly with the usual recitation of statistics for the previous half-year which would normally have sent the attendance home in buoyant spirits. Unfortunately, before this happy conclusion could be reached, there arose a rancorous item that today would be called a conflict of interests. A code of practice was being introduced under which shareholders would have to declare whether they were also suppliers to the company. Some transgressors were identified, the meeting turned very sour and ended in disorder. As a result, Alderman Nagle's attempt to pursue the matter of adequate meal breaks for the tram drivers and conductors was frustrated.

Inherited Liabilities

A liability inherited by the DUTC was the single lines laid by the NDST. While single-track tramways offered economies in the cost of construction, problems often arose afterwards. There was more wear and tear on the track than in the case of a double line, and there were also more sets of points, two per passing loop. Reaching the passing loop ahead of the car coming in the opposite direction was a pre-occupation for drivers who sometimes had serious altercations with their colleagues over right of way.

An avoidable accident on one of the single lines embroiled the DUTC in a court case. A recently married couple named Tyrrell boarded a city-bound car at the North Circular Road gate of the Phoenix Park around 7pm on Sunday 19th August 1883 and sat at the front of the lower deck. At one of the passing places, the tram in which the Tyrrells were travelling collided with another car, inflicting on Mrs Margaret Tyrrell back injuries of a permanent nature. The company's negligence was proved and the claimant was awarded £400 plus costs at a day-long court hearing in May 1884. In 1999 terms, Mrs Tyrrell's award was the equivalent of £27,727.

Great stress, indeed terror, must have been caused to tramway staff involved in accidents for which they were not responsible. If anybody was injured, the driver or conductor, and sometimes both, were arrested and, if not bailed, detained until they could be brought before a court. Unless obviously at fault or drunk, the unlucky tramwayman, represented by the DUTC solicitor, was then bailed to appear again, usually in one week. In the event of a fatality, the inquest would normally have taken place within the intervening period. With the well-nigh invariable exoneration of tramway staff, the charge would subsequently be dropped.

A typical example of this procedure affected a young man named John Reilly who was driving No 140, a Terenure car, along Harold's Cross Road on the evening of 4th August 1882. Near the junction of Leinster Road, he did not see a man lying on the tracks in time to pull up. This unfortunate man, William Lynott, was run over, suffering multiple injuries from which he died. Reilly was arrested, locked up and charged the following day but before his next appearance in court the inquest established that Lynott suffered from fainting fits and was wearing dark clothes when he fell on the roadway. Reilly, who had a good name with the company, was discharged and probably deemed himself lucky in the circumstances.

That no code of bylaws or regulations, however skilfully drafted, can cover every eventuality, is well illustrated by an episode which occurred in 1889. DUTC staff were concerned for the safety of an aged passenger, a resident of the Royal Hospital in Donnybrook, who used the trams regularly but caused them much worry. The matter eventually resulted in a letter being written to the passenger. 'The attention of the Board having been called to your very feeble state of health and the danger that may arise from your travelling alone I am directed to inform you that the Company must decline from this date to accept you as a passenger unless you are in charge of a person travelling with you.'

The Horses

In the early days of horse tramways, practice on horses varied from company to company. Some saw their animals as a valuable asset to be looked after carefully. Others followed a much less intelligent and humane path but learned in time that decently treated horses were still quite saleable even after several years' work. Acknowledging his acceptance of this at the company's meeting on 19th February 1875, the chairman of the DTC admitted that it originally worked its horses until there was no life left in them, getting 12s 6d for an animal's hide.

This cruel and stupid practice was short-lived in Dublin where tram horses were, generally, well treated. The horses, worth between £25 and £40, according to changing economic conditions, were usually about five years of age when put to tramway work which was regarded as heavy. Horses were carefully matched to work in pairs and a lazy animal inclined to let its mate take an unequal amount of the strain was quickly spotted, being then reassigned or sold.

The animals, up to ten in number required for each tram, were designated as a stud which was kept together and looked after by the same stableman. Carefully fed and housed, the horses also enjoyed the services of a veterinary surgeon. One double set of harness was kept for each stud and there was keen competition among stable staff in the matter of turnout and smartness.

At steep hills there was a trip or trace horse attached to help each team haul its tram up the incline. These animals belonged to a separate group assigned only to this duty and had their own special harness. The traceboys in charge of the trip horses were required by Dublin Southern District Tramways rules 128 and 129 to, 'on no account leave their horses... Horses going to or returning from work must be walked slowly... traceboys...must report an accident or injuries, however slight, that may have happened to their horses during work.' Trace horses were known as tippers to the tramway men.

Several steep inclines on the DUTC system required the services of trace horses. Among them were the canal bridges at Baggot Street, Charlemont Street and Portobello. Tippers were also needed at Newcomen Bridge on North Strand, Cork Hill, Mount Brown and from Dominick Street to Granby Row. At Phibsboro, a trace horse was stationed at Blackquire Bridge which spanned the branch, long since filled in, of the Royal Canal that ran under the present Phibsboro Library and through the linear park towards Western Way and Broadstone Station.

Two of the foregoing locations were regarded as sufficiently severe to be included in a list of places specified in Police Regulations (paragraph 20) made under the 1875 Dublin Traffic Act; 'No waggon, dray, cart, or other vehicle, when laden, shall proceed up Cork-hill…or Newcomen Bridge, save and except the animals yoked to any such vehicle shall be fully equal, without danger of injury or cruelty to such animal or animals to draw the same.'

An entire division of tramway staff was employed in serving the needs of the horses. There were employees responsible for storing and transporting huge quantities of feed and bedding, and disposing of manure. Some idea of the volume of this ordure may be gleaned from simple calculations based on the facts that the DUTC, at the zenith of its horse system, had 1,577 animals, each of which produced a minimum of 14lbs of manure each day, a total of nearly ten tons. As the tram horses were a minority of Dublin's total equine population, the dirt, the stench and the danger to public health can be easily imagined.

Responsible for all the company's horses, the DUTC's sole stable foreman had charge-hands reporting to him, one for each depot. The stablemen at the depots fed and groomed the horses, and changed them after each had done its quota of journeys which depended on the length of the particular line. A farrier and helper were available for each depot, while the DUTC also employed harness makers at Donnybrook and Nelson Lane (now Earl Place).

When offered for sale after about three years' service, tram horses were routinely bought by farmers and others who regarded them very highly. A horse auction was held at Kingsbridge (Victoria Quay) depot on the first Thursday of every month at two o'clock, and there was no reserve price on the animals.

In 1881, a large new granary was built at Kingsbridge depot, which was the animal resources headquarters of the system. This particular depot was also a repository for the great quantities of fodder required. On one occasion a tram which was missing for some time is reputed to have been found there under a mountain of hay.

All the horses were officially numbered, but they also had names and there was a very close bond between these animals and the men who had charge of them. Great pride was taken in their appearance and they were entered for various shows, especially those organised by the Royal Dublin Society. On these occasions DUTC horses were frequent recipients of prestigious prizes. For example, Dolly and Dot won a premier award in 1892, Daisy and Dandy repeating the success in 1895. Some of the medals they won are preserved by CIE at Heuston Station.

The indefatigable DUTC Chairman, Dr Carte, FRCSI, was interested in a wide range of subjects. His studies included vet-erinary medicine at least insofar as it concerned horses. The resulting very informative reports to the company's half-yearly meetings invariably gave details of the animals. The total in stock, the number bought and sold during each half-year, deaths, the horses' health and value and cost of feeding were all meticulously set out. These meetings of the DUTC and other big companies were fully reported in the daily newspapers.

Driver Training: A Love for Horses
One glimpse of life on the trams of over a hundred years ago concerns the driving of horses. Drivers were admonished to, 'drive their teams at a steady gait and with taut rein, keeping the right hand upon the brake at all times. They will stop their horses with the reins and not with the brakes. They must always start their horses slowly, not allowing them to trot until the car has moved at least twenty feet'. Speeds were in the order of four to six miles per hour, eight being sometimes reached by an enthusiastic driver with a fresh and energetic team.

A story has come down about an instructor who was endeavouring to train a prospective driver, an over-zealous individual who kept whipping the horses to a gallop instead of coaxing them up to the customary sedate trot. Despite the instructor's pleading, the would-be driver persisted in racing ahead until the senior man's patience gave out. He ordered his charge to stop, dismount and stick his finger in a pile of dung directly in front of the tram. Asked how it felt, the trainee replied, 'warm, why?' whereupon the harassed instructor bellowed, 'That's how you know you're too close to the car in front'.

Tram drivers were very good at their job and noted for their love of horses. But no matter how careful they were, others could cause them considerable pain and trouble as happened on the evening of Monday, 29th January 1883 when a tram travelling from Nelson Pillar to Glasnevin met what was described as a light vehicle on Glasnevin Road. This light vehicle went out of control and collided with the tram horses, a shaft penetrating the breast of one of the DUTC animals which was horribly injured and died within a few minutes. The driver of the light vehicle was arrested and charged with drunk driving. Reporting the accident, the *Freeman's Journal* also criticised the street lighting, pointing out that this had already drawn numerous complaints, the lamps being 100 yards apart.

Living Costs Drop, Fares Rise
The consumer price index continued to fall from 1872 towards the 1914 benchmark of 100. In 1881, when the Dublin United Tramways came into being, it stood at 103. In effect, the cost of living in 1881 was 3% higher than in 1914. By 1884 it had fallen to 97 and continued to drop during the rest of the horse tram era. Despite this, the DUTC increased fares in November 1883, provoking scathing press criticism, both editorial and from irate readers. The company was accused of taking advantage of winter by raising the 2d fare for inside passengers to 3d while leaving outside (upper deck) charges unaltered.

There was a short-term fall in passenger numbers and revenue but the company's monopoly position effectively meant that they could charge what the traffic would bear. James Lombard, who chaired the DUTC half-yearly meeting in August 1883, set his face firmly against lower fares. It had been suggested over and over again, he said, that 1d fares through the body of the city would yield a mine of gold. He ruled against this, contending that filling the cars with 1d passengers at Nelson Pillar would shut out longer distance travellers. He dismissed comparisons with London, which he said was too big to be used as a yardstick. Finally, he contended that stopping for 1d fares would impose a serious additional strain on the tram horses.

In January 1884 some concessions were made, penny fares being introduced somewhat tentatively. As a result, traffic increased to the extent that on Whit Monday, 2nd June, the DUTC recorded its heaviest loadings to date, 69,942 passengers being carried on that day. Reporting the figures, the *Freeman's Journal* noted that this feat had been achieved without a single mishap, reflecting great credit on the DUTC staff. At the company's half-yearly meeting held on 5th August, it was reported that the 1d fare was such a success that it had been extended progressively and would shortly be available on every DUTC tram. The company was also using omnibuses on a summer service from Rathmines to Merrion, encouraged by the very fine summer weather.

At the August 1884 meeting, Mr Begg, the shareholder who liked to ask unpredictable questions, enquired whether the company's tickets were printed in Dublin. Some early Dublin tram tickets were printed in England, possibly in London, a city regarded by Mr Begg as foreign. He was first told that they were not produced in Dublin but he pursued the matter further, finally eliciting that for the past three months they had been printed by Browne and Nolan, a local firm.

In September, it was reported that during the first week of that month, 58,209 penny tickets had been sold on DUTC trams. Judging from statements made at subsequent general meetings, this achievement persuaded the directors that increased passenger loadings with lower fares were preferable to lesser numbers at higher tariffs. Whether Lombard, the erstwhile staunch opponent of penny fares, displayed any embarrassment at the turn of events, is not recorded.

This DUTC two horse dray loaded with grain is believed to be at Kingsbridge, Victoria Quay. This depot was also the location of the animal forage stores. The driver's perch, giving a high degree of control over the horses, is noteworthy.
DUTC, Transport Museum Society of Ireland

The increase in journeys when potential passengers perceived the fares to be equitable was clearly illustrated by figures quoted at the DUTC meeting in February 1885. These referred to the week ending on 31st January in two successive years.

	1d	2d	3d	Total
1884	16,036	89,478	63,716	169,230
1885	55,138	96,503	59,922	211,563

The next shareholders' meeting on 4th August 1885 heard even better news. Mileage, at 1,075,985 for the first half of the year was up 28,000 on the previous six months, while passenger numbers had increased by 912,000 to 6,651,537, 1,763,640 of these had paid 1d fares. So enthusiastic did the DUTC become about penny fares that in April 1886 a discount scheme for prepaid tickets was introduced. A sheet of 12 tickets was available at its face value of 1/-, 20 12-ticket sheets could be obtained for 19/-, or a hundred for £4 10s 6d. By the time this discount scheme was offered, 70,000 penny tickets were being sold every week.

The Dublin Southern District Tramways Company

Blackrock, Kingstown and Dalkey, served by the Dublin & Kingstown Railway, became townships under the 1847 Town Improvements Act and were highly desirable residential locations. Kingstown was stated to have 17,500 inhabitants in 1878, while Dalkey had 3,667. The development potential of these areas attracted the attention of the Tramways & General Works Company Ltd, a prominent promoter of tramway schemes. To control a number of its smaller operating companies, T & G created Imperial Tramways to take over shares in the various concerns for which Tramways & General Works acted as contractors.

Imperial Tramways, which had as one of its directors T M McKay, Chairman of the Dublin Tramways Company, promoted the Dublin Southern District Tramways Company, with offices and a depot at 162 Shelbourne Road, where Ballsbridge Motors now has its premises. This company, which was to build two separate, and incompatible, tram routes, obtained its first Act in 1878 and had capital of £70,000. The Tramways & General Works Company received £70,000 in shares for building the DST lines.

One of the DSDT's two lines, with a gauge of 4ft 0in, ran from the bottom of Royal Marine Road in Kingstown to Dalkey (Castle Street), where a depot was built. This line opened on 19th March 1879. Among the reasons for the adoption of the 4ft 0in gauge was the narrowness of thoroughfares in the area. George's Street in Kingstown and Castle Street in Dalkey posed particular problems, especially for a double track tramway.

It will be recalled that, from its opening in October 1872, the Dublin Tramways Company's Sandymount line had taken considerable business from the Dublin, Wicklow & Wexford Railway, which worked the Dublin to Kingstown line. The DWWR had therefore adopted a strategy of resisting any proposed tramway it saw as a potential threat to its own lucrative monopoly.

This intimidating policy, clearly presaged at the DW & WR's general meeting of 19th February 1873, was roundly condemned by the newspapers and their readers. Despite this, the railway company indulged, for several years, in carefully orchestrated opposition, court actions and other tactics, some of them underhand, to stop tramway development between Dublin and Dalkey. By its successful objections to a standard gauge tramway from Kingstown to Dalkey, the DWWR ensured that through running, at least over the last two of the nine miles from Dublin, would be impossible.

The second DSDT tramway extended from Blackrock to Haddington Road where it met the Dublin Tramways Company's line from Sandymount to the city. This second DSDT line was to the Irish standard gauge of 5ft 3in, but was quoted by a contemporary tramway engineer as being to the English standard gauge of 4ft 8½in.

A branch of this Southern District line from Northumberland Road along Pembroke Road was in operation in 1879. It was intended that DSDT trams would travel further, along Baggot Street or Waterloo Road but the proposed service did not materialise because the Dublin Tramways Company would not grant the Southern Company running rights over its lines. The section of line from the Pembroke Road junction to Haddington Road connected the Southern with the DTC's Sandymount tracks at Beggar's Bush. Both the DTC and its successors objected to any proposals capable of providing competition. Intriguingly, another objector to the DSDT plans was Dublin Corporation.

Because the depot at Shelbourne Road was not ready in time for opening day, 16th July 1879, an arrangement was made with the DTC to provide horses, which brought the DSDT cars all the way from Blackrock to the city centre. When this agreement expired after about six months, the DSDT horses were changed at Haddington Road, its trams travelling into the city behind DTC animals.

The DSDT Haddington Road to Blackrock line as originally laid was single but powers were obtained in 1883 to install double track. In June 1884, the Southern District company obtained permission to lift the disused rails in Pembroke Road and relay them in Northumberland Road, thus doubling that section of the line.

The Blackrock & Kingstown

In 1883, yet another concern, the Blackrock & Kingstown Tramways Company, obtained powers to bridge the gap between the Dublin Southern's two lines. The directors were Robert Gardner and Robert Worthington, who provided capital of £26,000. The company had its registered office at 41 Dame Street, Dublin, the Secretary's name being given as Charles Harrell.

The Blackrock and Kingstown, because it could form the last vital link in any future through tramway service from Dublin city centre to Dalkey, was actively opposed by the DW & W. The railway company, anxious to maintain its virtual monopoly and regularly accused of charging extortionate fares admitted, in May 1883, that they had paid the expenses of a former Blackrock resident to come home from London for the purpose of opposing the proposed line.

Construction of the Blackrock and Kingstown was greatly delayed, legal action being taken at one stage to impede its progress. In September 1883 a letter in the *Freeman's Journal* pointed out that no construction work had yet taken place. On 29th April 1884, the same paper reported that the Kingstown Commissioners had been informed of the purchase by the company of several fast two-horse vehicles for use pending completion of the tramway. It was 23rd May 1885 before the line was declared ready for traffic, but another three months' delay then ensued.

The B & K's proposals for its double line down Royal Marine Road from the George's Street junction in Kingstown resulted in considerable friction. The Dublin Southern District company's existing line from Dalkey also turned down Royal Marine Road at this junction. Disagreements, normal between tramway companies in such situations, were complicated here by differences in gauge. Crossings between the 5ft 3in of the B & K and the 4ft 0in of the DSDT resulted in several disputes and delays, which further postponed the opening of the Blackrock line.

Finally, in August 1885 the line was cleared for opening. But the provision of stock by the Southern Company, envisaged in the Blackrock and Kingstown's enabling Act, did not materialise, nor did through running over the Southern's 5ft 3in gauge line to Haddington Road. The B & K depot was at Blackrock, the offices also being listed in 1887 at this address, 2 Newtown Avenue. It later formed an annexe and substation beside the larger DUTC depot built around 1908. This site now forms part of the Europa Cars premises.

Steam's Donnybrook Appearance

Right through the horse era, most tramway operators dreamt of alternatives to animal haulage. As some of the earliest experiments with steam traction had involved road vehicles it was inevitable that engineers would seek to substitute this form of motive power for animals at the earliest opportunity. Efficient tramway locomotives were designed during the 1870s and ousted horses on several lines in Great Britain. Many tramways were, however, tied to horse traction under the terms of their Acts and so had no choice in the matter.

As soon as steam haulage became a practicable alternative, tramway promoters included provisions for this in their bills, the subject being prominent in discussions on the Dublin Central Tramways bill. In June 1877, the Chairman of the Dublin Tramways Company was a member of a delegation who urged the President of the Board of Trade to grant powers for steam haulage on

existing lines. Unfortunately, there was considerable opposition to steam operation, despite smoke emission being controlled by the design of most tramway engines.

A certain level of genuine objections came from residents along any route on which steam was proposed. The real trouble, however, lay with horse owners and the vast equine industry, as important in the late nineteenth century as the motor business is today. These people were allergic to anything mechanical, as were many of the upper classes. It has been pointed out that they admired the Duke of Wellington, who had opposed railways some years previously because they might encourage the lower classes to move about.

The *Irish Times* of 21st July 1877, carried a comprehensive report on the first of two demonstrations carried out in Dublin by the tram locomotive *Pioneer*. 'The trial of Hughes's engine, which took place yesterday on the Donnybrook line, between Donnybrook and Morehampton-road, was witnessed by some thousands of persons…The experiment was a perfect success, and afforded the most convincing proof of the applicability of steam to tram-car locomotion…Shortly before one o'clock the Pioneer was driven from the Tramway Company's depot beyond Donnybrook to the road where one of the company's cars awaited it on the line. The appearance of the convenient, tight little engine was calculated to obtain for it the popular approval which was expressed by loud cheers. The engine differs entirely in appearance from that of the railway locomotive. It is less in size than a tramcar, is fitted with curtained plate-glass windows and is so framed that the machinery and wheels are entirely concealed. A small funnel, rising about nine inches above the roof, is almost the only indication that it is a locomotive. The tramcar to which it was attached was crowded inside and out – in fact, it carried over sixty persons…

'The engine and car proceeded at the rate of eight miles an hour – the speed limited by the Board of Trade – through Donnybrook and on to the Morehampton road. The engine was then detached from the car and placed in front of it in the direction of Donnybrook, and directly the return journey was made…the Pioneer is capable of running at the rate of fifteen miles an hour…while the engine was running at the rate of twelve miles an hour, was able to pull up within a distance of fourteen yards…A tram line for engines can be constructed at £1.500 per mile, while, owing to the cost of paving between the rails on lines worked by horses, the latter will cost £2,000 per mile…With its enclosing carriage the engine weighs four and a half tons. The average of a loaded tramcar is five tons, but the tramcar yesterday, with a freight of sixty-five persons, far exceeded that weight; yet it was drawn with great ease at a speed of about ten miles an hour.'

The paper listed the many prominent people who attended the demonstration and commented editorially on the demonstration and its future possibilities. It pointed out the high costs of horse operation, resulting in high fares and referred to the 'cost of buying fresh horses in substitution for those which are rapidly broken down by the irksome and slavish nature of the work…'

Apart from the Lucan and Blessington lines, where it was used from the start, steam would re-appear only briefly on conventional street tramways in the Dublin area, the horse reigning supreme for another 19 years.

The Dublin & Lucan

To the west of the city the Dublin & Lucan Steam Tramway Company began services from Parkgate Street to Palmerstown in June 1881. The ceremonial opening of the whole route to Lucan took place on 17th February 1883. The line, which was laid to the 3ft 0in gauge, ran on a roadside reservation for most of its length, the track being single, with passing loops. The depot and offices were located where Conyngham Road bus garage now stands. We will return to this line again, first on its electrification in 1900 and later, its acquisition and rebuilding, in 1928, by the DUTC. Its history is fully set out in *The Dublin and Lucan Tramway* by A T Newham (Oakwood Press). Apart from the difference in gauge which prevented through running, passengers transferring from Dublin trams had to walk from the Infirmary Road junction to board the Dublin & Lucan vehicles which terminated at the end of the Phoenix Park wall.

The Dublin & Blessington

The other steam-operated system in the Dublin area was the 5ft 3in gauge Dublin and Blessington, 19½ miles in length. It opened on 1st August 1888, replacing a horsedrawn mail car service between the GPO and Blessington. A four-mile extension to Poulaphouca was opened in May 1895. The D&BST had its terminus at Terenure, where it had physical connection with the DUTC. The D&B, too, is the subject of an Oakwood Press publication, *The Dublin and Blessington Tramway* by H Fayle and A T Newham. On the opening day, a special DUTC car left the GPO with the mails for the first Blessington tram from Terenure at 8.35am. An arrangement between the Blessington Company and the DUTC provided for through booking between the two systems. For an annual fee negotiated with the Post Office, the DUTC also transferred mailbags between the GPO and the Blessington line. Later, in electric days, considerable freight traffic was interchanged between the two systems. The Dublin & Blessington was the only tramway in the Dublin area to have double-deck bogie trailers, which were also top-covered. Up to three of these vehicles were regularly included in trains operating at peak traffic periods.

Steam on the Southern District

Taking advantage of provisions in the 1879 Tramways Orders Confirmation Act, the Dublin Southern District Tramways Company sought powers, on 13th July 1880, to use

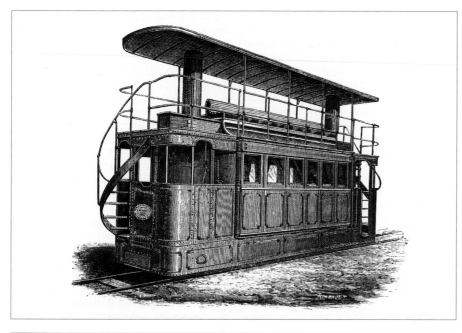

steam on its Haddington Road to Blackrock route. Following an inspection and declaration that the line was suitable for steam operation, the necessary licence was granted. This was for an experimental period of one year from 9th August 1881. Two Kitson locomotives, Nos 1 and 2, were ordered and a successful trial took place on Thursday, 21st July 1881.

A report in the *Freeman's Journal* on the following day gave details of the trial and included details of the locomotive. Weighing seven tons when ready for service, it had two cylinders with a 7¼in bore and 12in stroke. A casing or skirt protected the wheels and there was no smoke or steam, a condenser eliminating emissions and resulting in water consumption of 1½ to 2 gallons per mile. The automatic brake was capable of being set to cut in at a predetermined speed, in this case ten miles per hour, the driver knew his speed from an indicator. With its tramcar coupled up, the engine left the depot at Ballsbridge at 3pm and, 'made a very pleasant run to Blackrock and back, entering and leaving the various sidings without a hitch.' The distinguished passengers included directors and officials of the DSDT, the DUTC, the local authorities and Kitson's.

Although the steam experiment appears to have been technically successful, it encountered several problems. As might be expected, the horse lobby were opposed and appear to have logged every alleged instance of horses being frightened by the engines. These totalled 170, of which eight were stated to be serious.

On 28th January 1882, a memorial asking for the cancellation of the steam licence was presented to the authorities. The police, who were concerned with public safety, appear to have sided with the anti-steam activists.

Top left: **A Perrett steam car used on the Dublin & Lucan Steam Tramway in its early days. The original line was built to the gauge of 3ft.**

Centre left: **One of the steam tram engines of the Dublin & Lucan Steam Tramway Company poses for the camera. The company acquired seven 0-4-0 tank locomotives between 1882 and 1892.**

Bottom left: **A scene on the Dublin & Blessington Tramway. Unlike the Lucan line, this tramway was built to 5ft 3in gauge. The locomotive, which has a cab at either end to avoid the necessity of turning it round at the at the line's termini, is hauling three double-deck trailers.**
All photographs, author's collection.

Outside the company itself, there does not seem to have been any organised support in favour of steam operation. There was, however, one more very determined element of the 'anti' lobby, which probably overlapped with the memorialists; this was the railway company. In a file now in the Public Record Office at Kew, a civil servant wrote that the railway company was 'very sore' on account of the government, as it saw it, helping its rivals. The date of this observation is significant, 18th January 1882, exactly ten days before the anti-steam memorial.

In a report on the steam experiment, the Inspecting Officer, Major General C S Hutchinson, appears to have been satisfied with its conduct. He noted that the steam locomotives did not work between December 1881 and May 1882 and was prepared to allow the company's application for a further year's operation. Hutchinson also distinguished between those who objected on grounds of safety and those motivated by commercial considerations.

Unfortunately, Hutchinson had to stipulate that the speed should not exceed four miles per hour if the experiment was to be extended. This effectively killed off its advantages and in 1883 when the DSDT was given powers to double its main line, it was specifically refused permission to use steam. Two Wilkinson locomotives were said to have been ordered in 1884 but there is no record of whether they ever arrived and so far no reports of their operation have surfaced. In any event, the DSDT reverted, for the time being, to horse traction and was reported to have owned 26 trams.

Elite Districts, privileged passengers

The horse trams remained an almost exclusive preserve of the genteel and well-to-do classes identified by Maurice Brooks in 1873. Poorer people simply could not afford to travel and in any case most of them lucky enough to have jobs lived within walking distance of their employment. The level of fares and the fact that the trams were beyond the means of the less well-off was the cause of frequent criticism, and the most deprived areas of Dublin were never served directly by tramways. William Barrington's earnest wish that trams would enhance the lives of the poor remained unfulfilled.

The Tramwayman's Lot

Built to provide transport for anyone who could afford them, the Dublin tramways quickly became indispensable. They were heavily patronised and highly profitable for the DUTC, which constantly tried to attract even more passengers and succeeded mightily with the penny fare introduced in 1884. Another important factor was the well turned out vehicles drawn by smartly groomed horses, and staffed by crews who

were courteous and considerate. But whatever about the satisfaction of passengers, these crews, drivers in particular, enjoyed little comfort, standing on an open platform in all weathers. Their days were cruelly long and hard, the elements frequently adding to their physical discomfort. The following report of 4th January 1877 tells of what happened during a severe storm. 'The tramcar traffic on the Rathmines, Donnybrook and King's-bridge lines are not in any way interfered with. The Sandymount cars ran, with occasional interruptions from the flooded road, till the usual hour at night. The Clontarf trams left off plying at half-past one o'clock, and were unable to resume work until half-past four ...Mr William Anderson, Manager of the Dublin Tramway Company, gave anxious attention to the state of affairs during the day, in order that the public might not suffer inconvenience from the interrupted journeys of the cars, and he was efficiently assisted by Mr Gicks, the traffic superintendent.' An obvious feature of this report is a presumption that, whatever the weather, the men were expected to keep working until it became physically impossible to do so. This attitude contrasts starkly with that shown in the DUTC Chairman's detailed reports at half-yearly intervals about the health and sustenance of the company's horses. On those occasions, staff welfare was considered only when the subject was raised by concerned shareholders.

What was probably the most atrocious spell of weather in which the Dublin horse trams ever operated began on Saturday, 12th January 1894. A snowstorm, described as the worst since 1867, five years before trams first ran in Dublin, occurred that day, creating severe problems. Clontarf trams did not run out beyond the Howth Road junction and services on several other lines became intermittent as men and horses coped with the terrible weather conditions. Telegraph and telephone wires came down and there were several instances of conductors standing on upper decks holding up fallen wires so that their cars could pass underneath. On some lines, four horses were attached to each tram, with a fifth – the trace horse or tipper – to give added assistance up gradients. Despite the appalling conditions, an almost full service was provided. After the weekend, there was considerable flooding which once more made the tramwaymens' work very difficult.

The sufferings of the men in these and similar circumstances can only be imagined. Together with the ravages of working on the open-fronted vehicles in all weathers, their plight in regard to meal reliefs was frequently mentioned in letters to various newspapers, invariably pleading that they be better treated. In his highly critical leader about the Dublin Tramways Company on 18th November 1872, the editor of the *Freeman's Journal* had pointed out that the unfortunate tramwaymen did not even have time to fulfil their religious observances.

Paternalistic Autocracy

From its formation in 1881 to the First World War, the DUTC existed in a rigidly class-conscious world. Tramwaymen were bracketed by their employers with the artisans and daily labourers mentioned in the tramway acts. Some employers extended a modicum of well-meaning paternalism towards their workpeople, as in the provision of housing. In Dublin, with its appalling slum problem, this was a valuable and loyalty-enhancing perk. At the DUTC's annual general meeting of 2nd February 1887, the building of houses for tramway men at Terenure was rightly lauded, and a similar scheme was announced for Donnybrook.

Unfortunately, this benevolence was more than outweighed by the tyrannical autocracy endemic in contemporary management styles and practices. Their own shortcomings and the rights of their workers remained unrecognised by employers who failed to pay adequate wages or provide humane conditions in the workplace. In many industries, particularly transport, as we shall see later, technological progress actually worsened an already harsh environment.

On 16th January 1894, the DUTC Chairman, in unusually generous praise, said that the company's, 'conductors and drivers had proved themselves most admirable officials.' In an era when such employees were regarded as servants, the description 'officials' looks out of place. Its use could possibly be seen in the context of an event expected to take place on 25th January. This was a midnight meeting of the tramwaymen's union called in protest at plans by the Manager, William Anderson, to form a staff association.

Management, whose worst chimera was the ever-present likelihood of effective trades unions being formed, usually described organised labour as syndicalism or combinations to be resisted at all costs. In its efforts to stave off what it probably realised was eventually inevitable, flattery and cajolery were among the less hostile weapons employed. Over the years, managements in many industries made attempts to create staff associations through which they could monitor and influence workers' efforts to improve wages and terms of employment.

The DUTC was well aware of the conditions under which the men laboured, and of the widespread public concern at their plight. There were regular appeals by shareholders like Sir George Owens whose pleadings frequently referred to the 'unvarying courtesy and attention' of the staff, whom he called men of the best possible character.

Although treated less than humanely by their employers, the tramway staff was much better regarded by the travelling

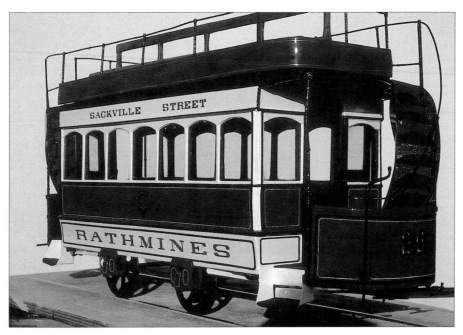

From 1887 to 1896, Spa Road works turned out highly standardised horse trams, those up to 1889 having knifeboard or back to back seating on the upper deck. This model of a knifeboard car may have been intended to illustrate the prototype, but is has also been suggested that it was produced for an 1891 court case. The model lay on top of a press in the CIE Club at Earl Place for many years, but was restored by Dublin Bus in 1987. Transport Museum Society of Ireland collection.

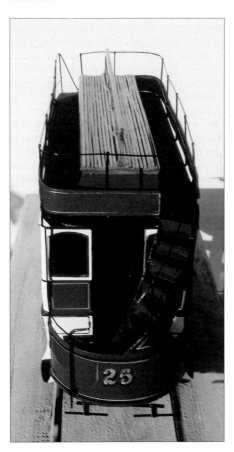

public. Regular passengers appreciated the personal attention they received. Apart from the numerous letters they wrote to the company and the newspapers appealing for better conditions, people showed their concern for the tramway men in a very practical way. Passengers on the various lines organised collections each December to give their drivers and conductors a well deserved Christmas box.

Consistent support for the tramwaymen by Sir George Owens and others finally bore fruit. At the company meeting held in February 1896 Dr Carte announced, to general approval, reduced working hours and more liberal mealtime arrangements for the men. He also recalled the numerous requests made over the years for the staff to be supplied with uniforms and announced, again amid widespread satisfaction, that this was now being done. The provision of uniforms was implicit in the Rule Books of most tramway companies, but was for years a dispensable option for the DUTC. In an age when most people were not well off, the provision of working apparel constituted a significant emolument.

As early as 1879, a newspaper correspondent had suggested that uniforms be issued to tramway staff, who at that time could only be identified by their licence badges and who were sometimes mistaken for passengers. Prior to 1896, at least some DUTC drivers wore greatcoats and bowler style hats bearing the company's initials. The decision to give the men uniforms was probably reinforced by what the directors saw on their visits to Europe and the United States where tramway staff were handsomely dressed.

Working Conditions: The Rule Book

Conditions of employment for those in all the tramway companies were very strict, a

good sense of what life was like being obvious from perusing the Rule Books, which were broadly similar for every undertaking. For example, the Dublin Southern District Company's 1894 edition contains a form of contract for all employees which runs to seven articles, all emphasising the employer's rights on the one hand and the employee's duties and responsibilities on the other.

The book then goes on to lay down the rules for the various categories of employee, General Rule No 2 stating that for any violation or other neglect of duty the workers 'may be fined a small sum, or may be suspended or discharged.' Inspectors' demeanour to their colleagues had to be courteous and considerate, guarding themselves against every jealous or unfriendly feeling (Rule 23).

Rule 45 required drivers to 'attend regularly, provided with uniform, badge, whip and whistle…10 minutes before the time appointed for their cars to start', while Rule 56 stated '…if any horse is, in the driver's opinion, unfit for work, he must report it to his foreman. This will free the driver from all responsibility.' Conductors, in compliance with Rule 70, had to 'report themselves…15 minutes before the time appointed for their cars to leave. They must brush the cushions, polish the windows and brass-work, and carefully see that the lamps, etc., are in good order'.

Both drivers and conductors were admonished by Rule 6 to 'be attentive to duty, observing every person as they proceed along the streets. Should they notice anyone looking at the cars as if undecided whether or not to ride, the driver or conductor should make a motion with his hand to attract their attention, calling out at the same time, 'car, madam?' or 'car, sir?' This would, many times, induce foot passengers to ride, and thereby increase the business of the company.'

A Scale Model: The Law's Bequest

For many years, a splendid but faded model of a Dublin horse tram lay in the Manager's office at the CIE Club in Earl Place. Soon after Dublin Bus was established in 1987, the model was extensively restored for display in the company's head office at 59 Upper O'Connell Street. Those involved in its refurbishment were amazed at the accuracy and standard of craftsmanship that had gone into it. It has been suggested that it may have been made to demonstrate, in miniature, features of the new generation of knifeboard horse trams built at the company's Spa Road works from about 1887 onwards. However, it is more likely to have been specially made for the case of Delany v DUTC, a lawsuit recalled in the 1995 Autumn/Winter issue of the *Northern Ireland Law Quarterly*. W N Osborough, in an article entitled *Recollections of Things Past:*

Trams, their Clientele and the Law, recalls the details of an action which in the days before workers' rights were acknowledged, could have had serious consequences for drivers and conductors.

On 18th February 1891 Conductor James Curran and Driver James Moore were the crew of a tram working on the Nelson Pillar to Phoenix Park line. On the North Circular Road, near its junction with Aughrim Street, a man named Delany attempted to board the moving tram. Because he was drunk, the conductor tried to prevent him from boarding by pushing him away. The DUTC man was enforcing the by-law which barred people under the influence of alcohol from travelling on the company's vehicles.

Before the driver realised what was happening and stopped the tram, Delany was somehow dragged along the road for some distance and suffered serious spinal injuries. He sued the DUTC and two trials followed. In the first, the jury disagreed, but the second found in favour of the plaintiff, awarding him £500 of the £3,000 he had claimed. But the verdict was overturned on appeal, James Curran's attempt to enforce the regulations and the duty of care being important factors in the litigation.

Protecting the Staff from Violence

Unprovoked assaults on transport staff are nothing new, as proved by reports of offenders brought before the courts well over a hundred years ago. A report in the *Freeman's Journal* on 12th July 1881 described such an assault on Driver John Quinn and Conductor John Conroy at Sandymount the previous evening. A passenger who had become ill was being assisted down the stairs by Conductor Conroy on his outbound car when a tram travelling in the opposite direction came alongside. On this car were two young men who for no known reason attacked both Driver Quinn and Conductor Conroy. The conductor was struck on the head with a stick, sustaining injuries which necessitated medical treatment. The two miscreants appeared before Chief Magistrate Charles O'Donel who fined one of them £2 for the assault on Driver Quinn or a month's imprisonment in default. The man who committed the more serious assault was fined £4 with a choice of two months in jail, the magistrate directing that £2 of the fine be paid to Conductor Conroy as compensation. £1 in 1881 was the equivalent of of over £65 in today's money.

How the Tram Evolved

Since George Shillibeer's omnibus of 1829 and John Stephenson's primordial 1832 tramcar, the two species have developed almost side by side, a revolution taking place when steam, electricity and the internal combustion engine replaced the horse.

Yet, even as the advent of mechanisation changed the mode of traction, the shape and structure of the vehicles displayed a continuing evolutionary progression. Tram and bus designs over the years have always copied and complemented each other; the first double-deckers were buses.

John Stephenson's tram consisted of three coach bodies mounted on a four-wheeled underframe with running boards at each side. In time, the separate compartments evolved into a single saloon with longitudinal seating and a door at the back. Like the primitive horse bus, it had the driver's seat, or perch, on the roof at the front.

Most early horse buses were box-like single-deckers with the entrance in the centre of the rear bulkhead and a step below to facilitate access. During the 1840s, enterprising operators found that they could increase seating capacity – and revenue – by putting box seats, reached by a ladder, on the roofs of their vehicles. Later, the rear step was extended to provide a platform for the conductor and a starting point for the ladder, which subsequently became a spiral staircase. Early versions consisted of a simple open framework, more substantial strings, risers and steps coming later.

Meanwhile, the tram became double-ended, thus eliminating difficulties at termini, where a platform at each end enabled the horses to be walked round a car while the driver and conductor exchanged positions. In the 1860s the double-deck omnibus inspired tram builders to produce double-deckers, with longitudinal benches inside. At first, the upper deck seating consisted of a longitudinal board on the top of the lower deck clerestory, the passengers sitting back-to-back and facing outwards. In time this developed into a more comfortable slatted seat with a backrest for the passengers; this came to be known as the knifeboard arrangement.

William Barrington, promoting his original tramway scheme, gave his vision of what a tram should be like, 'Commodious, well lighted and far superior to the horse omnibus it should also ... be well ventilated and upholstered'. From the start, virtually all the Dublin trams were double-ended, the horses simply being walked around to the other end of the car at each terminus.

Outraged Public Decency

Women were discouraged from travelling upstairs on the early double-deckers, Victorian prudery considering it immodest for female ankles to be seen by bystanders. The safety railings along the upper deck sides were fitted with decency boards, which also provided space for advertising. Thus began the evolution of a vehicle the descendants of which are so familiar to-day and whose upper deck panelling is still referred to as the decency boards by older coachbuilders.

Some people became very agitated by what they perceived as lapses in the maintenance of public morality. Their concern extended to tramway companies running what they regarded as unacceptably equipped rolling stock, as illustrated in a letter which appeared in the *Freeman's Journal* on 23rd April 1878.

Dear Sir – In the interest of womanly decency, may I ask of you and your contemporaries to use your influence with the Dublin Tramway Company that on such days as this, when the weather is so fine and the cars so crowded, they re-place upon the ladders leading up to the outside seats the canvas screening which was used during their first summer season here. This would prevent the positively scandalous scenes, which were witnessed today from the starting places of these conveyances...Yours truly, 'A Passer-by.'

First Generation Dublin Trams

The DUTC took over 137 trams from its three constituent companies. This number was made up of 82 DTC cars, with 30 from the Central and 25 from the North Dublin. Unfortunately, it is not possible to construct a reliable fleet list showing which trams were taken over from the constituent companies and how they were renumbered. It is most likely that the DTC stock retained their original identities, those of the other companies being renumbered. There were some single-deckers, mostly one-horse driver-only cars, but the bulk of the fleet consisted of 46-seat double-deckers seating 20 passengers inside (downstairs) and 26 outside (on top). The upper deck was reached by staircases, in most cases the simple spiral ladders already described, which turned anti-clockwise as one ascended. These trams also had access steps on both sides of the platform, passengers being requested to alight at the near or footpath side.

Virtually all of the trams operated by the pre-1881 companies were imported. The six bought by the DTC when the Cork system closed in 1875, were the only second-hand cars ever to operate in Dublin. The DTC carried out overhauls and major rebuilding at Terenure depot and there is evidence that some new trams were assembled there shortly before the 1880 amalgamation.

The DUTC repaired and rebuilt some trams at Terenure, which became the company's principal depot on its formation in 1880. Also, long after a new car works was established, some repair work was still carried out at Terenure. To make as complete a record as possible of the horse tram fleet, it is necessary to piece together information from contemporary newspaper reports, old photographs and the DUTC Car Repair Books. These volumes escaped destruction in 1922 because they were kept at Spa Road or Ballsbridge, where they were carefully preserved by Charles Ross until 1949. While pre-1889 details were sketchy, later work was more fully described.

Horse tram No 33, on the Palmerston Park (Upper Rathmines) line, at the King William statue in College Green. This car, which left Spa Road works in December 1885, was replaced by the first DUTC-built electric tram in September 1897. Heiton's Coals and Jeyes Fluid both continued to advertise on Dublin trams up to 1949 and on buses for several years afterwards. Lawrence collection, National Library

Although incomplete, the earliest Repair Book entries establish some basic facts. Several of the trams taken over from the old companies are recorded as 'existing' in 1882, with some clues as to their routes and origins. For example, No 28 was a Kingsbridge car, while No 34 was allocated to Sandymount, both were probably former Dublin Tramways stock. Nos 84 and 97 were respectively described as Harold's Cross and ex-Rathfarnham cars, suggesting both were ex-Central. Nos 127 and 128, referred to as Cabra trams, possibly originated with the North Dublin Company. The highest fleet number in the newly-formed DUTC was certainly 137.

Spa Road Works
At the time of the DUTC's inception, there was a strong and growing consensus in the business community about the need to encourage Irish manufacturing industry and create employment. There was no doubt about where the new company stood on this issue. In connection with a recent decision to organise an Irish Exhibition in Dublin a letter from William Anderson appeared in the *Freeman's Journal* of 30th August 1881. He wrote that the board of the DUTC had discussed the revival of home industries and was contributing £100 towards funding the Exhibition.

Always keen to expand local employment, William Martin Murphy was probably the inspiration behind the DUTC decision to build its own rolling stock, a sensible move in a city with an enviable coach-building tradition. Murphy frequently queried the logic of sending out of Ireland any work that could be done at home. He continued to preach and practise this doctrine of self-sufficiency throughout his lifetime.

In his August 1881 letter to the *Freeman,* Anderson had announced that the DUTC would display the first ever Irish-made tram at the planned Dublin Exhibition. Within a year of the DUTC coming into existence, a site was acquired at Goldenbridge, adjacent to the then existing tram depot and not far from the great Inchicore railway works. Thus was the Spa Road works established. At the half-yearly meeting of the company on 7th February 1882, the new workshops were reported as being built and that it was the company's intention to build all its own rolling stock in future.

No 138: The Harbinger
A detailed account was written about tram No 138, the Exhibition car. Its construction commenced on 31st May 1882; this is the earliest date quoted in the Car Repair records. No 138 was duly put on show at the Exhibition on 10th August. William Martin Murphy was one of the prominent citizens who organised this very successful shopwindow for Irish products. It greatly encouraged indigenous manufacturers and, as intended, proved an effective springboard for future 'Buy Irish' campaigns.

It is unclear whether No 138, the first tram built by the DUTC, was constructed entirely at Spa Road - some work may have been carried out at Terenure - but its completion was very significant. An *Irish Times* description of the car was reproduced in *The Nation* of 2nd September 1882.

'In the tramcar which is exhibited by the Dublin United Tramways Company will be found an indication of a strong desire and determination on the part of an important public body to do their own work at home. From top to bottom the car has been built in Dublin, and beyond all doubt it reflects the highest credit on everyone concerned in its construction, from Mr Nugent, the compa-

ny's engineer, down to the humblest workman under his direction. It is beautifully finished, the woodwork, ironwork, upholstering, fitting, painting and decorating being excellent specimens of good workmanship. This car is of full size, 23 feet 3 inches long by 6 feet 9¾ wide and 11 feet 6¼ inches high from the top of the roof seats to rails. The whole of the work has been made in the company's workshops, with the exception of the wheels and axles, which have been made by Messrs. Courtney, Stephens and Bailey, in this city. There are several details in the design of the car which merit attention. First, ventilation is secured by openings in the panelling of the roof, which are fully protected from rain and draughts by the formation of the top seat, which acts as a weathering to the interior roof of the car. Second, the handrail to the roof is formed as a girder to prevent the sagging which takes place in most tramcars. Third, the stairs to the roof are of strong construction, covered all round, and so made that passengers must leave on the 'near' side. Fourth, the 'draw bar' or portion of the car to which the horses are harnessed and the pole fastened; this is arranged with a coil spring to prevent sudden jerk to the horses which ordinarily takes place when starting. Fifth, axle boxes are completely closed in so as to prevent access of dirt, and also to retain a charge of air, which is taken up as required by the axles, saving the frequent application of oil by hand as is generally necessary.'

No 138 was renumbered 63 on 12th December 1882, the first in the long game of numerical musical chairs played by the DUTC over the years, and later still, on 5th February 1883 it became No 32 for the Kingsbridge line.

Following No 138's debut, the next Spa Road tram was a replacement. A new No 1 left the works on 19th April 1883, its cost being given as £163, the car it replaced was broken up on the following 27th December. Although at a later date, a reference to No 2 demonstrates that tramcar construction by the DUTC provided employment for people in other Dublin factories. A cryptic note shows that car No 2, a pre-DUTC vehicle, was sent, on 5th April 1886, for work to be carried out in Spence's Foundry, Cork Street. This engineering company was noted for its products, including the celebrated Geoghegan locomotives for the Guinness Brewery railways.

Car Costs and Improvements
Nos 1, 2 and 138, referred to above, all marked important stages in the development of the Dublin tram. As more new cars were built, there were modifications and experiments, ending in better and more

economical vehicles. There were slight variations in the cost of new horse tram bodies. No 1 cost £163, but No 19, which entered service on the Rathmines line in June 1883, came out at £156, while No 11, sent to work on the Terenure line in March 1885, cost £165.

Unfortunately, the newspapers of the period, notable for comprehensive reporting, often omitted one detail from their otherwise admirable coverage of DUTC trams in the 1880s. This was the fleet number, quoting which would have been a boon to a future transport historian reading the *Freeman's Journal* of 10th October 1884. The paper reported that a third new car from the DUTC's Inchicore works had been placed on the Donnybrook line. Emphasising that all work on the vehicle had been carried out in the company's own shops, it described the 'difficulty in retaining the rigidity and original form of a tramcar.' There followed a detailed description of the bracing, which would prevent the platforms from dropping, and the joints of the bodywork working loose.

The report described several other features of the new tram, revealed that it was somewhat shorter than those in general use, resulting in a lighter load to be drawn by the horses. A statement that two more cars of similar construction were approaching completion ended the report. The new cars were also referred to at the DUTC's half-yearly general meeting in February 1884, which was informed that while imported cars cost somewhat less than £200, Inchicore-built vehicles came out at £164 each. Another contemporary statistic, quoted at a meeting of the Engineers' Institute a month earlier gave the annual maintenance cost of a tram as £48.

A newspaper report in June 1885 described two more of the Spa Road cars. The DUTC has recently made several important additions to their rolling stock which will, no doubt, still further popularise this cheap and convenient mode of travelling. They have, at the same time, given a powerful stimulus to Irish industry, the new cars being, with the exception of the glass, exclusively of Dublin manufacture. On the Rathmines line, there are two of the new cars running, No 7 and No 10. They are easily distinguished by their light roomy appearance and admirable finish. They contrast most favourably with the imported article. They are only 2½ tons in weight, compared with 3½ tons of the older cars. With an improved system of iron bracing, the heavy woodwork of the sides has been disposed of, with

the effect of imparting an elegant appearance to the interior. The windows have been carried much higher, and the smothered gloomy atmosphere which is characteristic of the old cars, is no more. Ventilation is good and the windows amply covered. A judicious and efficacious use of polished Irish oak, ash and pitch pine, in addition to imported mahogany is used in the interior.

From Knifeboards to Garden Seats

Another exhibition was held in Dublin in 1885. Known as the Irish Citizens (or Artisans) Exhibition, this also included a DUTC tramcar, No 143, recorded in the Repair Books as being completed on 8th June at a cost of £175. It drew considerable praise and on 2nd September was examined closely by Charles Stewart Parnell, a strong proponent of Irish industrial development.

Earlier Spa Road horse trams were of the knifeboard type, but later vehicles were known as garden-seat cars, having a central gangway or aisle on the upper deck with double seats on either side. These seats had reversible backs, enabling passengers to face the direction of travel. Unfortunately, the incomplete records of horse-tram construction leave the building date of the first garden-seat car uncertain, but it was probably in or shortly after 1885.

No 28, built in 1886, is specifically mentioned as having garden (transverse) seats on top and may have been an experimental prototype for this type of car. No 111 is also referred to as having garden seats fitted, suggesting that it may have been rebuilt to allow a change from knifeboard seating. But whether of knifeboard or garden seat type, a distinguishing feature of all DUTC-built horse trams was the seven windows on either side.

The number of new cars built in the previous six months, but not their identities, was frequently given at DUTC half-yearly

shareholders' meetings. It has not so far proved possible to align this information with that contained in the repair books, as when Dr Carte informed the general meeting of 3rd August 1886 that three new cars had been built in the half year ending on 30th June. Of eight new cars recently built, he said that five were replacements for older vehicles and three were additions to the fleet.

From November 1885 when No 150 was placed in service on the Palmerston Park line, the rolling stock seems to have remained numerically static for a time. There is no written reference to horse trams numbered 151-154 but at least two of them appear in photographs, so the surviving records are tantalisingly incomplete. No 137 exemplifies the gaps in the DUTC records. It is written up as being scrapped on 8th August 1888 with no reference to a replacement, yet a horse tram with this number appears in a photograph of Grattan (Capel St) Bridge taken several years later.

About 40 trams are recorded as having been scrapped in the 1880s with no record of replacements bearing the same fleet numbers but there is ample photographic evidence that such vehicles went into service. Many knifeboard cars seem to have been rebuilt as such even after the introduction of the garden seat type. It is possible that some old upper deck structures were recycled into what were otherwise new vehicles.

There was a continuing requirement for knifeboard trams on the Sandymount line because of the low railway bridge on Bath Avenue. Approaching the bridge, it was the conductor's duty to ensure that top-deck passengers were seated while the tram passed under it. In the Merrion Square accident of November 1898 (see page 40), the trailer involved, horse car No 3, is yet anoth-

The first No 61, a horse tram inherited from the Dublin Tramways Company and allocated to the Clontarf line, was renumbered and reassigned to Kingsbridge depot in 1884. Its replacement, allocated to Clontarf on 9th May 1884 is seen here on what was probably an outing. There is no further official record of this vehicle. Birney collection

er of those shown in the records as having been scrapped several years previously, in this case on 26th February 1887, without a replacement being mentioned.

A Well Equipped Works and its Output

Spa Road was a source of pride to the DUTC for the skills of its craftsmen and the excellence of the vehicles they built. It was also a prime example of an enterprising indigenous industry that created considerable spin-off employment. The company's management was happy to demonstrate this whenever possible, as on Thursday, 7th April 1887 when a large party of invited guests toured the works and saw several cars being built or repaired. A report of the visit which appeared in the *Freeman's Journal* the next day contains an invaluable description of the equipment in the various shops and the work carried out in each of them.

Listed in the paper was everything one might expect to find in a well-equipped Victorian tram factory, from an Otto gas engine and 50-ton press, to the back-up tramway vehicles being built there. In horse car days, the service vehicles included forage vans and wagons, corn drays, road and handcarts, sand distributors and water lorries. Some long-defunct Dublin companies servicing the DUTC were also listed, among them Mitchells of Parliament Street (upholstery) and Strong & Sons of Hammond Lane who cast wheels, axleboxes and guard frames.

A series of 34 cars numbered 155-188, built between December 1893 and June 1897, may have replaced older vehicles with numbers lower than 150. Nos 129 and 130, scrapped in December 1892, are described as 'skeleton cars'. There are also references to other strange trams, such as No 15. This is shown as being at work in 1883, but became a workman's car on 3rd June 1886, serving in this capacity until 4th September 1886. The next entry records that it was broken up in June 1894, a new car with the same number emerging the following December. Workmens' cars and dining cars may have been the company's response to the frequently criticised lack of facilities for the staff and fare paying workmen. No 82, also referred to as a workman's car, was broken up on 21st April 1886; a new No 82 was in service on 27th July. When replaced by a new tram in April 1896, a month before the first electrics ran on the Haddington Road to Dalkey line, No 95 became a dining car, renumbered 171. It was subsequently rebuilt as electric tram No 75.

Apart from No 95, several other horse trams were renumbered, sometimes more than once, over the years. One which was involved in a convoluted series of identities was No 63. Shown as being broken up on 22nd August 1882, it was rebuilt, renum-

bered 138 and sent to the Irish Exhibition at Earlsfort Terrace in the same year. The reference 'rebuilt' is confusing, because the fleet records for No 138 specifically state that building of this car commenced on 31st May, nearly two months before its predecessor was broken up.

On 12th December No 138 became No 63 and was working the Kingsbridge line on 5th February 1883 when it received the fleet number 32. The number 63 was then given to car 19, which was replaced by a new vehicle. But this No 63 later went to Clontarf as No 32, causing further confusion. Meanwhile, a new No 138 was completed in December 1884 for the Terenure line. Events like this were frequently due to reasons of accountancy or the result of accidents and right through the history of the Dublin tramways there were also instances of unofficial renumberings, colloquially known as ringers. These were hard to discover and there were probably, instances where number changes went undetected by even the most astute observer.

Duplicates and Ghosts

Two other horse tram renumberings are noteworthy. One involves No 62, which became 162 in 1884 to distinguish it from a new No 62. The number 162 was far above the highest fleet number in use at the time and 'No 162' was in fact broken up on 28th July 1887, seven years before the numbers reached 162 and a new car received this identity. Adding one or more even hundreds to its original number, thus marking a supernumerary out from the regular fleet is a time-honoured practice in transport circles. Rolling stock thus treated was often referred to as being on the duplicate list.

While the highest fleet number carried by a DUTC horse tram was 188, the actual number of cars was officially put at 186. In 1896, up to 175 of these may have been serviceable (the official number for June 1896 was 170), but the true total of working vehicles could have been considerably less. Indeed, the *Railway World* of 11th May 1899 had quoted the number as 162.

181 horse trams are inferred to have been built at Spa Road. The first electric car No 33 of September 1897, was described in the official records as the 182nd Inchicore-built DUTC tramcar. This reference provides yet further proof of the many inconsistencies and gaps in the horse-car records, the electrics cars being far better chronicled. There is also a possibility that the works numbers recorded for the horse trams may have included departmental vehicles.

Horse Cars Listed as New by the DUTC

In the copies of DUTC records available to the author, the 128 new horse trams in the accompanying table are shown to have been built between 1882 and 1896.

1	20	62	82	107	136	157	173
2	21	63	83	108	138	158	174
4	22	64	84	110	139	159	175
6	23	65	86	111	140	160	176
7	26	66	87	113	141	161	177
9	28	68	88	117	142	162	178
10	31	71	89	119	143	163	179
11	33	72	91	120	144	164	180
12	35	73	95	121	145	165	181
13	46	75	96	122	146	166	182
14	48	76	101	123	147	167	183
15	49	77	102	124	148	168	184
16	54	78	103	125	149	169	185
17	57	79	104	126	150	170	186
18	58	80	105	128	155	171	187
19	61	81	106	135	156	172	188

This is 60 short of the nominal fleet and 49 less than the number of vehicles said to have been serviceable. As we have already seen, several trams recorded as being broken up without replacement did in fact have their numbers perpetuated on new vehicles. It is even possible that most of these can eventually be identified from photographs capable of being dated.

Nine of the listed trams (Nos 17, 46, 57, 77, 78, 79, 80 and 111) are recorded as being rebuilt, but were probably new cars incorporating some parts from their predecessors.

A total of 87 new garden-seat horse trams was built at Spa Road in eight years between June 1889 and June 1897. These cars constituted almost half the fleet. All but one, No 49, turned out in June 1894, were later rebuilt as electrics (see the Rolling Stock catalogue, page 142). An instance of the information deficit surrounding the horse trams occurs in a specific report of garden seat cars built in the first six months of 1890. Dr Carte categorically put the number at six, of which four can be positively recognised as Nos 17, 57, 77 and 81; the other two remain unidentified and were possibly rebuilds of older vehicles. The Chairman also mentioned that the garden-seat cars had led to a great increase in the number of, 'lady outside passengers'.

Normally, a horse tram was allocated permanently to a particular line and painted in a distinctive route livery for easy recognition. Colours included purple for Palmerston Park, cream or pale yellow for Donnybrook, green for Rathfarnham, and salmon for the 'Castle' tram. This ran between Westland Row and a siding in Palace Street, at the lower entrance to Dublin Castle and operated primarily for the convenience of civil servants.

Every tram had the name of the outer terminus painted on its rocker panels (the lower sections of the lower deck side panels) and repeated on the outside strings of the stairs. Advertising, painted or paper, was carried along the side and front panels of the upper deck, the sides sometimes carrying two displays, one above the other. Bullseye glasses in oil lamps at the saloon ends showed corresponding colours at night.

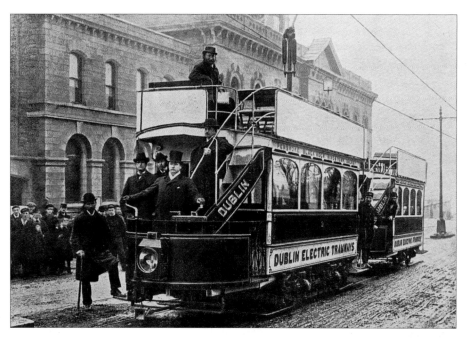

This well-known photograph records what was probably a specially staged occasion to mark the official inauguration of electric traction on the Dalkey line on 16th May 1896. Clifton Robinson stands at the controls of car No 2 coupled to its trailer outside the Town Hall in Kingstown. The platform party includes Robert Joule, the electrical engineer. The man on the top deck is Davy Stevens, a famous Kingstown personality of that era. BT-H Brochure

The advent of the tram was heralded by the jingling of bells on the horses' harness; even the trace horses at the steep gradients sported these embellishments.

Horse Tram Speeds

Questions are frequently asked about the service speeds achieved by various modes of public transport over the years. Even in horse tram days, velocity was frequently a matter for debate. Speeds are generally accepted as being between four and six miles per hour for horse trams, with occasional bursts of up to eight miles an hour. In his report of 1873, Parke Neville estimated the speed at five miles per hour, which was probably a carefully calculated average.

Although horse trams could not remotely match the speed of a train, railway companies worried about passengers being lost to tramways in pursuance of door-to-door times. Within the constraints of concerns about animal welfare, every attempt was made to achieve faster times. Speculation often arises about traffic speeds when the horse was king, but reliable information is very hard to get. There is, however, one record of an experiment carried out in Dublin, which helps to throw some light on a time, widely regarded as leisurely, when in fact delays irritated many people.

In 1884, considerable efforts were being made to speed up the mails between Britain and Ireland. Trains carrying the mails from Kingstown terminated at Westland Row, the line connecting that station with Amiens Street and Kingsbridge being in the future. In the meantime, transfer times from Westland Row to the other Dublin stations were deemed unacceptable. Because trams could provide a reliable link, a carefully timed journey was made on 13th October 1884 and reported in the *Freeman's Journal.*

On that Monday, a tram left Westland Row Station at 7.45am and, travelling via D'Olier Street and the South Quays, reached Kingsbridge Station 13 minutes later at 7.58. Another journey was made between Westland Row and Amiens Street, via Sackville Street, in eight minutes. A proposal to carry mailbags regularly by tram from Westland Row to the other stations never materialised, but the trial runs indicate a speed of just eight miles per hour. This was the maximum speed at which horse trams could be

expected to run and the 1884 trial trip must have been non-stop.

Complacency

The construction of a tramway invariably conferred a great sense of modernity on a road or district. Once the service became established and well patronised, it seemed as if the trams had always been there and would continue to run at their sedate pace for all time. Steam, acceptable on roadside and largely rural lines like those to Blessington or Lucan, impinged but little on the minds of those whose imagination stretched no further than the stable door. With steam kept at bay and alternatives like compressed air or gas showing little promise, the horse was invincible, or so they thought. But seven short years after Dublin saw its first horse trams, a new force was on the march, one destined to effect technological and social revolutions.

Developing the Electric Tramcar

Following the construction of Michael Faraday's successful dynamo in 1831, expanding knowledge and the development of ever more efficient electrical equipment turned the minds of scientists and engineers to the possibilities of electric traction. In 1879 Werner von Siemens demonstrated a reliable electric locomotive at the Berlin Industrial Exhibition. May 1881 saw his pioneering electric tramline, a mile and a half long, in use at Lichterfelde.

In September 1883, the world's first lengthy electric line began operation at the Giant's Causeway in County Antrim. Two years later, in October 1885, another Irish line, the Bessbrook & Newry, opened. A short time previously, on 29th September, the first urban electric tramway in these islands began working in Blackpool. This

operated on the conduit system, the trams having a plough-like attachment, which ran in a slot between the running rails. The plough collected current from a conductor rail laid in the conduit below the road.

The next major development in the United Kingdom took place in October 1891 with the opening of the Roundhay tramway in Leeds. None of the various methods of current collection hitherto used had found universal acceptance, but the Roundhay trams ushered in a new era. They took their current from an overhead wire by means of a sprung trolley pole topped with a wheel, which ran along the underside of the wire. Arguably one of the most important contributions to the evolution of the electric tramcar, this was among a host of features developed by Frank Sprague and introduced in Richmond, Virginia (USA) in 1887.

Sprague's, and other tramway developments, were watched carefully by the DUTC. Possibilities for mechanisation ranged from the fanciful to those with real potential. The latter included steam, cable haulage, gas, compressed air, accumulators (batteries), and mains electricity. Over a period of several years, the Dublin company looked seriously at the feasibility of various alternatives to the horse.

While steam had been considered but not pursued by the DUTC, the ability of one steam engine to replace up to 20 horses remained a powerful incentive to explore every possibility. Cable haulage and battery traction were also evaluated at different times. The company concluded, as early as 1884, that when electric motors became better developed, they would offer the best method of replacing horses. Electrification using Sprague's system won the day and the February 1887 half-yearly DUTC general meeting heard that the directors were already considering the conversion of the system. For Dublin it was now only a matter of time but it was the manner rather than the event of the new regime's inevitable arrival that was remarkable.

Opposition to the DUTC's Plans
In the early 1890s, the DUTC's horse tramway system was highly profitable, carrying up to 80,000 passengers a day and seemingly safe from competition. An impression of steady progress dominated Dr Carte's reports to the half-yearly general meetings during that period. For example, he was able to announce the building of six new cars between July and December 1890 at a total cost of £1,170. A total of 87 new trams was built in the eight years to 1897.

Concessions were obtained on taxation of the fleet which had been reduced to £468 per annum by 1891. In the following year Carte noted that stage carriage licences cost £212. In keeping with a larger and still expanding fleet, the number of horses in stock went up from 971 in 1881 to 1,099 ten years later. At the half-yearly DUTC meeting held on 21st July 1896, the company was reported to have 1,577 horses for its officially declared 186 trams, somewhat more than eight horses per car though a more likely figure is the '162 pair horse cars' quoted by the *Railway World* on 11th May 1899. This figure would also bring the ratio of horses to cars closer to the ideal 10 to 1.

Service improvements were introduced frequently. In 1891, a short extension of the Palmerston Park line brought trams up to the gates of the park. A new link through Lincoln Place was opened in August 1892. This became in January 1893 part of a circular route, in effect a rough oval, serving College Green and Westland Row at a 1d fare. Where possible, the opportunity to double existing single track was taken when reconstruction fell due. Despite earlier opposition from the Corporation, the Kingsbridge line along Essex Quay was doubled in 1892. The track across Grattan Bridge and the line from Berkeley Road to Phoenix Park was similarly treated in 1895.

The new Head Office at 9 Upper Sackville Street, at the junction of Cathedral Street, came into use on 1st January 1893. The previous premises opposite the GPO at 32 Lower Sackville Street was retained for the traffic and parcels departments. Profits from the ancillary services continued to improve. Tramcar advertising became ever more important and lucrative, while the parcel service went from strength to strength. In 1895, an agreement was made with the Dublin Wicklow & Wexford Railway under which the DUTC handled all parcel traffic on behalf of the railway throughout the coastal townships.

Serious arguments arose with the Corporation from time to time, as in the case of the Inchicore line through James's Street. In this dispute, which ended up in court on 21st January 1889, the Corporation had altered the level of the thoroughfare and ordered the DUTC to relay the tram rails to the same level as the new road surface. The company refused but the judge decided in favour of the Corporation, pointing out that tramway companies had responsibilities deriving from the great benefits that accrued from their operations. Following this judgement, Dr Carte was warned of the risks he took on the legal tightrope between the company's rights it was his duty to uphold and those of the Corporation. It was even suggested that he might become a guest in his own establishment, a reference to his position as surgeon to Kilmainham Jail.

Despite the continuing success of the horse system, the company's management was already firmly committed to electrification. The proposed change promised lower costs, greater carrying capacity, higher speeds and bigger dividends. As early as 1886, authority had been obtained to try out an electric car on the Terenure line south of Portobello Bridge, which was also the city boundary. This trial did not take place, due to objections from the Board of Trade. In the light of this and progress in other directions, a later proposal to operate an experimental electric car on the Dollymount route was also dropped.

In the early nineties senior DUTC officials visited several European cities to see electric trams at work. Dr Carte, William Martin Murphy, John Wigham, William Anderson and consultant H F Parshall, described as one of the most eminent electrical engineers, also went to the United States. There, they were particularly impressed by the developments which had flowed from Frank Sprague's success, noting the proliferation of both electric tramway systems and equipment manufacturers. In July 1893, the DUTC shareholders heard that the directors, encouraged by what they had seen on their trips abroad, were actively considering electrification. The ensuing period of deliberation ended in November 1894 with a formal decision to electrify. Paradoxically, following the DUTC's momentous decision, an extension to the horse system was opened in February 1896. This last horse line, to Dolphin's Barn was originally intended to be built as an electric route and became an embarrassment to the company during the electrification process.

On committing themselves to electrification, the directors faced considerable difficulties, some of them possibly unforeseen. While a few shareholders harboured residual doubts, it was announced at the half-yearly meeting on 22nd January 1895 that the system would go electric as soon as possible, with the Clontarf line the first for conversion. The following day, in an editorial supporting the plan, the *Freeman's Journal* expressed a sentiment often invoked a century later, 'The spirit of the age is all in favour of efficiency and speed.' Unfortunately, the DUTC seems to have overlooked two factors, politics and vested interests. Dublin Corporation, already at loggerheads with the company over several issues, was angry at not being consulted in advance and the DUTC directors may not have appreciated the sensitivity needed to handle a political public body that perceived itself as slighted. The vested interests covered a wide spectrum which we will encounter shortly.

The Corporation had welcomed trams to Dublin in 1872 but its relationship with the companies deteriorated over the years. DUTC management probably felt, however mistakenly, that its contribution to the city over the years, paying hefty rates and sundry other charges, maintaining miles of thoroughfare and providing a public service, entitled it to certain privileges. This was seen differently by the Corporation. Bad as things were in 1895, they got much worse after that.

The Dalkey Line Transformation
In the early 1890s, the contrast between travelling on the DUTC's integrated system and the disjointed tramways connecting Dublin with Dalkey could not have been greater. A tram journey from Nelson Pillar to Dalkey at that time was only for masochists. The Dalkey passenger took a Dublin United tram to Haddington Road, or, if in a Dublin Southern District car, endured a change of horses there. A change of vehicles was made at Blackrock and again at Kingstown, where a trip up or down Royal Marine Road was over double track of two gauges. The nine-mile journey from Sackville Street to Dalkey took more than two hours, compared to 35 minutes by train. By every means at its disposal, the DW&W strove incessantly to perpetuate this situation.

Two sections of this much derided four-part tramway service were owned by the Dublin Southern District Tramways Company, the subordinate of Imperial Tramways referred to earlier in this chapter. A wholly owned subsidiary of the Imperial Tramways group, the DSDT was only moderately successful. At its April 1887 annual general meeting held in London, it was revealed that the profit for 1886 had been £297 16s 5d and when a deficit for 1885 was covered, the surplus was reduced to £197 18s 11d. Among the factors blamed for this unsatisfactory state of affairs were 'the unfortunate condition of the country and the depressed state of trade.' However, the worst problem was the 'fierce opposition of the Dublin, Wicklow and Wexford Railway.'

Often referred to disparagingly as 'the English company', the DSDT was said to have offered its two unconnected and

A British-Thomson picture showing the engines and generators at Shelbourne Road, Ballsbridge which produced the power for the Dalkey line. This was claimed to be the first three-phase plant in Europe and was capable of driving 50 trams, each weighing ten tons, at eight miles per hour. Following completion of the Ringsend plant, the Ballsbridge equipment was dismantled in 1901. BT-H Brochure

incompatible lines to both the DUTC DW&W. The Blackrock and Kingstown was definitely offered to the railway company, but it is certain that acquisition of this or any other competing tramway would have been blocked by the Board of Trade. As things turned out, the B & K was acquired, on 24th August 1893 by Imperial Tramways for £7,500. As the Southern District was already wholly owned by this company, based in Bristol since 1892, and electric traction was obviously on the agenda, rapid developments were to be expected.

The next stage of the revolution was the appointment of Mr J Clifton Robinson (1848-1910) as Managing Director. Robinson, who lived at St Mary's Road, Ballsbridge during his Dublin sojourn, had succeeded Arthur Tyler as Manager of the DSDT in the autumn of 1892. A chartered engineer, Clifton Robinson was a gifted businessman and very experienced in tramway matters. Born in Birkenhead, he had worked as an office boy for G F Train when the latter introduced trams to London in 1861. He was involved in the Cork tramway project in the 1870s and was married a Cork woman.

On appointment to the Southern District company, Robinson pushed through an ambitious electrification programme. Finance was arranged in co-operation with the Thomson-Houston Company, which acquired a controlling interest. Robinson converted the Kingstown to Dalkey section to 5ft 3in gauge and relaid most of the line from Kingstown to Haddington Road. Here it should be mentioned that, while nominally 5ft 3in, most Dublin tramways were actually of 5ft 2 3/16in gauge. This allowed the wheels of standard gauge railway vehicles to travel on their flanges over grooved tramway track.

A generating station was built at Shelbourne Road, the equipment including three Babcock and Wilcox boilers working at a pressure of 140lbs per square inch, fired by Vicars mechanical stokers. There were four Willans compound condensing two-crank engines with belt drive. Two of these operated British Thomson-Houston (BT-H) 100kw four-pole generators, the other pair being matched to two six-pole three-phase generators. Current from the three-phase machines was transmitted at 2,500v through underground cables to substations at Blackrock and Dalkey, where it was converted to

operate the outer end of the line at the same voltage (500v direct current) as the sections supplied from the four-pole generators.

Dublin was among the first cities in these islands to have an electric tram service, and the Southern District installation, claimed to be the first three-phase plant in Europe, was regarded as a major achievement. Cooling water for the generating station was taken from the River Dodder, which flows at the rear of the site. The station was said to be capable of driving 50 cars, each weighing ten tons, at eight miles per hour.

The tramway was divided electrically into half-mile sections with feeders and section insulators at these intervals. Overhead work was installed by Robert W Blackwell of London and consisted mainly of pairs of traction poles with span wires to support the running wires, which were erected 22 feet above the road. The poles on this and most Dublin tram routes were tilted back slightly from the perpendicular to allow for a pull from the weight of the overhead. Well over a century later, many of the Dalkey line poles survive as lighting standards, still tilting in almost military formation and mostly retaining their decorated bases.

Robinson improved the existing depots at Shelbourne Road, Blackrock and Dalkey. At Shelbourne Road, where overhauls were also carried out, there was a very restricted entrance. Instead of a yard track fan with several sets of points branching from the incoming line, a traverser was installed. Running in a shallow pit at a right angle to the tracks, this was an electrically driven platform having rails that matched up with the incoming running line. A tram was driven on to the traverser and moved sideways to square up with and drive on to any of the several tracks in the depot, saving much valuable space and complicated pointwork.

Throughout its progress, Robinson's work was watched carefully by the DUTC, the July 1893 shareholders' meeting being informed that if the Southern District project proved successful, the Dublin United would follow.

A Grim Battle

Dublin became a notable battleground in the process of introducing electric traction. Because it was one of the earliest cities in the United Kingdom where electricity confronted the horse, this was to be expected. For any city to pioneer electric tramway development was one thing, but in the capital of an agricultural country, there were sure to be powerful vested interests ranged against it, was another. The electricity versus horse controversy was exploited skilfully by the inevitable coalition opposed to electrification. Manipulating public opinion shamelessly, in the process they battened on to people's legitimate fears, which obviously needed to be addressed. Passions were stirred, the level of debate rapidly descending to widespread mud slinging.

The most vocal antagonist was the Dublin Carmen's Union which represented the jarveys, who feared the electric tram because it could easily outpace their vehicles in a way its animal-hauled predecessor could not. A concern for animals, but for reasons very different from those of the jarveys, fuelled hostility among the less tolerant elements of the upper classes, who expressed fears about the trams literally frightening horses.

Spectres of the dire maladies caused by electric currents were conjured up. Terrible dangers would arise from speeding electric trams and fallen wires. Ruination of the streetscape by traction poles and overhead lines was inescapable. There was an understandable aesthetic concern about overhead wiring, aggravated by the insensitivity of

Above: **Dublin Southern District Milnes trailer No 34 and an unidentified motor tram are seen in Castle Street, Dalkey during testing of the line and staff training prior to the 1896 opening. This was the first trailer to be motorised. In November 1899 it became tram No 84 replacing the shortlived converted horse car that bore this number and was destroyed in the fire at Kingsbridge depot in August 1899. This No 84 worked from Kingsbridge for all its operational life, its balcony successor entering service on 30th April 1920.** BT-H Brochure

early overhead telegraph equipment as can be seen from many contemporary photographs in the Lawrence collection. Indeed, as early as 1897 plans were being drawn up to put some telephone wiring in built-up areas underground, feeding short lines of distributor poles.

Local authorities also had reservations about electrification proposals, anticipating increased expenditure in places where the horse companies maintained the roadway between the rails and for 18 inches on either side. Some of the councillors who came from rural areas had a further, more obscure agenda which would be adversely affected by a reduced demand for horses and everything they needed.

Anti-electric campaigners also forecast yet more unemployment, already a serious and seemingly intractable problem. Because horses were being replaced, they predicted lasting and irreparable damage to agriculture. Many of these arguments had been used in other towns where electric trams were proposed, but in Dublin they were poisoned by peculiarly bitter local political antagonisms.

The ensuing period of conflict was full of colour, an added dimension to the debate being the exciting prospect of competition to the DUTC's monopoly. Since 1872, Dublin Corporation had benefited considerably from the tramways, which contributed revenue and maintained considerable sections of the streets they served. The chance of increasing its income from tramways and extending its control over the operating companies was too good an opportunity for the Corporation not to seize. Competition and aesthetics were to be among its main weapons in this bitter battle.

Robinson's Achievements and Plans

With some difficulty, Clifton Robinson managed to satisfy four different townships – Pembroke, Blackrock, Kingstown and Dalkey, on the subject of overhead wiring, producing a neat and unobtrusive installation. He negotiated successfully on road reinstatement and maintenance, and convinced workers of the benefits that would flow from electrification. Savouring the prospects for more employment and improved social conditions, the artisans represented by the Trades Council wholeheartedly supported electrification.

Emboldened by the success of electric tramways elsewhere, encouraged by the likelihood of carrying many more passengers at lower fares and knowing the attitude of groups like the tradesmen, Robinson proposed extending his Dalkey line into the city. He envisaged running electric trams on streets parallel to those served by the DUTC, and extending his system to the north side. The details were set out in an advertisement, which appeared in the *Freeman's Journal* on 20th November 1895. A lengthy news report, together with a map, explained the scheme and showed how serious a threat the DSDT's plans were to the DUTC. Immediately below this report, some details were given of the DUTC's intentions.

The matter of electrification and the opposing schemes came before the Corporation at a meeting in December 1895. Representatives of the Trades Council attended to present their resolution in favour of Robinson, 'that having regard to the great and lasting benefits which the system of electric trams promoted by the Dublin Southern District Company would confer on the working classes in the districts generally, and with a view to promoting healthy

competition instead of sustaining a monopoly, the Trades Council hereby supports the project'.

The President of the Trades Council, Mr Richardson, presented the resolution and commended the company's scheme although some affiliated unions were opposed as they represented trades involved with horses. He pointed out that the Southern Company offered advantages never given by the DUTC or any other tramway company. The company proposed to cater more particularly for those districts in which the poorer classes of citizens lived. Mr Fitzpatrick, Vice President of the Council, noted that Robinson had offered an early morning service at a very cheap rate to bring working men to their employment and back in the evening. He contrasted that with the policy of the DUTC, whose routes at this time catered mostly for elitist elements in the community. He dismissed briefly the objections raised about the effect on employment of dropping horse traction concluding, 'We believe that the more facilities which are offered to the public to travel cheaply and expeditiously, the greater will be the prosperity of our city'.

The Secretary of the Trades Council, Mr Simmons, believed that electric trams would improve large areas of the city which were in a neglected and derelict condition. 'We do not expect', he said, 'that this scheme will restore the Coombe to its pristine vigour, but we consider that it will have the same effect in these places that tramways had in Drumcondra, and that it will lead to the erection of a better class of dwelling in the suburban districts for the working class, and improve those already in existence in the neighbourhood.' He said a lot of talk was heard about vested interests and against the current movement, just as people heard about Stephenson's railway and all the cows he would kill, but all those notions were now exploded. He referred to the overhead lines which would be necessary, 'As to aesthetic doctrine, we find that the Custom House exists as glorious in its beauty as ever, though the Loop Line crosses in front of it. These doctrines are nonsensical.'

Mr Dorman, President of the Independent Labour Party, also addressed the councillors. He conveyed an approving resolution passed at a public meeting of working men held at the Rotunda. This meeting had apparently been a stormy one, with two or three thousand people present. 'An attempt was made to destroy the meeting', Mr Dorman asserted, 'but at the time the resolution was passed there were still 1,500 working men present'. He said that the municipality could obtain a large income from electric trams to provide better dwellings for the working classes, pointing out that for some years Belfast had been receiving five or six thousand pounds from the privately owned horse tram system there. The new electric lines would also enable workers to go cheaply to the country with their families.

For several reasons, Dublin Corporation continued to drag its feet. In reality, its objection to overhead wiring fronted two more obscure ones, mollification of the horse lobby and a determination to abstract as much as they could in return for allowing electrification. There was moreover a deep-seated antipathy between William Martin Murphy and the Corporation. Murphy believed that public bodies should not interfere with or dabble in the private sector. He was critical of bureaucracy, expressing his views trenchantly on several occasions. Finally, the Corporation enjoyed the advantage of having two competing schemes, playing one company off against the other.

Dublin Southern v DUTC

Vigorous point scoring was the order of the day when Clifton Robinson and his opponent, Dr Carte, the DUTC Chairman, addressed the Corporation. Dr Carte denigrated the proposals 'of other people who proposed to cover the by-streets of the city with tramways'. Robinson riposted that the DUTC had flattered his company by scheduling some of the same by-streets for its own belated and halting schemes. DUTC fare reductions were branded by Robinson as being mostly mere trifling concessions. He also commented that the DUTC made no reductions for return tickets, except in the case of Glasnevin Cemetery.

Robinson dealt head-on with the old cry that had apparently been raised again that the Dublin Southern District Company was a 'new and foreign company'. The rivalry went on, but neither company succeeded in obtaining powers to operate electrically within the city boundary at that time. The DUTC was encouraged to run electric trams in the northern suburbs beyond the boundary, a widespread fear of electrocution now being given as the main reason for opposition. Alarmingly for the DUTC, the DSDT electrification appeared to be well on the way to realisation, and in February 1896 the DSDT brought a deputation of councillors and Corporation officials to Bristol, where electric trams were already running.

An interesting assessment of the opposition to electric tramways appeared in the *Kingstown Monthly* for February 1896. After referring to vested interests, the journal's editorial declared that, '...for years, the Dublin United Tramways Company have enjoyed the monopoly of the streets, and those the leading ones of Dublin and it is natural to expect that a determined attempt to introduce 'that soul of trade' opposition, and so destroy their monopoly, must of itself agitate the directors extremely. The city has been ornamented with posters, and strewn with handbills pointing out the evils to follow in the track of electricity; the lack of work; the injury to horse-breeders and corn-raisers, farriers, smiths and painters, all are to be ruined by this potent yet unknown power, electricity, yet in all the hubbub there has not been one word in defence of monopoly; the public interest has to be gained not by a fair statement of actual facts...but by an endeavour to enlist public sympathy in what is pleased to be termed the great cause of humanity...the extensions proposed are entirely new ones, affording a new source of employment to hundreds of workers...the electric company proposes a rapid form of locomotion at an exceedingly low figure, about one third of the fares of the United Company for similar distance, while the gaze of the public is ardently attracted to a fictitious statement about dangers and deathtraps. The proposals of the Electric Tramway Co involve a considerable step in the onward march of civilisation...which cannot fail to be a most potent factor in the upraising of the city.'

The Dalkey Opening

While the debate in the city of Dublin continued, work on the Dublin Southern electrification progressed relentlessly, although the company's plan to extend the line beyond Castle Street in Dalkey to serve Sorrento Road and Colimore Road was not realised. All the work, begun in 1895, was financed by the Thomson-Houston Company, formed the previous year. Eventually, a notice by the Dublin Southern District Tramways Company appeared in the papers. 'The Directors beg to announce the formal opening of the Electric Tramway between Haddington Road and Dalkey on Saturday 16th May 1896 when the Electric Motor Cars will run for passenger traffic.'

The ceremony took place with the Lord Mayor of Dublin, the Right Honourable R F M'Coy, at the controls of the first car, No 2. This hauled a trailer and carried very distinguished passengers including Clifton Robinson, the electrical engineer Robert Joule and, doubtless out of professional courtesy, William Martin Murphy. No 2 led four other motor cars, each with a trailer, in the great cavalcade which so spectacularly ushered in an exciting new era in Dublin's transport. Twenty motor cars and 20 trailers were available for service on the first day, a further ten motor cars and ten more trailers being delivered later.

Except for five of the motor trams, all 60 vehicles had Milnes bodywork. The 54-seat motor cars and 46-seat trailers are more fully described in the Rolling Stock Catalogue (see page 142).

The *Freeman's Journal* wrote on the opening day, 'the Directors have evidently made up their minds to make the very most of the traffic...a tram every ten minutes between Haddington Road and Dalkey is ample provision for the requirements of the public. From Haddington Road the service begins at 8am and runs to 11pm – a shade too early, however, to be of any use to theatre-goers. The fares are very modest indeed, Haddington Road to Merrion for a penny is certainly reasonable. Haddington Road to Kingstown for threepence, all the way to Dalkey for fourpence looks like business.' On Monday 18th May the same paper reported that, 'the speed is not excessive...it is worth noticing that the horses the trams encountered along the line seemed to regard them with perfect composure and complacency.'

An illustrated brochure was produced to mark the opening of the line and a most detailed description of the entire undertaking by Philip Dawson CE appeared in *Electric Railways and Tramways* (London, 1897).

BT-H Limited was responsible for the operation and management as well as the construction and equipment of the Dalkey line. The project broke the company which was liquidated in 1896, its place being taken by the new British Thomson-Houston Company Ltd, registered on 18th May 1896 just two days after electric trams began running on the Dalkey line.

Continuing Hostilities

A welcome for the electric trams was significantly absent in other quarters. The Dublin, Wicklow & Wexford Railway Company reduced fares and opened two new stations at Sandymount Avenue and Merrion in an effort to recapture lost traffic. They also watched the electric trams closely to ensure that they did not exceed the approved permitted maximum speed of eight miles per hour. The matter of speeds was to become the subject of a major inquiry in November 1898, the limits on various parts of the system were later set out in the staff Rule Book. Meanwhile, Robinson's ambitions were boldly proclaimed in the title 'DUBLIN ELECTRIC TRAMWAYS' emblazoned on his green and yellow (or cream) cars.

The DUTC brought the horse tram fare between Nelson Pillar and Haddington Road down to 1d. Animosity continued between the two tram companies, which, across the Atlantic prompted the *Street Railway Journal* to report. 'Bitter warfare has raged in Dublin during the past year between the Dublin United Tramways Company, which operates the principal system in the city and the Dublin Southern District Tramways Company, which operates a suburban line and has been for some time attempting to secure entrance into the city proper to develop a competing system. Both companies are applicants for electric privileges...There has naturally been a great deal of public discussion of this important question in Dublin, and the problem has been complicated by a desire on the part of the Dublin Council to exact heavy rentals from both companies in consideration of grant of franchises. The matter finally came to a head on March 3, when at a meeting of the Council, the whole matter was postponed for six months in order that the citizens may get further light upon the questions involved. One of the incidents of the discussion of the Council was a speech by the Lord Mayor opposing the grant of electric rights on the ground that it would be destructive to the country, as the farmers of Ireland had nothing to fall back on except the raising of oats and breeding of horses, and the result would be that in Dublin your beautiful Corn Exchange would be closed and your hay market abandoned.' The Lord Mayor apparently saw no conflict between accepting invitations to open electric tramways and then opposing their extension for partisan reasons.

The Dublin United Tramways Co (1896)

Robinson's bill to extend the operations of the DSDT was delayed in parliament, receiving a serious setback in June. Taking advantage of the lull in hostilities, William Martin Murphy lost no time in opening negotiations to avert expensive and destructive competition. A series of meetings was held to take the complicated legal and financial decisions necessary for the £243,000 purchase of the DSDT and the setting up of a new company, which was registered on 28th September 1896.

With this bold step there came into existence the Dublin United Tramways Company (1896) Limited, which for various reasons operated the old DUTC and DSDT as separate legal entities until 1905. William Martin Murphy JP, was Chairman, William Anderson was Managing Director; Richard S Tresilian AMICEI, FCIS, was Secretary and Charles W Gordon, Manager. Gordon, born in London around 1847, was a tramway manager of wide experience, much of it gained in mainland Europe. He was fluent in French, German and Spanish. This well qualified and determined management team immediately set about removing obstacles and pressing ahead with electrifying and extending the existing tramway system.

Garter belts surrounding the fleet numbers on the company's cars soon displayed the new title. One version of the new DUTC shield, appearing on documentation and, later, on cap badges, was divided vertically. The left side displayed the three castles from the city coat of arms, while the right side was divided in two; the upper quarter showed two horseshoes, the lower a stylised generator. The design of the device changed slightly over the years and a DUTC monogram was also widely employed. The title 'Dublin Electric Tramways', which had adorned Southern District tickets continued in use for some years under the DUTC ownership, but now appeared below the 1896 company's name.

Twilight of the Horse Tram

A glimpse of life in Dublin just before horse haulage began giving way to electric traction is afforded by the DUTC timetable for February 1897. Issued free, this contained a certificate from the publishers, Browne and Nolan, that 10,000 copies of the 'Time Table and Advertising Guide' were printed and delivered each month. Times and fares were given for each of the lines, examples being:

Route	First to Pillar	Last from Pillar	Fare
Clontarf	7.20am	11.40pm	3d.
Clonskea	8.00am	10.22pm	3d.
Drumcondra	8.30am	11.20pm	2d.
Dolphin's Barn	8.00am	11.07pm	3d.
Glasnevin	8.30am	11.00pm	2d.
Sandymount	7.30am	11.15pm	3d.

The only 4d fares were from Nelson Pillar to Rathfarnham by horsecar or Haddington Road to Dalkey on the electrics, still shown as being operated by the Dublin Southern District Tramways Company which was not wound up until 1905. 32 Lower Sackville Street and the Central Parcels Office at 62 Dawson Street continued under the auspices of the 1896 DUTC, as did the head office at 9 Upper Sackville Street, where the telephone number was Dublin 58.

Prepaid tram tickets were offered at a discount of 10%, or 5/- worth for 4/6d. School tickets were on offer at a 25% discount, 240 costing 15/-. A carry over from earlier times was the continued existence of a differential fare on the Westland Row to Kingsbridge Line, the fares quoted for this journey were 3d inside and 2d outside. Passengers were requested to report, in writing, any complaint of incivility or neglect of duty. They were also asked to save time by having the fare ready and to alight at the left or near side of the car, next the footpath.

The DUTC timetable, 36 pages including covers, contained timetables for the Dublin & Blessington Steam Tramway, highlighting the splendid scenery en route and at the Poulaphouca Waterfall. Passengers were advised to leave Nelson Pillar 40 minutes before starting times at Terenure, from here the first weekday train for Poulaphouca departed at 8.30am. Also set out was the timetable of the Dublin & Lucan Steam Tramway, with a weekday first departure from Parkgate Street at 7.30am

No less than five pages were devoted to details of the Parcels Express. This well patronised service provided for the collection and delivery of packages, charged by weight, all over the system and further afield by arrangement with the steam tramways and railway companies. In the case of the Blessington line, goods up to half a ton in weight could be carried through at special rates, obtainable on application.

J G Archer, a signwriter and decorator of 3, Whitefriar Place, offered in a full-page advertisement to paint and letter tram boards at moderate prices. The company's own advertising department was prepared to have its agent, Mr Byrne, call on prospective customers at any time, if desired. The Alliance Gas Company of D'Olier Street had coke for sale at 11/- per chaldron and broken coke for domestic use at 16/- a ton, exclusive of carriage, while the Dartry Dye Works had premises at Upper Rathmines, specially fitted with electric light and all modern appliances for dyeing, French-cleaning and carpet-beating. Other advertisements were for Bovril, Bolton's Whiskey, Kehoe, Donnelly & Pakenham's Hams, Bacon and Lard, and for Cameron's Painting and Decorating. On the back cover, B Hyam of 29/30 Dame Street, encouraged by the enormous success of his justly celebrated £2.2.0d. suit, offered overcoats, made to measure, for £1.15.0d. Related to the 1914 base of 100, the cost of living in 1897 has been estimated at 85; an 1897 £1 would be worth over £79 at 1999 prices.

Another interesting publication of this period was the *Dictionary of Dublin*, compiled by Cosgrave and Strangeways, and published by Sealy, Bryers and Walker. Chapter Six is entitled 'Dublin from a Tramcar'. This begins, 'Dublin is well supplied with tram lines, most of which start from Nelson's Pillar .... The Blackrock, Kingstown, and Dalkey electric system starts from Lower Abbey-street, and runs over Dublin lines to Beggar's Bush.'

This is clearly incorrect, because descriptions of the various tram sightseeing tours suggest publication prior to November 1897, 20 months before electric cars reached the Pillar from Beggar's Bush. However, it is possible that the compiler of the Guide may have expected difficulties with the Corporation to be overcome by the date of publication. The tramcars are described as well appointed and running frequently at moderate fares; it gives details of these for all of the 13 lines travelled, together with a catalogue of the sights on each of the trips.

Chapter Two

THE EARLY ELECTRICS

Tackling Problems

A tramway operator tackling electrification in the late 1890s faced a multiplicity of problems. Planning the system, sourcing finance and successfully negotiating the necessary legal powers were obstacle-strewn, tedious and expensive procedures. There was also the apprehension surrounding any new technological venture, with precious little precedent to guide those involved. We have also seen, in the previous chapter, how obstruction by the Corporation delayed electrification inside the Dublin city boundary. The programme was held up for nearly three years, but the DUTC's acquisition of the Southern District Company in September 1896 weakened the Corporation's position considerably.

Powerful lobby groups, especially those associated with the horse transport industry, were fighting the first battle in a war they were to lose over the following decades. Comprehensively identified by the editorial from the *Kingstown Monthly* of February 1896 quoted on page 35, they comprised a wide but largely discreet coalition of interests. In Ireland with its greater reliance on the agricultural sector, they obviously carried more clout than their fellows in industrialised countries, and maintained a rearguard action long after their cause was lost.

Numerous local interests had to be placated before electrification could proceed. There were influential individuals, such as Lord Ardilaun along the boundary of whose St Anne's Estate trams would run to Howth. Entire communities were represented by small local authorities like the Drumcondra Urban Council. Ultimately, these were all largely placated and what amounted to a co-existence agreement was reached between the DUTC and Corporation

The DUTC legislation of 1896 was followed by the Dublin United Tramways (Electrical Powers) Act of 1897. This gave the company authority to construct several sections, not already in existence, of what was to become the Cross Line from Lansdowne Road to Kenilworth Square. An interesting section of this statute specifically prohibited the company from blocking Castlewood Avenue, stipulating that trams should not stop there any longer than was necessary for passengers to board or alight.

With so many potential customers, pressure on equipment suppliers effectively created a seller's market, but only briefly, because within ten years there was massive surplus capacity in the electric tramway manufacturing industry. Despite all this, there were some positive factors in Dublin's case. The DUTC was luckier than most tramway companies in that its Chairman, William Martin Murphy, was himself involved in railway and tramway construction, while the company was one of the few having its own car-building facilities at Spa Road, Inchicore.

The Clontarf Electrification

On taking over the Southern District Company, the DUTC began implementing its well-thought out programme to replace its entire horse system as quickly as possible. Initially, because of the Corporation's objections to electric tramways, particularly the poles and overhead wiring, not yet being met, work on the first DUTC conversion began at the outer terminus of the Dollymount line, which had been the company's first choice for conversion in any case.

During 1897, a power station to the designs of the British Thomson-Houston Company was built at Clontarf on a site formerly occupied by the horse tram sheds and stables, construction being carried out by Mr R O'Connor. The new building, incorporating power station, car shed and repair shops was 166 feet long by 140 feet wide. Details of the installation were given in the January 1898 issue of the *Railway World*. Its most prominent feature was the chimney, an octagonal brick structure with a height of 112 feet. Clontarf Depot now a bus garage, retains little of its impressive brick facade behind the front offices erected by CIE in the 1970s. The power plant, capable of driving 25 trams, included three Babcock and Wilcox boilers. Water was supplied by two direct acting Worthington steam pumps, each capable of delivering 22,000 gallons per hour. There was a 10,000 gallon water tank in the boiler house, additionally, a 38,000 gallon underground storage tank ensured against failure of the public supply.

Three horizontal tandem compound engines, built by McIntosh and Seymour, and working at a pressure of 150lbs, drove the machinery. Each engine was coupled directly to a six-pole British Thomson-Houston generator, running at 135 revolutions per minute to produce 550 volts direct current, lighting current was also provided at 460 volts dc. Two cables fed current to the line, which was divided into five sections.

The standard height of the trolley wire was 21 feet above road level, but this had to come down to 17 feet to get under the stone arch railway bridge on Clontarf Road. The *Railway World* commended this feature to the Glasgow Tramway Committee, who had 'alleged that a somewhat higher bridge on their proposed line would render the use of garden seat cars impossible.' This incident well illustrates the willingness of the DUTC to go where others feared to tread.

A more traditional view of electrification was expressed by a shareholder at the DUTC half-yearly meeting on 27th July 1897. Referring to the Dalkey line, Dr Delahoyd lamented that, 'the great glaring illuminant *(sic)* on the electric cars formed such a mass of moving light that no horse could go in safety along that road.' The doctor's distress may have been deepened by a lengthy progress report on the Clontarf line which appeared in the *Freeman's Journal* on 10th July, forecasting somewhat optimistically that electric cars would be running to Dollymount in about three weeks.

Before the Clontarf line opened, 12 trams (Nos 21-32) with Milnes bodies on Peckham extension trucks were delivered. These had five windows on each side of the lower deck, as against four on the Dalkey vehicles. Always known as Clontarf cars, they had oak framing and weighed approximately seven tons. Fifteen trams were reported to be available for service by the time the Clontarf service began, the other three being Nos 33-36, the first electric cars built by the DUTC at Inchicore. Full details of these early DUTC electric trams can be found in later in this chapter and in the Rolling Stock Catalogue.

Heralded by a brief press announcement that, 'the Dollymount electric cars will commence to run this morning', the new trams began working between Dollymount and the city boundary at Annesley Bridge on 11th November 1897. While much of this boundary ran along the canals, extra territory was included on the north side. This dis-

Annesley Bridge Road, in the winter of 1897-98. The electrics began working the outer section of the Clontarf line on 11th November 1897, but objections by the Corporation prevented them from crossing the city boundary at Annesley Bridge until 19th March 1898. In this view, electric tram No 31 waits to cross over for its return journey to Clontarf. Horse tram No 170 may be preparing to return to Nelson Pillar, but the trolley of an electric car beyond it suggests that it might be working as a trailer. There is evidence of such operation being found on this route for a short period. Outside the wall on the right lay the infamous Fairview sloblands which Parke Neville sought to reclaim as early as 1873 but which were to remain a serious nuisance for several more years after this view was taken. *Tramway and Railway World*

trict was bounded by Jones's Road, Clonliffe Road and Poplar Row, also taking in the East Wall area. For four months the electric service terminated at Annesley Bridge, passengers continuing on towards the city centre by horse tram. The *Railway World* contrasted horse and electric operation;'...the lines already open enable the public to estimate how greatly increased will be their convenience and comfort when the entire tramway system has been provided with electric cars, and the dingy and lumbering horse cars have ceased to encumber the streets. There is a pleasing absence of more or less dejected animals, while the driver, now become the motor-man, bears unmistakable evidence of the effect that the altered conditions of employment invariably have upon the personnel of the staff. When the day of the tram-horse has passed, and the tramcar driver has acquired a recognised position as a skilled artisan, it will doubtless become a source of wonderment that some even of those who pose as the leaders and friends of the working man should have stood in the way of such a desirable change in the status of a large class of employees. Compare the wholesome surroundings of the car-shed and power-house with even the best kept of tramway stables, and another argument in favour of mechanical traction will at once be formulated.'

Whatever about those who opposed electrification for any reason, one group who enthusiastically supported it were the DUTC's shareholders. At the first meeting after the change on the Clontarf line, they learned that for a half-year in 1896, when the line was worked exclusively with horse traction, receipts were £7,216 from 1,124,801 passengers. But in the six months following electrification, 2,273,880 passengers contributed £12,114, an increase of 58% in receipts and 100% in traffic. It was calculated that, excluding track repairs, horse operation cost 7.84d per mile or 75.43% of income. The figures for the elec-

tric cars were 4.25d and 39.45%, respectively. This was the final and most effective argument in favour of electric trams.

Legislation, Litigation and Wayleaves

A second DUTC Act of 1897 involved the new company in litigation. The Pembroke Township Commissioners were empowered to rebuild Ballsbridge at the expense of the Tramway Company; the date recorded on the bridge is 1904. When the bill for £8,413 15s 0d was presented to the DUTC they offered £3,000 in settlement. This was refused, a court case followed and the tramway company had to pay £5,500 plus costs.

There was also the Rathmines and Rathgar Township Tramways and Improvements Act which gave the eponymous Commissioners power to purchase the lines in their territory on December 31st 1938, though by that date Rathmines, which became an Urban District in 1898, had in fact ceased to exist as an independent local authority. It furthermore fixed wayleaves at a flat rate of £1,000 payable after passage of the Township's Electric Power Bill; the amount would subsequently double to £2,000 annually.

A wayleaves dispute with Dublin Corporation was a much more complicated and long-drawn out affair, which rumbled on until 1925. When the Corporation withdrew its objections to electrification, a document known as the Wayleaves Agreement was signed. Under its terms, the Corporation would have the right to take over the tramway system after 40 years. Meanwhile, the company would be responsible for the maintenance of the roadway between the rails and for 18 inches on either side as heretofore and would also pay an agreed

sum of £500 per annum for every mile of track. But there were interminable disputes about what constituted a mile of track, single or double, what about sidings, or Sackville Street where there were veritable acres of track? So it went on until 1913 when agreement was reached but this did not become fully legal for another 12 years, when the company undertook to pay £15,000 annually.

Electrics to the Pillar – at Last

As soon as agreement was reached with the Corporation, work on erecting the overhead inside the city boundary began. One result of the agonising about overhead gear, the antagonism, as already noted, being partly due to a proliferation of very unsightly aerial installations by the embryonic telephone industry, was the use of more highly decorated traction poles from Annesley Bridge inwards. Examples, both of these and the plainer ones along the footpath outside Fairview Park, were still in position in 2000.

The first electric car arrived at Nelson Pillar on Saturday 19th March 1898 when an *Evening Telegraph* reporter wrote; 'I was a privileged passenger on the first electric car to enter the centre of Dublin City an event which took place this morning ...The officials of the Tramway Company had kept the fact very quiet that they intended to make their informal trip today before ordinary people were about but having got the necessary hint I was on the ground in good time and had the distinction of being the only unofficial passenger on the first electric car that was ever electrically propelled into O'Connell Street. We passed under the lee of Nelson at 7.10am exactly and negotiated the intricate and difficult wires at the turn with the greatest ease and success much to the delight evidently of the experts on board. Early as the hour was there was a crowd on the ground, partly composed of the Company's men working on the necessary changes in the line at the turning of Earl Street, but principally of the early population of citizens and citizenesses on their way to work with the inevitable sprinkling of slightly sarcastic Jehus and more or less judicially critical gendarmes...The experiment was most successful and gives every promise that early next week the electric service on this line will be in full working order from the Pillar to the Bull.'

On Monday, 21st March, the *Evening Herald* carried the following paragraph in its 'Current Topics' column:

'Yesterday was rendered notable by the opening to the public of the electric tram between the Pillar and Dollymount. The fine day and the agreeable mode of conveyance attracted a large number of passengers and there is every probability that the new line will become as popular as that to Dalkey. A temporary permit from the Board of Trade was obtained for yesterday's running but it is expected that the regular authority will be granted this week.' Within a few days, the Dollymount line, like all public transport services, came to be taken for granted. During its first year of operation, there was some working of trailers on the route.

Highs and Lows

Even at this early stage, Dublin was regarded as being very advanced in electrification. The *Railway World* commented harshly on London councillors' defence and proposed extension of horse traction, saying that, 'The Londoner would appreciate rapid and pleasant conveyance to Kew and Richmond as much as the people of Dublin enjoy the run to Kingstown or Clontarf, and it is encouraging to note that new efforts are just now being made in that direction by the same enterprising managers who introduced electric traction in Dublin and Bristol.' This complimentary reference was, of course, to Clifton Robinson and his team.

During July 1898, side by side with reports of Orange demonstrations and the centenary of the 1798 Rebellion, the newspapers carried frequent references to trams. Strong views of a kind still being expressed by the passengers of a hundred years later exercised the pen of JK in a letter to the *Evening Herald*; 'May I ask for space...to say a few words in condemnation of a very objectionable habit on the part of young men and I regret to have to say, old ones too from whom a better example might be expected. I refer to the growing habit of smoking in tram cars and in railway carriages in and around this city. These ill-conditioned 'gents' without leave or licence, plant themselves on the front seats and puff their tobacco smoke and ashes

in the eyes of people who go out to inhale a breath of fresh air and even for females, have not the least consideration. Oh for the manhood and chivalry of former days, even forty years ago when no man would smoke in company of a lady nor in the daytime on the public street. Might I now suggest to the manager of the DUTCo that a notice be placed in each tram car inviting these gents to take a back seat and to observe the rules of common courtesy.'

On Wednesday 6th July, in the Southern Division Court, a tram passenger named William Williams, described as a master mariner, appeared before Mr Swifte. He was fined 5/- and ordered to pay 15/- compensation for refusing to pay the fare from Haddington Road to Sackville Street after travelling that distance. He had also assaulted Conductor J Shaw and upset his cash bag, spilling the takings, 5/- of which was lost.

The Tramway Sports were held in Ballsbridge on Saturday, 9th July, an advertisement in the previous day's *Evening Herald* announcing that the programme would include athletics, cycling and tug-of-war competitions. First-class catering was offered at modest prices, there would be a prize fund of £200 and admission was 6d or 1/-; reserved tickets could be obtained from conductors at 1/- before the day itself.

Dalkey Electrics Reach the Pillar

On the following Tuesday, 12th July, the first electric car to reach the city centre from the south side came in from Dalkey. Probably because people were now becoming more familiar with electric trams, this inauguration commanded less space than the first electric arrival from Clontarf four months earlier. A news item in that day's *Evening Herald* headed 'Extension of the Electric Tram System' simply said, 'All details

having been fully completed between Nelson's Pillar and Haddington Road, the electric tramcars began running from the place indicated in O'Connell Street this morning, thus forming a through communication between the city and terminus at Dalkey. The advantage to the public of the extension will be fully appreciated inasmuch as it avoids the annoyance of having to change from one series of cars to another, and intending visitors to the coast will be enabled to gratify their desire in the future without the slightest inconvenience.'

In fact, the Nelson Pillar terminus was not immediately accessible to trams coming in via D'Olier Street, at that time the only route for electrics south of O'Connell Bridge. This was due to a serious subsidence of the roadway at the south side of O'Connell Bridge during work on the Main Drainage scheme. This major project had been in progress since 1895 and consisted, among other works, of laying large interceptor sewers along the North and South Quays. Its effect was to end the continuous obnoxious discharge of sewage into the River Liffey opposite virtually every street running on to the Quays. The DUTC timetable for December 1896 records that the North Quays line was closed during construction of the City Main Drainage and reminded passengers that there was an alternative service on the South Quays (Kingsbridge) line.

All horse trams coming from the south side terminated in Westmoreland Street during the period of the 1898 subsidence. The electrics turned back in D'Olier Street. The new Dalkey cars initially ran from Merrion Square via Westland Row, Great Brunswick Street and D'Olier Street, not being routed through Nassau Street and Westmoreland Street until 12th October.

In the autumn of 1898, then, there were two operational electric lines, nine miles

Approaching the Parkgate terminus is No 28, one of the twelve trams (21-32) with Milnes five-window bodies obtained for the Clontarf line in 1897. No 28, later transferred to Kingsbridge depot on Victoria Quay, is here working the North Quays line from Parkgate Street to O'Connell Bridge. It displays the white square which was the symbol for this service, which became route 24 in 1918. The presence of a Scotch or Verity lighting pillar at the corner of Infirmary Road places the earliest possible date for this photograph to 1904. No 28, never vestibuled, was still allocated to Kingsbridge in 1917 and was replaced by a new open-top car in March 1919.
Lawrence collection, National Library

from Nelson Pillar to Dalkey and four to Dollymount. They were powered by the generating stations at Shelbourne Road and Clontarf, nominally capable of driving 50 and 25 cars respectively. According to the records, 68 electric trams had been available in July 1898 and conversion of horse cars was proceeding rapidly at Spa Road. By 30th September the number of electrics had reached 78, at the end of December there were 89.

Early Electric Accidents:
Merrion Square and Dalkey
Following the extension of electric traction to the city centre in July 1898, the Sandymount - Bath Avenue - Nelson Pillar horse service was cut back to Haddington Road, where Sandymount passengers transferred to the electrics. They felt hard done by, their complaints being articulated by Alan Shaw of Tritonville Road in the *Evening Herald* of 25th October. He pointed out that passengers changing between electric and horse cars were being overcharged, frequently having to pay twice for journeys which had previously been a single fare stage.

There was a further problem for those travelling to the city, when loaded electrics did not stop, leaving Sandymount passengers to wait for the next tram at the Northumberland Road/Haddington Road junction. By the time of Shaw's letter, there were more motor trams than trailers, and the DUTC tried to improve the service by having electrics haul the Sandymount horse cars as trailers into the city.

Late on Sunday evening, 27th November 1898, tram No 64 was operating from Kingstown to Nelson Pillar, with Motorman Patrick Donnelly and Conductor Patrick Reddington. Among the passengers was a married couple, Charles and Mary Dunn of East James's Street, who travelled outside. At Haddington Road, No 64 picked up Sandymount horse car No 3, with Driver Joseph Quinn and James Shaw, the conductor assaulted the previous July by a passenger who refused to pay his fare.

At the stop near Holles Street, Mrs Dunn alighted and the trams resumed their journey. Some short distance further on, Charles Dunn rose from his seat and tried to leave the moving tram. He staggered or slipped on the platform, fell off and was run over by No 3, sustaining fatal injuries. The accident was reported in Monday's papers and on the following day, 29th November, an inquest was held, being fully covered in that day's *Evening Herald*. Constable Fitzgerald (32B) was the principal police witness and detailed evidence about operating horse cars as trailers was given to the coroner, Dr J E Kenny.

The conductors operated independently of each other and the horsecar or trailer driver's sole function when on tow was to apply and release the brake as necessary.

Driver Quinn saw Charles Dunn's fall but was unable to hold his trailer against the pull of the motor car. Motorman Donnelly, on the electric car, said that he had travelled 70 to 80 yards from the stop, unaware of what had happened until he heard shouts and the signal bell ringing above his head. He stopped immediately.

Summing up, the Coroner stated that this was the first fatal accident involving an electric tram in Dublin. He also hoped that it would be the last and tried to impute some blame to Conductor Reddington. The jury did not agree with this view, finding that none of the tramway men was at fault. They also commended Mrs Dunn to the kind consideration of the Tramway Company.

Dr Kenny criticised the speed limit of eight miles per hour which he thought should be reduced rather than increased, even if this inconvenienced passengers. Speed limits for electric trams were a widely discussed topic at the time and led to an inquiry. As could be expected with any revolutionary new form of transport, accidents attracted more attention than was the case in later years.

The Coroner at the Merrion Square inquest also pointed out that if a trailer had not been on tow, the fatality would not have occurred. The jury concurred about the trailers, recommending that their use be discontinued. Following a limbo period in which at least some were used as horse trams, all 30 trailers were rebuilt as motor cars. Twelve were dealt with late in 1899, the remaining 18 following in the early months of 1900.

Although the Merrion Square accident was the first involving an electric tram in the city of Dublin, it was not the first one on the Dalkey line. On the evening of 18th July 1897, a young woman named Maggie O'Donnell (25) was cycling in Dalkey when she got trapped between tram No 15 and a horse-drawn car. Her bicycle wobbled, throwing Ms O'Donnell, who was run over by both No 15 and its trailer. The tram had to be lifted to free the unfortunate victim, who regrettably died from massive injuries. Both the tram crew and the driver of the horse vehicle were charged in connection with the accident, but a verdict of accidental death was reached at the inquest.

Accidents Aboard Trams
Several accidents, like that at Merrion Square, originated or happened aboard trams. In early electric days, alighting passengers sometimes appear to have confused the trolley rope with that for the bell. An instance of this occurred on 30th July 1899 when car No 33, en route for Nelson Pillar, was approaching the railway bridge in Amiens Street. The conductor was upstairs collecting fares when a passenger pulled the trolley rope. He failed to hold it, the trolley

sprang up and damaged the overhead, bringing down the running wire. Three men received electric shocks necessitating hospital treatment but, luckily, nobody died.

The rope-pulling passenger was charged under the bye-laws but discharged after the magistrate had considered all the evidence and criticised the DUTC. Straps later replaced bell ropes but were always placed towards the outer edge of the platforms. Some years later, a passenger reached for the bell strap on a Dalkey car, missed it and overbalanced. He fell out on to the roadway, sustaining fatal head injuries.

The commonest passenger accidents involved stumbling or being thrown about by sudden braking. Such incidents were comparatively rare on the slower horse trams, but their number increased after electrification. Some accidents in early electric days were caused through people not yet being familiar with the movement, especially the rapid acceleration and braking of the new trams. Repercussive actions taken against the company caused it to look very carefully at every incident.

In July 1899, William Martin Murphy expressed concern at the 'vain attempts of some newspapers...to create a feeling of danger in the public mind in connection with the working of the tramways.' Two years later, he opined that 'An idea was abroad not long ago that the Tramway Company was fair game for any description of claim, no matter how much the claimants were themselves to blame.' This attitude, he said, had resulted in the company successfully appealing some dubious awards made in the lower courts.

Pushing The Programme Ahead
The programme to provide Dublin with a first-class electric tramway system in two phases - electrification of the existing horse system followed by extensions and new lines - was now well under way. Despite difficulties in providing new trams, track, overhead and feeder cables, the first phase would be virtually completed in less than 16 months. This was made all the more creditable by the delays encountered in a vital element of tramway infrastructure, the construction of a major new power station capable of supplying all the company's needs. Most of all, to do everything that was necessary meant learning new skills and working in a completely new environment. Dublin's tramway men rose magnificently to the occasion.

A period of considerable frustration ensued, during which enough new trams were available, overhead gear and electrical feeders were in position - but the changeover from horse traction was held up by slow progress in building and equipping the new Ringsend power station. There were various other problems too, such as the long-drawn out dispute with the former Drumcondra Town Commissioners, succeeded by Urban District Councillors in 1898. This had its basis in the perceived intention of the DUTC to leave the Drumcondra line as single, a legacy of the North Dublin Street Tramways Company.

William Martin Murphy referred to the availability of electric power at the shareholders' meeting on 26th July 1898. He expressed the hope that it might be possible, pending completion of the Ringsend plant, to deal with the North Quays, North Circular Road, Rathmines-Pembroke and perhaps the Donnybrook lines. This turned out to be unduly optimistic. Pushing the available resources of power supply to the limit, the DUTC managed to introduce electric traction on only two of these routes before Ringsend became operational.

The impatience of the DUTC's management at the delays experienced in replacing horse traction comes through in a brief report carried by the *Evening Herald* of 22nd August 1898: 'The trams from Rathmines to the sea ran today for the first time. In a short time the horse cars will be replaced by the electric ones'. This was the genesis of the present No 18 bus service.

Frustration was further increased by a sequence of events surrounding the North Quays line. Following its closure during the laying of the parallel interceptor sewer, this line was reconstructed and electrically equipped, but had to re-open as a horse-operated service by 1st November 1898. However, the company's morale was partially restored on 22nd November, when the line from Nelson Pillar to Phoenix Park via Phibsboro went electric.

The 89 electric trams available at the end of 1898 exceeded by 14 the number capable of being driven by the combined output of Ballsbridge and Clontarf. A service availability rate of 90% would have reduced the number and these 80 trams, while drawing more power than the designed capacity of the generating stations, allowed just one more changeover to take place. With this next conversion, which took place on 23rd January 1899, the first cross-city service connecting distant suburbs came into being.

The line from Donnybrook to Nelson Pillar via Merrion Square and Nassau Street was joined to the already electrified one between the Pillar and Phoenix Park. The last line to begin electric operation for more than seven months, its introduction was a very important event in the development of the electric tramway system.

Following his tribute to Dr Carte, who had died suddenly in April, William Martin Murphy proudly told the shareholders on 22nd July 1899 that the introduction of electric services between the Phoenix Park and Donnybrook had resulted in a reduction of one third in fares, while receipts had gone up by half. He also predicted confidently that 'horse tramways will be relegated to the domain of ancient history.'

Ringsend Generating Station

An efficient, efficient generating station and power distribution system are fundamental to successful electric tramway operation. Dublin was very fortunate in the choices made and effected. Consulting engineer H F Parshall accompanied a deputation of directors to the USA to obtain equipment for the DUTC generating station. He then designed the installation, the building of which commenced in October 1898. Situated at Ringsend Road on the western section of what is now the parking area beside the bus garage, it was ready for use on 16th August 1899, being commissioned 12 days later. However, it was still incomplete, and did not come into full operation until the following year. When fully equipped, Ringsend enabled the smaller installations at Ballsbridge and Clontarf to be closed, on 3rd January and 14th February 1901, respectively. From those dates, these former generating stations became substations to

Ringsend, the redundant electricity production machinery being sold.

The front of the Ringsend plant faced the road, the rear being a few feet from the Grand Canal Company's dock. The main buildings consisted of a boiler house and engine room placed side by side. The engine room building, containing the offices and stores, was 182 feet long by 80 feet wide, while the boiler house measured about 134 feet by 76. Because of the close proximity of the Grand Canal Dock, an ample supply of water for condensing purposes was available, while 400-ton cargoes of coal from Scottish collieries could be brought alongside. To accommodate the vast amount of machinery utilised, including the necessarily lofty coal hoisting tower, the buildings were very high and the two 224-foot chimneys of the station became a familiar landmark, being known as the Twin Sisters or the Heavenly Twins.

Planning, Distribution and Protection

As we have already seen, electrification of the Dublin tramways was planned in a most comprehensive manner. Details of the routes and the all-important current distribution system were set down from the beginning. A comprehensive report on the Ringsend power station in the *Street Railway Journal* for April 1898 was accompanied by a plan of the distribution system. The underground feeder cables were carried in conduits or ducts manufactured and laid to very strict requirements, much of which survives today as part of the underground telephone cable network. Electric tramways were initially regarded unenthusiastically by telephone engineers. There were two reasons for the fears of the telephone authorities. One was the danger of

The junction of Nassau Street and Dawson Street in the very early days of the electric trams. No 3, one of the 1896 Milnes cars, is outbound for Dalkey, while American car No 146 is going from Terenure to Nelson Pillar. No 3, vestibuled in 1903, was replaced in 1910, while a Standard Saloon took 146's identity in October 1926. The side bracket pole on the right has a white section denoting a stop. The square base gas lamp pillars, replaced in this area around 1904 but familiar in Dublin for another 50 years, are also conspicuous.
GEC Alsthom

contact between a telephone line and tram wires. An early instance is recorded on 22nd January 1897 when a gale broke two telephone wires beside the Dalkey line near Monkstown, blowing them across the tramway overhead. In the course of his report, telephone Engineering Inspector Mr Louth wrote; 'About a quarter mile nearer Dublin, a pole blew over and fell with all its wires on to the trolley wires…At this latter point, several horses were caught by the telephone wires…and two animals have since died…and I have heard that the Tramway Company will hold the NTC (National Telephone Company) responsible for what happened.'

Following this and other incidents, various methods of dealing with such problems were devised, essential safety apparatus being installed. The other difficulty experienced by the telephone service arose from the tramcar's return circuit to the power station being via the running rails. The current often found a path of lesser resistance through the lead cable sheaths of underground telephone cables, entering at one point and leaving again some distance away. At the exit point, electrolysis occurred, which soon perforated the lead and let water in. The tramways responded by improving rail bonding and installing negative boosters in the return path, though despite this the problem persisted.

A very important and eerily prophetic paragraph in the April 1898 *Street Railway Journal* report reads; 'In the subdivision of the cables, as controlled from the power house, the object has been to provide alternative routes for cars approaching or departing from the centre of the city in case of emergency. For instance, any car approaching the railway terminus near Harcourt Road from Dolphin's Barn, Terenure, Palmerston Park or Clonskeagh has three independently controlled routes by which it can reach the Trinity College area, and in case of a fire or mishap on its ordinary route, it can be sent on either of two others. Again, any car arriving in Clare Street from the south has an alternative route from there to O'Connell Bridge. The principle is carried on throughout.'

As already explained, the Dublin electrification programme was carried out in two stages, the original horse system with some minor extensions from 1897 to 1901 and over the following five years, the introduction of new routes. Completion of the Ringsend power station removed a major obstacle to completing the electrification programme. With the current per car calculated at 16 amps, the new station initially had a capacity to drive 200 cars, as against 50 by Ballsbridge and Clontarf's 25.

Over the years, Ringsend was constantly upgraded and improved. P S Sheardown, MIEE, described it in detail for a British Association Handbook to the Dublin District in 1908. Sheardown, who was in charge at Ringsend, recorded that the boiler house by that time contained 12 Babcock and Wilcox boilers, arranged in six pairs and equipped with a mechanical stoker. The boilers worked at a pressure of 150lb. per square inch and space had been left for additional units if required. There were six Allis vertical cross-compound open-type engines, four being coupled direct to 550-volt direct current generators, the fifth to a 2,500-volt three-phase generator and the sixth to both 550-volt direct current and 550-volt alternating current machines mounted between the cylinders. A later addition was a Willans turbine, coupled to a 1,000-kW Westinghouse 2,500-volt alternating current generator.

Dublin: A World Electricity Leader

Dublin Corporation's sophisticated electricity installation complemented that of the DUTC, for many years making the city a mecca for electrical engineers. The Corporation, which was the supplier of electricity to home and business consumers, had made astonishing progress with this service. A new generating station at the Pigeon House, massive in the terms of the period, was commissioned in 1903 to replace the pioneering

installation at Fleet Street. The Pigeon House plant was one of several projects to beneficially affect the future shape of Dublin's development for over a quarter of a century.

Unfortunately, the electricity service was a deep source of ideological differences between the DUTC and the Corporation. The company was anxious to provide the service, the functions of electrical supply and transport being frequently combined under one authority. There were, in fact, several potent arguments in favour of this arrangement, the situation in Dublin being out of line with that in many other cities. The DUTC had offered to take over the Corporation's electricity service in 1897. Three years later they claimed that consumers in Cork, where the same company performed both the electricity supply and transport functions, had power at 2.93d per unit as against 7d in Dublin. William Martin Murphy, who was a director of the Cork undertaking, constantly and vigorously championed private enterprise against public ownership. He availed of every opportunity to express his views, in the process constantly antagonising Dublin Corporation.

The Overhead Installation

Dublin Corporation's initial opposition to electrification, already described, resulted in great care being taken to ensure that the overhead wiring and poles would be unobtrusive and aesthetically pleasing. Three types of decorated base were used plain, bulbous, and fluted, the last manufactured by the Dublin firm of Ross and Walpole whose foundry also turned out innumerable lamp standards. The poles were formed of steel tube in three sections shrunk together when hot and under pressure. The bracket arms were made from steel tubes two inches in diameter and had decorative scroll work by the Dublin firm of J & C McGloughlin, specialists in ornamental ironwork. The standard spacing of poles was at 120ft intervals.

Poles on the Dollymount route beyond Annesley Bridge, outside the city boundary until 1900, and the Dalkey line beyond Haddington Road had span wires fixed direct to the poles. On sections of the Clontarf sea front, some span wires were carried

A rare early workshop scene in Ballsbridge. Trams 32 and 65 are on jacks for truck repairs or replacement. No 32, a Clontarf 1897 Milnes car, was vestibuled in 1902 and was still on its original route in 1917. It was replaced by a new tram in January 1919. The 1892 horse tram 135 became electric car No 65 in June 1898 and was based successively at Ballsbridge, Donnybrook, Terenure and Kingsbridge. Never vestibuled, its number was taken by a new balcony car in 1922. Also visible in this picture is Water Lorry No 2. Birney collection

A Thomson-Houston picture of Ballsbridge before the inauguration of electric traction. Motor trams 1 and 16 are to the left, while No 8 is centre stage with two trailers, 24 and 26, on the right. These became DUTC motor trams 194 and 229 in 1899 and 1900 respectively. The traverser pit is just visible in the foreground. Preston collection

by wooden telegraph poles on the inland side of the road, an arrangement that probably did not endear itself to those objecting to overhead work in the city area. Throughout Rathmines, Pembroke except for the Dalkey line, and all of Dublin City the span wires were fixed to cross arms embellished with decorative scrollwork. In narrower streets there were poles on one side only, these having side arms extending out over the track. Such poles were even more elaborately adorned with scrollwork. Most poles were surmounted by a finial consisting of a ball and point.

Centre poles were initially erected in several locations. These were gradually replaced in most streets over the years, having become an obstruction to the increasing volume of traffic and much later, a particular hazard to growing numbers of motor vehicles. They were actively discouraged by the Board of Trade and the Corporation insisted that lamps be placed on them to show their presence up at night. In a report criticising unsatisfactory aspects of the electrification work then being pressed ahead, the *Evening Herald* of 24th October 1899 stated that 'another piece of undoing was the taking down of centre poles that had been removed from Harcourt Street and Camden Street and the substitution of side poles.'

In some locations there were centre poles with very long side arms, as for instance in O'Connell Street, spanning three parallel lines on either side. Because they were not a hazard to other traffic, these poles remained in position throughout the entire electric tramway era. The use of side arms longer than 16 feet on any other street was banned by the Board of Trade at an early date, but the regulations were not retrospective, thus absolving the DUTC from having to replace existing fittings.

Power Control and Distribution

Delivery of abundant current from the power station to the cars by way of the feeder system and overhead wires is arguably the most vital component of successful tramway operation. The two original outlying stations on the DUTC system, at Ballsbridge and Clontarf, changed in character and function early in 1901 when current generation was concentrated exclusively at Ringsend. Most of the Dublin termini were within four miles of Ringsend and operated by direct current at 550 volts by means of

underground cables, which fed the overhead at half-mile intervals. The law required that tramways be broken electrically into these divisions. The feeds were easily recognised by the presence of a street box beside a pole, heavy cables running up the column and out to the running wires. The wires were fed in both directions for a quarter of a mile from the feeds, section insulators being installed halfway between the feeds, known to the tramwaymen as boosters. The advantages of this arrangement were that voltage loss was minimised and in the event of an overhead failure only a comparatively short section of the line was affected. Trams frequently produced spectacular flashes at boosters and section insulators, much to the delight of small children.

Dalkey terminus was 9.1 miles from Nelson Pillar and Howth 9.5 miles. Both routes required special arrangements. The switchboard at Ringsend had five direct current generating panels with 19 dc feeder panels. Two rotary converters with the appropriate switchboards could be used for changing alternating to direct current or vice versa. There was an ac substation at Blackrock, half way along the Dalkey line and a smaller substation at Dalkey.

Clontarf operated the outer end of the Howth line, which we will meet on page 46, equipped with a motor generator set operating on 2,500 volts, there being also three small rotary converters. The power cables under the streets were carried in the ducts already described, the manhole covers on which were easily recognisable by their circular covers with segmental framing and wooden block fillers. Some of these remained in position in 2000. Later covers, such as those still to be seen on Clontarf Road, were castings with the company's initials on them.

More Conversions

Following an interruption of more than seven months in the electrification programme, the commissioning of Ringsend Generating Station triggered the rapid demise of the horse trams. By the time the process resumed in August 1899, the 89 electric cars available at the end of 1898 had been joined by the 50 American cars, Nos 121-170, and 20 more Spa Road-built trams. Some of the latter were about to travel over routes they had already traversed in their previous existence as horse trams.

The resumption began on 28th August when electric trams took over on the line to Terenure via Rathmines. There was a slight hitch in the morning when a car derailed in Nassau Street, but the service was soon restored. Everything then went well until the evening, when tram No 108, driven by Motorman P Morse, became derailed at Rathmines. Ten other cars were held up and theatre goers who were delayed on their way to the city derived much amusement from watching the re-railing of the errant No 108.

On 4th September the Inchicore line changed over, this electrification being a double bonus for the DUTC. The route from College Green to Goldenbridge had been especially hard on horses because of the numerous gradients along the way. Its conversion also put Spa Road works on an electrified route.

Three services were converted during October, the first being known to the DUTC at that time as the line from 'Rathgar to the Sea'. Later, it became familiar to Dubliners as the Cross Tram route because it met, crossed or shared the tracks of ten other services. Sections of it had existed in horse days and an Act of 1897 had given the DUTC powers to construct the remainder. It had been

The first DUTC line to be electrified, that to Dollymount, was changed over in two sections: Dollymount to Annesley Bridge in November 1897 and onwards to Nelson Pillar in March 1898. This intriguing 1897 picture of Clontarf depot shows the refurbished horse car depot to the right, with a seven window car inside and an engineering vehicle, a water sprinkler, in front. Today, a modern facade and offices front this impressive building, now a Dublin Bus garage (see page 37).
BT-H Brochure

horse operated for about 12 months, but on 12th October 1899 a prime DUTC ambition was realised when the electrics began plying between Lansdowne Road and Kenilworth Square over what today is part of the No 18 bus route. One of the lines with which the Cross Tram connected, that from Terenure through Harold's Cross to Nelson Pillar, went electric on 16th October.

A second cross-city service was reported in the *Evening Herald* of 24th October. 'This morning the Palmerston Park trams commenced to run by electricity, and the line is now worked in conjunction with the Clontarf system. The cars are now running continuously between Upper Rathmines just outside the entrance to Palmerston Park, and Dollymount. The advantage of a rapid service of tramcars between these far distant suburbs will be highly appreciated by the residents in both. The system of amalgamating two hitherto distinct lines is chiefly useful in enabling passengers to pass from the concluding section of one of the routes to the opening section of another without interruption, thus tending towards cheaper and more convenient transit in the central parts of the city.' Trams working this route travelled from Amiens Street via Talbot Street, Gardiner Street, Beresford Place and Lower Abbey Street, bypassing Nelson Pillar. This service was the first of several attempts at connecting the Clontarf line and Amiens Street Station with other points on the tramway network. Unfortunately, people from both ends of the route grumbled about not being able to board already crowded trams going either way in the city centre. These complaints resulted in the service being cut back to its separate north and south side components.

Discommoded Citizens

Eagerly looking forward to the new milieu, people were understandably irked by any perceived hiatus in the pace of the changeover. During this difficult period when both types of car shared the same tracks, horse trams often held up a following electric, to the dismay of the passengers and crew on the newer vehicle. There were also several valid complaints about the behaviour of selfish objectors who held up progress on the various lines.

The DUTC regularly came in for severe criticism, especially over the state and impassability of streets while new rails and cable ducts were being laid, and overhead wires were being erected. Discommoded people reacted in different ways, as evidenced by two unhappy citizens who ended up in court in contrasting circumstances.

Guests in the Central Hotel took exception to night work in South Great George's and complained to Mr Mayhew, the Manager. Having got little satisfaction from the tramwaymen, Mayhew doused them with a hose, giving John Corcoran an especially severe drenching. Realising that he was in trouble, Mayhew gave the men £2.10s the following day but excluded Corcoran, who took him to court. On 18th October 1898 the Recorder found that although Mayhew was imprudent, he had been provoked and awarded Corcoran compensation of 10s 6d, the equivalent of £42 in 1999.

Thomas Sexton of North Frederick Street objected to the noise and inconvenience caused by round-the-clock reconstruction work outside his house during 1899. Having tried unsuccessfully to negotiate, he took the company to court. On 1st November, he was granted an injunction, with costs, preventing the DUTC from doing any work outside his house on any night between 9pm and 6am the following morning.

However, on the plus side the provision of extra work in a city with a horrifying unemployment problem was widely acknowledged. The new regime presented the travelling public with far more advantages than handicaps though for some people,

many of the benefits were cancelled out by what they saw as negative developments. One innovation that caused considerable resentment was the establishment of fixed stopping places, which many people found irksome. Horse trams had normally halted to suit individual convenience, agile passengers jumping on and off while they were in motion. A major advantage of fixed stopping places was an ability to exploit the higher speed of the electric cars. To forestall complaints, staff members were instructed to look after passengers who might need special consideration.

Yet More Change-overs

On October 18th the North Quays line, electrically equipped but operating as a horse service since November 1898, finally changed over. It initially carried a service which continued past O'Connell Bridge to Westland Row. This afforded passengers who would normally use the as yet unconverted South Quays line from Kingsbridge to Westland Row a faster journey. Another significant development took place on 9th November when the Harold's Cross electric service was extended northwards past Nelson Pillar to Drumcondra.

December 1899 saw two conversions, starting with the Clonskea line on the 1st. The second, effected on the 4th, came as a particular relief for the DUTC which, two months earlier, had been much criticised over the Dolphin's Barn section of the route involved. It will be recalled that the line from Leonard's Corner (Clanbrassil Street) to Dolphin's Barn was the only major new horse route constructed by the DUTC (see pages 19-20). Opened from Dolphin's Barn to Nelson Pillar as late as February 1896, this service was cut back to Harrington Street for a long time in 1898 for two reasons. These were the widening of Wexford Street and the line's own reconstruction. Unfortunately, much of the track renewal was carried out with the lighter rail used on horse lines. While this was being dug up again to enable heavier rails to be laid, passengers had to make the best of the situation.

The gall of the Dolphin's Barn passengers, compounded by having to travel on an antiquated horse service over part of a route already electrically equipped, improved dramatically on 4th December. Their new electric cars now began running through the city centre and on to Glasnevin. There was a new terminus here, the line being extended north-westwards from Botanic Avenue to the Holy Faith Convent gate opposite Ballymun Road. With this change-over, horse trams ceased to use Nelson Pillar as a regular terminus.

The conversions continued into the early weeks of the new century. Electric trams took over on the College Green to Drumcondra line on 5th January 1900. On 16th January the South Quays line went electric, the service operating from Kingsbridge via Westland Row and Earlsfort Terrace to Hatch Street, at its junction with Harcourt Street. Horse trams were finally banished from the city centre by these January change-overs. The last conversion in this major phase of the programme took place on 9th February when electric cars on the Harold's Cross line began working beyond Terenure to Rathfarnham.

A resume of the change-over to electric traction was given to DUTC shareholders at their meeting on 13th February 1900. They learned that the electric cars cost 4d less per mile to operate then their horse-drawn predecessors, this works out at £1.23 at 1999 prices. Dates on which electric cars began working on the various routes were also listed, but some of these were unfortunately quoted inaccurately in the press. The number of electric cars was put at 180, with another 70 expected by August 1900.

Reconstruction of the track prior to electrification enabled the DUTC to double as many of the remaining stretches of single line as was practicable. In a submission to the Board of Trade on 25th September 1899, the company pointed out that the following sections had been doubled: Dunphy's (now Doyle's) Corner to Glasnevin, Harold's Cross (Dodd's Buildings) to Rathfarnham, Belgrave Square to Palmerston Park, Sandford Church to Belmont Avenue Clonskea and Capel Street (Ryder's Row) to Drumcondra.

In a few locations, stretches of interlaced track, overlapping lines in opposite direc-

tions, were dictated by road widths. Tracks at Castlewood Avenue, Charleston Road and Appian Way on the Kenilworth Square to Lansdowne Road route had this feature, while a particularly busy place so afflicted was George's Street in Kingstown. There were also a few lengths of single track on less busy lines; some of these were later doubled.

Nearly There – Congratulations
Except for the section of the Sandymount line from Beggar's Bush outwards, the DUTC's extensive horse system had been converted to electric traction in a little over two years. Considering the delays caused, first by objections and then in the completion of the generating station, this was a notable achievement. At the end of the electrification programme, the DUTC shareholders were told, in a brief review, that the profit of £20,000 which had been made in 1881, the DUTC's first year of horse operation, had doubled in its last one, 1896.

In the introductory paragraph of a major article on the Ringsend power station in the American *Street Railway Journal* of 5th May 1900, A C Shaw wrote, 'The Dublin United Tramways Company may well be congratulated upon the practical completion of its magnificent system of electric tramways, which may safely be said to be the most extensive and most complete in the British Isles.'

Well-deserved congratulations were also extended to the company's staff at the DUTC shareholders' meeting in February 1900. Special reference was made to the men in the company's employment, especially those in the Traffic Department. These were mostly long-serving employees, interested in electric traction, 'who displayed great skill and aptitude for their new duties.' It was revealed that, almost every week, Manager C W Gordon experienced continuing difficulties in trying to get enough

trained men as each line changed. Men being laid up with flu or drafted off to South Africa to fight in the Boer War exacerbated the situation. Extra staff had to be taken on to enable daily shifts to be shortened, while drivers and conductors with long service were awarded an increase of 2/- per week.

The Growing City: New Boundaries
Under the provisions of the 1898 Local Government Act, the townships surrounding the City of Dublin achieved Urban District Council status. The former Town Commissioners were now replaced by elected councillors. However, the level of services they could provide, and the expansionist ambitions of Dublin Corporation, effectively circumscribed their viability and independence. Along the southeast coast, Pembroke, Blackrock, Kingstown and Dalkey became Urban Districts. Rathmines, which shared some services with Pembroke, became one of the more powerful UDCs. Clontarf, Drumcondra and Glasnevin on the north side, and New Kilmainham to the south-west, enjoyed their enhanced status for only a short time, being overtaken or, as they saw it, engulfed by the Dublin Corporation Act of 1900. Under the provisions of this statute, they were incorporated into the city, as were areas of the county, such as Donnycarney and Crumlin. While the boundary extension was less than the Corporation had hoped for, the result nevertheless more than doubled the municipal area, from 3,733 acres (1,510 hectares) to 7,894 acres (3,194 hectares).

The administrative shape of the Dublin conurbation, for that is what it would become with the absorption by ever-spreading suburbs of previously separate, self-contained villages like Glasnevin or Donnybrook, was now more or less fixed for about

Two apparently similar trams, but with very different origins, at Northumberland Road in the early days of electric operation. No 47, a 54-seater was the seventh electric tram built by the DUTC. Dating from 1898, it was vestibuled c1915 and replaced by a Standard Saloon in 1926. No 37 began life as horse tram No 21 in July 1889. In December 1897 it was the second of 86 DUTC horse trams to be rebuilt as an electric. Its seating capacity of 46 was increased by four when it was vestibuled in October 1903. It too was replaced by a Standard Saloon in 1927. Tramway and Railway World

30 years. Much of this development would be facilitated by the electric tramway system, people being encouraged to live along or near the extended and improved routes.

Developments Elsewhere in Ireland

To place the Dublin system in the wider context of electric tramway development in other parts of Ireland up to 1901, three other undertakings in operation before the end of the nineteenth century must first be acknowledged. The pioneering Giant's Causeway and Bessbrook & Newry lines, mentioned in the previous chapter, had been operating since 1883 and 1885 respectively.

A very early urban electric system was that in Cork. The Cork Electric Tramways and Lighting Company had obtained permission to provide the city with electric power and lighting, a primary condition of its supply franchise being that it should also deliver a public transport service. The Cork Electric Tramways began operation in December 1898 on six routes radiating from the Father Matthew Statue, serving Tivoli, Summerhill, Blackpool, Sunday's Well, Douglas and Ballintemple, the latter being extended in 1902 to Blackrock. The Cork fleet eventually totalled 35 cars operating over 9.8 route miles of 2ft 11½in gauge track. The depot and power station were at Albert Road. William Martin Murphy was a director of the company, which was controlled by the British Thomson-Houston Company Ltd. Apart from the DUTC system, three other electric tramways also began operation in the Dublin area at the beginning of the twentieth century.

The Dublin & Lucan Electric Railway

To the west side of the city, the Dublin & Lucan Steam Tramway Company had been operating its 3ft gauge line since 1881 (see page 23). This tramway had encountered

many difficulties since its opening and by the mid-nineties it required substantial renewal. A formal decision was made in 1897 to electrify and the name of the company was changed to the Dublin & Lucan Electric Railway. A curious decision at the time was to alter the gauge to 3ft 6in, for which there are two plausible reasons. First was a distrust of the DUTC, which it was feared might try to take over a 5ft 3in gauge tramway instead of simply issuing through tickets from O'Connell Bridge to Lucan. The terminus of the DUTC North Quays line, which had been extended to the gates of the Phoenix Park on electrification, adjoined the Dublin and Lucan at the Parkgate Street Conyngham Road junction. There was also the practical matter of adapting some of the steam trailer stock to the gauge proposed, which would have been difficult if not impossible with a move to 5ft 3in.

Dublin & Lucan tracks were on a roadside reservation for most of their length. Starting from Conyngham Road they followed the Phoenix Park side of the road as far as Riverside where they crossed to the south side, recrossing just beyond the Chapelizod Gate. The line hugged the eastern parapet of the bridge over the Liffey and continued along the south side of the road to Lucan, where there was a depot. The Dublin & Lucan Electric Railway built a power station at Fonthill. This building, now a factory, is an important example of Victorian public utility architecture.

The Dublin & Lucan Electric Railway opened on 8th March 1900. In addition to commuters and some goods traffic, the line catered for a large volume of tourist and leisure traffic. In 1912, it was extended half a mile to Dodsboro (Spa Hotel). This length was a partial revival of an extension to the original steam tramway connecting Lucan with Leixlip, but which had been abandoned some years earlier.

In 1900, the DL&ER had five open-top double-deck cars supplied by Dick, Kerr and running on Brill maximum traction bogies. Four were 62-seaters, one a 66-seater and they were claimed to be the first eight-wheeled electric cars in Ireland. They certainly had the largest seating capacities yet seen here on electric trams. The line on which they ran will come back into our story at a later date (see pages 97-100).

Clontarf & Hill of Howth Tramroad

A very important line with a complicated history was the Clontarf & Hill of Howth Tramroad, not to be confused with the Hill of Howth Tramway of the Great Northern Railway (Ireland). A tramway to Howth via Killester and Raheny had been proposed as early as 1890 but four years were to pass before the project began to assume the shape in which it eventually materialised. This envisaged an end-on connection with the Dublin United line at Dollymount, the distance from there to Howth (East Pier) being about five and a half miles.

When the DUTC had first applied for powers to electrify its own system in November 1894 it was expected that the Dublin company would enter into reciprocal arrangements with the Clontarf to Howth concern for power supply, provision of rolling stock and through running. The necessary powers were finally obtained in 1898 and the Clontarf & Hill of Howth Tramroad Company Limited (CHHC) was incorporated. William Martin Murphy was a director, but resigned within a short time.

Numerous complexities surrounded the construction and early operation of the Clontarf & Hill of Howth Tramroad. First there were difficulties with Lord Ardilaun, along the sea frontage of whose property at St Anne's the line would run, this is the route of the present day James Larkin Road. Lord Ardilaun imposed very stringent conditions. Access to the foreshore and his private rifle range were understandable enough provisions, as were stipulations that the free flow of the Nanniken and Santry Rivers should not be restricted. Fences of agreed design were to be erected and the traction poles were to be to an approved, considerably embellished design.

One of the line's more difficult problems stemmed from the condition that the track was to be single opposite St Anne's and cars might not stop along this section to pick up or set down passengers. This resulted in a

Dublin & Lucan Electric Railway bogie car No 14. When the line was regauged to 3ft 6in and converted to electric traction in March 1900, it boasted the first electric bogie trams in Ireland. No 14 lasted until the closure of the line in 1925.
Kennedy collection

This posed photograph from the first decade of the twentieth century shows one of the GNR's Hill of Howth trams, en route to the Summit, on the overbridge at Howth railway station while below, No 301, a city bound Clontarf & Hill of Howth car, pauses for the photographer. In earlier years the Howth cars and a few four-wheelers had their headlamps on the lower dash panels with the fleet number above them. Straw boaters proclaim the season to be summer, it is a great pity that we have no means of giving names to the tramwaymen and passengers in the picture. Irish Railway Record Society

very long stretch without passing places and the extremely rare use on an electric tramway of the train staff system. Regular practice on single track sections of railway, this required that a section could not be entered unless the crew was in possession of a staff, only one of which could be in use at any time, the others being locked in frames at either end of the section. In the case of the tramway, more than one car could travel in the same direction, protected by a staff on the last car in the convoy. The instruments were located in huts at Dollymount and Raheny, while there was also a semaphore signal at Dollymount.

From Raheny (Watermill Road) the line was double and on sleeper track, with railway fencing as far as Blackbanks. Before this there was a double-track depot adjacent to the end of Fox's Lane. It reverted to single track with passing loops on joining the road from Raheny at Blackbanks and continued on a reservation on the sea side of the road. Curves in the wall and a wider footpath still mark the locations of the former loops at Kilbarrack Cemetery and Baldoyle Road. At the latter point there was an extra long passing place with an intermediate crossover to facilitate the special cars laid on for patrons of the Metropolitan Race Company's meetings at the former Baldoyle racecourse.

There was some further double track after the turn at the Claremont level crossing and the line then carried on past Howth railway station to the terminus at East Pier. A financially unfortunate feature of this tramway was that as it ran beside the sea for more than four miles between Fairview and Sutton, it had only half a catchment for this distance. Somewhat more cheerful from the viewpoint of costs was that, except for a short rise over the Royal Canal at Newcomen Bridge, the entire line from Nelson Pillar to Howth was nearly level for all of its length.

A poignant memorial from the construction of the Howth line may be seen in the graveyard at St Mary's Abbey in Howth. In that quiet resting place is a plot known as the Strangers' Bank, where the bodies of shipwrecked sailors were buried in bygone days. A ganger employed in building the

Howth line, whose name was said to be unknown to his colleagues, died during the work and was buried in the Strangers' Bank. His friends, anxious to commemorate him, have left us an exquisitely eloquent grave marker in the form of two pieces of tram rail.

The Clontarf to Howth line opened on Thursday, 26th July 1900. At a time when electric tramway inaugurations had become routine, the *Evening Mail* carried a fairly detailed report the next day. Dubliners and visitors from further afield had sampled the new service on its opening day. There was a running time of 45 minutes for the nine miles from Nelson Pillar to Howth for a 5d fare. The cars were described as being vestibuled 75-seaters. There was a 15-minute frequency on the line, later lengthened to half an hour during off-peak periods. In addition to regular commuters, the Howth line carried heavy leisure traffic from the day it opened.

On 28th July 1900, just as the line was getting into its stride, a court heard a claim for £50 damages by a man who had been injured by a falling wire near Dollymount on 11th May. He was awarded eight guineas, a guinea being the equivalent of £1.1s.0d. Three days after the opening, a passenger who had just alighted from a tram found a young man named William Duffy lying on the track with serious leg injuries. He was taken to Nelson Pillar in a tramcar, being transferred from there to Jervis Street Hospital by Fire Brigade ambulance, a facility introduced the previous year.

The Clontarf & Hill of Howth operated at first as a completely separate system, with a crew change at Dollymount for trams working through from Howth to Nelson Pillar and vice versa, the changeover point at Dollymount was known as 'the Junction'. Along with the crew change, the Clontarf company

issued its own titled tickets between Dollymount and Howth. The Clontarf & Hill of Howth Tramroad Company bought 12 open-top bogie trams, details of which are given in the Rolling Stock Catalogue on page 143.

A working agreement of April 1899 governed the early relationship of the Clontarf & Hill of Howth concern with the DUTC, later altered by a supplementary document dated February 1902. Under the terms of this, the change of crews at Dollymount was abolished, the DUTC taking control of CHHC staff and also assuming responsibility for maintaining the permanent way and lighting equipment. From 1902, the DUTC issued their own tickets to Howth passengers, the name of the CHHC being shown as a subtitle to that of the Dublin company. Further important changes in the operation of the Dublin to Howth line in 1907, are recorded on page 72.

The Hill of Howth Tramway
The third line to be built outside DUTC control around the turn of the century and in later years easily the most famous, was the Hill of Howth Tramway. The full story of this legendary system is told in R C Flewitt's book '*The Hill of Howth Tramway*' (Transport Research Associates 1968). It is introduced here to round out the developments of the electrification era

The Howth branch of the Great Northern Railway (now part of the DART system) runs along the north shore of the Howth peninsula, Sutton and Howth stations being two miles apart. To the south of this stretch of railway lies the Hill of Howth, the road journey across the summit between the two stations being about five and a quarter miles. Incipient residential development, increasing tourism and the potential of the breath-

In the graveyard at St Mary's Abbey in Howth is the Stranger's bank, the last resting place of unidentified shipwreck victims. Here also lies a man who worked on the construction of the Dollymount to Howth tramway. In memory of this nameless soul, his colleagues marked his grave with two lengths of tram rail. *Transport Museum Society of Ireland collection.*

taking views from the Hill were all factors which persuaded the GNR to build the tramway. It opened in two sections, Sutton to the Summit (three and a quarter miles) on 17th June 1901 and Summit to Howth (two miles) on 1st August. The depot and power station were at Sutton. While not part of the Dublin United system the Hill of Howth Tramway is too important to dismiss in a couple of short paragraphs and is therefore the subject of Chapter Six. In the meantime, however, some facts will set it in the context of the early twentieth century and its relationship with the Dublin-Howth line.

The Howth Electric Tramway, as it was called by the GNR, ran partly on a roadside reservation on the Sutton side of the Hill, employing sleeper track with bullhead rails. It crossed the Clontarf and Hill of Howth line at two points, but there was no physical connection between the two. The GNR line was the full 5ft 3in gauge, the Clontarf to Howth line, as explained earlier in the context of the DUTC lines, was $^{13}/_{16}$ of an inch less.

At Sutton there was a diamond crossing using grooved rail in setts, and also an insulated section in the Dublin line's overhead where it crossed that of the GNR. At Howth Station, the Hill line crossed the main road and the DUTC tracks on an overbridge, whose abutments are still in position, bringing the GNR trams into the station yard. At Sutton Cross, Dublin trams travelling

towards Howth yielded to Hill of Howth cars, the latter gave way to DUTC trams coming from Howth.

Local authorities had the right to use tramway poles as public lighting standards and did so extensively, indeed several hundred former traction poles are still in use as lamp posts, throughout the city. The Dublin & Lucan Electric Railway and the Hill of Howth Tramway both supplied current to domestic consumers in their areas, as well as to local authorities for public lighting. A particularly interesting situation arose along the main road leading into Howth, where the poles on the Dublin to Howth line carried traction current from the DUTC station at Ringsend and a lighting supply generated by the GNR at Sutton.

New DUTC Lines:
Proposed and Realised
At various times during the horse tram regime, additions to the system were suggested but never built. With the onset of electrification, extension of several existing lines was considered and some totally new ones were also proposed. An extension effected immediately upon conversion was that of the Glasnevin line from Botanic Avenue to Ballymun Road corner, while others took place following completion of the electrification programme.

A number of eminently sensible extensions to the system were proposed but never implemented. These included a continuation of the Inchicore line to Bluebell and connecting the Parkgate Street and North Circular Road termini by a loop through Phoenix Park, serving the Zoo and the RIC depot. New lines canvassed but not built would have linked Finglas and Swords to the network. However, some new routes and extensions did materialise in the first six years of the new century, beginning with those to Sandymount via Ringsend and from Capel Street to Ballybough.

Sandymount via Ringsend
From the introduction of the horse tram service in 1872, all traffic to and from Sandymount had gone by way of Bath Avenue, and the previously unfashionable area of Ringsend had been ignored. In 1900, a new tramway connecting Sandymount with Nelson Pillar by the most direct route through Ringsend was opened in two stages. This new line ran through areas of considerable population and passed several major industries, including glass factories, the Gas Works and Hammond Lane Foundry which all fronted directly onto it. It also put the maritime village of Ringsend firmly on the tramway map. Apart from its logic in the network this route could be claimed by the DUTC, sensitive to criticism as primarily a provider of transport for the better off, to cater for working class people. It also served

the DUTC power station in Ringsend, where in time there was also established a permanent way and engineering materials yard.

The Sandymount via Ringsend line could not operate as a through service until the bridge over the entrance to the Grand Canal Basin near Boland's Mills was replaced. This work was carried out by the DUTC which had most of the iron and steel work for the two-lane swivelling structure cast or fabricated by Ross and Walpole of North Wall. Special fittings were designed for the overhead to ensure the automatic restoration of electrical continuity after each opening of the bridge.

Trams began working between Sandymount and the new Victoria Bridge on 4th July 1900. While work on the bridge was in progress, trams terminated at either side, Inchicore cars working to and from the city side of the gap. When the structure opened, on 18th March 1901, Sandymount cars began running through to Nelson Pillar, and the Inchicore services were cut back to Westland Row. The completed Sandymount route through Ringsend reached Nelson Pillar via Great Brunswick Street, D'Olier Street and O'Connell Bridge. Great Brunswick Street was officially renamed Pearse Street on 1st November 1920. A small two-track horse-car depot at Gilford Road, later adapted for the electric single-deckers working the Bath Avenue line, was unable to cater for the double-deckers allocated to the Ringsend route. A new three-track building for these cars was therefore built adjoining the existing Gilford Road premises.

The narrow roadway and awkward footpath at Victoria Bridge caused a heart-rending accident on 29th June 1904. Two little brothers, Joseph (4) and Patrick (3) Ward, were accidentally thrown out of their pram at the kerb and struck by the fender of tram No 89, driven by William Ryan. Both children died, one at the scene, his brother later in hospital. Shocked but reliable witnesses, some of whom did their best for the unfortunate children and their minder, were able to provide evidence exonerating the deeply shocked motorman.

A New Route: Ballybough
Following the Rathfarnham conversion in February 1900, the only remaining DUTC horse-operated line was that between Beggar's Bush and Sandymount. Much of the year 1900 was spent in consolidating the work already done and preparing for a completely new electric service, which opened on 1st October. This was the Ballybough line, which had its western terminus at Parkgate Street and followed the existing North Quays line to Grattan Bridge. It then turned into Capel Street, still following existing lines to Great Britain Street (renamed Parnell Street in 1911). It left the Drumcondra

line at this junction, running through Parnell Street, which had not previously been served by trams. Carrying on past the Rotunda Hospital, it crossed Sackville Street, and went on via Summerhill and Ballybough Road, to terminate at Clonliffe Road.

Often referred to as the back street route, the Ballybough line epitomises those so described and argued about during the electrification debate in 1895. None of the section from Capel Street to Ballybough appeared on the first current distribution map produced in connection with the Ringsend generating station project in 1898. The Ballybough service ran through some of Dublin's most cruelly disadvantaged areas. Summerhill and Gardiner Street were truly the epicentre of the terrible poverty so searingly dramatised by Sean O'Casey, suffering the most intense unemployment and deprivation. Bearing in mind the level of wages in vogue at the turn of the century, it is almost a certainty that the few people from that area lucky enough to be at work could have afforded to even think about travelling regularly by tram.

This line was, more likely, intended to generate traffic from the better-off Clonliffe Road, Ballybough and Fairview districts. Its Ballybough terminus is also something of a mystery, because it was originally intended to continue through Fairview Strand, connecting with the Howth line at Fairview Corner, as part of a plan to have a branch from the West Pier at Howth providing a through service to the Fish Market.

The Last Horse Trams: Electric Single-Deckers on Bath Avenue

Only the truncated Sandymount via Bath Avenue line remained operated by horse trams after the Rathfarnum electrification in 1900. This carried on for another eleven months mainly because of its unique vehicular requirements though the cars ceased running to the city centre when the Dalkey electrics were extended to Nelson Pillar in 1898. Now operating from Sandymount Tower only as far as Beggar's Bush, its outer end was further curtailed when the Ringsend line electrics began running to Sandymount Tower in January 1900. It was then restricted to working between Haddington Road and the junction of Londonbridge Road with Irishtown Road. By that time, the few remaining horse cars had less than a year to live.

No 304 was one of the twelve Preston built cars, numbered 301-312, supplied to the Clontarf & Hill of Howth company in 1900. The reversed Peckham trucks, with the driving wheels near the centre of the car, can be seen clearly. The frame of this vehicle was used in a new No 304, to a DUTC four window design, which left Spa Road works in 1922. IRRS collection

While double deck horse trams could negotiate the notorious Bath Avenue railway bridge with caution, electric cars, sitting higher on their trucks, could not. Single-deckers were therefore needed, and three, Nos 252, 253 and 254, were duly turned out from Spa Road in December 1900. They are more fully described on pages 53 and 54 and in the Rolling Stock Catalogue. The final change-over from horses took place on 14th January 1901 when Nos 252 to 254, the only single deck electrics cars in DUTC service, began to work between Nelson Pillar and Sandymount via Bath Avenue.

On the last evening of horse traction, 13th January, there was an accident when a man named Ralph Patterson was knocked down by one of the trams. His injuries included two broken legs, some contemporary reports even said, erroneously, that he died. Police Inspector Thomas Grant was a passenger on the car and gave evidence when the driver, Thomas Treacy, was charged at the Southern Police Court, remanded on bail and subsequently exonerated.

A report headed **DUBLIN TRAMS – THE LAST OF THE HORSE CARS** in the *Evening Herald* on 14th January included a valediction to the horse era; 'The last trace of the old system of horse-haulage on the Dublin tram lines has now disappeared with the withdrawal of the one link with the past which remained over from the nineteenth century, namely the little connection by horse car between Northumberland Road and the Star of the Sea Church on the Sandymount route. The company have signalled the new era by the removal of this slight anachronism, and last night one solitary pair of quadrupeds, the only remnants of a once powerful squadron, ambled along by Beggar's Bush on their final journey. This morning electric cars were put on this line, and their advent was naturally hailed with much satisfaction by the travelling public...'

Replacement of the horse trams over four and a half years resulted in a rapid depletion of the DUTC's animal stock, changing over a service using ten trams could result in the disappearance of up to a hundred horses. As we saw in the first chapter, the considerable back up for the animals comprised a significant industry, including grooms, harness makers and farriers, and of course suppliers of feeding stuffs and bedding.

Such losses were compensated for by growth in other areas of employment, mechanics, electricians, linesmen, suppliers of lubricants, to quote some direct replacements as closely as possible. A comparison can be made between William Anderson, said to have been the toughest of all the buyers of animal feed at the Dublin Corn Exchange, and later DUTC purchasers of coal for power generation; the method of haggling remained the same, only the merchandise being different.

For many people, a great deal of sentiment vanished with the horses and there are several stories of sad partings. When the last of 156 horses were being taken away from Terenure, a harness maker named John Malone stood with a bridle in his hand and tears in his eyes. But as the last horse passed him it is said to have gently plucked the bridle from his hand, cheering him up. Many of the horses are believed to have gone to the Glasgow Tramways and there is a story of one horse resolutely refusing to go up the gangway of the emigrant ship at North Wall. A passing tramwayman recognised the animal and called out 'Go on, Sandymount' whereupon the horse willingly went aboard the vessel.

In 1900, the DUTC reported a deficit of £13,366 on the sale of its tram horses. On 31st July, the shareholders were told that

109 horses remained in service with the company at that date, 22 of these being employed on the Sandymount line. The rest were used on parcels traffic or general cartage and tower wagon haulage. It was expected that, following the electrification of the Bath Avenue line, about 70 horses would remain in DUTC service.

Anatomy of a Tram

On page 27 we looked at how horse trams had evolved up to 1896 when Dublin's last vehicles of that type were built. The line of structural development continued straight into the electric era, the new cars having bodywork very similar to that of their horse-drawn predecessors. The story can now be taken further as we examine the salient features of an electric tramcar.

Like their animal-hauled forerunners, Dublin's electric trams were double-ended, they could be driven from either platform in either direction, all the necessary accoutrements being installed on each platform. These consisted of controllers, canopy switches, hand brakes, sanding mechanism and advance warning gongs, plus a bell push or strap for the conductor's use. The ends of the tram were referred to as No 1 End and No 2 End, each having its identification painted on the rear of a staircase riser at eye level.

Tramcar Trucks and Bogies

The running gear under an electric tram normally consisted of either a rigid four-wheeled truck or two four-wheeled bogies. Dublin used both types, four-wheelers being used exclusively in the early days. The entire first generation DUTC fleet, up to and including No 293, was made up of four-wheeled or single truck cars. Most trams had two motors geared directly to the driving axles, every Dublin electric car was so equipped.

Companies in the United States, where electric traction technology was very advanced in the late 1880s, supplied much of the early equipment especially trucks and bogies. There were several leading manufacturers, trucks of whose design were later made under licence in Britain and other European countries.

All DUTC electric trams up to and including No 224 were mounted on Peckham trucks, but that of No 225 bore the name of DuPont. This American company franchised several others to manufacture running gear of its design, one being Lorain Steel whose products were sometimes referred to as Lorain trucks.

About 50 of these were bought by the DUTC and initially placed under trams in the number range 225-293. Later, when truck changes commenced, DuPonts were fitted to several cars which had originally been on Peckhams.

Being as self-sufficient as possible, the DUTC also produced some trucks of its own. The foreman in charge of the truck shop, Harold Brierley, was a resourceful individual who put much effort into empirically modifying and improving running gear. He paid particular attention to DuPont trucks, which became the pattern for those made by the DUTC. Sometimes called Brierleys, these were officially known as Inchicore or DUTC trucks and carried the words 'DUTC, Builders, Inchicore' on their axlebox covers.

Later, there were also Peckham Extension trucks, Peckham No 10s and numerous others of various makes described as 'modified'. At least one BECC truck was bought by the DUTC and placed under No 270 in 1903. An early DUTC example of a Brill-trucked four-wheeler was No 18 in 1907. After the First World War, Brill 21E trucks were used increasingly and in time were to be found under more than half the fleet.

Driving the Car

Current came from the overhead wires through the trolley wheel. The heads in which these were fitted could be either fixed or swivelling, the latter being standard in Dublin. From the trolley wheel the current passed through a cable in the trolley pole and then via the canopy switches and fuses to either controller. This had two handles, one for Off, Forward or Reverse, the other working through a series of notches which regulated the flow of current to the motors, thus governing the speed of the car. There were series and parallel notches, and a rheostat or resistance dissipating the heat generated during series operation. The electrical circuit back to the power station was effected through the tramcar wheels and the rails. Braking notches were also provided on the controller.

The hand brake was operated by a swan-neck handle on a spindle with a pawl and ratchet, applying the wheel brakes through chains and linkages. The sanding gear, used to assist adhesion on slippery rails, consisted of hoppers under the seats in the four corners of the lower deck; these had pipes discharging just above the rails at the platform side of each wheel, sand being discharged by activating a pedal on the platform. A second platform pedal operated the warning gong.

An important feature of each tram was a full-width gate under each platform. In the event of anybody falling in front of the car this would lift on coming in contact with the accident victim. On raising, it triggered a mechanism that dropped a tray fitted below the saloon bulkhead of the platform. This was intended to scoop the person up, thus preventing more serious injury from the car's wheels or truck frame. Widely known as the lifeguard, the mechanism, once acti-

vated, could be reset from the platform. The driving, or leading, platform of a tramcar was closed off by a trellis gate to prevent unauthorised access, the door to the interior being kept closed; passengers boarded and left by the trailing or conductor's platform.

All Dublin electric trams up to the late 1920s had longitudinal seating on the lower deck, the passengers having their backs to the windows. There was also a movable seat placed behind the closed saloon door at the leading (motorman's) end of the car. Upstairs (officially 'Outside'), the central aisle had double seats on either side, with a single seat outside the trolley standard, which was offset so as not to obstruct the gangway. The seats had reversible backs, turned over by the conductor at each terminus, thus enabling passengers to face the direction of travel; there was a fixed seat, usually for three, against the end panel at either end of an unvestibuled tram.

The seating arrangements varied at the ends of the upper decks on trams from different builders or batches. In Dublin, top-covered trams were of three types: Balcony cars which first appeared in 1904, totally enclosed Standard Saloons (1924) and Luxury Saloons (1931). All of these trams had their upper-deck transverse seats in pairs, the trolley pole being fixed to a horizontal roof-mounted trolleybase.

A tram's seating capacity was sign-written above the entrance to the lower deck on each platform as follows: 'Constructed to carry 22 inside and 24 outside', the figures varying according to the size of the car. It is noteworthy that the upper deck was always called 'outside' and that this practice continued to the last years of the tramways, when open-top cars were but a memory.

Trams were licensed by the police, a carriage plate being fixed to the outside lower panel of the bulkhead, usually at the No 1 end. This was a cast brass shield showing the car's licence number. Up to 1925, it bore a crown and was issued by the Dublin Metropolitan Police. From 1925, with the incorporation of the DMP into the Garda Siochana, the symbol changed to the three castles of the Dublin City arms. Apart from this change, the plates remained virtually the same throughout the existence of the tramways. When buses received the then new-style oval aluminium carriage plates in the thirties, the trams retained their brass shields.

The First Electric Cars

The Dublin Southern District rolling stock orders totalled 30 motor cars and 30 trailers, all except five being built by G F Milnes of Birkenhead. Motor cars 1-20 were mounted on 6ft wheelbase Peckham trucks, the cars were just over 27 feet long with two 27hp motors geared direct to the axles. The motors were type GE800 and the controllers, type K2.

Seating capacity was 53, 29 upstairs and 24 below, and the matter of odd seat numbers is worthy of note. Most open-top electric cars had a single seat beside the trolley standard, but from very early in the electric era Dublin cars also had an uneven number of seats downstairs. This was due to a movable single seat placed inside the saloon door at the driving end of the car and moved to the opposite end at the start of the return trip. It was known as the mushroom seat, toad stool or piano stool, was much loved by children and remained in general use until 1938 when it disappeared following objections from the company's insurers.

Twenty trailers, Nos 21-40, also came with the first Southern District delivery. These were slightly smaller than the motor cars, probably 24ft 5in long, and as built had 46 seats, 22 inside and 24 on top. They were later rebuilt as motor trams, and when dealing with the period 1896-1900 it is important to distinguish them from motor trams with the same numbers delivered later in 1896.

The other five DSDT-ordered motor trams built by Milnes were Nos 41-45; the earliest official references to them is dated March 1898. The final five, Nos 56-60, were built by London North Metropolitan, to whom the construction appears to have been subcontracted by Milnes; these cars were not delivered until 1898. The remaining ten trailers were Nos 46-55 and, like the earlier stock of this type, were later rebuilt as motor trams. Fleet integration, vehicle delivery sequences and the subsequent renumbering of motorised trailers has led to some confusion about the identities of the early electric trams.

Twelve Milnes cars ordered by the DUTC in 1896 became Nos 21-32, thus duplicating some of the trailer numbers during the period 1896-1900. These 12 cars differed from the DSDT vehicles in having five side windows instead of four and at 27ft 3in, they were also longer than Nos 1-20. They were allocated to the Clontarf line on its electrifi-

cation in November 1897 and, isolated operationally from the Dalkey line until September 1898, were always referred to as 'Clontarf' cars. Nos 21-32 were also the last new trams to have route details painted directly on to the bodywork.

Trailer operation was short-lived in Dublin, being confined to the Dalkey and Clontarf lines. The use of trailers was discontinued following the fatal accident at Merrion Square in November 1898 described on page 40. On that particular occasion the trailer was horse car No 3. Conversely, there is photographic evidence of trailers being used as horse cars between the date of the Merrion Square accident and January 1900.

The First Inchicore-Built Electrics
On taking over the Dublin Southern District Company and proceeding with electrification the DUTC adopted the numbers of the Milnes and London North Metropolitan powered cars, Nos 1-32, 41-45 and 56-60, as the beginning of its electric fleet register. The new company was, of course, faced with the problem of ensuring an adequate number of vehicles for the electrification programme. In September 1897 the first electric tram to be built by the DUTC emerged from Spa Road. It was No 33, a 54-seater on a Peckham truck. Two similar cars, Nos 34 and 35, followed almost immediately.

The next electric tram, No 36, was completely different. It was a motorised rebuild of horsecar No 126 originally built in 1891 and which now, with an expenditure of £70 in modifying the body, became an electric 46-seater on a Peckham truck. Because the DUTC had been actively contemplating electrification since 1887, it has been said that the 87 new horse trams turned out

between 1889 and 1896 were built with probable conversion in mind. Eighty six of these cars, No 49 was the exception, received similar treatment up to June 1901. Some of them were destined to have chequered careers as electrics. No 49, formerly horsecar 66 and originally built in June 1889, was the oldest, and 234, previously No 188, the newest. The full list of the conversions with new and old numbers in the Rolling Stock Catalogue, illustrates the well-nigh impossible feats of memory demanded by an acquaintance with Dublin tram fleet numbers. After the build-up of the initial stock, in which numbers were allocated more or less in the order in which cars arrived, new vehicles simply took the numbers of those they replaced, a procedure which was to have sometimes interesting results.

Outside Builders
Between Milnes motor cars, ex-horse trams and new Spa Road construction, there were 55 electric trams by June 1898. Coinciding with the delivery of the five London North Metropolitan vehicles, there came the first of 34 from another outside builder. This was the highly respected Dublin coachbuilding firm, Browne's of Great Brunswick Street, the City Wheel Works. Some deliveries from Brownes, who had not previously built trams, were rather slow. At first, the relatively small size of the coachworks was probably a contributory factor, but Browne's had become quite proficient by 1902, when they were able to build a tram in less than three months.

A report in the *Evening Herald* on 6th September 1898 dealt in detail with the building of trams by Browne's. It began by noting that the substitution of electric

Displaying the Maltese Cross symbol of the Drumcondra via Harold's Cross line, No 67 stands at Rathfarnham terminus. Horse car No 110, built in October 1890, was electrified as No 67 in June 1898 at a cost of £104. First allocated to Inchicore, it was working from Terenure depot by 1909, was never vestibuled and was replaced by a new car in December 1923. The motorman's greatcoat buttons up to the neck, thus affording him more protection than that allowed to the conductor. Both men wear kepi caps. The ticket boy's only item of uniform is his overcoat. The musical instrument case carried by the conductor probably belong to the man sitting on the platform step. Birney collection

One of the Thomson-Houston views taken to highlight the excellence of the Dublin electrification programme just before the turn of the nineteenth century. Built as horse tram 163 in June 1894, No 82 emerged as an electric car in November 1898 and was based at Kingsbridge (Victoria Quay) depot. It was scrapped in 1921. The highly decorated centre traction poles are noteworthy, as are the lamps placed on them. The care taken with the design of the overhead installation was largely dictated by the intrusiveness of the huge double and triple telegraph poles visible above the roof lines of the buildings on Bachelor's Walk. The marker lamps on the traction poles were lit by gas. GEC Alsthom

power for horse on the tramway system had necessitated the acquisition by the company of a very considerable number of motor cars. It continued, 'All who are interested in the promotion of Irish industries would naturally wish to see these cars built in Dublin and it is satisfactory to learn that though the company have been obliged to obtain several of them from America they have had many of them made in the city where their operations are carried on and they are apparently determined to have as many more constructed here as is found possible. They are entitled to every credit for having given Irish workmen a chance of showing what they can do, seeing that is so much the fashion of the hour to look abroad for almost everything in the way of manufactured articles. On the other hand they have reason to be satisfied with their patriotic action for they have not only got stronger and more beautifully finished vehicles than those which have been imported…' The writer then went on to the subject of cost, noting that Mr Joseph Browne of the City Wheel Works, 'has been able to meet the foreigner and beat him.' The article continues, 'According as the cars are built by Mr Browne they are wired by the electricians of the company, under the direction of Mr Towell and when handed over by the builder they are fitted with the electrical apparatus at the Company's power station at Ballsbridge.'

Six Browne cars were reported to be running with a seventh just delivered and five others being proceeded with as 'as rapidly as possible.' This statement is obviously in error, because the company records show only three Browne-built cars, Nos 61-63, as entering service in 1898, the remaining 31 being delivered between 1900 and 1903. The *Herald* pointed out that the name of the firm was painted on these cars so that passengers could compare them favourably with the American vehicles. Here again the report is suspect, because the first American car, No 121, is shown in DUTC records as being imported some months later.

The *Herald* described the layout and equipment of the City Wheel Works and concludes with some details of how the trams were constructed. 'The framework of the new motor cars is made of Irish grown oak…everything from the laying down of the framework to the forging of the sheet iron for the platforms and the iron rails for the seats on top is done on the premises…The glass for the new vehicles has been supplied by Messrs. Dockrell and the lamps have been made by Mr Phillipson of Stafford street.'

Any impatience arising from delays at Browne's seems to have been outweighed by William Martin Murphy's satisfaction at having 34 good trams built by a local supplier who made every effort to meet the DUTC's requirements. He was, however, highly critical of delays by well established overseas builders. His views were expressed trenchantly at the company's half-yearly meeting in February 1901 when he referred to 12 trams that, 'might or might not come, the only cars that would ever come into Dublin again built outside it.' Murphy may have expressed himself awkwardly, but his meaning was clear. Whatever the circumstances, the man meant what he said, apart from eight trams built by Browne and nine bogie cars purchased in 1906 (see page 75), some 375 trams built for the DUTC between 1901 and 1936 all came from its own works at Spa Road.

It has been suggested that Browne's could have been sub-contracted by Milnes to build some Dublin trams. The appearance and dimensions of cars from the two builders are strikingly similar and the laying-down dates for some Browne cars follow the date of Murphy's comments to the DUTC shareholders in 1901. It is also within the bounds of possibility that the Milnes trams numbered 41-45 could have been completed by the City Wheel Works. The cryptic and inexplicable first entry for all five cars in the Repair Books records them as entering the works on various dates between March and October 1898. No such remarks were written about any other new tram bought by the DUTC.

A batch of 50 cars, Nos 121-170, was built in the United States of America. It has so far proved impossible to identify the builders, who were probably sub-contractors to British Thomson-Houston. These trams were delivered, probably crated in partly knocked down condition, early in 1899, before electric traction took over on some of the lines for which they were intended. All of the American cars were 54-seaters on Peckham trucks.

The Shortest-Lived Electric Tram

Dublin's shortest-lived electric tram was the first No 84. It had started life in June 1891 as horse tram No 79, and was rebuilt as electric car No 84 in December 1898 at a cost of £104. Allocated to the Kingsbridge depot on Victoria Quay, it was one of several cars on shed on the afternoon of Saturday 19th August 1899. Kingsbridge was also the central grain and hay store responsible for supplying all the DUTC's horse tram depots. A fire broke out here, spreading to the electric depot where at least two trams were damaged. No 84 was destroyed, only its twisted framework remaining.

The new No 84 which appeared in November 1899 was the first fruit of a further rebuilding programme, this time involving the 30 trailers. These had ceased running behind motor trams following the accident in Merrion Square in November 1898, some of them serving temporarily as horse trams. With the impending demise of the horse services, motorising the trailers began when No 34 was transformed into the new No 84 at a cost of £120. Twelve trailers were rebuilt as motor trams by the end of 1899, the remaining 18 following interspersed with 30 horsecar rebuilds, in 1900.

Vestibules: No 91 – The Coffin

A further stage in the evolution of the Dublin tram came in December 1899 with the appearance of No 191, a vehicle of major significance. This was the first Dublin tram to be vestibuled, that is, fitted with full-length platform canopies and windscreens – it was also among the earliest such cars anywhere, and claimed, wrongly, by some commentators as a world first. Extending a tram's upper deck over the platforms increased the seating capacity, usually by four. With one known exception, No 35, all vestibuled DUTC trams built before 1931 had reversed stairs that ascended clockwise.

No 191 had several other new features, the most distinctive being the continuation of the rubbing strake or moulding dividing the waist and rocker panels along the sides right up to and around the dash, which thus had clearly separated upper and lower panels. This was one of the features which over the years would make the DUTC tram as characteristic of Dublin as the Custom House or the Four Courts: few things can be as redolent of any city as its own distinctive transport vehicles. No 191 had the somewhat flattened dashes that were to be a further distinguishing mark of the Dublin tram, but unlike later cars on which they were curved, No 191's were hexagonal, and so the car quickly became known as the Coffin.

Excepting the Dalkey and Clontarf cars as delivered, the early electric trams had detachable destination boards on the rocker panels, colour coded according to route, with a rectangular board above the platform at either end. No 191 went a stage further, having at each end a revolving box lit from within at night, and with destination names painted on removable glass panels. This arrangement also appeared on some other cars. No 191 served for a time as a special car, used by the directors and other dignitaries on important occasions. This vehicle, the body of which cost £237 to build and was mounted on a Peckham truck, was the 202nd car to be built by the DUTC, but it was to be completely outclassed by the 203rd.

The Directors' Tram

While put in hand at the same time as No 191, the 203rd Inchicore tram did not emerge until June 1901. It never had a fleet number and is additional to the numbered

A rather fuzzy photograph showing No 191, the DUTC's first vestibuled tramcar, built in 1899. This tram, known as the Coffin, from the shape of its vestibules, was initially used to transport the directors of the company and their guests. The occasion of the photograph is not known. A new No 191, incorporating parts of the original car, was built in 1918 and later went through a series of transformations leading to its becoming a balcony vehicle in 1930. It was withdrawn in 1939. Birney collection

cars listed as being built at Spa Road. This transcendent car was the Directors' Tram, one of the most exotic vehicles to be encountered on any system. Unique among Dublin trams in having three windows between the bulkheads, this was one of the most famous trams ever built. The body cost £160, while a further £387 was paid to Clery's for furnishings. Fittings included interior window pillars carved like classical columns, a drinks cabinet and folding tables supported by carved busts of angels. The window glass was bevelled plate, there were rich window curtains, blinds and miniature lamp clusters. In each of the 12 ventilators, two above each window, was a coloured etching of a Dublin scene.

Instead of the company garter, the Directors' Car carried the Dublin City arms, the Three Castles, on its sides, the only tram ever to be adorned thus. It had no headlamps, and the dash carried DUTC company monograms; the letters U and T were superimposed on each other with the other two to either side, thus identifying the car as DC, no prosaic fleet number here. The destination box, illuminated at night, permanently displayed 'Special', and the upper deck was surrounded by elegant wrought iron railing with brass medallions. There were 12 armchairs in the saloon of the Directors' Tram, and at least as many swivelling chairs on top, each with a carved company monogram. The car's original Peckham truck was replaced by a DUTC one in 1909 when the tram was valued at £900. In addition to being used by the directors and their guests, it could be hired for special functions.

Improvements

From mid-1900 all Spa Road cars except Nos 252, 253 and 254 were built with vestibules, those from No 225 onwards having them from new or upon conversion from horse

cars or trailers. Nos 225-228 initially had experimental non-standard vestibules. Two years later began the process of converting the older trams into vestibuled cars and although open-fronted vehicles were to be seen for another 20 years, they became increasingly rare with the passage of time. There were of course exceptions to the standardised designs like No 35 which, as recorded earlier, managed to retain its original direct stairs after conversion.

The standard dash layout for vestibuled trams had the headlamp in the upper (waist) section with the number below, but a few early cars had this reversed, including Nos 8, 16, 24 and 58. In a fleet which always abounded with interesting and individualistic vehicles, such exceptions having characteristics out of the ordinary merely heightened interest for the observer. The presence of particular trams or groups of cars in photographs can often help the historian to date a picture because one or more of the vehicles may exhibit features known to have existed only during a particular period.

Single-Deckers

For the electrification of the Bath Avenue line in January 1901 there arose a need for single-deckers. Electric cars had less overhead clearance than their horse-drawn predecessors and so the very low railway bridge near Beggar's Bush dictated the shape of the new rolling stock. As already noted, three former horse cars were therefore rebuilt as electric single-deckers, becoming Nos 252, 253 and 254. They entered service on 14th January and were joined in July 1904 by No 49, which had been converted from a horse car to an electric double-decker in 1898. This was the first of several further double-deckers to be cut down for the Bath Avenue route up to 1932. Originally 21-seaters, at some stage these trams acquired

Above: **An early view of the Directors' Tram, built in 1901, on its original Peckham truck with primitive safety guard and decency boards around the upper deck. The truck was changed to a DUTC one in 1909 and the tram also lost its decency boards, revealing the full glory of its upper deck railings. This unique car survived to the end of the tramways and was sold complete, except for the seats, in 1950. Following severe fire damage, it was acquired by the Transport Museum in 1988, placed indoors and awaited restoration in 1999.** *Tramway and Railway World,* Transport Museum Society collection

three seats on each platform where the stairs was located in a double-decker. Only the seats at the trailing or conductor's end were normally occupied, the cars then being regarded as 24-seaters.

Final Build-Up of Four-Wheelers

Following the emergence of the single-deckers, there was a pause in the delivery of new double-deckers from Spa Road until No 255 was turned out in June 1901. These were a mixture of converted horse cars, with new construction by Browne and the DUTC. Up to No 280 were available by the end of 1901, Nos 281-293 following in 1902. Of the 52 new cars constructed at Spa Road up to 1903, Nos 99-108 had five windows. The other 42 had four, all further DUTC trams built up to 1931 having similar fenestration.

The Howth Cars

Twelve trams were built for the Clontarf & Hill of Howth Tramroad at the Electric Railway and Tramway Carriage Works, Preston. At the time of the order, it was expected that the DUTC would have 300 cars. Because of the close association between the two concerns, to avoid any confusion or duplication of identities, the Howth cars were numbered 301-312.

These trams ran on eight wheels, being mounted on Peckham bogies of the maximum traction type. Each bogie had two big wheels 30in in diameter, to the axles of which the motors were geared. The two small or pony wheels, 20in across, carried only about 30% of the car's weight, thus giving the bogie type its name. With individual bogie wheelbases of 4ft 6in and a total wheelbase of 17ft 11in, such cars rode very steadily and were still capable of negotiating sharp curves. As originally delivered, these trams had their larger driving wheels nearer the centre of the car but the bogies were later reversed.

Nos 301-312 had six windows between the bulkheads and their original livery is generally accepted as being terracotta or plum. Beyond those facts, however, there has been some confusion about the bodywork of these trams, with obvious discrepancies between what was reported to have been ordered and what was actually delivered. A drawing in the *Railway World* of 11th May 1899 shows 'under construction' an uncanopied, unvestibuled car with direct stairs; the cars are also stated to have been under construction for the DUTC. The tram in the drawing was a 77-seater (41/36) with transverse seating on both decks but photographs taken about the time they entered service depict the cars as vestibuled and with indirect stairs. It is also most likely that the lower deck seating was longitudinal.

Curiously, with the exception of No 301, every one of these cars is recorded as being overhauled by 1904. The earliest reference in the Car Repair books is for January 1902, when No 302 received major attention following a fire. Nos 301-312 were later fitted with partitions dividing the lower deck into smoking and non-smoking compartments. This prompts further questions about their seating capacity. In their original condition, they had headlamps below the fleet numbers and were not fitted with destination boxes.

Constantly Changing

To describe all the rolling stock on the Dublin tramway system at any particular period could fill a book, the best that can be done in a general history such as this is to provide snapshot glimpses of the fleet at important stages of its development. Lists of vehicles such as the first electric fleet in Section One of the Rolling Stock Catalogue became obsolete almost as soon as its subjects entered service because of developments like vestibuling and truck changes. The latter practice was described by Charles Ross, last chargehand at Ballsbridge works, as akin to playing musical chairs. This was due to the continuous improvement, replacement and re-equipping of the fleet and the many experiments undertaken by the DUTC in its pursuit of excellence.

Many of the original cars had their running gear changed within a very short time of going into service, and as will be recounted later (see page 77), a look at what happened to one or two individual cars was astonishingly complicated. Read in conjunction with later rolling stock lists, this summarised account of the fleet as it remained until the autumn of 1904 will help in understanding its composition. Another practice to be borne in mind is that of renumbering cars, raised by the DUTC from an occasional necessity to a frequently employed art form. Officially recorded instances and observations by alert spotters are set out in Section Eight of the Rolling Stock Catalogue making up as accurate a list as can be put together.

Accidents and Road Safety

When the horse was the basic unit of transport, there were few rules of the road and most people simply did as they pleased. Such laws as existed were widely flouted, concepts of road safety being decades away in the future. At the very dawn of mechanical road transport, people in charge of horses were understandably ignorant of dangers not hitherto experienced. They were therefore totally unprepared for the arrival of electric trams, the first self-propelled vehicles to appear in any numbers on the streets of Dublin.

Drivers of horse-drawn vehicles can be seen in many old photographs travelling on the wrong side of the road. Well used to weaving their way from one side of the road to the other, carters failed to grasp the fact that the faster electric trams should be treated more cautiously than horse-drawn ones, and that motormen were less likely to acquiesce when conflicts arose. The risk of accidents was further increased by the reaction of some horses, terrified by their first encounters with electric tramcars.

Inevitably, there were many collisions between trams and other vehicles in early electric days. The newspapers regularly carried reports of accidents, which usually resulted in carts or vans being badly damaged, horses injured and carters hurt. The DUTC were sometimes accused of insensitivity, with certain reporters depicting a David versus Goliath situation.

In a January 1897 court case, taken by the owner of a trap (the name widely used in Ireland for tub carts) which had collided with a tram, each side claimed that the other driver had run into its vehicle. The judge found against the Tramway Company, severely criticising the behaviour of tramway motormen, especially in George's Street in Kingstown where the traders were apparently at loggerheads with the company.

Another typical story appeared in the *Evening Herald* of 13th November 1899, headed '**YET ANOTHER – BIG TRAM SMASH IN RATHGAR** – CART SMASHED – TRAM DERAILED'. 'One of the electric cars (256) coming from Terenure to the city at about 5.45pm when midway between Rathgar Catholic Church and Grosvenor Road dashed into a horse and cart…smashing the cart in pieces…the horse was apparently uninjured…The driver, who was violently thrown to the ground and appeared dazed, complained of injuries to his hand and to the back of his head. The electric tram was derailed…and turned across the road. The traffic was of course blocked, and the scene of the accident became crowded with people. Eventually…the injured tram…was hitched on to other electric cars, which succeeded in drawing the first car on to the line.'

In the interests of accuracy, it should be pointed out that if the tramcar number quoted above was correct, this accident could not have happened before June 1901, the month in which No 256, a rebuilt horse car, entered service. It is more likely that the tram involved was No 156, one of the American cars commissioned in 1899 which was was allocated to Terenure depot. Some other reports of accidents helpfully recorded correct tram fleet numbers, as in January 1900 when No 81 was in collision with a cart in Rutland Square.

A more than usually objective and concise report headed, '**ACCIDENT ON THE ELECTRIC TRAMWAY AT KINGSTOWN**', appeared in the *Freeman's Journal* of 30th May 1898.'On Saturday evening, at Summerhill, Kingstown, electric motor car No 1 collided with and overturned a horse attached to a coal dray, breaking the harness of the horse, bending the springs of the dray, and throwing to the ground two coalmen…It appears that the horse and dray crossed out of Martello Avenue in front of the tram car, and the collision could not be averted.'

Speeds
Horse tram speeds of five or six miles per hour were easily exceeded by the electrics, the success and momentum of which created an ill-assorted range of disgruntled, prejudiced groups and individuals. Some, like the jarveys and the Dublin Wicklow & Wexford Railway had lost out heavily, first to the horse trams and then to the electrics. Others simply hated anything not pulled by a horse, their hostility further aroused when the primitive motor vehicles of the period were freed, in 1896, from the requirement of having a man with a red flag walking in front.

Eight miles per hour was the permitted speed on the Dalkey line, Clontarf being allowed ten. While eight miles per hour was little better than the top speed of a horse tram at the gallop, the sharp acceleration curve of the electric cars gave them a decided advantage even at low overall speeds. The antipathy of the opposition was stoked up at the prospect of a city dominated by electric trams, which might be allowed to travel even faster. In contrast, this prospect of accelerated travel was fervently desired by tramway passengers and managers who foresaw a situation in which fewer trams could carry more people at higher speeds.

The only method of estimating the speed of a tram was by counting the number of poles it passed in a given length of time. The Rule Book informed motormen that, 'if you pass six poles in one minute, the speed is practically eight miles an hour.' They were advised to, 'note the speed frequently so as to know accurately at what rate the car is running.' The DUTC's application for an increase in the speed of its trams resulted in a Public Inquiry held in November 1898 at which a weird assortment of interests, including the Blackrock Cowkeepers' Association, were represented by some of the most eminent lawyers of the day. The proceedings began in the DUTC offices at 9 Upper Sackville Street but moved to the Four Courts at the behest of some of the objectors, apparently because the legal luminaries would feel more at home there.

Eventually, varying speed limits on different parts of the system, with a maximum of 12 miles per hour, the same as that allowed for early motor vehicles, were agreed. In the interim, the argument about the difference in permitted speeds on the Clontarf and Dalkey lines was resolved by allowing ten miles per hour between Haddington Road and Williamstown, with eight remaining the maximum for the rest of the way to Dalkey.

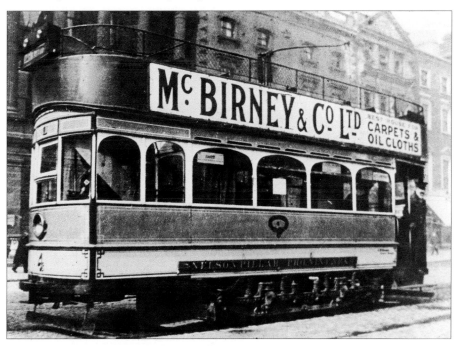

Vestibules, platform canopies and windscreens, became a standard feature of new or rebuilt Dublin trams from June 1901 onwards. Although not extended to the entire fleet, widespread vestibuling of most previously open fronted cars, about 220 in number, was achieved over a period of 20 years. No 4, one of the original Dalkey electrics of 1896, seen here in Upper Sackville Street, was converted in 1903. This tram was scrapped in 1922, its number being taken by the former No 124 of 1919 which lasted until 1939. The company in the advertisement, McBirney & Co Ltd, ran a department store located in the present Virgin Megastore building on Aston Quay. Gratwicke collection, East Ham Public Libraries

Chapter Three

THE GOLDEN AGE OF DUBLIN'S TRAMWAYS

A Stratified Society

There was a brief pause in tramway development following the disappearance of the last horse tram in January 1901. The interlude affords an opportunity of looking at the social environment in which the Dublin tramways blossomed. Socially, during those pioneering years of electric tramways in Dublin, from 1896 to 1913, rapid technological progress took place within a community paralysed in an apparently insoluble permafrost of status and snobbery.

It is very difficult to appreciate the extent to which the population was stratified in the early part of the last century. A code of rigid if unwritten rules regulated peoples' lives and, in the language of the time, nobody dared to move above his or her station in life. A look at workers in general and the Dublin tramwaymen in particular puts the realities of those so-called good old days into stark perspective.

The DUTC was very typical of most large commercial organisations of the period. At the top of the tramway social order were the directors, managers and professionals like accountants and engineers being somewhat lower down. These people enjoyed comfortable lifestyles, the home addresses of the DUTC's top four being significant. William Martin Murphy lived at Dartry, R S Tresilian at 32 Eglinton Road. C W Gordon's home was at 59 Merrion Road and William Anderson's at 71 Northumberland Road. Among directors' perks were special travel passes, coveted gold medals bearing their names and worn on their watch chains.

Each level in the pyramid was socially insulated from the ones above and below and there were also certain barriers between people with similar living standards. An example would be that a manager from an administrative background was socially superior to one who had once been a tradesman. Far down the managerial and administrative scale were junior clerks and others who, through ability, hard work, the right connections, or sheer social climbing ability, might, in time, make it to the top. A man's background could be positively determined as soon as he said whether he went to work or went to business.

An article in the *Tramway and Railway World* of 5th May 1910 gives a good picture of the DUTC's organisation, staffing and operation at that time. The opening paragraph sketched the historical background and revealed that the company was now operating over 55.275 miles, the total track length being 100.762 miles. The directors included William M Murphy JP (Chairman), William Anderson (Managing), Alderman W F Cotton, Percy B Bernard, R S Tresilian FCIS, AMICEI (Secretary), the General Manager was C W Gordon.

Several of these men will be remembered as having had long and exemplary careers in the industry. Anderson and Tresilian had worked for the pre-1881 companies. The unified company they built up became one of the United Kingdom's leading horse tramway operators, then rose to even greater heights in the electric era. They were justly boastful of what they had created. Tresilian's pride in the company comes across clearly in his statement that '...the DUTC was practically the pioneer in the United Kingdom of modernised electrical traction'.

Frontline Staff

Passengers on a transport system normally encounter three types of official: drivers, conductors and inspectors. From the operator's point of view these are the front line personnel on whose behaviour the undertaking must depend for goodwill and custom. The DUTC's grasp of this fact comes across clearly from reading the Rule Book issued to employees. It also demonstrates vividly the structure of the Traffic Department which was responsible for the staff just mentioned. The General Manager had a number of officials below him, among them the Traffic Superintendent in control of the inspectors, who may be divided roughly into three categories.

Supervisors

Depot superintendents were senior inspectors responsible for rostering and supervising the men who drove and conducted the trams. They dealt with minor disciplinary matters, referring more serious transgressions upwards. They also had to co-operate closely with the Depot Foremen who were responsible for the electrics, mechanical equipment and bodywork of the trams, and who, although they belonged to the Engineer's Department, had some authority over the drivers and conductors.

The other main areas of activity for inspectors were in timekeeping and ticket checking. Duties included seeing 'that the cars are properly cleaned and equipped, and that the employees serving on the cars are thoroughly qualified and fit for duty, that their uniforms are clean and tidy and that the passengers are treated in a polite and becoming manner'.

Ticket checkers were particularly enjoined to use great patience and politeness in carrying out this duty; '...the public view, for the most part, the revision as superfluous and somewhat irksome'. Discretion was another quality demanded of controlling officials, as supervisors were referred to in the Rule Book; '...it is expected that they possess the necessary tact to guard their authority with their inferiors through firm, becoming conduct'. They were also admonished that they, 'in all their duties must proceed with great circumspection and quietness, in order to avoid anything in the shape of a disturbance...They must always guard themselves against exaggerated reports of any kind, and must confine themselves strictly to absolute facts.'

Platform Staff: Regulated Lives

It has been said that men working for concerns like the DUTC were owned by their employers and a perusal of the 1902 edition of the 'Standard Rules and Regulations for the Guidance and Government of Officials and Employees' tends to bear this out. The Preface begins, 'Applicants...must be able to read intelligently, sign their name legibly, and perform simple arithmetical operations; must be of temperate habits, and lead reputable lives...must join the employees' Benefit Society...All desirable applicants are accepted only on trial, and are placed in actual service without pay, under the instruction of skilled and competent employees, for a period of three or four weeks.'

Rule 2 says: 'Controlling officials must give those below them in the service an unceasing good example by great activity, attention, moderation, and reputable lives. They must endeavour by tact and warning to prevent young beginners from falling into careless ways, and in some cases where this has happened to try to lead them back to a sense of their duties'. There is much more in the same vein.

Newly trained crews had to act as spares or benchmen at first, attending at the depots early in the morning and being available at certain other times to replace men not going on duty. It was made absolutely clear that there were more men available than jobs and staff turnover was fairly high. Under Rule 28 the following were considered good grounds for dismissal, 'Insubordination, failure or refusal to obey orders or rules of the Company, lying, violent temper, the habitual use of obscene or profane language, slovenly personal habits, drinking intoxicating liquor, smoking, or reading newspapers while on duty, discourteous conduct towards passengers, failure to collect fares, making false or dishonest returns, failure to make out promptly reports of accidents, running into an open point, rere-end collisions, reckless running ahead of time, permitting unauthorised persons to operate car, incompetence or inattention to duty.' Reckless running ahead of time, keeping as near as possible to the car in front, was known as close poling, a term still used today.

A man could spend up to six years on the bench during which he got nine shillings per week. A beginner had to lodge a £20 guarantee, give references for the previous five years and work his first six weeks free.

On appointment, a conductor received £1 1s 6d and a motorman got £1 8s 0d, 25% less than the rates paid in Belfast or Liverpool. This partly explains staff turnover and why there were so many Irishmen working on the Liverpool trams, where the excellent training given by the DUTC was much appreciated. Liverpool, which had a municipal tramway system, was severely criticised by the DUTC for poaching. Just before 1913 this was said to involve two hundred men in a year. Money was deducted from the wage packet for various items; 2/- for 20 weeks towards the cost of the uniform, renewable every two years when the old one had to be given back. A further 6d was taken for the Rule Book and the same amount for sickness benefit. There was a 3d levy in case of death, while a licence to drive or conduct cost 2/6d with a 1/- annual renewal fee.

Crews got one day off in 12 (later ten) and could work between nine and 14 hours a day, according to their positions on the roster. In the event of being summoned to Head Office on a disciplinary charge, they had to attend on their day off, a deeply hated imposition which continued beyond the end of trams nearly 50 years later. Meals were taken at the terminus or depot and were usually brought to a pre-arranged place in a billy-can or lunch box by a member of the family.

The DUTC gave preference to men from the country for employment as motormen and conductors, it being William Martin Murphy's firm belief that they were healthier, better educated and of stronger moral fibre than Dubliners. Most of them were deeply religious. In 1904 a visiting papal representative noticed that tramwaymen, on passing a church, would make the sign of the cross. So impressed was the Pope on hearing of this that he granted special indulgences to Dublin tramwaymen performing this pious practice.

Social Status

In horse days, carters or draymen did not enjoy great social status and tram drivers were regarded as being not much better. They admittedly had a regular job, sometimes with such emoluments as a greatcoat and hat, but it was nevertheless a menial occupation. The arrival of the electric trams improved their status significantly. For one thing, they were no longer drivers, they had training and skill in the new age of self-propelled road vehicles and their title was that of motorman, a job description imported from the United States which inspired so much early electric tramway practice and nomenclature throughout these islands. Being at the controls of an electric tram created a feeling of superiority which was resented by horse drivers, especially jarveys who disliked the new vehicles intensely.

Howth line tram No 308 at Clontarf depot before the First World War with a conductor and inspector. The difference in the colour and style of the uniform coats are noteworthy, but both officials are wearing kepis which were standard headgear for all uniformed DUTC staff at that time. No 308 was destroyed at the junction of North Earl Street and Sackville Street during Easter Week 1916. Its replacement did not appear until December 1920. Birney collection

Left: **This picture and that on page 61 were
taken from the same viewpoint. It shows
Grafton Street in the first decade of the
twentieth century. The two trams going
towards College Green are Nos 270, nearest
the camera, and 231. Coming towards the
photographer is No 252, one of the single-
deckers which worked the Sandymount via
Bath Avenue service. Both this and No 231
were former horse cars, beginning life as
Nos 4 of December 1890 and 101 (1896)
respectively. Both trams were converted to
electric operation in 1900. No 270 was built
by Brownes in 1900. New vehicles replaced
these three trams in 1910 (231), 1922 (270)
and 1928 (252). Following withdrawal, No
231 was converted for further use,
becoming haulage wagon No 20.**
Lawrence collection, National Library

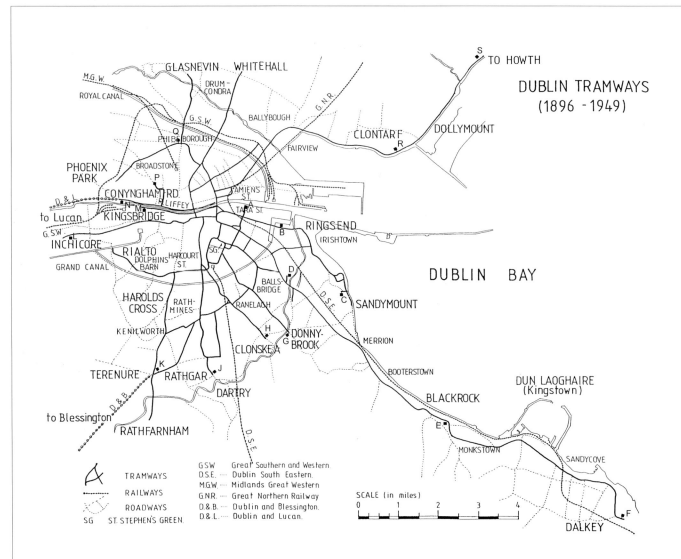

The conductors too, came up in the world and because of additional duties such as looking after the trolley rope and other equipment they were regarded as having more skills and responsibilities than in former times. Crews, collectively known as platform staff, were now dressed in smart uniforms which invested them with status and authority. In winter they wore stylish greatcoats, the motorman's being buttoned to the neck for protection from the elements on the open platforms of the day. Both wore a kepi style cap in winter but during the summer months the conductors and inspectors exchanged this for a straw boater.

The company badge, which at that period was made from cloth, was worn on the cap. The motorman carried his enamel police licence badge while the conductor had a shamrock-shaped cast licence badge fixed to the strap of his cash bag. The original issue of these badges, dating back to horse tram days, had a crown, the word 'Conductor' and the badge number.

The Rule Book

Rule books were updated as required, the DUTC 1902 edition already quoted from being an excellent reflection of how transport peoples' lives were governed in the early years of the century. Thirty rules were set out applying to both conductors and motormen. Some of these would not look out of place in a modern context, referring to matters like signing on, checking rosters and so on, and one or two would be strikingly apposite today, for example, 'When the Fire Brigade, Ambulance, or the Company's Emergency Waggon is running in the street, the cars must be stopped until such vehicle has passed'.

Motormen and conductors 'must conform to Time-table in running their cars, and be particular in making the time points as laid down'. It was also their duty to look out for passengers; furthermore, 'when on the stand at terminal points and when approaching passengers at night, Motormen and Conductors must announce, in a clear and distinct tone of voice, the destination and route of their car.'

Conductors had to remember 27 special rules covering their behaviour in situations that ranged from giving information and issuing tickets to dealing with drunks and coping with accidents. The conductor was in charge of the car, being responsible for time keeping, reversing the seat backs at termini, and changing destination displays. Most importantly, the conductor also looked after the trolley, turning it at the terminus in the direction indicated by small notices at each end of the tram so that it always trailed the vehicle. He then swung the rope into a retaining pigtail at upper deck waist level and tied it off, neatly but loosely, on the platform. The conductor was specifically required to keep a grip on the rope at junctions and crossovers where dewirements were most likely.

The Motorman's Duties

Motormen's instructions were very comprehensive, beginning with an exhortation to study, 'the motor-car, its trolley connections, motors and controllers, and to the detection and prevention of defects in them'. The rule book continued, 'the abuse of motors by too rapid handling of the controller has been dwelt on ever since electric tramways were first inaugurated, and every competent Superintendent realises the importance of instructing Motormen not to turn on current too quickly. At the same time nearly every Superintendent laments the difficulty of getting his men to observe at all times the rules about slow starting.'

Accidents could and must be avoided, the reader was told, and '...good judgement...avoiding risks...will prevent accidents. The moment any person, wagon, or other obstacle is seen on the track, Motormen must bring their car under such control, that it can be stopped immediately...do not approach any vehicle closer than twenty-five feet.'

Any obstruction in the rail groove, which might cause the car to jump, had to be removed to avoid breaking wheel flanges. The gong was to be sounded at least twice before passing cross streets, 75 to 100 feet from the junction, or to call attention to the movement of the car. Ensuring that sand boxes were full, use of the hand and electric brakes, and how to stop the car safely on hills, were all covered. Particular attention was given to right of way, trams were not permitted to pass on sharp curves, the car on the outside track having priority.

Precedence and Bell Signals

When two cars arrived at a junction at the same time, the tram on the main line took precedence. A speed of two miles per hour was prescribed over curves, points and crossings. Points had to be checked for their proper setting and a tram was not to be stopped under a section insulator. Motormen were not permitted to leave the platform without taking the controller handles with them, throwing off the overhead switch and applying the handbrake. In wet conditions they were never to run a car fast enough to splash water up on the motors, being advised to turn the current off and coast where possible. Among other duties, motormen also had to see that headlights were working with clean glass and they were never to leave the depot without three extra fuses. Further instructions explained how to cope with mechanical and electrical faults.

Before reversing a car, the motorman had to give a three-bell signal to the conductor, meaning, 'backing car, conductor to see road is clear and give the usual starting bell.' The final section of the book dealt with speeds, equating miles per hour or yards per minute with the number of poles passed as the trams did not have speedometers. Passing four poles in one minute was the equivalent of three miles per hour, six represented eight miles per hour, and nine poles, 12mph. This was up on the eight mph, which was the maximum in the early years. It was also the speed to which early motor vehicles were restricted.

Regulations and Bylaws

Board of Trade regulations specifying speeds of two, three, four, five, seven or eight miles per hour allowed on various places on the system were given. Examples include eight mph in Thomas Street and Irishtown Road, seven in South Great George's Street and Capel Street five in Talbot Street or on Capel Street Bridge; four around most curves; three down Cork Hill or Mount Brown and two at various junctions and potential accident blackspots. It must be recorded, however, that speed limits were not rigidly adhered to.

Coping with Traffic Congestion

Unlikely as it may seem, serious traffic problems existed in Dublin even before the horse tram era. William Barrington catalogued the chaos in 1871, a one-way tram system in Merrion Row, Ely Place and Hume Street in 1873 providing further evidence of its existence. There were even suggestions in the late 1870s that the College Green statue of King William III be moved to facilitate horse tram operation. An 1875 Dublin Traffic Act empowered the Commissioner of the Dublin Metropolitan Police to bring in bylaws which came into force in 1876. They were revised in 1895 and again in 1903, tram drivers and conductors being listed among those on whom obligations were specifically placed.

We have already seen how the introduction of the electric trams took horse traffic unawares. Traffic discipline took some time to impose, chances were taken and increasing numbers of drivers, very few of them tramwaymen appeared before the courts. One rather unlucky motorman was fined 5/- on 24th May 1907 for allegedly letting his tram strike a constable at the junction of Dame Street and South Great George's Street. This tramwayman was genuinely unlucky, because there was strong evidence that the policeman carelessly stepped backwards against the tram.

Even before motor vehicles began to make their presence felt, the increased tram traffic after the electrics appeared caused the authorities to start taking stock. As early as 1899 there was a proposal to move back the railings of Trinity College so that Grafton Street and Nassau Street could be widened. By 1912, when motor traffic was on the increase, it was reported that the eight DUTC services using Grafton Street resulted in 159 trams passing through that street every hour.

The DUTC Departmental Structure

The *Tramway and Railway World* of 7th July 1910 published a paper prepared by

R S Tresilian for the Tramways and Light Railways Association on the occasion of a visit to Dublin. Included was a primitive organisational chart showing four DUTC departmental heads reporting directly to the board. In addition to R S Tresilian (Secretary) and C W Gordon (General Manager), these were P F O'Sullivan, MICEI (Engineer) and P S Sheardown, MIEI (Electrical Superintendent). Property, accounts, materials and advertising were all within the Secretary's domain, while the Manager was responsible for traffic, the fleet and its maintenance. Permanent way and buildings came under the control of the Engineer, while the Electrical Superintendent looked after overhead lines, power generation and transmission and maintenance of plant. To manage all these and other aspects of the business, all the departmental heads had subordinates. The Secretary had six, the Manager four, the Engineer and Electrical Superintendent two each.

Mr M Maher, the Traffic Superintendent, and his deputy, were responsible for 820 staff: 50 inspectors, 326 conductors, 326 motormen, 50 washers and 67 others. They looked after 318 tramcars, plus the 12 belonging to the Clontarf and Hill of Howth concern. Mr T Brierley, whose name was given to some DUTC fabricated tramcar trucks, was in charge of the Body Shop, with Mr D Moy overseeing the Electrical Shop. The total support staff was given as 2 foremen, 3 clerks/timekeepers, 25 fitters, 33 menders and other mechanics, 29 bodymakers and carpenters, 18 painters, 58 car cleaners and 7 sundry, a total of 175 men.

At the power station, Mr Sheardown had R L Hughes as Mechanical Engineer and K Quaney as assistant in charge of cables and overhead lines. The staff consisted of 4 engineers, 3 engine drivers, 4 clerks and storemen, 9 greasers; there were 6 stokers, 4 fitters, 31 bricklayers and labourers, and 9 sub-station attendants. There were, in total, 70 men in this department. Details of the power station, described earlier on page 41, were brought up to date in the article and a series of tables broke down the costs involved in electricity generation in February and March 1910.

Craftsmen

The craftsmen who worked for the company were, in the structures of the time, very much lowest middle class. They included mechanics, coach builders, trimmers, carpenters, electricians and a myriad of other crafts calling for exemplary skill and dedication. Pride in good workmanship was an inculcated ethic of the period. Coach painters, for example, would go through the rituals of mixing, applying and rubbing down up to ten coats on a tramcar, which would then be varnished to give a finish unobtainable in to-day's spray paintshops.

Most of these craftsmen would have served an apprenticeship of seven years indentured to a master of their particular trade. Severe lifestyles were imposed on indentured apprentices, although conditions varied from trade to trade or between individual masters. Strict working standards were set for apprentices and their personal lives were also regulated. Getting drunk, gambling, attending theatrical performances, fornication or marrying without the master's permission were among the mortal sins that could lead to summary dismissal.

By the turn of the century, changes were taking place because formal education in special institutions had begun. Kevin Street Technical School had opened in 1887, that at Ringsend (then in Pembroke Township) six years later. These establishments, the ethos of which took some years to become established, instilled a pride with their training which was palpable even 40 years later in men who had learned their skills at that time. Several crafts and skills, some of them not formally recognised but important nonetheless, were peculiar to the activities of the company.

All the familiar practical jokes, such as being sent for the long stand or the glass hammer, were played on apprentices, but the trainees were taught to know their own worth. They were also warned to mind their own business. Strict demarcation lines were maintained between the trades and apprentices. Those following one trade were actively discouraged from trying to learn anything about the work of another, even in situations where skills needed to cross over. Charles Ross, who was a fitter, recalled being ridiculed and intimidated by an electrician on being told to examine a tram for leaking current.

The Overhead Lines Department was very progressive and made a significant, and patented, contribution to tramway technology with a simple but effective device which was widely adopted. In the early years of electric tramways it was found that when an overhead running wire broke it was nearly always at a suspension point. A fallen wire, as we saw in the case of the Amiens Street accident (see page 40) was a widely feared occurrence with possibly dire consequences. The problem was examined by the Overhead Lines Engineer Kerr Quaney and the Chief Engineer Mr Kirwan. As a result they developed a simple anchoring device which in the event of a wire breaking near the suspension point, prevented it from falling on to the tram or the street. Known as the KQ patent anchoring device, his ingenuity brought no financial rewards to Kerr Quaney.

Permanent way, the track, pointwork and the section of roadway between the rails and for 18 inches on either side, involved a numerous staff working for the Permanent Way Engineer. These included the paviors who laid down the stone setts and whose trade almost died out until the recent revival of such paving for streets in conservation areas. The Ringsend power station had on its eastern side a large vacant site, now occupied by the bus garage, which was used for materials storage in the early years of the century. It appears on the 1909 Ordnance Sheet as an open site containing a small building, but within a few years it became a well-organised permanent way and overhead equipment yard with extensive workshops and stores.

Other aspects of the DUTC's operations called for such diverse tradesmen as harness makers who made cash bags and bell straps or brass founders to manufacture trolley heads and headlamp rims. Between Spa Road, Ballsbridge, Ringsend and the various depots a truly comprehensive range of skills was to be found. Another craft of the period which, like that of the pavior, almost died out but is now happily thriving again, was that of the signwriter, who painted so much of the lettering on the trams.

Bottom of the Pyramid

For a large segment of the population, Dublin in the early 1900s was a city of festering tenements, below subsistence wages and high unemployment. Social welfare was for the future: the first (means-tested) old age pension was not introduced until 1908, unemployment and sickness benefit following in 1911. After a harsh working life, if one was lucky enough to have a job, and having endured conditions in the appalling slums, there was the daunting prospect of the workhouse for any individual who survived into his or her sixties.

From this background and lifestyle came the vast pool of poor labourers, the 'daily labourers' of the Tramway Acts. They were taken on and sacked again at the whim not just of masters, the term often used to describe employers, but frequently of corrupt underlings. Completion of work on the tramway system and the main drainage scheme swelled further the numbers of these unemployed men, many of whom joined the British Army out of cruel economic necessity.

The DUTC was probably as good as most big employers at the time but the labourers who tended craftsmen, slaved at the power station, cleaned yards and depots, sweated on the permanent way or performed other lowly tasks, were generally treated very badly. The daily or weekly paid labourer who had a compassionate foreman or supervisor was a fortunate man and there were many humane overseers who endeavoured to sustain the dignity of these unfortunate people. The institutionalised humiliation of the lower orders in the tramway company can best be illustrated by the fact that the motormens' and conductors' uniforms that were replaced every two years were re-issued to the men who maintained the track.

In the first decade of the twentieth century the general rate for labourers could be as low as 15/- per week but the average was around £1. A T Newham records that the man who washed the Howth trams was awarded an increase in 1903 bringing his wages from 15 to 18 shillings per week. Three years later the highest skills could command £1.15s 0d. but every effort was made to avoid paying such rates.

The lowest paid in regular work were the apprentices. Kathleen Corcoran (*née* Levins), mother of the author, earned 2/6d per week and was constantly reminded of how lucky she was to have a job. These rates are worth putting in juxtaposition to the six, nine and 12 shillings per week for tram fares paid out by 'A Family Man' in his letter to the *Irish Times* in June 1872, quoted on page 11.

Welfare

In the nineteenth century and the first half of the twentieth, Dublin had one of the most appalling slum housing problems in Europe, with many people forced to live in one-room tenements. The conditions exposed by Sean O'Casey in his plays were not exaggerated. Even when resources were made available it would take the Corporation decades to eliminate the scandal. Meanwhile, a modicum of responsibility to their staff was recognised by some companies, among them the DUTC.

We have seen in earlier chapters how a selectively paternalistic DUTC began providing houses for its employees as early as 1885. Records show that in the first decade of the century these cottages cost £150 each to build. In several of the schemes there were some larger houses, usually two-storey, for supervisory staff. Formerly known as Tramway Cottages or Tram Terrace, virtually all were renamed in the fifties and sixties. These houses were systematically sold off by CIE and many are now occupied by people who are proud of the tramway connection.

Contrasting sharply with the open-top, unvestibuled car it is following, No 261 travels down Grafton Street. Built at Spa Road in June 1901, this tram was allocated to Clontarf until 1905 when it received its top cover. This picture was taken shortly after it was assigned to work the Dalkey line in June 1905. Coming south is No 245, originally horse car 88 of April 1896, rebuilt as an electric in December 1900. It, too, is on the Dalkey service and about to try overtaking the sidecar occupying the tracks, a common practice by the jarveys who wilfully obstructed the trams on a regular basis. While No 261 was replaced in 1921, 245 lasted until June 1932 when a new Luxury Saloon took its number.
Lawrence collection, National Library,

A form of closed shop prevailed in the DUTC in that sons of employees were given preferential treatment in employment opportunities. School leavers were taken on as ticket pickers, clearing the floors of the cars at the termini: in those days used ticket boxes were not fitted to the trams. If found to be satisfactory employees, the ticket pickers were later promoted to the Parcels Express or as messengers. In time they could go on to be trained as conductors or motormen.

Physical Hardship

Tram conductors and motormen on the unvestibuled cars of the early electric era endured physical hardship of a kind now thankfully in the distant past. Working on cars with open platforms, hard enough in horse days, became more intolerable with electrification. A light shower in a gentle breeze on a slow moving horse tram became a storm-whipped deluge on a much faster electric car. Unvestibuled trams, although declining in numbers, were a fact of life until the early 1920s. The hardship these caused crews, an accepted part of life before the First World War, was practically enshrined in the philosophy of some contemporary managers.

Attitudes of the time are well-expressed in W A Agnew's *Electric Tramcar Handbook for Motormen, Inspectors and Depot Workers*. The Introduction states that; 'the motorman must be physically strong enough .... to withstand the constant exposure to the weather on a car platform.

He .... must rigidly abstain from stimulants during working hours, and pay attention to the ordinary rules of health and good living. A motorman.... must necessarily keep himself in fit condition, otherwise he risks being put aside for abler men....Tramway managers are always ready to recognise good men and retain their services, while being just as anxious to get rid of ignorant and unsatisfactory men who are always in trouble.'

Chapter VI, *On the Road*, has this; 'First Essentials – Motormen should remember that as public servants they may often find it necessary to exercise great patience and self-control in performing their duties and in dealing with dissatisfied people, but they will usually find that a cheery and polite reply will do much towards soothing down any dispute which may occur.'

The Night of the Big Wind

During the long build-up to the events of 1913, the men accepted, albeit with growing frustration, the physical hardships identified by Agnew. This sheer stamina was but part of the price they paid in their struggle for a very frugal existence. Devotion to duty and the concept of public service were paramount. Rarely was their ability to rise to the demands of unusual and cruel circumstances as vividly illustrated as in the hours and days after the evening of Thursday, 26th February 1903, the second Night of the Big Wind.

Some necessarily brief reports appeared in the papers of 27th February, but on the following day more detailed accounts were published. The *Irish Times* stated that, 'Within living memory no such storm has visited Dublin and its environs as that which raged from about ten o'clock on Thursday night to six o'clock yesterday morning....last tramcars were eagerly besieged by people hurrying home…'

What it was like to stand on the platform of an unvestibuled tram in those conditions is hard to imagine. Detailed reports from various areas of Dublin, its suburbs and the rest of the country, set out catalogues of injuries and damage on a terrible scale and in several instances mentioned what were obviously heroic efforts on the part of tramway staff and others in the public services. Another report in the same paper, citing innumerable instances of fallen trees, added, 'As a necessary adjunct of this record of destruction, telegraph poles and wires were also frequently lying prostrate on the ground, and what is an altogether new element in the havoc of a storm, in certain districts the electric tram poles were bent hopelessly out of the perpendicular.'

Fully restoring the overhead, which bore the brunt of the storm, took several days and one maintenance man was injured in the course of cutting up a fallen tree at Blackrock. Several examples of ingenuity by resourceful but anonymous tramway staff were mentioned, and a fine compliment was paid to the system generally, 'The facility with which the Tramway Company were able to divert traffic round by alternative routes bears high testament to the excellent plan on which the various connections

throughout the city were made when electric traction was introduced'.

A Period of Leisurely Progress

The hectic activity that culminated in the replacement of the DUTC horse trams was followed by a period of more relaxed progress. During that time, a period of consolidation, improvements were made to the way in which the electric tramways operated. Within the social structures outlined earlier, some details of the tramway system in operation are worth a look. These illustrate the relationships between DUTC staff and passengers, how peoples' attitudes evolved and provide some insights into daily life at the beginning of the last century.

The success of the electrification programme can be gauged from comparisons between 1896, the last year in which the DUTC worked horse trams only, and 1902. This was the first year of exclusively electric operation, although it should be borne in mind that the 1896 figures omit the Haddington Road-Dalkey line. In 1896, 175 operational horsecars (162 according to the *Railway World*) ran 3,163,968 miles, carrying 24,402,462 passengers and earning £147,845. In 1902, 292 electric trams (this figure includes many cars which came into service only in the course of the year and several not ready until December) travelled 6,796,976 miles, their 47,044,451 passengers contributing £240,225 in revenue. Miles run had doubled since 1896, passenger numbers almost so.

Because of its own prestige and the high profile of its system, the DUTC could justifiably use the names of its directors and senior officers as a guarantee of excellence. A contemporary advertisement set out the routes on either side of a photograph of Nelson Pillar, described as, 'the centre of the Dublin tramway system'. Below were listed the directors: Wm M Murphy JP, Chairman; Ald W F Cotton JP, DL, MP; Joseph Money, JP; William Anderson, Managing Director, and Capt C Colthurst Vesey. Also named were the Secretary, R S Tresilian AMICEI, FCIS, and the Manager, C W Gordon.

A New Guide to Dublin

Shortly after completion of their principal electrification programme the DUTC published a *Guide to Dublin and Suburbs*, written by R S Tresilian. This guide has on its cover the city crest together with photographs of Ringsend power station and the DUTC head office at 9 Upper Sackville Street. It contains illustrations from the Lawrence collection plus several more, which were probably commissioned by the company.

The booklet includes a folded map and starts by describing the city, its public buildings, churches, theatres and other prominent features. All of the headings are in an

attractive Gaelic script and much of the decoration is Celtic, very much in keeping with the spirit of the period. The descriptions of the noteworthy features along the various lines are similar to those in the publication *Dictionary of Dublin* of 1896/97 and referred to earlier (see page 36).

An intriguing feature of the DUTC booklet is a route numbering system, which did not appear on the cars and, as we shall see, was to be overtaken by something very different in 1903. Meanwhile the numbers and lines were listed as follows:

1 Nelson's Pillar - Dalkey
2 Nelson's Pillar - Howth
3 Nelson's Pillar - Terenure via Rathmines
4 Nelson' Pillar - Palmerston Park
5 Nelson's Pillar - Clonskea
6 Donnybrook - Phoenix Park
7 Dolphin's Barn - Glasnevin
8 Rathfarnham - Drumcondra
9 Kingsbridge - Hatch Street
10 Parkgate Street - O'Connell Bridge
11 Inchicore - Westland Row
12 Parkgate Street - Ballybough
13 Kenilworth Road - Lansdowne Road
14 Nelson's Pillar - Sandymount
15 College Green - Drumcondra
16 Nelson's Pillar - Irishtown via Haddington Rd

At the beginning of the electric era, the unvestibuled or open-fronted trams carried spacious painted destination boards on the canopies above the platforms. These showed the name of the terminus in large capitals, with an even bigger and decorated initial letter. Detachable destination boards were fixed to the rocker (lower side) panels of the cars, a finger pointing in the direction of the terminus described at either end of the board. The background colour of these boards was different for each route; some of the colours perpetuated those used in horse tram days.

Scrolls and Symbols

Starting with the revolving illuminated boxes on car No 191, the DUTC carried out further experiments, meanwhile watching developments elsewhere. During 1903 linen roller blinds, or scrolls as they have been known in Dublin ever since, were introduced on the trams. They were in glass-fronted, backlit boxes and showed the final destination in white letters on a black background. The destination boxes were mounted above the panel previously used to display the large destination boards, the space thus vacated now being given over to advertising. Conductors carried a special key, usually in a loop on their cash bag straps, to turn the blinds at each terminus. Conversion of the fleet to the new system took some time.

On top of every destination box a pair of

prongs carried an easily recognisable and removable symbol indicating a tram's route. These coloured metal symbols differed in shape and colour for each route: only services which did not meet could have similar shapes. There were squares, triangles, hearts and other shapes, the initial issue being listed below.

Route	Symbol
Sandymount via Ringsend	Green Crescent
Kingstown	'K' on Green Shamrock
Dalkey	Green Shamrock
Donnybrook-Phoenix Park:	
via Merrion Square	Two Blue Diamonds
via Stephen's Green	Two Blue Diamonds with
(1906)	Horizontal White Bar
Clonskea	Two overlapping Yellow
	Discs
Palmerston Park	White Circle
Dartry (1905)	Red Triangle, with
	Vertical White Bar
Terenure via Rathmines	Red Triangle
Rathfarnham-Whitehall	Green Maltese Cross
Kenilworth Sq-Lansdowne Rd	White Square
Glasnevin-Rialto	Brown Lozenge
Inchicore-Westland Row	Brown Oval
Kingsbridge-Hatch Street	White Square
Ballybough-Parkgate Street	Two Red Diamonds
O'Connell Bdge-Parkgate St	White Square
Dollymount	Green Shield
College Gn-Drumcondra	Inverted White Ace of
	Spades

Trams travelling outwards from College Green to Drumcondra through Capel Street and returning via North Frederick Street and O'Connell Bridge displayed the inverted white Ace of Spades listed above. Cars running inwards through Capel Street and outwards via O'Connell Bridge and North Frederick Street displayed a red bar on the Ace of Spades.

Above every destination box (and later incorporated into its top) was a pair of bulls-eye lenses displaying a coloured code at night. This was different for each service, thus enabling people to distinguish cars on the various routes. The principal reason for these symbols and coloured lights was the high incidence of illiteracy still prevailing just after the turn of the century.

Unfortunately, no newspaper accounts covering the introduction of the symbols have as yet come to light. So far as is known no official company reports survive and until now, only one reference has turned up in accounts of DUTC general meetings. This occurred on 27th July 1909 when a shareholder suggested the adoption of route numbers but he does not appear to have pursued the subject. The Dublin symbols were unique in these islands, the only other known instance of anything similar being in Cairo. Today, Amsterdam uses distinguishing colours in its numeral scrolls, as do some other cities.

There were two Dublin services which never carried symbols. One was that to Sandymount via Bath Avenue, worked by instantly recognisable single-deckers. The other was the Howth line, not under DUTC control when symbols were introduced and worked by distinctive bogie cars. The Howth cars, however, displayed a colour code at night. When trams were operating on special services, they normally showed no symbol and the plates were usually removed when a car was not in service. The centre pages of the timetable showed the symbols in colour.

Royal Visits and Staff Bonuses
While commuters and regular leisure traffic provided a satisfactory level of profits for the DUTC, the company made strenuous efforts to capitalise on every special event that materialised. Royal visits were easily at the top of the list and the company was a major beneficiary of five such occasions in the early years of the century.

Queen Victoria came to Ireland in April 1900, the first time the reigning monarch had been to Dublin for more than 50 years. Her visit was a great State occasion of the type that brings large crowds of people to the various public ceremonies laid on at such times. The DUTC rose to the occasion, carrying very large numbers of extra passengers. The pattern was to be repeated on four further occasions up to 1911. King Edward VII made three visits, in 1903, 1904 and 1907, while King George V came to the city in 1911. During each of these Royal visits, huge demands were made on the tramway system. In recognition of their strenuous efforts and the extra profits earned, bonuses were paid to the men.

The Whitehall Extension
North of the Tolka, there was little development in the Drumcondra area prior to the 1900 city boundary extension. This attractive district, less than two miles from Nelson Pillar and with obvious immediate potential, provided a rare instance of tramway construction in Dublin opening up an area rather than following its development. An important section of what would later become recognised as the backbone of the cross-city system and less than three-quarters of a mile long, the extension sent trams beyond the former horse tram terminus at Botanic Avenue to where Whitehall Garda Station stands today.

Opened on 7th September 1903, the Whitehall extension served Ormond Road, Church Avenue and Home Farm Road where there was incipient development. Otherwise, the area was largely rural, with several large tracts of institutional lands still not built on 96 years later; Griffith Avenue was over 20 years in the future. As originally laid, the Whitehall extension was single

track with passing places at Ormond Road and Wellpark Avenue and a run-around loop at the terminus.

Company Staff and Passengers
In the pre-1914 social structure described at the beginning of this chapter, when having a job was widely regarded as a privilege, working people were usually seen by their employers as ciphers or units of production capable of being readily replaced. The DUTC's treatment of staff under this labour relations philosophy contrasted starkly with its attitude to passengers, who represented profit and were therefore pivotal in the company's scheme of things.

An ethos of public service under all conditions was inculcated into the staff and in pursuit of this, they also observed strictly their place in society. In this environment, all transactions between people from different social backgrounds were strictly formal and proper. Yet, in an era when so many people flattered their perceived superiors while lording it over those seen as inferior, there was widespread respect for tramwaymen. With few exceptions, passengers appreciated the excellence of the service and the courtesy of the staff.

The regulations under which public transport operated in the early twentieth century still look strikingly appropriate today. There were rules prescribing walking pace speed past stopping places within the city boundary while, 'within the zone between Sackville Street and College Green where the streets are very wide, cars will stop at any point'. While stops were generally well indicated - 'Wait here for Car' or 'All Cars stop here' - in outlying districts a discretionary power was left to the conductor. This allowed for trams to halt other than at stopping places to oblige elderly or infirm people or women with children, especially in bad weather and after dark. Caring for vulnerable people after dark, in an age when public lighting was grossly inferior to what we are familiar with today, was very important. It should also be remembered that fear of the dark was heightened by the innumerable superstitions with their attendant fears that were still well nigh universal less than a hundred years ago.

Because personal hygiene was not as important a hundred years ago as it is nowadays, the resulting atmosphere in a crowded tramcar is not hard to imagine. If he thought it necessary, a conductor was therefore authorised to open the front saloon door to let fresh air in. However, he could do this only if every passenger consented; a single dissenter meant that the door stayed closed.

Fare Collection and Tickets
A vital element in revenue from fares is the honesty of both staff and passengers. Shortly after his London bus service started in

1829, George Shillibeer is said to have estimated that ten per cent of the fares collected never reached him. To change this undesirable situation, a rapid and foolproof method of fare collection and lodgement was sought for many years. We have seen how William Barrington adopted Shawson's Patent Fare Box on the North Dublin Tramways and William Anderson of the Dublin Tramways Company introduced prize draws. The most important advance in fare verification, however, came with the invention of the Bell Punch in 1878.

The Bell Punch literally punched a hole in a pre-printed ticket, its position relative to information on the ticket showing how far the passenger was entitled to travel. Each time the punch operated, a bell rang, thus assuring both passengers and staff that a ticket was being issued. The earliest punches were pistol-grip machines, in time ousted by the more compact box type, designed in 1889. Carried on a shoulder strap, this became one of the most widely used of all ticket machines, was standard DUTC equipment from 1911 and outlasted the Dublin trams by some years. Training in the repair and servicing of punches was provided by Alfred Williamson, a major ticket printer and punch manufacturer who never printed tickets for the DUTC but hired punches to them. In the 1930s punch maintenance and repairs were carried out at Conyngham Road depot.

DUTC tickets were printed by different companies at various times. Dublin based suppliers included Browne & Nolan, Sealy, Bryers & Walker and Falconers. Before and around the turn of the century, the London firm of Whitings printed tickets for Dublin. There were different colours for each value: in Dublin, the initial protocol was 1d blue or grey, 2d white, 3d pink or mauve, 4d green and 5d yellow. Later, the 1d became white, blue being the colour for 2d fares.

Until 1918, the tickets were known as geographicals, separate issues being printed for each route. These showed the various stages that could be travelled for the value of the ticket. To cover every value and variation, huge stocks of tickets had to be maintained, at least 230 different styles have been identified by Eugene Field. This figure excludes several types such as workmens' and special events issues. A single printing could produce millions of tickets.

Tickets were identified by prefix letters and a four digit serial number. There was also a separate extra letter for additional classification. Because numbering always started at 0000, the difference between the numbers of the first ticket issued and the next to go represented the total already sold. Conductors were issued with packs of tickets in hundreds, together with waybills. At termini and city centre fare stages, they recorded on their waybills the numbers of

tickets issued on the previous journey, reconciling sales with the cash in their possession. On boarding a tram, an inspector usually examined the waybill before checking passengers' tickets. The DUTC never stapled its tickets with a nail in the pad; nailing was intended to prevent fraud. This was most unusual in these islands and such unbound ticket packs continued to be used even in CIE days, but only in Dublin city services.

Every conductor had a metal box in which to carry his punch and tickets while going to and from his duties. This also contained a punch cleaner, a wafer-thin metal wedge for clearing the slot on the punch into which tickets were inserted for cancellation. The box was handed in to the depot clerk at the end of a shift, the waybill showing the number of tickets of each value issued on every journey; the cash had to match. Conductors were responsible for the safe keeping of their cash bags as well as the punch shoulder straps and breastplates.

Behind a movable cover on the front of the punch there was a small aperture into which a pin could be inserted to open the machine. Doing this tore a coloured paper seal bearing a number known only to the depot clerk who had issued the punch. This simple security trick was backed up by a further device consisting of a small box inside the punch and which contained the clipping from every ticket issued. In the most extreme instances of dispute, these could be sorted and counted.

As none of the lines except Howth and Dalkey had fares higher than fourpence, conductors placed the most commonly issued tickets, 1d and 2d, in fifties or hundreds back to back in an elastic band, threepenny and fourpenny blocks were then placed at the sides facing outwards. This arrangement formed a neat four-sided bundle, which fitted easily into the cash bag; except in isolated, much later, instances, Dublin tram conductors did not use the mousetrap type ticket racks found elsewhere.

In the event of further ticket values being required, conductors simply made up another bundle. The need for a second bundle applied particularly on the Dalkey and Howth lines where 5d tickets were used and returns were also offered. In later years at least, return tickets had a highly distinctive patterned background to the printed information and on handing one up the passenger received a 'Return Voucher', a ticket printed in red.

A passenger discovering after a short distance that he or she had taken the wrong tram and had not yet paid a fare was not to be charged. Old tickets were not to be allowed lie about in the car, the conductor being instructed to call the attention of the ticket boys at the termini who were to clear

them from the tram. As noted in on page 61, these boys frequently came from tramway families, some being the sons of deceased staff members, and they were to be found all over the system for many years. After serving a satisfactory period of probation at these duties, followed by further experience as messengers, they could be offered adult employment as conductors or motormen.

The bitterest confrontations between the DUTC on the one hand and passengers and the Corporation on the other concerned fares, an always controversial subject since horse tram days and one that will arise again at several future points in this book.

Prosecutions and Bye-Laws
Fare evasion was the most frequent reason for legal action by the DUTC. A passenger who initially managed to evade the conductor but was subsequently challenged was usually given a chance to pay the fare. Others brazened it out or tried to ridicule or abuse conductors and inspectors These were the ones who usually ended up in court. The company's policy was to select a number of the worst cases arising in a given period and bring the defaulters to court. Even then, apologies and payment, if forthcoming, were usually accepted and the case was dismissed.

Some fare evaders tried to bluff their way out of court with half-truths, lies, and sheer brass neck, as reported regularly in the press. There were also defendants' solicitors who tried to mock the law, the company and its employees on technicalities. Excuses ranged from tickets thrown away because the passengers concerned saw no reason to retain them to not being able to read the fare table or the bye-laws on display being out of date.

One case which came to court on 4th December 1903 involved a Rathgar based butcher who went into the city on one morning every week. He travelled on one of the two cars that left Terenure at 5.30 and 7.00 and had special fares for, 'mechanics, artisans and daily labourers', maintaining such a service was part of the agreement reached with the Corporation in 1897. The full fare for the journey was 2d but the butcher, who would have been regarded as belonging to a superior class, paid only the artisan's 1½d for the inward journey. After hearing detailed arguments, the magistrate pointed out that he was going to a lot of trouble to save a yearly total of 2s 2d and dismissed the charge on receiving a guarantee that he would pay the full fare in future.

Although potential passengers, as many as possible, were the company's aim, they too were regulated by bye-laws. The DUTC's original ones of October 1881 were replaced on 1st May 1903 by a new code of 30 rules, signed by the Company Secretary and approved by the Board of Trade.

Under these bye-laws, passengers were not allowed to smoke inside a tramcar or to play or perform upon any musical instrument. No person in a state of intoxication was to be allowed to enter or mount upon any carriage, nor could anybody swear, or use obscene or offensive language. Spitting was strictly prohibited, as was causing annoyance or nuisance to any other passenger. People with infectious or contagious diseases were barred and, if found, could be removed summarily from the tram. Those whose dress or clothing might be injurious or offensive had to travel outside (on top). Vandalism was comprehensively proscribed, as was interference with any part of the tram or its equipment. Payment of fares, retention of tickets for inspection, carriage of dogs, the powers and responsibilities of staff and officials, all were covered. The penultimate bye-law set out the penalty for a breach of the code – a fine not exceeding 40 shillings.

In times past, spitting was a habit more universal than it is to day. Generally condemned as a cause of spreading various diseases, its prevalence was partly attributable to the widespread chewing of tobacco. The enamelled DUTC notices prohibiting spitting were rather awkwardly worded, proclaiming that 'Spitting is prohibited in or on the cars.' Wits observed that the admonition as shown did not rule out spitting off the cars, a habit sometimes practised by wayward passengers on the upper decks.

Company bye-laws and regulations, and the fares applicable to the line being travelled, were prominently displayed in bulkhead frames at either end of a tram's lower deck. To put the passenger's rights and obligations beyond all doubt, most tickets carried the legend, 'Issued subject to the Company's Bye-laws.'

The conductor was responsible for checking the car on taking it over and had to perform certain rituals on laying it up in the depot at night. The final section of the conductor's instructions listed the bell signals to be given to the motorman, one to stop, two to start, three for 'car full'. Four bells meant 'stop at once, without causing a jerk', while six signified 'stop, trolley off', or to avoid an accident.'

Public lighting was either poor or non-existent in outlying areas in the early years of the century. A lamp was therefore mounted on a pole at most tram termini. While this re-assured people waiting for a tram during the hours of darkness, its more important function was to assist the crew. Because no light emanated from the tram while its trolley was removed from the wire for turning, the lamp supplied essential illumination.

Each tramway lamp had a cluster of five 110-volt bulbs wired in series and thus compatible with the 550v direct current supply. Tramcar lighting circuits were similarly wired. Putting the trolley back on the wire was a most unpleasant chore in bad weather, with perhaps a series of misses, giving rise to a recitation known euphemistically as the tram conductor's litany. Urinals were also provided at most termini, and shelter was provided for the timekeepers, who whistled each car on its way and accepted items for the Parcels Service.

Employees on Company Business

An enduring feature of the Dublin trams was the Employee's Pass. Metal discs, mostly circular but also square or diamond-shaped, were issued to staff travelling to and from work or sent out on company business. Styles and materials changed over the years, brass and aluminium being the most common; a small hole enabled the pass to be attached to a key ring or watch chain. The passes carried serial numbers, some of which may have corresponded with an employee's staff number. Strictly non-transferable, they bore the name of the current General Manager, were to be used only for official purposes and usually stipulated that the bearer was to travel 'outside only' - on the upper deck.

Literary Acclaim

Electrification of the Bath Avenue line in 1901 completed the first stage of providing Dublin with a tramway system regarded as one of the best in the world. In his autobiography, the novelist L A G Strong illustrates just how quickly it became an accepted amenity in the life of the city; and he also conveys the niceties of etiquette in those distant days; 'The conductor had barely time to take their pennies when they were at the church. Then, he might rest from the exertion, for twenty old ladies and gentlemen in their Sunday clothes were not to be hustled off a tram in the year nineteen hundred and one. When the tram had well and truly stopped, the church-goers would arise, stiffly, and with some parade of mutual assistance. Next came a polite mutual surrender of precedence, causing, in the narrow gangway, almost great difficulty as a panic. Only one person could alight from the tram at a time, and all the ladies got down backwards – while to such old gentlemen as had already achieved the conductor's platform was presented the distressing alternative of remaining where they were, in everybody's way, or of getting off before a lady. It all required two minutes, if not three: and the conductor, child of his age and clime, stood in the road, helping the ladies in all friendliness and respect, by the guidance of his arm or the official assurance of his person and uniform; confirming Christian ratepayers in their belief that all was well, and that the tram, marvel of an enlightened age, yet creature of their needs, would not proceed until the last of them had been safely deposited in the road.'

Unfortunately, depositing passengers in the road was to be part of the tram's undoing several decades later when other forms of transport would challenge its very right to exist. Meanwhile, the Dublin trams were to find a place in one of the world's greatest literary works, as is recounted below.

The Dublin Trams and Traffic in 1904

It sometimes happens that a major event can be taken almost in isolation from those that preceded and followed it. In terms of Dublin tramway history, the mythical

No 154, one of the 50 American-built cars Nos 121-170. No 154 is recorded as being allocated to Dartry between 1908 and 1911, which is probably when this picture was taken outside the depot. This tram was vestibuled in September 1915 and was replaced by a Standard Saloon in 1926. The conductor and timekeeper are wearing straw-boaters, the motorman has a kepi, and the ticket picker's hat appears to be too big for his head. Birney collection

happenings of 16th June 1904 fall almost at the end of the lull between the opening of the Whitehall extension in the autumn of 1903 and the introduction, in October 1904, of the DUTC's first top-covered trams.

'Before Nelson's pillar trams slowed, shunted, changed trolley, started for Blackrock, Kingstown and Dalkey, Rathgar and Terenure, Palmerston Park and upper Rathmines, Sandymount Green, Rathmines, Ringsend and Sandymount Tower, Harold's Cross. The hoarse Dublin United Tramway Company's timekeeper bawled them off: – Rathgar and Terenure! – Come on, Sandymount Green! Right and left parallel clanging and ringing a double-decker and a single-deck moved from their railheads, swerved to the down lines, glided parallel. – Start, Palmerston Park!'

This extract from *Ulysses*, is James Joyce's description of the multiple tramway termini at Nelson Pillar on Bloomsday, 16th June 1904. Probably the most comprehensive, it is one of several references in *Ulysses* and other Joycean literature to the Dublin trams. Generally very exact, there are occasional and understandable minor inaccuracies, but they are insignificant when compared to the unbridled licence exercised by some writers about early twentieth century Dublin. A description of the city's public services and especially the tramways in 1904 may, therefore, not come amiss.

The motor car was still a primitive and temperamental machine, so much so that around Bloomsday the Hon C S Rolls and Henry Royce were beginning their legendary partnership in search of excellence. The Motor Car Act of 1903 had decreed the introduction of registrations throughout the United Kingdom from 1st January 1904. Dublin County Borough had been issued the RI mark, the County Dublin mark, IK, also covered Rathmines, Pembroke, Kingstown and the other urban districts, including Howth which had not yet achieved that status.

In Dublin County Borough only 31 new motor cars and 81 motorcycles were registered in the April to June quarter. Motor lorries were almost non-existent and the only British commercial vehicle makers of the time still in business in 2000 were Dennis and Foden. The latter built steam wagons and traction engines, which in 1904 would have handled heavy haulage. Arthur Guinness, Son and Company was already using steam wagons and would shortly begin buying motor lorries. For road maintenance, steamrollers were being increasingly used.

Water, Drainage and Cleansing
Work on the Dublin Main Drainage scheme, inaugurated in 1895, was being pushed to a conclusion. The two interceptor sewers on the North and South Quays were almost complete but pending the 1906 commissioning of the system, sewage continued to discharge directly into the Liffey. Shortly to become storm overflows, the river outfalls

meanwhile continued contributing to the infamous Liffey smell, causing gross pollution in the process. Rathmines and Pembroke had a joint drainage system flowing by gravity to Londonbridge Road pumping station, being there lifted to a high-level sewer which discharged into Dublin Bay at Whitebanks on the South Wall.

Far worse, however, than the city drainage system was the method of refuse disposal. Collection was by two-wheeled horse drawn carts or skips, which were used to carry the material to South Gloucester Street or Stanley Street depots. There was a modicum of incineration at Stanley Street but from South Gloucester Street the bulk of the refuse was transferred to a barge called the *Eblana*. This discharged in the bay, adding to a filthy mess which, in certain weather conditions, was washed back in with each incoming tide. The important role played by the tramway system in ridding Dublin of this environmental horror is described on page 72.

Gas and Electricity
Already well established when the first horse trams ran in 1872, the Alliance and Dublin Consumers' Gas Company was the sole source of town gas in the Dublin area in 1904. This monopoly, formed by the merger of three smaller concerns, had its head office in D'Olier Street where the Irish Gas Board is still located in the year 2000. The manufacturing plant and gasholders were at Sir John Rogerson's Quay, Great Brunswick (now Pearse) Street and Barrow Street. While it was still the major energy supplier, its dominance was already being challenged by the extension of electric public lighting and the rapidly growing use of electricity in domestic and business premises. Electricity had, paradoxically, been introduced to Dublin in the early 1880s by gas interests, but it was the Corporation which eventually inaugurated a full generation and supply service.

The service provided by the Electricity Department was one in which the Corporation took justifiable pride. It began in 1892 with a generating station in Fleet Street, replaced in 1903 by the much larger Pigeon House plant. The principal streets had been lit by arc lamps since 1892 but changes were now taking place. In 1904, the original arc lamp columns or pillars as they are known, were having their top-mounted lanterns replaced with elegant swan-necks which have stood the test of time and still grace the streets today.

Similar fittings topped the splendid 'Scotch' or Verity columns, introduced in 1903 and now a hallmark of the city. By Bloomsday, more than three quarters of the initial order for 400 of these distinctive columns had replaced gas pillars, many of which were re-located to streets previously

badly lit or with no illumination at all. During more than 30 years of arc lighting the vertical carbon cylinder below the lamp cowl would distinguish both types of pillar. Rathmines and Pembroke had their own distinctive designs of lighting pillars, supplied from electricity generating stations at Rathmines Town Hall Yard and South Lotts Road, respectively.

There were four methods of domestic lighting. Many new houses were wired for electricity and older ones were also being connected, the supply fed through underground cables. As explained in Chapter 1, the Corporation objected to overhead wiring on aesthetic grounds and as long as they were responsible for electricity supply, they refrained from erecting poles for overhead distribution. Many middle class residences had gas lighting, usually on the ground floor only; oil lamps were an alternative or supplementary light source. Candles were used upstairs, and Kathleen Levins, the author's mother, recalled sitting at a bedroom dressing table in 1904 reading Bram Stoker's *Dracula* by candlelight and being afraid to look up into the mirror. In poorer homes, candles were the only form of lighting.

Post and Telecommunications
Postal services were excellent in the early years of the last century, with several deliveries each day and a listing in *Thom's Directory* of all post boxes, together with the times at which they were cleared. The Post Office also operated the telegraph service, many post offices being designated as telegraph offices. The principal ones in the city centre were at the GPO and College Green. Responsibility for telephones was divided between the Post Office and the privately owned National Telephone Company, soon to be taken over by the Post Office.

Emergency Services
Around Bloomsday, Dublin Fire Brigade was in a state of transition. Headed by the innovative Captain Thomas Purcell, it had recently opened two new stations at Buckingham Street in 1901 and Dorset Street in 1903. Negotiations were in progress to acquire a site for another station at Thomas Street and in May 1904 the Corporation took possession of a site at Tara Street. On this would rise the new Central Station which opened in 1907. In the meantime the headquarters were at Chatham Row, where the School of Music is now.

The front line appliances included three Shand Mason steam pumps, a 66-foot aerial ladder and two ambulances, all horse-drawn. The remaining escape station ladders, due to be phased out, had been modified to enable them to pass under the tramway overhead wires. The street alarm-box system was being extended, especially on the north side. The street alarms consisted of bell pulls in glass-fronted boxes mounted on truncated square base lamp pillars. To summon the Brigade, the caller broke the glass and pulled the handle. This rang a numbered bell in the fire station and the caller remained at the box to guide the fire crew on their arrival. Rathmines, Pembroke, Blackrock and Kingstown had their own separate Fire Brigades.

The Dublin Metropolitan Police
Apart from changes in personnel, uniforms and some station locations, the Dublin Metropolitan Police of 1904 was recognisably the same force that had been responsible for law enforcement when the first horse trams ran in 1872. The police divisions were much the same, albeit expanded to cover the extra territory taken into the city by the 1900 boundary extension. A and B Divisions policed the south city, E covering the township areas from Irishtown through Pembroke and Rathmines to Kilmainham. F was responsible for Kingstown, Blackrock and Dalkey, while G was the Detective Division. North of the Liffey C and D Divisions had been greatly enlarged to serve areas such as Glasnevin, Drumcondra and Clontarf.

Railways, Public Hire and Licensing
Turning to public transport, in 1904 Dublin was served by four mainline railway companies. The Great Southern & Western Railway had its headquarters at Kingsbridge from which it served the south and west. It also maintained the Inchicore railway works where locomotives, coaches and wagons were designed and built. Broadstone was the principal station of the Midland Great Western Railway whose lines ran to the west of Ireland. Its Broadstone works performed similar work to Inchicore, although on a smaller scale. The Great Northern Railway (Ireland), serving Belfast and the north west places of the country, had its terminus at Amiens Street. Across the river at Westland Row was one of the capital's two termini of the Dublin, Wicklow & Wexford Railway whose works was nearby at Grand Canal Street. Its second Dublin terminus was at Harcourt Street. In 1907 this company changed its name to the Dublin & South Eastern Railway.

Kingsbridge, Amiens Street and Westland Row were connected by the Phoenix Park tunnel and the Loop Line over the Liffey while the southside stations were served by a tram route running from Kingsbridge to Hatch Street via Westland Row. Taxis had not yet appeared, but horse-drawn cabs and sidecars were to be found at the stations and on various hazards or stands throughout the city. These vehicles, and the trams, were supervised by the Dublin Metropolitan Police, whose Carriage Office issued licence plates and badges.

Throughout most of the tramway age, conductors wore the shamrock-shaped licence badge on their cash bag shoulder strap. In horse days drivers displayed a large oval enamel badge, however this is missing in many photographs of motormen from the electric era. While drivers and conductors were licensed in the horse era, there was initially some doubt as to whether the police really had any licensing powers over electric trams, which, legally, were mechanically propelled vehicles. This was resolved in 1897, with tramcars, motormen and conductors all coming under the licensing system. There is evidence that the number of Dublin trams always exceeded that of carriage plates, which appear to have been switched around between the cars at various times.

The Tramways
Outside the city, three tramway systems independent of the DUTC afforded connections with it: the Dublin & Blessington and the Dublin & Lucan. At Sutton Cross and again at Howth railway station, the GNR Hill of Howth Tramway crossed the Clontarf company's Howth line which connected with the DUTC at Dollymount. Dublin had bidden farewell to its last horse tram in 1901, long before many other places had started to electrify and, three years later, the DUTC tramway system was one of the city's glories. As befitted such a splendid undertaking, the track layout in Sackville Street was extensive and complicated. Two sets of double track crossed O'Connell Bridge from D'Olier Street and Westmoreland Street and on the north side of the O'Connell Monument there was a double scissors crossover with four lines coming from beyond Abbey Street, which a tram could enter from either direction.

Nelson Pillar was known to Dubliners simply as 'the Pillar'. Countless appointments were kept there over a period of 158 years. In public transport, it was of outstanding importance and in the tramway era was the hub of the system. It was referred to as Nelson's Pillar in Joyce's time, but the 's' and its apostrophe were dropped in later years. The four tracks coming past the Abbey Street junction became six between there and the Pillar, the four inner ones going through a series of crossovers to form four terminal stubs right in front of the Pillar's entrance door. From these stubs began the journeys to all but one of the southside destinations listed by Joyce.

Not mentioned in the extract from *Ulysses* on page 66 are Dolphin's Barn, Rathfarnham, or Donnybrook. These connected by cross-town services to Glasnevin, Drumcondra and Phoenix Park, respectively, and ran past Nelson Pillar on the outer two of the six tracks just described. One of the southside destina-

tions mentioned by Joyce did have a cross-city service to a northern suburb. This was Harold's Cross, from where trams ran to Whitehall, in 1904 a lonely rural terminus just beyond the present Garda station. On the north side of the Pillar (behind it, as explained earlier), there was a less elaborate track layout, but also with terminal stubs. From here, by way of North Earl Street, trams departed for Dollymount and Howth. It has been calculated that a tram could make upwards of 60 different movements between O'Connell Bridge and Rutland (Parnell) Square.

There was a complicated but neat overhead scheme in the street, the decorated poles having a variety of arms and brackets. The most noteworthy were those between Abbey Street and the Pillar which spanned six tracks. While not as busy as in previous times, College Green was also an important terminus with an impressive track layout, handling cars for Whitehall and various short workings, mainly on the Inchicore line.

The DUTC Guide
The DUTC's 1902 *Guide to Dublin and Suburbs,* (see page 62) would have been still regarded as reasonably up-to-date two years later. Printed at the ABC Guide Office, 53 Upper Sackville Street, the book begins with a very brief summary of Dublin's history. Twenty-two pages then describe buildings and places of outstanding interest in the city, while the next four list places of amusement, principal churches and hotels. For fuller details of the many places of interest and beauty in and around Dublin, however, readers of the *Guide* are referred to the Cosgrave and Strangeways *Dictionary of Dublin*.

Fifty-four pages are dedicated to a route-by-route description of the tramway system. History, architecture and topography are covered, and there are references to the other tram services encountered along each line. The last two pages, 83 and 84, are devoted to the DUTC's Parcels Express service, with city centre premises at Dawson Street and Cathedral Street. Two respects in which the book had been overtaken by events since 1902 were the extension of the Drumcondra line to Whitehall and the introduction of the route symbols in 1903.

Nothing comes more clearly out of the *Guide*, which would have been invaluable to an expatriate writing about Dublin, than the DUTC's pride in its tramway system. In the introductory pages, it said that, 'The topography of the city and suburbs lends itself excellently to street car traffic; the streets and roads – none of them very hilly – radiate in all directions from the centre, situated practically at O'Connell Bridge, and by following the routes given most of the places interesting, either from an historical or pictorial aspect, can be easily and comfortably visited.'

The next paragraph is most specific, 'The cars – the best of their kind in the Kingdom – run to all the suburbs, and a frequent service is provided, all worked by electricity, generated at probably the most up-to-date and perfectly equipped station in Europe, situated at Ringsend (Route No 14) and for permission to visit which application should be made at the Secretary's Office, 9 Upper Sackville Street.'

Kingstown and Dalkey are the only places of interest outside the city mentioned in the *Guide's* preliminary list of buildings and notable locations. They were served by the premier line, designated Route No 1 in 1902, but carrying a shamrock symbol in 1904 (with a K superimposed for trams going only to Kingstown). 'NELSON'S PILLAR to DALKEY – distance 9 miles – Cars run every 5 minutes', read the headings to the text which follows and is typical of that appearing about every route, and is worth quoting. Joyce is said to have written to a friend in Dublin asking him to travel on the Dalkey line and send him the ticket.

'The cars start from **Nelson's Pillar** (close to the General Post Office), at the junction of Upper and Lower Sackville-streets, and passing through Lower Sackville-street, in which are the statues erected in memory of **Sir John Gray**, the originator of the Vartry water supply to Dublin, and of **Daniel O'Connell**, 'The Liberator', this being the work of the great Irish sculptor, Foley, and then cross **O'Connell**, formerly **Carlisle**, Bridge, where, at the junction of D'Olier and Westmoreland-streets, is the statue of **Smith-O'Brien**; passing through **Westmoreland-street**, and at the junction with College-street, by the statue of **Thomas Moore**, the great Irish poet, they come to College-green, with the statue of **Grattan**, the **Bank of Ireland**, **Dame Street**, on the right, and **Trinity College** on the left, with statues of **Burke** and **Goldsmith** in front; through the lower part of the fashionable **Grafton-street** (the Bond-street of Dublin), they turn off along the **Trinity College Grounds**, to the left, through Nassau-street, with the **Kildare-street Club** and Kildare-street on the right, in which is situated the **National Library** and the **Science and Art Museum**; Leinster-street, with the **Leinster Club** on right, and Clare-street; then along Merrion-square, with what was formerly the **lawn of the Duke of Leinster's house** on the right, through Lower Mount-street to the Canal-bridge, and at Haddington-road cross the **city boundary**, where they enter the Pembroke Township…'

Without full stop or paragraph break, the narrative continues: '…thence they pass along Northumberland-road and Pembroke-road, with the **Trinity College Botanical Gardens** on the left (immediately at the junction of Lansdowne and Pembroke-roads); thence over Ball's-bridge, crossing the **River Dodder**, and from whence can be had a very pretty view of the **Dublin Mountains**, by the show-yards of the **Royal Dublin Society**, where the celebrated **Irish Horse Show** is held each year, along the Rock-road, close to the sea, through the villages of Merrion and Booterstown and the town of Blackrock, along Monkstown-road and past **Monkstown Church**, through Kingstown main street, close to the landing stages of the **Cross-Channel Mail Boats**; Sandycove, Bullock, and into Dalkey, where the line ends.'

Three separate paragraphs follow; 'In close proximity to Dalkey is the celebrated Victoria Park, Killiney, thrown open to the public in commemoration of her late Majesty Queen Victoria's first jubilee, and from which the most magnificent views of Dublin Bay and the surrounding country can be had…the time occupied in going to Dalkey from Nelson's Pillar and returning is about 2 hours and 20 minutes.'

The Trams, Tramwaymen and Fares of Bloomsday

On Bloomsday, all Dublin trams were open-top double-deckers, with the exception of the single-deckers working the Bath Avenue line. The highest fleet number on a four-wheeler was 293, which was new in December 1902. Because rolling stock was continually being improved, there were already 79 vestibuled four-wheeled trams and the records show nine more, Nos 12, 18, 29, 40, 44, 49, 56, 60 and 252, as being in the works during that month. No 252 was one of the single-deckers from the Sandymount via Beggar's Bush and Bath Avenue service. Four of the 12 bogie cars 301-312 from the Howth line, Nos 304, 306, 311 and 312 were also off the streets, recorded as being under overhaul in June.

The DUTC livery of ultramarine and ivory was elaborately lined out in red and gold. Trams carried extensive advertising, external displays being on colourful enamelled plates screwed in manageable sections to the decency boarding and the upper deck dashes of vestibuled cars. Displaying the most famous brand names of the day, these enamelled advertisements were very much an art form in their own right much sought after by collectors in later years. Until the 1930s, paper advertisements were generally confined to window bills, most of which faced inwards to be read by the passengers. However, there were exceptions, as in the case of the large window bills publicising the Royal Dublin Society's shows at Balls-bridge which faced outwards.

Being summer, conductors and inspectors would have worn straw-boater hats, the motormen retaining their kepis all the year round because these were less likely to be blown off on a breezy day. Cancelled by the Bell Punch, tickets were of the geographical type, with separate issues for each service and having the stage points listed, the reverse carried advertisements, Prescott's Dye Works being the most frequently encountered. The most expensive single fares, those to Dalkey and Howth, cost 5d, while the majority of termini were 2d from the Pillar and most cross-town journeys, for example Dolphin's Barn to Glasnevin, were 4d all the way. Contemporary ticket colour coding was 1d blue or grey, 2d white, 3d pink or mauve, 4d green and 5d yellow.

The consumer price index, related to the 1914 base of 100, had risen from a historic low of 83 in 1896, to stand at 92 around Bloomsday. The 2d and 5d fares paid by Leopold Bloom's fellow-citizens on 16th June 1904 would be approximately 62p and £1.55 respectively at 1999 prices, a Bloomsday pound would have been worth nearly £75 in 1999.

Time Zones and Timekeeping

As noted by Joyce, trams were sent off from the Pillar by a timekeeper or dispatcher, in 1904 the holder of this office was the legendary Richard Delaney, whose name is, unfortunately, not recorded by Joyce. This worthy, as noted in *Ulysses*, invariably ordered departures by calling out destinations rather than motormen's names or car fleet numbers. Known as 'the Captain', Delaney was a native of Co Laois who had started his career with a three-year stint in the police, followed by five years on Wilson's omnibuses. He transferred to the Dublin Tramways Company when Wilson's buses were replaced in 1872 and had been through all the subsequent changes on the tramways. Richard Delaney was famous enough to be profiled in a series called 'City Celebrities', in *The Lepracaun*, a humourous magazine in December 1906.

Delaney's memory for departure times was prodigious. He is reputed never to have consulted a timetable or running board but he kept a sharp eye on the famous clock on the traction pole in the centre of the street just down from the Pillar. His successors, and most timekeepers at other termini, normally used whistles to start trams on their journeys. Tramway staff who had watches were expected to have them in good order and synchronised with this DUTC clock.

On Bloomsday, Dublin time differed from that in London. Prior to the advent of railways, there had been great discrepancies in the observance of time, each locality more or less following its own rules. The resulting confusion was rectified by the 1880 Statutes (Definition of Time) Act, which laid down Greenwich Mean Time as the standard throughout Britain. However, this left Ireland in a separate time zone 25 minutes behind GMT, a situation that lasted until 1916 when GMT became universal throughout these islands. Local time was adjusted each day, electrically from Greenwich Observatory, by the fall of a timeball on the roof of the Ballast Office at the junction of Westmoreland Street and Aston Quay.

Symbols, Bullseyes and Scrolls

Leopold Bloom observed, 'The tram which went from Glasnevin to Rialto bore a brown lozenge badge to indicate its route. From Nelson's Pillar to Sandymount was indicated by a green crescent. A green shamrocked tram bore you to Dalkey, a green Maltese Cross from Rathfarnham to Drumcondra. Two blue diamonds decorated the tram which linked Donnybrook to the Phoenix Park and a white circled tram reached the quiet pools of Palmerston Park. It didn't, therefore, matter whether you could read'. Thus James Joyce described the outstanding feature of the Dublin trams, introduced in 1903 and described on page 63.

The illuminated headcode, two red lights for the Howth service, may well be the reason for one of Bloom's experiences in Nighttown, 'Through rising fog a dragon sandstrewer travelling at caution, slews heavily upon him, its huge red headlight winking, its trolley hissing on the wire'. The description sandstrewer has two possible meanings. One involves grit being forcefully dislodged from the rail groove by a tram's wheels or the deposit of sand from its four sandboxes to assist either braking or adhesion. It is more likely, however, that litigation still fresh in public memory around Bloomsday inspired Joyce's words.

Under their empowering Acts, horse tramway companies were responsible for the maintenance of the roadway between the rails and for 18 inches on either side. They also sanded this section of the roadway to prevent horses from slipping, but following the change to electric traction, the DUTC ceased sanding. A man named Fitzgerald who was injured when his horse slipped in Grafton Street successfully sued the DUTC. During the initial case and several appeals, evidence was given that sand on a dry surface was prone to being blown about in the breeze caused by a passing tramcar: was this Joyce's sandstrewer?

Another acute observation occurs in the Lotus eaters: 'a heavy tramcar honking its gong'. Honking is not a term usually associated with any bell, but one that is cracked, rusty or caked with dirt would lose its resonance and produce a very unmusical effect as described by Joyce. The reference to a heavy tramcar is also intriguing and is indicative of Joyce's capacity to distinguish the 116 converted horse cars and trailers, especially those remaining unvestibuled, from the

larger and more massive looking cars built as motor trams. There was a range of lengths too, from the former trailers at around 24ft 6in to the American cars which were 4ft longer. A vestibuled American car would certainly have looked massive and heavy compared to an open-fronted ex-trailer.

A Power Failure

A further observation in *Ulysses* concerns a failure of the traction current supply in Sackville Street: 'At various points along the eight lines tramcars with motionless trolleys stood in their tracks, bound for or from Rathmines, Rathfarnham, Blackrock, Kingstown and Dalkey, Sandymount Green, Ringsend and Sandymount Tower, Donnybrook, Palmerston Park and Upper Rathmines, all still, becalmed in short circuit.' Incidents like this happened from time to time and were irritating for tramway staff and passengers alike, but due to the separation of the overhead lines into insulated half-mile sections, rarely affected cars along greater distances.

Joyce's references to the tramways include four apparent errors, one of them perhaps intentional. The possibly deliberate one concerns the company's name, quoted as the Dublin United Tramway Company, whereas the official name used the plural 'Tramways'. Omitting the 's' was a common colloquialism, made quainter by the tendency of many Dubliners, when using the full title, to add a syllable to the word United, pronouncing it 'un-inited'. Most of the time, however, people simply referred to the DUTC as 'the Tram Company'. Other common misnomers included 'Chapelizard' (Chapelizod), 'the Izoo' (Zoo) and 'the Copperation' (Corporation).

In *Ulysses*, there are two destination anachronisms. The first occurs in the reference to Upper Rathmines, quoted in the

extract from *Ulysses* on page 66. This had appeared on horse trams plying the Palmerston Park route and may have been used on some of the early electrics. However, the electric service usually understood to serve this area and leaving the Terenure line at Rathmines to operate along Upper Rathmines Road en route to Dartry, did not commence until 27th January 1905.

Another discrepancy occurs in the description of the lozenge-badged car en route to Rialto. In 1904, this tram would have gone only to Dolphin's Barn, the Rialto extension not being opened until 20th May 1905. Finally, in the passage describing the power cut, Joyce refers to eight lines of trams whereas there were only six parallel tracks in Lower Sackville Street.

The trams carried handsomely painted removable and reversible destination boards on their rocker or lower side panels with a different background colour for each line. The lettering on these was gold, shaded, and with a hand at either end pointing in the direction of the named terminus. These boards were targets for removal by students on university rag days and other occasions, when conscientious crews frequently took them inside. Many years later the noted humourous essayist John D Sheridan, in a valediction to the trams, referred to a motorman in these circumstances as having his household gods safely aboard.

'Line' was the title universally used to describe the company's tracks to the various destinations. The word 'route' did not become general until the bus era. Also noteworthy is the use of the word 'car' to describe a tram. This goes back to horse days and was not confined to Dublin, although here it is still used among bus people and also Fire Brigade, Ambulance and

When the Whitehall extension, stretching from Botanic Avenue to the present Garda station at Griffith Avenue, was opened in September 1903, the line ended in open country. This was a case of a tramway facilitating rather than following urban expansion. Initially encouraging progress was unfortunately delayed by the tumultuous events and depression of the years 1913-1930. By the latter date development had finally caught up with the tramway. When the Drumcondra line closed in 1939, development had also taken place beyond this once lonely terminus, but from Binn's Bridge outwards the trams ran through an area that even today has large tracts of undeveloped institutional lands. Here the crew of No 199 pose with their charge, the picture probably dating from the 1910 to 1918 period. This tram started life as Milnes trailer No 54, being electrified and renumbered in June 1900. It was working from Clonskea depot in 1905, but by 1910 had transferred to Cabra (Phibsboro), which provided vehicles for the College Green to Whitehall service which closed in 1918. Birney collection

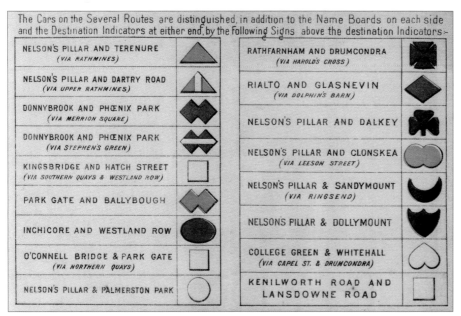

The symbols chart as it appeared in the centre of the timetable. Variations such as the Kingstown K or Express S were not included and the services that did not have a symbol were not even mentioned, such as those to Howth and Sandymount via Bath Avenue. The symbols first appeared in 1903 and were replaced by route numbers in 1918.

Cleansing Department personnel. Another anachronistic description which persisted among older Dubliners up to the end of the tramway era was to call depots 'tram stables', a clear hangover from the days of horse traction.

Depots, Parcels and Backup

DUTC running depots in 1904 were at Sandymount, Ballsbridge, Blackrock, Dalkey, Donnybrook, Clonskea, Terenure, Inchicore, Kingsbridge (Victoria Quay), Cabra (Phibsboro) and Clontarf. An important facility provided by the company was the Parcels Express, the efficient delivery service with rates starting at 2d. Parcels could be handed in at most of the depots, at agencies or Tram Stations, these were the timekeepers' offices at some of the termini. Packages were sent by the next tram and transferred to other routes as necessary. Collection could be from the DUTC or its agent or the parcel could be delivered for an extra fee. Special tickets were issued, 2d for the carriage of a parcel, 3d for a bicycle.

In addition to the ordinary running depots, the DUTC had its generating station and a site for a permanent way yard at Ringsend and the tram building works at Spa Road. In Nelson Lane, now Earl Place, and on the site of the CIE (Dublin Bus) Restaurant and Club, there was a premises housing horse-drawn tower wagons and other emergency equipment. As described in Chapter One, Shelbourne Road was both a depot and an overhaul works, the latter, with its traverser, was known to tramway men as 'the Yard'. Because Cabra also had an inconveniently restricted entrance, this depot, too, was equipped with a traverser.

Electrically Operated Points

A most interesting passage in *Ulysses* occurs as Leopold Bloom sits in a horse-drawn cab

at Westland Row. 'A pointsman's back straightened itself upright suddenly against a tram standard by Mr Bloom's window. Couldn't they invent something automatic so that the wheel itself much handier? Well but that fellow would lose his job then? Well but then another fellow would get a job making the new invention?' The pointsmen were frequently boys, like the ticket pickers and messengers, hopefuls for future employment as motormen or conductors.

Safe and practical automatic points, a Holy Grail of tramway engineers, were the subject of patents in America as early as 1892. In September 1902, Messrs. Tierney and Malone, electrical engineer and foreman respectively, of the Dublin United Tramways Company began their own experiments. In May 1903 a unit was installed at the Londonbridge Road junction, Tierney and Malone carrying out exhaustive tests and eventually patenting their invention. Later adopted widely on other tramway systems, this was one of many developments contributing to the pioneering reputation of the Dublin tramways. Under an agreement concluded with the Corporation in 1904, more than 40 sets of automatic points were installed in the city within a short period.

A brochure on the point controller explained that the device was electrically operated and could be applied to any existing system of points. The point was normally set for the main line and cars staying on that line would not have to move the point, but trams going on to the diverging route would always move the point for themselves and set it back again after going through. During daylight hours, motormen could see the point moving before they came up to it, but at night a signalling device on a convenient pole assisted them. This consisted of two green lights side by side with a red one between. With the left hand green and red showing together, the points were set left,

while the right hand green with the red indicated that the right hand lines were open. All three lights out warned of jammed points, in which case the motorman would open the box on the pole and remove a set of fuses, thus rendering the points operable by a point iron.

A contact or skate in the overhead some distance before the junction and another beyond it effected electric or automatic operation. The equipment included an electro-magnet mounted on each side of the point blade and when one of these magnets became energised, the point was turned. When a motorman wished to turn a point he was approaching, he drew power from the overhead while the trolley passed over the skate, causing current to reach the electromagnet and turn the point. But if the points were correctly set for his tram, the motorman coasted under the skate. While the installations were a great improvement on the situation observed by Leopold Bloom, they had their faults and were eventually superseded by newer and more advanced mechanisms. But whether James Joyce knew about the 1903 Londonbridge Road installation at that time or included Bloom's musings with the benefit of hindsight must remain a matter for speculation for the literati.

Bloom also speculated about the possibility of carrying livestock from the cattle market straight down to the North Wall by rail. This idea could also have come from Joyce's knowledge of post-1904 tramway developments in operation by the time he wrote *Ulysses*. In this instance, a later decision by the DUTC to handle freight resulted in some livestock wagons, mainly from the Dublin & Blessington, being employed for cattle market traffic. However, no rails were ever laid on the North Circular Road east of Berkeley Road and cattle droving, from the markets down to the North Wall, continued to be a major nuisance well beyond the end of tramway operation.

Bloom's Wider Choices

Completing the range of trips available in the Dublin area on Bloomsday, outings could be planned on other tramways, all accessible by DUTC services. From Terenure, reached via either the Harold's

Cross or Rathmines lines, the Dublin & Blessington Steam Tramway operated throughout the day, certain services working through to Poulaphouca. Trams on the North Quays line from O'Connell Bridge connected with the Dublin & Lucan Electric Railway's services at Conyngham Road, while cars on the Dublin to Howth route enabled transfers to be made with the Hill of Howth Tramway at Sutton Cross or Howth Railway station.

Joyce, Fascinated by Vehicles?

Joyce seems to have been fascinated by trams and makes succinct references to them in other works. In *Dubliners*, for instance, published in 1914, Dame Street is described in *After the Races*, 'busy with unusual traffic, loud with the horns of motorists and the gongs of impatient tram-drivers.' These and the other sounds to be heard in our streets at different times - motor horns would have been conspicuously absent on Bloomsday - are again referred to in *Counterparts*, when Farrington's head was, 'full of the noises of tram-gongs and swishing trolleys…'

That hallmark of the Dublin tram, the moveable seat or piano-stool placed behind the motorman's door engaged Joyce's attention in *Clay*. En route to Nelson Pillar, Maria found that the tram was full and she had to sit on the little stool at the end of the car, 'facing all the people, with her toes barely touching the floor.' James Joyce's great interest in all the vehicles to be found on our streets may well have been stimulated by his stint as an early motoring correspondent and chronicler of the famous Gordon Bennett race of 1903.

Extensions: Dartry, Rialto and Lower Baggot Street

Two important extensions to the tramway system were made in 1905. On 27th January, a new line was opened southwards from Rathmines, leaving the Terenure tracks to run along Upper Rathmines Road. It turned left and then right at Highfield Road to carry on up Dartry Road, terminating opposite Orwell Park. Cars operating to here from Nelson Pillar were sometimes said to be going to Upper Rathmines, this had been the official destination on Palmerston Park horse cars. The destination boards displayed the words 'Nelson Pillar-Rathmines-Dartry' and the symbol was the Terenure red triangle with a vertical white stripe.

An attractively designed depot was erected at the terminus, having outside it an office with a large window opening on to the road. This was occupied by the inspector and timekeeper and is still known as the Ticket Office. From the Highfield Road junction, a connection was laid in to Palmerston Park enabling trams working between there and Nelson Pillar to reach Dartry depot where they were henceforth shedded. Transferring Palmerston Park trams from

their previous base at Clonskea depot saved a considerable amount of dead mileage. The DUTC also built several houses at Highfield Road for the men attached to Dartry depot.

An unchronicled disappearance some time after this was the former Dublin Central Tramways premises at Rathfarnham Road, Terenure. The label 'Tram Shed' for this three-track ex-Central Tramways building on the 1909 Ordnance Sheet contrasts with 'Tramway Depot' on the same map for the larger Dublin Tramways premises opposite St Joseph's Church on Terenure Road.

The second route extension of 1905 took place on 20th May when trams on the Dolphin's Barn line began running further westwards along South Circular Road. The new terminus was at Rialto, bringing the Glasnevin cars to a point just short of the bridge spanning the now-closed Grand Canal branch from James's Harbour.

On 14th May 1906 a new service was introduced between Phoenix Park and Donnybrook, running up Dawson Street rather than on by South Leinster Street and Merrion Square. On turning left at St Stephen's Green and passing the Shelbourne Hotel, the new route traversed existing rails to the corner of Upper Merrion Street, continuing along Lower Baggot Street over new tracks. It rejoined the existing Donnybrook line via Merrion Square at the corner of Fitzwilliam Street. This new service used the existing Donnybrook to Phoenix Park blue double diamond as its symbol, but with a horizontal white band. Another extension to the system, believed to have been made around the turn of the century, was a double line from Ballsbridge along the frontage of the Royal Dublin Society grounds in Anglesea Road to facilitate showtime traffic.

The Belfast Electrification

Dublin's trams cannot be considered in isolation from other happenings in the city, throughout Ireland or further afield. Tramway developments of great importance, which took place in Belfast in the early years of the century, yield critical comparisons and contrasts with Dublin and therefore merit close attention. Belfast had its first horse tram service in 1872, the same year as Dublin. The system was operated by the Belfast Street Tramways Company, which in 1878 changed the city's track gauge from the Irish standard 5ft 3in to the unusual local one of 4ft 9in, and had among its directors William Martin Murphy.

Electrification was considered from 1896 onwards and not immediately proceeded with, but an Act of 1904 authorised the Corporation to acquire and electrify the system. Accordingly, Belfast Corporation Tramways assumed responsibility on 1st January 1905 for some 33 route miles, including track from sources other than the Street Tramways Company. 170 horse trams and

two horse buses were also acquired. This system was almost identical in terms of mileage and rolling stock to the DUTC in 1896.

The Belfast electrification was put in hand instantly and carried out with remarkable speed, the first ceremonial trip by an electric car took place on 29th November 1905 and by 5th December the system was in full operation. Initially 170 new trams were bought, but as in Dublin a number of horse cars, in this case 50, were rebuilt as electrics. Because so many comparisons and contrasts between the two systems were to be made during the tramway era, subsequent Belfast developments will be referred to in later chapters.

Track Renewal and Improvements

Back in Dublin, the Dalkey route was easily the busiest on the DUTC system. While it had been largely relaid in preparation for its electrification in 1896, there were defects. The rails laid at that time were originally joined by fishplates, which proved troublesome. As a result, 12½ miles were electrically welded in 1904 at a cost of £8,000, so successfully that the same procedure was, eventually, applied to the rest of the DUTC system. A length of single track in Monkstown Road which should have been tackled by the Southern District Company had to be doubled by the DUTC.

The rails used on the Dalkey line proved to be insufficiently heavy for their purpose, especially when heavier eight-wheeled or bogie cars were introduced. Relaying was therefore undertaken around 1907, when rails on straight track were reckoned to have a lifespan of 20 years. It was anticipated that crossings, curves and stopping places would often require renewal in considerably less than half that time. Good track facilitated higher speeds and the DUTC was anxious to exploit all such possibilities.

The DUTC system after 1906 consisted of about 54 route miles, mostly double track, much of which was shared by two or more services. On the south side of the city particularly, was a route network which boasted many intricate junctions and connections. One of the most spectacular installations on a tramway system is a Grand Union. This is a double track layout at a cross-roads where trams approaching the junction from any of the four directions can go straight through or turn right or left. Dublin had two unusual offset examples, one at the junction of Morehampton Road, Waterloo Road, Leeson Street and Appian Way. The other offset installation was at the Appian Way, Ranelagh and Charleston Road junction.

There were several other junctions which, although less impressive, were nevertheless very busy and interesting. Combined with a generous distribution of crossovers these made the system extremely versatile and adaptable to short workings, unusual traffic demands or alternative routings. The benefits flowing from this example of fortuitous foresight were to be fully exploited a few years later in completely unexpected circumstances.

House building continued at a sedate pace in the affluent townships and southern suburbs, an advantage from the tram company's viewpoint being that much of it was on or adjacent to the tram routes, creating a higher density of traffic. Building development in the City of Dublin was rather slow in the period between 1900, when the city boundary was extended, and the First World War. The South Circular Road area around Dolphin's Barn and beyond was active, Inchicore and Kilmainham sluggish.

On the north side, while there was some building in the North Circular Road, Phibsboro, Glasnevin and Drumcondra areas, a problem was the huge tracts of land owned by religious orders which were unlikely to be developed for housing. Apart from the village at the end of Vernon Avenue and a few terraces, Clontarf still consisted of some high quality roads like St Lawrence's Road and Haddon Road. While incorporation of the area into the city did produce a drainage scheme leading in time to hinterland development, the coast road remained somewhat unattractive. This was largely due to the section between the stone arch railway bridge and the Bull Wall being still prone to periodic flooding.

The Howth Line
The Clontarf & Hill of Howth Tramroad, whose line ran from the DUTC terminus at Dollymount to Howth (East Pier) had, as described earlier, been the subject of complicated agreements with the DUTC in 1899 and 1902. Following more negotiations, the DUTC leased the Howth line from the Clontarf & Hill of Howth Company in January 1907 at, from 1908 onwards, an annual rental of £3,000. The Clontarf company's rudimentary depot at Blackbanks, a corrugated iron shed, became an outstation to Clontarf DUTC depot around this time and was used to house permanent way vehicles and materials and trams not in service.

From 1907, the Howth line operated as an integral part of the DUTC system, the trams carrying the DUTC crest. The large destination boards which originally adorned the upper dashes of the cars were replaced by advertising and they later acquired standard DUTC-style destination boxes. No symbol appears to have been allocated to the route, although the supplementary light code of two reds, graphically described in *Ulysses*, was carried.

Howth trams showed 'Dublin' rather than 'Nelson Pillar' on their scrolls, a feature also found in later years on some Dalkey line cars. Return tickets were available

between Sutton or Howth and Nelson Pillar as early as 1903 and limited stop cars serving only Dollymount, Vernon Avenue, St Lawrence's Road, Fairview and Amiens Street, also operated from 1903. Fast timings with limited stops were greatly facilitated by the steady riding of the bogie cars used on the Howth line. As we shall see later, express trams also became an even more prominent feature of the Dalkey line when eight-wheeled cars became established there too.

Corporation Workings
On page 13 the unpleasant sloblands at Fairview, where the park is today, were described. Also recorded were proposals by the then City Engineer, Parke Neville, to fill in the area with refuse. His idea of using the tramway system to carry this material to the site, which was years ahead of its time in 1873, again became a live issue after 1901. The primitive refuse collection and disposal methods used in the city around that period have also been outlined. Following the development of the electric tramway system and the 1900 boundary extension, which brought Fairview into the municipal area, the Corporation actively sought ways and means of improving matters and dealing with the sloblands.

The destructor plant at Stanley Street was enlarged and modernised. Invoking its powers to utilise the tramway system, the Corporation laid track from the North Quays line up Queen Street, Redcow Lane and North Brunswick Street into Stanley Street depot. Here an extensive layout incorporating sidings, pointwork and wagon turntables was installed. Several sidings and points were also laid in South Gloucester Street depot and connected to the existing tracks at the Pearse Street/Westland Row junction via Petersen's Lane, Townsend Street and Lombard Street East.

On collection by horse-drawn carts, refuse and street sweepings went to the depots at Stanley Street or South Gloucester Street. At Stanley Street, it went straight into the destructor, the clinker and ash being then loaded into tipping wagons bought specially for refuse disposal. There was a fleet of about 70 such vehicles, together with three electric locomotives. The refuse from South Gloucester Street, mainly a paving depot but to which some of the wagons were allocated, was ferried to Stanley Street for burning.

While the Corporation had rights to the use of the system and possessed its own locomotives and wagons, it could not provide traction current. Negotiations were therefore conducted with the DUTC, which supplied the necessary power. William Martin Murphy announced the agreement at the DUTC shareholders' meeting on 25th July 1905 when he hailed the new refuse dispos-

al arrangements as highly beneficial to the health of the citizens. He also pointed out that the DUTC was supplying the current at 1½d per unit, well below the rate charged to its customers by the Corporation.

Most of the Corporation work was carried out at night after normal tramway traffic had ceased, as was haulage of the incinerated material to Fairview. Here, specially constructed branches led into the sloblands with spurs, which could be altered to suit requirements. From 1907 to 1925 when the service ceased and new refuse collection arrangements were made, the triangular area between the Tolka, the road from Annesley Bridge to Clontarf Road and the railway was filled in to provide the base for the beautiful amenity which Dubliners enjoy today.

Parcels and Freight
Friction arose regularly about what the DUTC would allow passengers to carry free on the trams. The company operated an extensive and profitable parcels service, and obviously would not have been keen on freelances using the trams to deliver packages. Some enterprising individuals who spotted an opportunity here fell foul of the DUTC. As a result, from 1st October 1908 new regulations came into force setting out in detail what could be carried free and what would incur a charge.

Passengers were not allowed to carry with them, without paying, any parcel or package, only personal luggage not exceeding 28lbs in weight being excepted. The whole subject was aired at the company's general meeting on 2nd March 1909 when the Chairman said that the growth in parcel receipts was partly due to, 'payment for heavy parcels carried by passengers, a new and hitherto overlooked source of revenue which promises to yield a permanent addition of a thousand a year...'

Workmen's tools or materials, hawker's baskets, bundles of washing and messengers' packages, were not deemed personal luggage. Parcels of a bulky or inconvenient size or considered objectionable could not, under any circumstances, be allowed to accompany a passenger, but had to be sent by the company's Parcels Express system.

A charge of 2d per item would be made henceforth except for the personal luggage already mentioned and two other classes of specific items. These were packages of workmen's tools not exceeding 28lbs weight and not more than two feet in length and six inches wide. Returned empties, if accompanied by the passenger by whom they were originally carried when full and paid for on the outward journey, were likewise exempted. A concession was made for three small parcels carried by a messenger and tied together. These would be charged for as one item.

Season Tickets

Season tickets were introduced in 1911 on the longer lines to Dalkey and Howth, with validity periods of one, three, six or 12 months, as a direct response to railway competition. It is noteworthy that the places favoured by season ticket facilities, Dalkey, Kingstown, Sutton and Howth, all had railway stations capable of offering competition. On the Howth line, there were different rates for 'Gentlemen, Ladies and Ladies (Wives of Subscribers)'. Further reductions were offered for under-18 sons and daughters of subscribers, while school children were offered season tickets at a discount of 25% off ladies' rates.

Weekly tickets for travel between Howth and Nelson Pillar cost 4/-, Sutton to the Pillar was 3/-. A monthly season ticket for travel between Howth and Nelson Pillar cost 18/- for a man, 12/- for a woman and 9/- for a wife, the corresponding rates for Sutton were 14/6d, 9/8d and 7/3d. The yearly ticket for Howth was £7.10s for a man, £5 for a woman and £3.15s for a wife, the rates for Sutton were £5.12s.6d, £3.15.0d and £2.16s.3d.

The Dalkey line season ticket list as shown in the June 1912 timetable was less complicated, showing no womens' or wives' rates. The Dalkey rates were, one year £9.10s, six months £5.5s, three months £2.15s. The Kingstown fares for the same periods were, respectively, £8.10s, £4.15s and £2.10s. Members of one family buying more than two season tickets were allowed further discounts, three season tickets got ten per cent, four or more 15 per cent. The full distance fares on the Dalkey and Howth lines were 5d single, return tickets being available for 8d, Kingstown was 7d return. A 6d return was available to and from Sutton; return tickets costing less than 6d were not offered.

Major Events: A City of the Empire

Among all the incompatible streams and strata of society in pre-1916 Dublin, significant segments displayed their loyalty to the Crown. Up to 1914, Dublin was very much a city of the Empire, with daily displays of military splendour as groups of soldiers marched ceremonially between the many barracks in the city and their various duties at Dublin Castle, the Bank of Ireland, or other important establishments.

Throughout its existence, the DUTC, ever anxious to increase revenue, laid on special services in connection with major events. Up to the First World War, army displays and visits by naval squadrons occurred frequently, bringing out large crowds, which led to heavier traffic on the tramways. However, even these were outdone in numbers of spectators and travellers when reigning monarchs came to Dublin.

King Edward VII visited Dublin three times during his reign, in 1903, 1904 and 1907. The King's 1907 visit included a visit to the great Irish International Exhibition at Herbert Park, which was open from 4th May until 9th November. William Martin Murphy was the leading figure in organising this enormous and hugely successful event, which attracted two and three quarter million visitors in five months.

Commenting on the Exhibition traffic – described as unprecedented - at the DUTC general meeting on 4th February 1908, Murphy spoke of the abilities of tramways to convey passengers to and from the gates. In his opinion, they never failed to meet the heaviest demands. He said that he had observed methods of dealing with passengers travelling during rush hours by railways and tramways elsewhere under similar conditions, 'and I must say I never saw anything better done than the way in which the Exhibition traffic was handled.'

The Last Royal Visit – and a Tragic Accident

The last royal visit to Dublin by a reigning monarch was that of King George V in July 1911. It lasted for several days, drawing thousands of people to numerous ceremonies and special events. On Saturday, 8th July, the DUTC carried 340,000 passengers and operated 104 special cars. On Monday, 10th July, the *Irish Times* reported, 'Five hundred cars would not have met the demand for these specials and the Manager had to close the lists more than a week ago. Twenty-five specials were also used for facilitating the movements of the Police. The magnificent generating plant, to which some important additions have recently been made, and the cable system for distributing the electric current were proved to be capable of dealing with loads well in excess of any demands made on them.'

Sadly on the following day, 11th July, the *Irish Times* carried a harrowing report headed **YOUNG WOMAN BURNED TO DEATH – SHOCKING ACCIDENT ON A DUBLIN TRAM.** 'Elizabeth Johnson (28) of Drumcondra was on one of the trams plying between O'Connell Bridge and Parkgate Street to cater for the thousands who visited the Royal Review in Phoenix Park when her dress caught fire. In the ensuing terror and confusion, another unfortunate young woman fell from the tram and was injured. Meanwhile, despite the heroic efforts of several fellow-passengers and bystanders to smother the flames, Elizabeth Johnson sustained fatal burns. She was taken to hospital where, before her death a few hours later, she told her father 'there was a flash...'

The inquest was inconclusive, with conflicting stories and a theory about a cigarette causing the fire. DUTC officials gave evidence of testing the tram's trolley and its fittings which they found to be in good order but nobody could explain the flash that terrified several eyewitnesses. Many years later, Kathleen Levins, who lived opposite the Johnsons in Upper St Brigid's Road and knew the family well, recalled the accident clearly and was positive that a flash or spark from the overhead wire caused the death of this ill-starred young woman.

Fares Again: a Newspaper Investigation

As we have seen several times already, Dublin tram fares had always been a subject of controversy. In 1872 the Dublin Tramways Company was empowered by its Act to charge 1d a mile with a 3d minimum but this discouraged short distance passengers. The stage system was then brought in, the 1d fares introduced in 1884 proving a bonanza for the DUTC. In spite of that success, a clearly mercenary shareholder, one S N Robinson, told a shareholders' meeting in July 1888 that the fares were too cheap.

An official photograph of No 313, the first DUTC Balcony Bogie tram of 1906 and the prototype for the Dalkey Windjammers. Fitted with a saloon top in 1929, it was the only Balcony Bogie tram so treated, the company opting for the modern Luxury Saloons. No 313, visibly taller than the other Bogie Standards, was scrapped at Ballsbridge in 1944. Fayle collection, IRRS

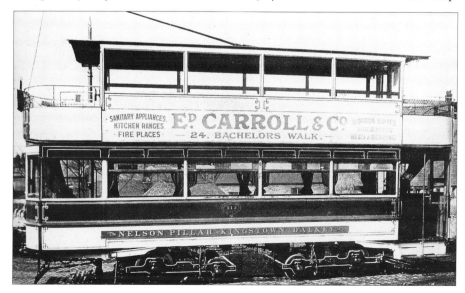

Water Lorry No 4, the building date of which is uncertain, was mounted on a Brill truck. In addition to its normal duties, it also served as a snowplough, as evidenced in this pre Second World War picture. This vehicle lasted to the end of the tramways in 1949 and was subsequently used as a static water tank at Mellifont Abbey in Co. Louth for many years. Fayle collection, Irish Railway Record Society

Charges were the subject of negotiation with the Corporation when the Clontarf line was being electrified and the DUTC was endeavouring to gain access to the city for electric trams. At that time, the principle was established that no fare from Nelson Pillar to the city boundary, typically a mile and a half, was to exceed 1d. As a result, fares to the outer termini on the shorter lines were 2d from Nelson Pillar, Rathfarnham and Dolly-mount were 3d. The DUTC always maintained that the fares were more generous than the statutory minimum.

The DUTC was frequently criticised over its fares, which were alleged to favour only the middle classes and highly invidious comparisons were made with charges elsewhere. A sustained campaign for lower fares, which ultimately petered out, was mounted by the *Evening Telegraph* in the autumn of 1912. The DUTC, having stated its position, simply allowed the crusade to continue until it ran out of steam.

In what was probably its most informative offering on the subject, the *Telegraph* of 7th September devoted a whole column to an article about fares. The first three headings read, **DUBLIN TRAMS, Compared With Other Cities Fares Seen at a Glance.** Simple line diagrams compared the relative distances allowed for specific fares in various cities, and the article is worthy of extensive quotation. 'We have prepared a number of diagrams which illustrate at a glance the difference between tram fares in Dublin and those in other cities. The diagrams are constructed to scale and are an exact representation of the proportionate lengths of the fares in the different places. The comparison is made between Dublin and one Irish city, Belfast, eight English and four Scottish cities and towns. The trams in four of the thirteen centres serve a larger population than the Dublin United Tramways Company, and the population served by the trams in the remaining nine centres is less than that served by the

Dublin trams. There are no halfpenny fares in Dublin and no children's half fares. It will be seen that in every case except Cardiff and Chester the halfpenny stage for children exceeds the penny stage in Dublin, the excess ranging from 33 per cent in Bradford to four times the Dublin distance in Belfast. That is, a child is carried one and one-third the distance in Bradford and four times the distance in Belfast that he is charged a penny for in Dublin. The ordinary penny stage exceeds those of Dublin by 50 per cent in Leeds, Glasgow, Belfast and Hull, and increase until in Dundee the ordinary penny stage is over one hundred per cent longer than in Dublin. The penny morning stages exceed those of Dublin by eighty-three and one-third per cent in Cardiff and by two hundred and thirty-three per cent in London.

HALFPENNY STAGES, 'The halfpenny stages, shown to scale in this diagram range from half a mile in Aberdeen, Halifax, Sheffield and Leeds to 1.15 miles in Glasgow.

DUBLIN	None
HALIFAX	_____
ABERDEEN	_____
SHEFFIELD	_____
LEEDS	_____
LONDON	_____
AYR	_____
GLASGOW	_____

PENNY FARES
Comparative lengths of the penny stages are illustrated in this diagram. They range from one and a half miles in Dublin, two and a quarter in Belfast, to 3.14 in Dundee.

DUBLIN	_____
LEEDS	_____
BELFAST	_____
GLASGOW	_____
HULL	_____
ABERDEEN	_____
LIVERPOOL	_____
LONDON	_____
DUNDEE	_____

CHILDREN'S HALFPENNY FARES
Children under fourteen years of age are carried for half-price in Belfast and in most English towns and cities. The following diagram shows at a glance the comparative lengths of the children's stages in a number of these towns, the population of which is equal to or less than that of Dublin. The stages vary from one and a half miles in Cardiff and Chester to 6 miles (Glengormley route) in Belfast.

DUBLIN	None
CHESTER	_____
CARDIFF	_____
BRADFORD	_____
LEEDS	_____
ABERDEEN	_____
SHEFFIELD	_____
HULL	_____
DUNDEE	_____
BELFAST	_____

PENNY MORNING STAGES
'In several cities there are penny morning stages up to 9am available for everyone, and especially intended for business men, city clerks, typists, artisans, etc. They vary in length from two and three quarter miles in Cardiff to 5 miles in London. The ordinary one and a half mile exists in Dublin. This diagram shows the comparative lengths of these morning penny stages:-

DUBLIN	_____
CARDIFF	_____
HULL	_____
HALIFAX	_____
LEEDS	_____
BRADFORD	_____
BELFAST	_____
ABERDEEN	_____
GLASGOW	_____
LONDON	_____

Dublin tram fares, controversial even as the tramways opened in 1872, continued to be a source of grievances on countless occasions in the years that followed. In 1912, the *Evening Telegraph's* criticism merely articulated a widely held view that DUTC fares were too high.

One fundamental and highly significant difference between Dublin and all the other cities quoted by the newspaper must be noted. With a partial exception in the case of London, every one of those other cities had a municipal tramway system. These were planned, built and operated to encourage urban development and provide a low-cost service for all the citizens. With gas and electricity, tramways were often one of the essential public utilities developed and owned by progressive local authorities. By contrast, Dublin Corporation controlled electricity only, gas and the tramways being the preserves of commercial companies whose principal objective was profit.

The 1914 Civic Exhibition
One of the last major events to take place in Dublin prior to the First World War was a Civic Exhibition held in the Linenhall Barracks (off Bolton Street) from 15th July to 31st August 1914. Although much smaller and more limited in scope than its 1907 Herbert Park predecessor, this was also an attractive and well-attended affair for which the DUTC laid on a special tram service. Passengers could travel from College Green via Dame Street, Parliament Street and Capel Street at a flat fare of 1d. Yet again the ease with which this exhibition could be serviced was demonstrated by the versatility of the system. Linenhall Barracks was also accessible from Nelson Pillar via Parnell Square, North Frederick Street and Upper Dorset Street.

As mentioned in the Introduction, it has been necessary to group various sequences of events into chapters to attempt thematic continuity. The result is that several parts of our story overlap, and the 1914 Exhibition chronologically belongs to a later chapter, its inclusion here probably appearing to be an anachronism. However, as our story unfolds, readers will appreciate that its somewhat premature appearance is because it was almost the last event of an old order already drastically changed for Dublin and about to disintegrate for the rest of the world.

Top Covers
The development of the Dublin tram up to the end of 1903 was examined in Chapter 2, see pages 50 - 54. The DUTC fleet of numbered passenger cars then totalled 293, and there were also the Clontarf & Hill of Howth Company's bogie cars numbered 301-312. Improvements were constantly being made to the rolling stock, particularly by vestibuling previously open-fronted vehicles. It is now opportune to look at the next stage in the evolution of the Dublin tramcar and the fleet renewal programme which began in 1910. Among the cars shown as being in the workshops on Bloomsday were Nos 49 and 252. No 49, a double-decker and former horse car, was being rebuilt as a single-decker to provide an extra tram for the Bath Avenue service. It was also vestibuled at this time, as was No 252, one of the three one-time horse cars which had become the first electric single-deckers in 1900.

While praising the great advance in urban travel represented by the electric tramcar, The *Irish Builder and Engineer* of 8th October 1904 asked if there was any place more dreary than the top of an electric car when the rain was beating down. Surprise was expressed at the tardiness of the DUTC in tackling the problem and unfavourable comparison was made with Manchester where top covers had been purchased for a hundred trams. The case was pressed home relentlessly, pointing out that there were, 'many people to whom the uncovered top of a tramcar is a death-trap in cold weather, but who would readily patronise it if some shelter from the chilling blast were afforded.'

The idea of covering upper decks had been around for some time. Even in Dublin there were double-deck trailers on the Dublin & Blessington with open-sided top covers and in 1903 a primitive roof was fitted to a Dublin & Lucan car. Despite an apparent lack of progress, the DUTC actually had the situation well in hand. At the half-yearly general meeting in July 1904 the Chairman mentioned that several forms of weather protection had been examined. As a result, top covers similar to those used in Liverpool and Leeds were being fitted to DUTC trams at Inchicore even as he spoke. These were Nos 29 and 44, easily the most important in the group listed as being out of service on Bloomsday. They reappeared in October, not only vestibuled but top-covered as well, the DUTC's first such cars.

In Britain, as in the Manchester instance quoted by the *Irish Builder and Engineer*, top covers were being offered commercially for fitting to existing open-top cars and over the next few years the numbers of roofed DUTC double-deckers would increase dramatically. As on subsequent DUTC top-covered cars, Nos 29 and 44 had sliding doors in their end bulkheads, which were directly over those of the lower deck. The roofs did not extend beyond the saloon, the end balconies being completely open.

Fifty-seven seaters, Nos 29 and 44 were allocated to Ballsbridge depot for the Dalkey service, always considered the Premier Line. During 1905 ten more cars, Nos 257-262, 286, 291-293, were fitted with DUTC manufactured top covers, of which at least the later ones established a feature to be found on DUTC roofed, or balcony cars, for many years. This was an extension of the roof to form a short canopy, about 18 inches long, over the balcony at each end of the upper deck.

Around this time some cars were fitted with DUTC trucks, a local development of the DuPont design. The company bought about 50 DuPonts and subsequently manufactured similar trucks, but with modifications based on the DUTC's operational experience. Sometimes referred to as Brierleys, their axle-box covers proclaimed the

DUTC as the makers. The frequent changing of trucks and equipment was too widespread and complicated to describe here, but is more fully set out in the Rolling Stock Catalogue (Section Eight, Table 8B).

The Preston Dalkey Bogie Cars
The DUTC's proclamation of self-sufficiency in rolling stock in February 1901 did not result in a complete ban on outside purchases. The capacity, riding qualities and speed of the Preston-built bogie cars 301-312 working the Howth line greatly impressed the company, which saw similar vehicles as an obvious choice for the Dalkey service. The result, in 1906, was the supply of nine large tram bodies to the DUTC by the Electric Railway and Tramway Carriage Works Ltd of Preston.

Always known as Preston cars, these vehicles were mounted on Peckham maximum traction bogies. Like the earlier Howth cars, they were distinguished by having six windows per side in contrast to the four found on Inchicore built stablemates. Their top covers were built at Inchicore, the seating capacity was quoted as 73, 31 inside, 42 outside. Parcel racks were fitted inside.

Seven of these trams were numbered 294-300, filling the gap between the highest-numbered four-wheeler and the Clontarf & Hill of Howth open-toppers 301-312. The other two received the fleet numbers 316 and 317. No 294, the first of the batch, left the works on 31st July 1906, the last to enter service, No 317, emerging in April 1907. These were the last passenger trams supplied by an outside builder to the DUTC.

The First Inchicore-Built Bogie Cars
Although numerically higher, the DUTC's first indigenous bogie tram left Spa Road six weeks before Preston car No 294. This historic prototype, No 313, from which would evolve all DUTC eight-wheeled cars built during the next quarter century, was outshopped on 13th June 1906. It was the first of 15 similar vehicles, Nos 313-315, 318-323 and 325-330, turned out over the succeeding two years for the Dalkey line.

An enlargement of the DUTC's four-wheelers, but in some respects redolent of London and Blackpool cars, it had four windows between the bulkheads and a top cover with short canopies over the end balconies. Excluding the movable stool, No 313 was a 73-seater, its lower deck longitudinal seating capacity of 30 divided by armrests into three five-passenger sections on each side. Most of the later DUTC bogie trams with longitudinal seating were fitted out similarly.

Development by the London County Council of the largest tramway system in these islands was in progress at that time. This necessitated building great numbers of cars with a standard specification for bogie

Dublin's first top-covered tram was No 29, built by Milnes in 1897. It entered Spa Road works in April 1904, reappearing in October, vestibuled and top-covered. No 44 was similarly treated and in 1905, the DUTC placed top covers on ten more trams with the roof extended about 18 inches over the balconies. In this photograph, No 29 displays the Dalkey route symbol, a shamrock, though this tram was later transferred to the Donnybrook line. It was replaced by a new top-covered car in 1924 which was rebuilt as a Standard Saloon four years later. *Tramway and Railway World*

design, which could be turned out by selected manufacturers. The technically advanced and forward-looking DUTC appreciated the advantages of what was known as the LCC class 4 maximum traction bogie and made it virtually standard for its future needs. Bogies of this type were supplied to the DUTC by Mountain and Gibson of Bury, Lancashire. Following M & G's demise the company had similar but sturdier trucks, a DUTC derivative of the LCC Class 4, made by Hurst, Nelson of Motherwell in Scotland.

The cost of No 313 including wages was: body £290; top cover £80, bogies £118, electrical equipment £227, a total of £715. Eight more trams, Nos 314-5 and 318-323, were turned out during the following year. All of these vehicles, suspiciously claimed in 1907 to be using ½d worth of current per mile, were allocated to the Dalkey line, on which bogie cars were eventually to work the entire basic timetable. The DUTC bogie cars are listed in Section Two of the Rolling Stock catalogue.

Combining the company's own ideas with design features from other sources and the essentially 'Dublin look', these trams epitomised excellence. Addressing the DUTC shareholders on 30th July 1907, William Martin Murphy said, 'These fine cars are well adapted for the traffic on the Dalkey line and we are satisfied that the pleasure of travelling in them has brought us an accession of passengers for that reason alone.'

Always finely attuned to every nuance of the tramway scene, Murphy was clearly acknowledging, at a very early date, the existence of transport tourists and their contribution to revenue. Kingstown, ever jealous of its reputation as the 'Premier Township', now had the best trams, the Dalkey line revelling in its Premier Line status.

Bridge Restrictions
For many years, the type of tram to be used on various Dublin services was determined by clearances under railway bridges. Every one of these structures presented a serious obstacle to the early top-covered cars. The Dalkey line was free of overbridges, as were both of the Donnybrook to Phoenix Park alternatives via Dawson Street and Merrion Square. The Terenure and Dartry services through Rathmines encountered no overbridges, nor did the Rathfarnham route via Harold's Cross. The line from Rialto to Glasnevin had no overbridges, nor did that along the North Quays.

Other routes were not as fortunate. Apart from the infamous Bath Avenue railway bridge, which dictated the use of single-deckers on that line, there were several other difficult locations. The direct route to Sandymount, via Ringsend, encountered a railway bridge carrying the Loop Line over Great Brunswick (Pearse) Street. Nearby, the Loop Line bridge at Westland Row posed problems for the service between

Kingsbridge and Hatch Street and for cars connecting Westland Row with Inchicore.

Two bridges on the Harcourt Street to Bray railway line, at Ranelagh Road and Charleston Road, precluded the use of top-covered cars on the Palmerston Park line. The Charleston Road bridge also affected the Cross Tram service operating from Kenilworth Road to Lansdowne Road. On the north side of the city, the Ballybough and Drumcondra routes both passed under railway bridges.

As far as clearances were concerned, the most difficult route was on the north side, with seven bridges between the city centre and Howth. Immediately on leaving Abbey Street, trams heading for the Howth line encountered bridges at Beresford Place and Lower Gardiner Street. Like the regular scheduled cars coming from Nelson Pillar via North Earl Street, they next went under the Talbot Street Bridge, followed by the one at Amiens Street and another at North Strand Road. Next came the Great Northern Railway's stone arch bridge at Clontarf Road, the seventh and last bridge at Howth station being the one carrying Hill of Howth cars over the Dublin to Howth tramway.

Although overhead wires were ideally set 22 feet above street level, they came much lower passing under bridges and in some instances were offset to improve clearance. Before open-top cars passed under railway bridges, their conductors were instructed to request that upper-deck passengers remain seated.

While not affected by overbridges, the introduction of bogie cars on the Dalkey line necessitated a small but crucial alteration at the entrance to Dalkey depot. The gateway, which was still in position in 2000, was very narrow. It barely allowed enough clearance for the larger four-wheelers at either side of the entrance, where the outside corner of these vehicles came close to the pillars. To accommodate the swept inter-bogie overhang of eight-wheelers traversing the insides of curves, the brickwork of the left-hand gate pier had to be chamfered. The resulting angle provided just sufficient leeway for these trams as they negotiated the gateway.

Fleet Reaches Maximum Number

The great exhibition of the arts, commerce and industry, already referred to on page 73, took place on the site of the present Herbert Park at Ballsbridge from May to November 1907. For this major event, the DUTC built a special open-top bogie 76-seater, No 324. The lower deck was exactly the same as that of the top-covered cars and set the standard to which all the Howth vehicles would eventually conform. The upper deck panelling, railings and seating were similar to that of the ubiquitous four-wheelers. This splendid tram demonstrated the company's wish to provide cars of similar quality to the Dalkey ones throughout the system, but taking into account the restrictions imposed by bridges. Originally mounted on M & G bogies but later on Brill 22Es, No 324 had an interesting career and will reappear later in the book.

No 324 was followed by six more balcony cars, the entry into service on 1st October 1908 of the last one, No 330, being a significant milestone in the history of the Dublin tram. 330 was the highest fleet number ever carried by a Dublin tram and from now on every new tram would take the identity of the one it replaced. On completion of No 330 the DUTC, which four years previously had only open-top vehicles, possessed 36 top-covered trams, 24 of them being eight-wheelers.

The DUTC is said to have estimated the number of trams ultimately required to provide a full service to be around 290, with a ten per cent float to cover overhauls and new construction. This would bring the total to 319, to which must be added the 12 Howth cars and explains the highest fleet number being 330. In practice, the maximum requirement was probably nearer to 260 cars and when old trams were withdrawn, their fleet numbers frequently remained vacant for long periods, sometimes several years. Conversely, there are a few instances of the old and new co-existing for a short period.

Improving the Fleet

A problem with the four-wheeled tram was its very short wheelbase - in Dublin 5ft 6in or 6ft 0in - in proportion to the overall length of the car, usually about 28-29 feet.

The majestic lines of a Dalkey Windjammer, No 328, dating from 1908, are shown to great effect in this *Evening Herald* picture taken at Blackrock in January 1942. This was the last of the short-canopied bogie balcony cars, AE's 'high-built glittering galleons of the streets'. Following representations from Dalkey line passengers, the DUTC reprieved this tram and offered it to the National Museum.
Transport Museum Society of Ireland collection

The longest wheelbase of any Dublin four-wheeled tram up to 1931 was 6ft 6in. As a result, these vehicles pitched and swayed at speed. Longer wheelbase trucks improved matters on straight track but encountered difficulties on curves. Several possible solutions to the problem were tried on various tramway systems.

Bogies were an attractive alternative to single trucks but costlier to purchase and maintain and were seldom fitted to cars less than 30 feet long. The DUTC did, however, experiment with bogies on the shorter vehicles. In 1907 car No 262, one of the earliest balcony four-wheelers, had Brill bogies fitted but these were removed very quickly. In 1909 open-top car No 18 ran briefly on Brill bogies. The famous No 324, which we have already encountered, later acquired similar running gear. It is probable that the same pair of Brill 22E bogies was used under all three of the trams just mentioned.

A compromise between the single truck and bogies was widely sought, a truck which would allow for a degree of articulation. One solution, apparently promising the advantages so eagerly desired, was the Barber six-wheeled patent radial truck. In November 1911 No 286 was taken into the shops and, according to the repair books, surrendered its Peckham truck and equipment to car 293, and was made ready to receive a radial truck. This had a total wheelbase of 11ft, promising obvious advantages in terms of ratio to overall length. Thus fitted, No 286 duly operated on the Donnybrook line for some weeks early in 1912, but the results do not appear to have been satisfactory and the car reverted to four-wheeled running gear.

Trucks and electrical equipment were

changed frequently, tram No 18 being a good example of how complicated things could become. This 1896 vehicle had its original Peckham truck exchanged for a Brierley in 1905, but two years later it received a Brill, which in turn was transferred to an engineering vehicle, sand car No 11, in 1909. The Brill bogies already referred to were then fitted to No 18 but these also went to the sand car, following which No 18 was put on to a Peckham truck from car 117. This was finally replaced by new running gear of the same make in 1914.

Although No 18 was an extreme case, it illustrates the difficulties of trying to record fully the career of a DUTC tram. Furthermore, there is evidence that not all modifications were written up. A better documented change around this time was the provision of a fifth single-decker to join Nos 49, 252, 253, 254, on the Bath Avenue line. This was No 234, a former horse car electrified in 1900 which began work as a single-decker on 29th January 1909.

Vestibuling of formerly open-fronted cars continued for many years, great attention being paid to their structural condition. Seventy of the four-wheeled trams existing at the end of 1903 were built with vestibules. Of the remaining 223, 34 had been vestibuled by 1910, and some of these had been modified as early as 1902. About 12 more trams were dealt with between 1910 and 1914 and 15 were replaced by new vestibuled cars. Apart from protecting the crew and improving its appearance, this increased a tram's seating capacity by four.

Analysing the Rolling Stock

The DUTC's stock of trucks and bogies has always been a problem for tramway

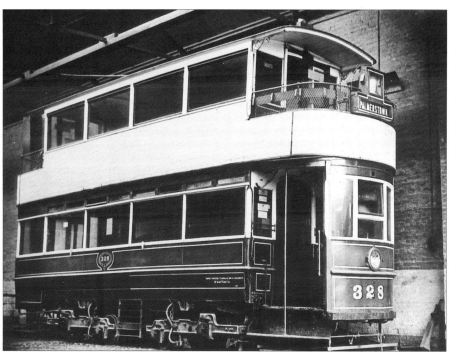

observers and historians. Much effort has been expended and frustration suffered in trying to reconcile available lists with what was known to be in use at various times, but there are always discrepancies. Fully verifiable assembly of all the details will prove more difficult as time goes on and it is, unfortunately, now unlikely that a complete and definitive list can ever be produced. However, in July 1910 *Tramway and Railway World* published a summary of what it believed was the composition of the DUTC stock of running gear:

Trucks	Bogies
225 Peckham Cantilever	13 pairs Mountain & Gibson
50 DuPont	8 pairs Peckham
16 DUTC (Brierley)	6 pairs Hurst Nelson
2 Brill 21E	(on order)

Motors were quoted as GE52 (77 pairs), GE58 (168 pairs), GE60 (2 pairs) and GE80 (34 pairs with six more on order) and Westinghouse 220 (13 pairs). There were also some GE800 motors. Controllers were mainly of British Thomson-Houston B18 type, but there were 23 pairs of B13s and some General Electric K2s on the oldest cars.

A reduction in maintenance costs reported to the shareholders in July 1909 concerned wheels. Chilled iron wheels had been universal on first generation trams, but were now being replaced by steel wheels which had been adopted as standard. While initially costlier than iron wheels, the steel replacements had proved far more durable.

The number of trucks lines up exactly with the number of four-wheeled cars (293) in service at the beginning of 1910, but omits service vehicles and the Directors' car. The list is clearly incomplete: including the Howth cars, there were, early in 1910, 37 bogie trams, but only 27 pairs of bogies are accounted for. However, a quick check shows how some of the discrepancies may have arisen. It is possible to make a grand total of 53 DuPont trucks, but the closely related DUTC type, believed to have been constructed at Ballsbridge, complicates matters further. It should also be pointed out that in 1910-12 a replacement programme, detailed below, was carried out involving 15 trams. The six pairs of Hurst Nelson bogies on order could be for either the 1910 or 1911 deliveries of new vehicles.

Anyone who has ever worked on assembling statistics for a report, often working to a deadline, will appreciate how easy it is for inaccuracies to creep into such a compilation. Figures produced for accountancy and engineering purposes can differ considerably and because of the widespread practices of ringing fleet numbers and rebuilding various components within the DUTC, it is unlikely at this remove in time that absolutely accurate conclusions can be reached in this or similar situations.

Bogie Cars and Express Services

Between 1908 and 1912, 15 first generation trams, all except two being former horse cars, were withdrawn. By then, it had been decided to operate the basic timetable of the Dalkey line exclusively with bogie cars. There were already 24 balcony bogie trams, plus the 12 four-wheelers previously mentioned. The ever increasing traffic on the Premier Line called for several more large capacity vehicles. Fifteen more top-covered bogie cars were therefore built.

The new deliveries were spread over three years. Six (Nos 79, 81, 83, 85, 183 and 231) came in 1910, a further six (Nos 64, 70, 71, 113, 117 and 220) in 1911 and three (Nos 3, 91 and 185) in 1912. These trams were all fitted with magnetic track brakes. The first two, Nos 79 and 81, were built with short canopies, but the other 13, and all later balcony cars had full length roofs.

The original ten top-covered four-wheelers were allocated to the Dalkey, Donnybrook and Terenure lines. As new bogie cars progressively took over most of the Dalkey workings, the four-wheelers were reassigned to the other two routes.

Experience with successful express or limited stop services on the Howth line from 1903 (see page 72), obviously presaged similar arrangements for the Dalkey line as soon as conditions would permit. Reconstruction of the Dalkey line and entry into service of the new cars enabled the company to introduce 'Express' trams. Morning and evening, several limited stop runs were undertaken, passengers paying a minimum fare of 3d.

Strategically sited loops and crossovers at Ballsbridge and Booterstown Avenue enabled ordinary service cars to clear the line for the expresses, which ran four and a half miles non-stop between Merrion Street and Blackrock. The trackwork at Ballsbridge had been laid in 1907 to accommodate exhibition traffic. A large red board on a side panel beside the platform left nobody in any doubt as to the character of a 'Special Car', and the normal Dalkey line symbol, a green shamrock, was embellished with a large red 'S'. For a long period the regular performers on this outstanding duty were Nos 79, 85 and 183.

While not as famous as their Dalkey counterparts, the express, or 'Limited Stop' Howth cars had their own special characteristics. These trams would 'not carry passengers inside who are travelling less than a 3d section. Local passengers paying not less than a 2d fare will be carried on the outside of these cars provided there is room.' Howth expresses overtook Dollymount cars at Fairview, crossovers enabling stopping cars to clear the line. A Howth resident, writing in the *Evening Mail* in August 1954, recalled that while two cars were normally passed at Fairview, a third one was usually overtaken before reaching Dollymount ter-

minus. This passenger also stated that 50 minutes was the time allowed for regular services on the Howth line, with 40 for the expresses, but that the latter usually ran the nine miles in 35 minutes.

Because of all the Howth cars being open-top, and the very exposed nature of the line between Fairview and Sutton, windswept journeys could frequently be expected by upper-deck passengers. As an experiment, the DUTC therefore fitted glass windscreens and side shields to car No 307, which left the works thus equipped in May 1913 and operated in this form for three years. The upper deck seating is said to have been altered to a perimeter arrangement for the duration of the glass screening, but this is not recorded in the repair books.

The Windjammers

To Dublin tramwaymen, the Dalkey balcony cars quickly became known, for several reasons, as 'Windjammers'. A feature of these trams was a canvas sheet on each platform which could be unrolled and fastened to close off the stairwell, thus protecting the motorman from the elements. The similarity to a flapping sail probably inspired the nickname, the nautical likeness being further emphasised by the trolley rope, sometimes called the rigging, plus the ship-like swaying of a Dalkey eight-wheeler at speed. A slight creaking from the tram's timber joints contributed yet another element to the sensation of being on board a ship.

There was also the opening mechanism for the upper deck windows, all four of which on each side were wound up or down simultaneously by a wheel on the balcony bulkhead, somewhat like a ship's wheel. The sight of a tramcar ablaze with light swinging through the dimly lit streets of the period would have been likened to that of the luxury liners that so caught the public imagination around that time. Such allegories were not lost on the poet George Russell (AE), in the section of whose book *Poems 1903-1930* devoted to 'The City' the following lines appear;

'Mine eyes beget new majesties: my spirit greets
The trams, the high-built glittering galleons of the streets
That float through twilight rivers from galaxies of light.
Nay, in the fount of Days they rise, they take their flight,
And wend to the great deep, the Holy Sepulchre'

Freight Traffic

For about 15 years from 1909, freight traffic of various kinds was a significant feature of the DUTC's operations. The company already had a lucrative parcels service and had used locomotives and wagons to carry its own materials since the early days of electric traction. The concept of commercial freight services appears to have been enunciated for the first time at the shareholders' meeting of 2nd March 1909. William Martin Murphy referred to 'a new item of revenue', saying that a Mr Nash had found a supply of sand on his property at Howth and opened up a trade for its disposal in the city. He believed the tramway system could handle this and also build up a large trade in carrying coal, which became another major component of the DUTC's freight traffic.

Coal was carried in quantity. One well-known firm of coal merchants, Heiton's, had tracks laid into their yards at Ringsend. Here coal was unloaded from cross channel colliers into tramway wagons for haulage to the Heiton yard at Kingstown and other destinations. DUTC traffic also included stone, building materials, hardware and sundries. Livestock was transported to the Dublin cattle market, situated on the North Circular Road between Prussia Street and Aughrim Street. Some of the cattle wagons came from Dalkey, others from the Dublin & Blessington Steam Tramway.

In addition to the sand from Howth, quarry material from the various pits along the Blessington line was handled. A Drumcondra resident recalled a load of gravel being deposited from a tramway wagon at the junction of Clonliffe Road in the twenties, very early in the morning; the gravel was then barrowed down the road to a house in course of being extended. Another type of traffic from the Blessington line was farm and dairy produce, especially milk, which came in creamery cans or churns and was transferred to DUTC passenger cars at Terenure for delivery to shops in distant suburbs.

All these goods operations reached their peak before increasing traffic congestion and the availability of vastly improved motor lorries from 1918 onwards rendered them less acceptable and uneconomical. While they were operational, they required the use of much interesting rolling stock, which became inextricably mixed up with the engineering or departmental vehicles of the DUTC. Both appear later in this chapter and in the Rolling Stock Catalogue.

Engineering and Goods Trams

From the early days of tramways, there were to be found on every system non-passenger vehicles used for a great variety of duties. Some were purpose-built, others converted from withdrawn trams eking out a twilight existence before going to the scrapyard. Several tramway systems had sizeable fleets of such vehicles, but on the Dublin tramways they proliferated, bequeathing multifarious puzzles to the vehicle historian.

The DUTC's back-up fleet, numbered separately from the passenger stock, began with three open water cars, Nos 1-3. Bought at the dawn of the electric epoch, these were simply motorised tramway trucks with a driving platform at each end and a large square tank in the middle on which the trolley standard was mounted. They were later joined

by another, more sophisticated, vehicle, No 4, which was on a Brill truck and had an overall roof covering the large cylindrical tank. An eel was reputed to have lived in the tank of this car for several years.

One of the obstacles to satisfactory cataloguing of DUTC non-passenger stock is the duplication of fleet numbers. Here No 4 is a good example; a second vehicle bearing this number was a motorised tower wagon, which probably operated on the Howth line. By the time the Dalkey line was being relaid around 1907, No 5 was in use. This appears in several photographs and seems to have combined the functions of locomotive, mobile office and canteen.

Because minimal details are extant, purpose-built DUTC works cars are a particularly dangerous subject on which to pontificate. Even more recondite are the withdrawn passenger trams, which continued to exist in support roles. In some instances, their very existence is revealed only by references to truck or equipment transfers with passenger cars. The whole subject is rendered even murkier by a seemingly capricious fleet numbering system. Conventional works car numbers originally began at 1 and appear to have continued in a reasonably logical sequence as far as No 12. By then, the inauguration of the freight service created a requirement for more non-passenger stock. This coincided roughly with the first fleet replacements.

Withdrawn passenger trams relegated to engineering or freight duties, but retaining their original fleet numbers complicated matters considerably. With the growth of traffic and the relative independence of some departments, it is easy to see how vehicle stocks, and numbering, could get out of hand. Those responsible for the permanent way, overhead maintenance, stores, breakdowns and freight could all justify claims for rolling stock, some of which had to be adapted for specific duties.

Apart from the essential support vehicles acquired in the early days of the electric system, the first converted passenger cars appeared, predictably, shortly after the new bogie trams for the Dalkey line brought the fleet up to its maximum numerical strength of 330 in 1908. Several of the 15 trams replaced by new bogie vehicles in the period 1910-1912 underwent complicated truck and equipment exchanges about the time of their withdrawal. Most of them are shown in the records as 'lying' or 'shedded' at various depots, suggesting that they provided at least parts for future departmental vehicles. It was standard practice to fit the vestibules, platform structures and anything else salvageable from old passenger trams to works vehicles. Charles Ross recalled the proficiency of the DUTC engineering staff in this art, plus their ability to successfully 'ring' numbers on the vehicles concerned.

Both the DUTC and the Dublin & Blessington Steam Tramway Company also maintained fleets of goods wagons. So great was the exchange of freight between the DUTC and Blessington systems that the Blessington company's yard at Terenure was wired up at an unknown date. An electric locomotive of unknown provenance and doubtful ownership but which was certainly on a DUTC truck, shunted in this yard.

Recycling Old Trams

Mechanical engineering people in transport have long been renowned for their ingenuity in adapting superannuated passenger vehicles to other uses. As will be obvious from what has already been stated, this practice was raised almost to an art form in the DUTC. It was very easy for engineers and others to argue convincingly for the retention of vehicles, which would otherwise have been scrapped. When the freight service began, the requirement for locomotives and freight wagons made things even easier and provided the necessary cover for some quite unorthodox re-incarnations. Sometimes these were renumbered into the service fleet, but they often retained their original numbers. They were frequently replaced surreptitiously at a later date by a suitably renumbered, more recent withdrawal. Charles Ross averred that there were more ringers than originals among the works cars.

Self-propelled goods wagons with a motorman's cab at each end were a common sight on the Dublin tramways. Above the wagon body, a gantry supported by the cab roofs carried the trolley. These adaptable vehicles, of which there were several, could work as solo wagons or locomotives. Also used to tow disabled passenger trams, they have properly been described as the bridge between commercial and departmental works cars. Fortuitously, the beginning of the company's freight operation coincided with the withdrawal of the 15 trams replaced by the new Dalkey Windjammers around 1910. Thus, a varied fleet of relatively cheap locomotives was available.

While the opportunities presented on withdrawal of the 15 four-wheeled trams replaced by the 1910-1912 balcony cars were quickly exploited, they went hand in hand with a policy of recovering all serviceable items for further use. The bodies of two of these trams were transferred to other trucks, renumbered, and saw service for several more years, the trucks and electrical equipment from at least three more being retained for future use. A further trio, Nos 64, 113 and 231, became, respectively, a snowplough, a breakdown wagon and a haulage wagon, the latter being renumbered 20. Verifiable details of all the DUTC engineering and freight vehicles are set out in the Rolling Stock Catalogue.

As we have already seen, a large stock of four-wheeled wagons was maintained by the DUTC. These were of various types and numbered in a series of their own, the highest number appears to have been in the late sixties. While most were purpose-built, there was at least one, which consisted of the lower deck floor and motorless truck of a former passenger vehicle. This was probably the ultimate in salvaging the last remnants of a once-proud tramcar.

From the earliest times the company employed horse-drawn road vehicles. They owned a variety of such items and in the first years of the electric trams even some specialist appliances were horse-drawn, such as tower wagons and sanding machines. By 1911 the company had purchased their first motor tower wagon, a chain-driven, open-cabbed Commer. Further motor vehicles were bought as time passed and these, too, will be referred to again; a list appears in Section Ten of the Rolling Stock Catalogue.

Depots and Storage Capacity

On coming into existence in 1880, the DUTC took over nine horse-tram depots. The Dublin Tramways Company handed over five, at Terenure, Sandymount, Donnybrook, Kingsbridge and Clontarf. Cabra and Inchicore were former North Dublin Street Tramways premises, while Clonskea and Rathfarnham Road (subsequently closed) originally belonged to the Dublin Central Tramways. In 1896 three more depots, at Ballsbridge, Blackrock and Dalkey came from the Southern District Company. Finally, Blackbanks, subsequently used only for storage or maintenance vehicles, was taken over from the Clontarf & Hill of Howth Tramroad.

From the beginning of the horse tramway era, it was normal for all the rolling stock to be housed at night or while out of service. This practice continued after electrification. The maximum number of horse cars, 188, was soon surpassed, the electric fleet growing to 330 by 1908. The electric cars were also longer than their predecessors, bogie cars by nearly 30%, thus creating difficulties. Various procedures were adopted to deal with the situation. Several horse depots were updated and improved to accommodate electric trams. In some places, as at Sandymount, a new depot for the electric cars was built beside the existing one. At Clontarf, the electric depot erected in 1897 covered some ground previously occupied by stabling for the horses. A new running shed was built beside the car works at Spa Road for the Inchicore line. A completely new depot was opened at Dartry in 1905, while over the next four years Donnybrook was extended and land was purchased for the extension of Cabra. To accommodate the new bogie trams, a 30-car depot was built at Blackrock beside the former horse

era shed which was inadequate to cater for large electric cars.

DUTC practice contrasts with that in other cities, especially those with municipally owned tramway systems, where very large depots were favoured. Belfast, for example, had only seven depots (including the Sandy Row works) for a fleet about the same size as that of the DUTC. The comprehensive article about the Dublin tramways published in the *Tramway and Railway World* for May 1910 contains a table setting out the capacities of the various depots:

Depot	Cars	Depot	Cars
Terenure	48	Clontarf	26
Rathfarnham Rd	7	Dalymount	62
Clonskea	23	Kingsbridge	24
Donnybrook	24	Inchicore	20
Ballsbridge	40	Dartry Road	27
Blackrock	36	Sandymount	18
Dalkey	12		

Rathfarnham Road, the former Central Tramways Company depot referred to in Chapter One and stated in the notes accompanying the table to be out of use, can be discounted. This gives a total capacity for 367 cars, 37 more than the number in the passenger fleet. There would, however, also have been the engineering and support vehicles.

The large allocation at Dalymount, usually known as Cabra although it was located at Phibsboro, is significant. Apart from Clontarf, this was the only depot on the north side and provided vehicles for the Phoenix Park, Glasnevin, Drumcondra and Whitehall services. Not mentioned is the Clontarf & Hill of Howth depot at Blackbanks, a simple two-road structure not used as a running shed but as a store for permanent way equipment and cars not in use.

Harsh Lives

The conditions of employment for tramway staff were, as we have seen, a source of resentment from the earliest days of the DUTC. There had been a strike in the Dublin Tramways Company as early as 1873. To settle this and subsequent disputes, minor concessions were made from time to time, usually on an ad hoc basis. But conditions of employment and discipline remained obstinately harsh. Every Rule Book was based on a standard model that hardly changed over the years. Tramwaymen, who had been the subject of more than one abortive attempt to organise since 1890, were among the weakest of all workers in terms of industrial muscle. A lack of alternative employment encouraged the DUTC in its efforts at getting the most out of the men while giving the minimum in return.

In August 1898, a letter signed 'Fair Play' appeared in the *Evening Herald*; 'Sir, – Allow me through the columns of your influential paper to

bring before the public at large a grievance at present in existence among the drivers and conductors of the Donnybrook line, whereby they were hardshipped by a change in the running of the cars on the above-mentioned line. Some months ago the drivers had, I learn from a reliable source, 32 minutes to go into Nelson's Pillar and start back, and also to pay in at the office the proceeds of the journey which they were after completing. Now the authorities have put on two extra journeys, making the amount 12 instead of ten; and in order to complete the 12 journeys they have reduced the time to 28 minutes to perform the half journey, which leaves the men no time to take their meals, unless they take them on the car.

'I was very much surprised a few days ago to see the conductors and drivers taking their tea on the back of the car, having no other way of taking it. I fear the men's constitutions will ere long give way if this scandalous system is continued, and I am told if they get sick they won't be believed. The men should put their heads together and form another union, and see if they cannot get fair play. It is a scandal to see such a willing and obliging lot of men treated in such a manner – men who, if they were only treated half well enough, would not grumble. I am surprised at the company for putting on such long hours on their men. If they were a company who would give their men a holiday to encourage them, or let them attend some of these demonstrations; but the poor tram-men never get a day, not even a Sunday, and the majority of them have on that day to do without a particle of food the whole day long. I hope and trust this will come before the eyes of all the travelling public, in order that it may give them an idea of how the poor men who work the system are treated'

In the early years of the last century, governed by the class system described earlier in this chapter, most workers continued to endure these draconian lifestyles. Lack of security, low wages, hopelessly inadequate health and welfare provisions were but some of the factors dominating too many peoples' less than frugal existences. Added to this was the sheer physical hardship, dramatically illustrated by W A Agnew's concept of the ideal motorman standing on the front of an unvestibuled tramcar in the worst of weather (see page 61).

Balanced against this were the very moderate expectations of most workers at that time. Their aspirations included a regular living wage, a roof over their heads and the health and happiness of their families. An intrinsic part of their ethos was loyalty, both to their employers and to one another. This fidelity was accompanied by the camaraderie in adversity so strikingly illustrated in James Plunkett's *Strumpet City*. Another characteristic of a worker's loyalty was respect for authority, accepted as a natural right by employers who failed to reciprocate similarly, or to respond positively, to ever clearer danger signals. A further quality employers generally, and the DUTC in particular, failed to appreciate was the congenital sense of public service displayed by so many transport people.

This photograph was used on the cover of an advertising brochure for the Tierney-Malone automatic point (see page 70). It shows No 330, numerically the highest numbered tram in the DUTC fleet, in Nassau Street with the railings of Trinity College as a backdrop. This tram, built in 1908, was replaced by a Bogie Luxury Saloon in 1934. Author's collection

Following the example of Sir George Owens in the 1890s, several distinguished citizens and DUTC shareholders regularly took up the men's case in the next decade. Michael Davitt was one, another was William Leahy TC, who spoke frequently at DUTC general meetings. When Councillor Leahy pleaded for the men on 28th July 1902, he was challenged by an irate shareholder demanding to know, 'is this gentleman really a shareholder at all?' Always sensitive to criticism, the DUTC was particularly disconcerted around that time by a newspaper letter from Davitt and charges that C W Gordon had threatened the staff.

The men's plight was well recognised in 1913 by Archbishop Walsh who said that the discipline was too severe for an independent concern, being military in character. He also regretted that promotion depended on favour and the plasticity of employees rather than efficiency and seniority. But while most were glad to have employment in those first years of the century, working people were becoming more aware of both their rights and their capacity to exercise them. For the time being, however, they accepted the social scenario already described, but this compliance would soon be diluted in the fight for better pay, working conditions and personal dignity.

Larkin Versus the Employers
There were further attempts, as in 1903, to unionise the tramwaymen, but they remained one of the industrial groups who had made least progress in obtaining a fair deal. It was stated that the Dublin tramwaymen worked longer hours than their counterparts in any part of the United Kingdom and that their attempts to meet the board had been rebuffed. At that time, they had every twelfth day off; other grievances included having to work more than nine hours a day, and split duties, a scandal that caused enormous distress.

The DUTC employed three crews for every two trams in the fleet and were adamantly opposed to having two crews for each operational car. It was pointed out that split duties, always a sensitive public transport problem, were widespread in the

DUTC and one quoted example required a man to begin work at 8.40am and not finish until 11.15pm. In the cocooned world of a status quo where nobody in authority appeared to think that change could ever come about, the DUTC seems to have been particularly unprepared for what would inevitably happen.

James Larkin arrived in Ireland in 1909 and organised many groups of hitherto lowly esteemed workers into the Irish Transport and General Workers' Union. His first overtures to the tramwaymen in 1911 were not entirely successful, reluctance to join being due to fear for their jobs and the as yet unproved efficacy of the Union. Management closely observed every activity in which the men engaged, controlling even a series of concerts they organised. There were also several attempts to enroll the men in a company sponsored staff association.

Two years later, 1913 ushered in a decade, which would determine the future of the world, and of Ireland in an especially decisive way. Dublin would be the centre of the action in this country, and the tramway system, its management and staff were to be involved in, or affected by, ten years of tumultuous events, which can perhaps be best dealt with together. Predictably, industrial strife was the first of the many tribulations about to be endured.

The Lock-Out
The terrible fears of the workers had much to do with the DUTC's policy of keeping as many staff as possible permanently anxious about their futures. DUTC Chairman William Martin Murphy was also head of the employers' organisation, which was resolutely opposed to trades unions and prepared to fight to the finish. Anybody who

complained, showed spirit or tried to organise his colleagues could be sacked on the flimsiest pretext, and the men were constantly reminded of this. But such a situation could not continue indefinitely, only one spark being required to ignite an uncontrollable conflagration.

In normal circumstances, the mens' requests might have been negotiable. These were, an all-round wage of £1.10s per week, a day off in every eight, time and a half for Sunday duties and pay day to be on Friday. The collision of Murphy's and Larkin's strong personalities guaranteed total entrenchment and polarisation in the titanic struggle just about to start. The immediate cause of the dispute now turned on the principle of union recognition rather than the type of issues that were usually at the centre of an industrial dispute.

Serious trouble in the DUTC began with a series of meetings during June and July 1913 when tramwaymen joined the ITGWU, at the same time as workers in the *Irish Independent* newspaper, also owned by William Martin Murphy. He sought undertakings from his employees that they would resign from the Union and promise not to join it in the future. They were also once more encouraged to negotiate through the frequently advocated staff association.

Forty *Independent* employees were sacked on 15th August, the paper was blacked by other workers who were then locked out and a series of increasingly dangerous disputes broke out in quick succession. Two days later a hundred alleged union members were dismissed by the DUTC and on the 21st the Tramway Parcels Express was suspended. What had started out as a series of skirmishes now turned into a major war.

During the apocalyptic 1913 labour troubles, some trams remained in service, usually crewed by DUTC officials or strike-breakers. Here No 282, built at Spa Road in 1902, is accompanied along Annesley Bridge Road by members of the Dublin Metropolitan Police. *Evening Telegraph*

The biggest losers in the wake of 1913 were probably the Dublin Metropolitan Police, whose brutality during the strike earned them the implacable hatred of the workers. The subsequent granting of free tram travel to policemen, generally thought to be in recognition of their support for the DUTC during the lock out, served to intensify this enmity.

The Second Merrion Square Accident

In view of the industrial relations disaster to be explained, William Martin Murphy's address to the shareholders' meeting on 3rd February 1914 was clearly going to be difficult. It was made even more fraught by having to deal with an event, which had taken place less than 48 hours earlier, the worst accident ever to happen on the Dublin tramways. While there were some notable mishaps, the Dublin tramways had an excellent safety record throughout their years of operation, until now.

The DUTC's most serious and dramatic accident occurred on the evening of Sunday, 1st February 1914. Balcony bogie car No 295, with Motorman Downes and Conductor Kavanagh carrying 26 passengers - it was later stated in court that the number was 39 - was outbound on the Dalkey route. Just before 9.30pm, it reached Merrion Square, from which the Donnybrook line diverged opposite Holles Street Hospital to run along Merrion Square East. As the car was running on the main (straight) line through the facing points it left the rails, probably because of a malfunction.

No 295 ran along the roadway for a short distance and overturned. At that period, several eminent medical men lived in the vicinity and on hearing the crash, a number of them were quickly on the scene, rendering vital first aid to the injured. No fewer than 13 famous doctors were named in the papers on the following day. In all 22 people were injured, six were in a serious condition, including one unfortunate passenger who died later. The motorman escaped unscathed but the conductor suffered a head injury. Ambulances from the Dublin and Pembroke Fire Brigades and the Dublin Metropolitan Police, plus some cabs, ferried the injured to Sir Patrick Dun's and Baggot Street Hospitals.

Badly damaged, No 295 was righted, put back on the rails and towed to Ballsbridge. It was extensively repaired at a cost of £212, a new top cover costing £104. The car's original trucks were transferred to No 294. It

The Extended Struggle

The Union, which was trying to organise all the workers in the various departments of the DUTC, regarded the generating station staff as vital in a spectacular planned shutdown of the system. Throwing the right switches would immobilise the entire tram fleet instantly. Failing to persuade this group, Larkin carefully chose the time of his next tactic for maximum effect. The Dublin Horse Show began at Ballsbridge on Tuesday, 26th August, and what happened at 10am that day is told in Sean O'Casey's *Drums Under the Windows*. 'On a bright and sunny day while all Dublin was harnessing itself into its best for the Horse Show, the trams suddenly stopped. Drivers and conductors left them standing wherever they happened to be at a given time of the day when the strike commenced....They came out bravely, marching steadily towards hunger, harm and hostility, just to give an answer for the hope that was burning in them'.

This episode is also dealt with in a scene in James Plunkett's play *Big Jim*. The impact of the dramatic scenes of that morning tends to obscure the fact that only an estimated 700 out of a total staff of 1,700 took part in the strike. Supervisors, workers who did not join the strike and others hurriedly recruited, kept a service of sorts going, but there were attacks on trams, which were given police escorts. The bitterness caused at this time was to endure for many years, its consequences for employers and trade unions alike still affecting industrial relations up to the end of the century.

The dispute spread with amazing speed. Around the end of August nearly 25,000 people were said to be locked out, on strike or disemployed in Dublin. On 31st August, 1st September and again on 21st September, there were serious disturbances, or riots, according to the perspective of the reporter, in which 50 policemen and nearly 500 civilians were injured. Two of the injured subsequently died. Dublin port was

closed to cross-channel traffic from 12th October to 10th December, and no settlement had been reached by the end of the year, despite intensive negotiations.

Widespread unrest continued up to 19th January 1914 when the strike ended. Embittered and sullen, the DUTC strikers, or those of them acceptable to the company, were humiliatingly forced back to work, only to get caught up almost immediately, in further momentous events. Many of them became members of, or at least sympathisers with, the Irish Citizen Army, the revolutionary organisation most closely identified with the labour movement, which was destined to play an important role in the events of Easter Week 1916.

On this occasion, the employers won a pyrrhic victory. The workers were back, but had frightened their bosses who realised that they could never again employ the same tactics in any future dispute. They also knew that, in time, the workers would come to understand their own worth and the power they could wield in another confrontation, having learned lessons from the one just ended. Even the most moderate of employers appeared to be ambivalent, pitching their pronouncements to the mood or viewpoint of their audience.

Differing newspaper presentations of the discussion on the lockout at the DUTC annual meeting held on 3rd February 1914 can lead to diametrically opposing conclusions. According to the *Freeman's Journal*, William Martin Murphy told the attendance that he felt no sense of triumph and, ironically, reported progress in the provision of workers' houses. An account of the same meeting in the *Irish Independent* was very different in tone and content. It quoted several triumphalist speeches, demonstrating well the extreme stances taken by many of the shareholders who were frequently employers from other companies.

received new Hurst Nelson bogies, and left the works on 23rd September. In its rebuilt form, No 295 was the first short-canopied balcony car to have its roof extended to full length.

1914: Divided Loyalties

Following moves to introduce Home Rule in 1912, the rival Ulster and Irish Volunteers staged confrontations with the government. An already volatile situation was made worse by gun-running at Larne and a later, similar exercise at Howth. On Sunday 26th July 1914, a large party of police and soldiers presented themselves at Clontarf depot. They demanded transport to Howth, intending to thwart the arming of the Irish Volunteers.

The Depot Inspector was Patrick Clifford, who had started his career as a conductor on the horse trams and stayed with the DUTC until his retirement in 1941. He would not allow four-wheeled Clontarf trams to carry the security forces beyond Dollymount and was unable to provide crews for any bogie cars that might have been available. Nor could he assist them to get in touch with Dublin Castle, the telephone having mysteriously gone dead. By the time matters were resolved the arms and ammunition had long left Howth.

The First World War began in August 1914, further stirring up the kaleidoscope of clashing loyalties in Ireland. William Martin Murphy was a nationalist and supporter of John Redmond, leader of the Irish Party and believer in the inevitability of Home Rule as soon as the war was over. Redmond, in a September 1914 speech, exhorted Irishmen to join the British Army. The policies and actions of the DUTC reflected the philosophy of Murphy who supported Redmond's efforts. One result was that tram No 242 was decked out with flags, banners and posters, touring the system and encouraging men to come forward. 'Recruiting Office' proclaimed a banner on the lower dashes of the car, while the ends of the upper deck carried two large signs saying 'Irishmen enlist today' at either side of a shield bearing a crowned harp. No 242 was ever afterwards referred to as the Recruiting Car.

Easter 1916

When the Rising or 'Rebellion' as it was called at the time began on Monday 24th April 1916 the tram service was operating normally. One group of insurgents travel-

ling to the General Post Office from Harold's Cross commandeered a tram, some reports stating that they insisted on paying their fares for the journey. There were several cars at Nelson Pillar terminus, as confirmed by Kathleen Levins who, when the first shots were fired, was waiting at the Pillar to meet friends and go away for the day. Services were soon suspended, some trams were abandoned where they stood and a few were used as barricades. A photograph exists of No 18 with another, unidentified, car so employed at St Stephen's Green. The fighting lasted about a week, a cordon being placed around the city and martial law declared.

During the Rising, 186 civilians and 124 military and police personnel were killed, with 614 and 397 wounded, respectively. The dead included one DUTC employee on duty, a carter named James Hogan, who worked out of the company's stables at Nelson Lane (now Earl Place). He went to work as usual on Monday and turned in again on the Tuesday but was sent home by his foreman. Later that day, at the foreman's request, he returned from his home at 31 Upper Rutland Street to keep the stableman company. On Thursday 27th he left the premises briefly in the morning and again in the evening to buy milk. This was against the wishes of the foreman and, tragically, James Hogan was shot down in North Earl Street.

Damage caused during the insurrection was appalling, and on 29th April the worst conflagration ever seen in Dublin up to that time took place. It consumed practically all the east side of Lower Sackville Street, Eden Quay, Middle and Lower Abbey Street and

several other streets. No 308, a Howth bogie car that had been abandoned at the junction of North Earl Street and Sackville Street, was destroyed. Another total loss was No 72, an unvestibuled former horse car burned out on Usher's Quay.

The *Freeman's Journal* was not published during the Rising. When it reappeared on 5th May, the lead story was headed 'The Complete Story of Sinn Fein Insurrection'. This gave details of events as seen by ordinary citizens and contained several references to the trams. Describing the scenes at the GPO around noon on Easter Monday, it noted that, 'the situation was so amazing that the public quite failed to appreciate its gravity and jokes were freely exchanged between passers-by and the insurgents'. Trams ran on most routes until about 2pm that day.

By Monday 8th May, most routes were operating again but the next six years would see further, innumerable, interruptions to the service. Also on 8th May, a big clean up began, when it was reported that dangerous buildings were cordoned off and some were still smouldering, despite heavy rain. Martial law was in force between 8.30pm and 5am, but the tram service was practically a full one. Military pickets remained on the outskirts of the city. The police and military inspected passing trams, passengers being examined cursorily to see that none of the missing insurgents was among them.

Imaginative Reporting

Under the heading 'Dublin Rebels and the City Tramways', a highly colourful report in *Tramway and Railway World* on 11th May stated: 'As a result of the insensate rebellion of the Sinn

Bedecked with advertising material, tram No 242 appeals for men to join the British Army in College Green during the early days of the First World War. Known for years afterwards as 'The Recruiting Car', No 242 was originally trailer No 27, being electrified in 1900. It was replaced in 1922.
Birney Collection

Fein organisation in Dublin which broke out on April 24, the services of the Dublin United Tramways Company were at once suspended, and it was not until May 4 that the running of the cars was resumed on some of the routes. On St Stephen's Green the overhead wires were knocked down on Easter Monday and three cars came to a stop. The vehicles fell into the hands of the rebels, who entrenched themselves and lined the trenches with the cushions from the cars. Partly owing to the destructive tactics of the rebels and partly owing to the military operations for gaining possession of St Stephen's Green, several cars were badly damaged. The body of one was entirely destroyed, nothing but parts of the truck and some ironwork remaining.' (**The car just referred to was No 72, destroyed on the South Quays**). The report continued, 'Wherever the conspirators and their dupes took up a position, they fired on all traffic, and tramcar after tramcar was riddled with bullets and small shot. One body of the rebels seized the power station, and in numerous places portions of the overhead equipment were destroyed in order to render the tramways useless. The wrecked cars were still at St Stephen's Green on May 3. One of the signatories of the 'Republican Government' was an ex-tramcar motorman.' Like much else in this report, the reference to an ex-tramcar motorman was inaccurate. The signatory in question was Sean McDermott who had been employed as a conductor by Belfast Corporation Tramways and of whom a photograph exists with BCT car No 135.

A Slightly More Realistic Report?
Four weeks later, in its 8th June issue, *Tramway and Railway World* gave a less lurid account of the Rising as it affected the tramways. 'On Easter Monday, April 24 at 12.30pm, immediately after the Sinn Fein rebels had occupied the principal buildings in Dublin, the Tramways Company started withdrawing their cars from the streets, and at 2.30pm most of the vehicles were returned safely to the different depots. In Sackville Street one of the Howth cars was stopped and the motorman and conductor were covered with revolvers and ordered to leave. An endeavour was made to upset this car by hand to form a barricade for Earl Street, but the attempt failed. Then a charge of dynamite was put beneath it and exploded, but it did lit-

tle or no harm. Eventually this car was burnt owing to the adjoining houses having caught fire and fallen upon it. Another car was caught on the South Quay and was also burnt in the same way. Minor damage to four or five of the cars was done by rifle fire. There was no direct attempt to damage cars except for the rebels' 'military' purposes. One motorman, however, in running his car out of the danger zone, was seriously wounded, while another employee, who was coming from a city depot, was killed by rifle fire from the General Post Office. Several tramwaymen were wounded by stray bullets in the vicinity of their homes. The trolley wires suffered most severely; several miles were brought down all over the city by rifle fire. Several tramway standards were damaged by shell fire....at the corner of O'Connell Bridge and North Quays....a shell passed right through the pole. Subsequently this standard, as well as the others damaged, were filled up with concrete reinforced with steel rods on site.

The day after the outbreak the Sinn Feiners surrounded the power station, and eventually entered and ordered the employees to leave. All of the intruders carried revolvers, and some of them displayed a revolver in one hand and a dagger in the other. They gave the engineer on duty an hour to clear out, under penalty of death, and ordered that the whole of the works were to be shut down. This was exactly what the management had decided to do themselves. The rebels were apparently satisfied that their wishes were carried out, as they did not return. The staff, however, kept in occupation of the station in its shut-down state throughout the whole of the fighting, notwithstanding the heavy rifle fire in the district, which was one of the most stubborn in resisting the troops and was the last to be conquered. No attempt was made to do any damage to the power station.

'On May 2, immediately after the burning of the General Post Office, the fires in the power station were restarted, and on May 3 the greater part of the undertaking was in working order. Sniping was very prevalent throughout the whole of tramways area, which made it uncomfortable for the men repairing the overhead wires, but by May 5 practically every feeder was temporarily repaired and the full car service was restored as far as the military authorities would allow it to run. General Maxwell had drawn a cordon around the whole city, and would not allow the cars to pass more than two bridges – one on the south side and one on the north side.

'The amount of damage to the rolling stock, including the two cars destroyed and injuries to six other cars mainly breaking of glass by rifle fire did not much exceed £1,500. The total damage to the overhead equipment amounted to about £500. Considering, however, the amount of property that the company owns throughout the city, such as the various depots, and the large number of cars, the shareholders may be congratulated on their good fortune in escaping so lightly. The actual stoppage of the services was from 12.30pm on Easter Monday, April 24, until May 3, and this cessation of traffic constituted the company's most serious loss.

' The Howth car already referred to as being burnt...as well as the smaller one destroyed on the South Quay, was eventually towed home on its own wheels. The field coils were rendered useless, but the armatures are apparently not very much the worse. Notwithstanding that the metal melted from all the bearings, the two trucks are not beyond repair. No damage was inflicted on the truck as a result of the attempt to blow the car up.'

Trying to Restore Normality
The DUTC's efforts to restore normal services took place against a wider background in which business and commerce strove to get back to where they had been prior to the Rising. A number of businesses disappeared altogether and others were a long time recovering. It took several years for some premises to be rebuilt and in the meantime companies which could afford to do so, operated from temporary and often unsuitable premises. The DUTC resumed its parcels service as quickly as possible and later in 1916 was advertising in the papers:

'Vans or Messengers will call at Warehouses, Shops, Offices &c at arranged hours for the Collection of Parcels and Prompt Delivery will be made at the following rates:

4lbs	3d	56lbs	7d
14lbs	4d	84lbs	9d
28lbs	5d	112lbs	1/-
42lbs	6d		

Telephone: Dublin 745'

The two trams damaged beyond repair were later replaced. Only one other vehicle is recorded as undergoing extensive repairs, but it is not possible to connect this with any specific incident. Whatever happened, the Repair Books show that four-wheeled Balcony car No 291 was the subject of, 'extensive repairs costing £158,' in June 1916. This was expensive work, which would have come to around £7,400 at 1999 prices.

The remains of Howth line car No 308, blown up at the junction of North Earl Street and Sackville Street following the Easter Rising in April 1916. A short distance away down North Earl Street, the unfortunate DUTC employee James Hogan was shot down as he went for supplies during that fateful week. Author's collection

At the company's 1917 general meeting, the Chairman remarked that the DUTC had got off relatively lightly in April 1916. He expressed special thanks to Mr D Brophy, the Traffic Manager, whose efforts had saved the company's offices, referring to the Rising as, 'a state of warfare at their own doors…a disaster without parallel in the history of the city.'

The Effects of War
Although slower in their effects than indigenous trouble, developments accruing from the wider European conflict also had grave results for Ireland and Dublin's tramways.

One effect was the coming into force in February 1918 of the Lighting Restrictions Act, arising from official fears of German raids by air or sea. Trams operating on seaside lines were required to have the upper sections of their windows, on the sea side at least, painted blue to obscure their interior lights. This affected Dalkey, Sandymount, Dollymount and Howth cars particularly. A contemporary photograph of No 271 shows the tram's windows painted in accordance with the regulations. No 263, also working the Dollymount line in 1918, is stated in the Car Records to have had its stairs, roof and platform blackened. Fear of submarines was however well grounded. On 10th October 1918 the *RMS Leinster*, en route to Kingstown from Holyhead, was sunk by a German submarine with the loss of 501 lives.

During 1918, Britain's all-out war effort was affected by escalating unrest throughout Ireland, leading to a shift in relationships between the two islands. Outside Ulster, public opinion, initially hostile to the 1916 Rising, had changed radically with the execution of the leaders. Increasing repression of what government agencies regarded as subversion and resistance to conscription worsened an atmosphere in which any sympathy English people may have felt towards Ireland all but evaporated. Following the 1918 Sinn Fein election victory, strong feelings led to the War of Independence. Urban guerrilla warfare broke out in Dublin. Through the same streets in which this vicious and episodic conflict took place, the trams, a symbol of civilised normality, continued to operate.

Management Uncertainty: Cutbacks
Before the situation began to deteriorate seriously in the last year of the war, the DUTC's 1918 annual general meeting took place on 6th February. William Martin Murphy was less than enthusiastic about the company's performance, noting that while receipts had gone up considerably, so also had costs. He pointed out that despite an increase in traffic, the year 1917 produced £25,000 less profit than 1912, regarded by the company as the last year of normality.

Implicit in this statement was an acknowledgement of how cataclysmic the events of 1913, the last year of peace, had been. Further unrest, by now widespread among the DUTC staff, was seen by many as unfinished business carried over from 1913. For any leaders of industry who studied labour unrest and politics, the outlook was made even more uncertain by workers' actions in other countries and especially what wider consequences might follow industrial or civil unrest.

Increased traffic encouraged the DUTC to hope for further improvement, and the Chairman also announced plans to invest in more goods wagons, with freight traffic becoming more profitable. At an industrial conference held later in 1918, on 11th September, there were proposals to link the tramways with the port. Howth was a source of gravel transported over the system to distant suburbs, and it was suggested that consideration be given to laying spurs into various business premises so that freight traffic would not interfere with passenger services.

It was nonetheless conceded that some types of traffic could now be handled better by motor vehicles and that the high density of traffic on the Dalkey line was a deterrent to increased goods operations. It was claimed that loads of 10-20 tons could be moved most economically by tram. This was true at the time, but something unforeseen by the DUTC was the growth in both the numbers and carrying capacity of lorries. Nor could anybody anticipate the effects of worsening traffic congestion on tramway operation generally.

Despite any optimism expressed by Murphy and others, the DUTC cut back progressively in various ways during the war, particularly over a period of several months in 1918. The expresses were already gone, now return tickets were abolished on the Howth and Dalkey lines. Fares were increased generally, the stages being shortened and a 1½d fare introduced from 27th April. This fare, known as the three ha'penny, was represented by an orange ticket. Passengers were advised to consult notices at tram stops about the changes. A series of curtailments on 2nd April saw the Inchicore service cut back from Westland Row to College Green.

There were frequency reductions on other routes, for example, to six minutes on the Terenure line, with three-minute headways between Rathmines and Nelson Pillar. Even before the service reductions, the trams were frequently overloaded during the evening rush hour when people were going home. Successive cutbacks made the situation so bad that in January 1919 'McD' complained to the *Irish Times* that he found it necessary to take a tram from his place of work to Nelson Pillar. This was in order to be sure of getting a place on a car travelling

in the opposite direction over the same route towards his home.

The First Track Closure
Several services were withdrawn on 21st March 1918. Trams ceased running between Donnybrook and Phoenix Park via Baggot Street and Merrion Row. To compensate, trams from Clonskea, operating through Appian Way and Leeson Street to Nelson Pillar, worked on to Phoenix Park (North Circular Road), with a through fare of 4d.

Also withdrawn, but without a replacement, was a service introduced as recently as November 1916 and intended to rectify a defect in the route system. This arose from Amiens Street station being served only by Dollymount and Howth line trams which had their city terminus less than half a mile away at Nelson Pillar. As a result, there were no through services from Amiens Street on to the many lines running elsewhere throughout the city.

The corrective service began at Fairview, running via Talbot Street, Gardiner Street and Lower Abbey Street to Westland Row. It was extended at both ends on 17th February 1918 to St Lawrence's Road and Hatch Street, thus serving three railway stations. Closed on 21st March, in its extended form it was Dublin's shortest-lived tram service, being in existence for only 32 days.

Also withdrawn was the Nelson Pillar-Sandymount service via Bath Avenue, worked by single-deckers. Another suspension was the Parkgate Street to Hatch Street service, the final restriction being that of the Kenilworth Square to Lansdowne Road service, the cross route, which was cut back to operate only from Castlewood Avenue to Lansdowne Road.

All of the suspended services were replaced in one form or another at a later date, with one significant exception the College Green to Drumcondra line via Capel Street. This was the first time the DUTC ceased serving any length of track, and one of only three places on the north side providing alternative routing. However, the rails through Parliament Street, across Grattan Bridge and from the Parnell St junction through Bolton and Upper Dorset Streets to the junction of Blessington St and North Frederick Street junction were, most fortunately, retained for a few years.

Wages and Costs
Another unpleasant effect of the war was its impact on the cost of living, as borne out by the official index. Calculations are usually fixed on the year 1914 with its base of 100. The figure had increased to 123 in 1915 and to 146 in 1916. In 1917 it was 176 and in the four years to 1918 it had more than doubled to 203. Wages also increased, but far short of the spiralling index and there was panic among Irish industrialists and businessmen

Probably photographed during the relaying of the Dalkey line in 1907, Water Lorry No 3 is here in use as a locomotive. Behind it, also coupled to permanent way stock, is No 5. Referred to in the car records as an attendance wagon, this multi-purpose vehicle which served as locomotive, site office and dining car, was much rebuilt. Renumbered 22 and described as a haulage wagon, it certainly existed in 1933-35, during which time its consumption of current is recorded. The wagon immediately behind No 3 consists of the lower deck sides and running gear of a former horse tram. M Tierney, Transport Museum Society of Ireland collection

during 1918 at the prospect of pay rates reaching the inflated British levels caused by severe labour shortages. Although they did not command the same newspaper coverage as the higher echelons, the pressures on people lower down the social scale were also very severe.

Statistics quoted by William Martin Murphy at the DUTC annual general meeting on 5th February 1918 threw some light on the company's performance in the previous five years. Comparing 1917 with 1912, receipts had increased by £51,106. However, the expenses for 1917 were £76,503 up on 1912, while profits were down £25,397.

Unskilled men were said to be earning between £3 and £5 per week in Britain during the Spring of 1918. Faced by the threat of industrial action, the DUTC, in a pre-emptive strike, published its rates of pay. Of 358 motormen in the company's service, 313 first-class men got the top rate of £1 19s 6d per week, 19 in the second class received £1 18s and 26 in third class got £1 14s 6d. The 364 conductors included 163 'A' class at £1 17s 6d, 103 first class £1 16s 6d, 34 second class £1 14s 6d and 64 third class who received £1 11s 6d. The DUTC, whose low 1913 pay rates had increased by less than half the rate of inflation, pleaded inability to pay. They pointed out that men going on strike would have to give two weeks notice before their engagements can be ended.

The effects of all the foregoing on the DUTC were considerably exacerbated by the constant threat to fuel supplies. Coal, on which industrial and domestic users alike were almost totally dependent at that time, was essential for the generation of traction current. Availability and distribution were strictly controlled during and for some time after the war by the government's Coal Controller. The situation was also adversely affected by a shipping deficit, causing ever more severe shortages of all imported materials, including coal.

A booklet issued by the DUTC in August 1918 to its motormen and conductors set out clearly the company's genuine anxieties 'respecting the Working of Controllers and the Economical Use of Power and Consequent Saving of Coal'. In its introduction the booklet said, 'The careful Motorman will use as little electricity as possible....The chief article used in making electricity is Coal. When Coal is once burned it is gone for ever. When you save electricity you save Coal, and when you waste it you waste Coal.'

'It takes about 4lbs of coal to make one Unit of electricity. It takes an average of one and a half units to drive a car one mile, and in an average day's work of 100 miles a Motorman may therefore use 5 to 6 cwt. of Coal. If by more efficient and careful driving 1 cwt. of Coal per car per day is saved, and that is quite possible, it would make a difference of 9 tons per day – equal to a saving of 17 per cent – through more efficient driving of the cars alone this saving would represent about £6,000 in a year.

'When Coal of better quality than any we can get now was delivered into the bunkers at 9/- per ton the question of Coal Saving was not one of very great importance. When inferior Coal got to its present price of 36/- per ton it became a very grave question for the Company. It has now become a matter of supreme consequence to save coal by every possible means in our power owing to the restrictions on supply imposed by the Coal Controller, which might result in a much greater reduction in the number of cars allowed to run, or in a complete stoppage, if the Coal consumption is not reduced. The booklet went on to plead for intelligent, and consequently, economical driving, setting out exactly what sections on each line were to be traversed in series, parallel or coasting settings of the controllers.

Tramwaymen won some improvements in pay and conditions in 1919. A wage increase of 5/- per week was granted in April, followed by the introduction of an eight-hour day from 1st August. This necessitated the employment of an extra 200 men, but another threat to coal supplies resulted in up to 180 of these being served with redundancy notices in October. The immediate cause was a railway strike in England, which virtually stopped the transport of the vital fuel. This led to severe service cutbacks from 2nd October when the Kenilworth Square to Ballsbridge and Ballybough to Parkgate Street services were suspended. Clonskea cars ran only to Nelson Pillar and the Dalkey expresses were withdrawn. Services on all routes ceased at 8.30pm in the evening, but the reductions lasted only until 8th October, following the end of the railway strike. The Kenilworth Square and the Dalkey expresses did not yet re-appear, however.

Living Dangerously

The quality of life, already miserable enough for most people, deteriorated as the War of Independence escalated during the latter half of 1919. Murders, many of them random, made people fearful, tramwaymen feeling particularly vulnerable. Then things got even worse with the imposition on 23rd February 1920 of another curfew. People within the Dublin Metropolitan Police District were required to remain indoors between midnight and 5.00am During the year the times were altered as the hours of daylight lengthened and fell back again, midnight to 3.00a.m. from 30th June and 10.00pm to 5.00am from 23rd November. Because of the number of incidents in the city, a very restrictive regime came into force on 1st April 1921, people being forced to stay off the streets from 8pm to 5am. These conditions made things extremely difficult for the DUTC and its staff who had to get to and from work during curfew hours. They were subject to harassment and frequently provided cover for people involved in the troubles. The DUTC made every effort to alert people to the dangers of the time. The cover of the timetable for May 1921 carried the legend 'Subject to Curfew Regulations'. With the time and fare details for every route the following exhortation appeared: '**NOTE – For Departure of Last Cars during 'Curfew', please See Notice in Company's Offices and Depots.**'

Citizens going about their lawful activities rightly feared for their safety as they moved in and around Dublin during those dark days. Nobody knew when he or she might accidentally get caught up in a raid or gun battle and innocence was no guarantee of personal safety. Some perhaps felt safe when travelling by tram, but even here there was always the danger of witnessing or becoming involved in some horrific incident.

That was exactly what happened on the morning of 26th March 1920. Conductor Patrick Kearns left Dalkey terminus at 9.20 on car No 83, loaded with 'business men, clerks and respectable citizens.' At Simmonscourt Road, one of several alighting passengers pulled the trolley off the wire, immobilising the tram. To the horror of the passengers and bystanders, a man named Alan Bell, a retired magistrate working in a sensitive area at Dublin Castle, was dragged off the tram and shot dead. At the subsequent inquest, one witness testified that Kearns had been threatened, but he denied this; tramwaymen were unfortunately at risk from both sides in the conflict.

Company instructions to staff about what to do in the event of a tram being stopped and boarded by the Black and Tans were straightforward. In no event were crews to put their own safety or that of passengers at risk. Whatever their personal feelings they were to conduct the raiders through the car quickly and courteously, calming any possible altercation between searchers and passengers.

The late Joe Greally recalled that he was collecting fares on the top deck of a crowded tram in South Great George's Street on a summer day in 1920 when they were stopped by a patrol. Making his way towards the stairs to get to the platform as quickly as possible, he was horrified to see a pistol suddenly land in his cash bag. Thinking fast, he managed to hide it in the destination box as he started down the stairs. Trying to appear normal, he was petrified while he accompanied the raiders through the tram. After getting the Black and Tans off the car without further incident, Joe returned to the destination box, intending to retrieve the pistol and address some strong words to the inconsiderate coward who had put him in such danger. As he opened the box, two pistols fell out. The passengers stared at him impassively so he turned both weapons in as lost property and heard no more about them. Subsequently, he learned that the gun in the destination box trick was a speciality of Michael Collins, who often travelled on the Dalkey line. On these occasions, Collins usually rode on the front balcony, thus having a good view of the road ahead and close to the destination box in the event of a raid.

The Civil War

The tragic 'Split' that followed the Treaty of December 1921 granting independence to the Irish Free State inexorably degenerated into armed conflict. Inevitably, ordinary, blameless citizens suffered yet again, people in Dublin being especially subjected to further needless cruelties. On 14th April 1922, a group from the side opposed to the Treaty took over the Four Courts. They continued in occupation until 28th June when the National Army began a bombardment that lasted until 30th when, following a massive explosion, the building was totally destroyed by fire. Worse was to come on 5th July when the east side of Upper Sackville Street was completely destroyed by fire.

Among the buildings ruined was No 9, at the corner of Cathedral Street. Acquired from Scottish Provincial Insurance in 1892, this Victorian Gothic structure with its distinctive turret was the headquarters of the tram company. Two statements made by DUTC Chairman Joseph Mooney at the annual general meeting on 13th February 1923 sum up much of the aura of a terrible era which, most people hoped, was ending. Referring to the destruction of 9 Upper Sackville Street, he mourned the loss of 'all our valuable records, going back to the formation of the company.' Staff records and a priceless photographic collection were among the irreplaceable archival material destroyed. He also paid tribute to the tramway staff, 'Men who carried out a lot of work with their lives in their hands, work carried out at the point of a bayonet.'

The gutted remains of the buildings were rendered safe over several days, the shell of the DUTC offices being demolished by steel ropes attached to a traction engine. Although its offices were gone, the company's ability to overcome calamities and adapt to new situations was strikingly demonstrated around this time. Following the destruction of the Four Courts, law sittings were transferred to King's Inns, accessible from Henrietta Street. To facilitate people travelling there disused sections of the former tram route from College Green to Drumcondra were brought back into operation, thus serving Henrietta Street. That a service could so easily be provided amply demonstrated the versatility of the city centre tramway network.

Winning Through

Ireland suffered multiple traumas in the decade up to 1923. The 1913 labour struggle, the First World War, the 1916 Rising, the War of Independence, the Civil War - any one of these on its own qualifies as a shattering event. These events affected Dublin directly and the city's tramway system was at the epicentre of much of the action. That the DUTC survived virtually intact, still providing a good service when so many tramway systems were threatened with oblivion, is even more remarkable. That it was still generating profits and was about to enter a fresh period of renewal, is unique.

A city's public transport system has three partners, management, staff and passengers. In surviving the terrible ten years just reviewed, whatever credit was earned by the DUTC management was largely, some would say totally, cancelled out by the happenings of 1913. To the other two parties must go most of the plaudits; between those two there was a strong bond of friendship and understanding. A paragraph from the *Evening Herald* summed up the esteem in which the Dublin tramwaymen were held: 'The social spirit and good fellowship which exist among the tram men of the city contribute in no small degree to obtain for the tram system, which is one of the notable features of Dublin, its high reputation for efficiency and comfort.' When the decade of turmoil ended in 1923, these words were surely as true as when they actually appeared, on 6th March 1903.

In this picture, taken in Sackville Street during the War of Independence, the crowds milling round obscure some of the action involving British soldiers and an armoured car. The nearer Windjammer has a short canopy, the other car having a full length roof. Both trams have the route number plates introduced in 1918 but retain bullseye lamps in their destination boxes. Author's collection

Chapter Four

A TROUBLED DECADE

Changes at the Top

A much overused but nevertheless true cliché proclaims that after the First World War the old social order was gone for ever. In Ireland, its demise coincided with an evolving political situation which led to radical rearrangement of the governance of the island. Within the tumult affecting every organisation in what would become the Irish Free State, the Dublin United Tramways Company and its staff also entered the new era under a changed management.

Following its reconstruction in 1896, the first serious loss suffered by the DUTC was the death of Dr William Carte in 1899, right at the dawn of the electric era. Carte, prominent in the tramway world since the mid-1870s, was survived well into the new century by his colleagues William Anderson and Richard Tresilian, respectively Managing Director and Secretary of the DUTC. The other senior figures straddling the transition from horse trams to electric traction were General Manager Charles W Gordon, with the company since 1897, and Chairman William Martin Murphy.

The first of this group to pass away was Anderson, who died on 31st August 1910 in his 71st year. He appears to have been genuinely mourned by the staff, more than 300 uniformed tramwaymen and 30 inspectors marching in his funeral cortege. Following Anderson's death, the DUTC came to rely more heavily on the great strengths of R S Tresilian and C W Gordon. Both men made strenuous attempts to avert the 1913 lockout, addressing staff meetings at which they tried to dissuade the men from embarking on what they saw as a disastrous course of action. Later they tried hard to restore the company's position and its reputation as well as striving to repair shattered internal relationships in the wake of 1913.

C W Gordon, an early riser, frequently carried out early morning inspections of tramway depots and installations. An enthusiastic horseman, he usually rode on these daily rounds, accompanied by his coachman, also on horseback. On 27th May 1915, he left his home at 59 Northumberland Road around 7.00am After inspecting a tramway lamp at Pembroke Road, he fell from his horse in Herbert Park, suffering

fatal injuries. Two days later, on 29th May, Richard Tresilian also died following a brief illness. The *Irish Independent*, in its obituary of Tresilian, referred to 'the remarkable progress of what is admitted to be one of the most perfect tramway systems in the world, one taken as a model on which many other cities endeavour to mould theirs.'

William Martin Murphy, who had been deeply affected by industrial, political and personal events since 1913, and had been in declining health, died on 26th June 1919 at the age of 74. His son, Dr William Lombard Murphy, was co-opted to fill the vacancy. The chairmanship passed to the Rt Hon L A Waldron, who was in office for a comparatively short period; he died on 27th February 1923 and was succeeded by Joseph Mooney.

Despite the tradition of blaming Murphy personally for every industrial grievance in the milieu he personified so vividly, it must be pointed out that differing public and private personae can be found in one individual. That he happened to be a powerful and determined leader of the Employers' Federation is undeniable, it is also arguable that many of those he represented were far more extreme than he was. Whatever the light in which he has been portrayed, Murphy's personal courtesy and consideration cannot be denied. Politically, he was very much a nationalist, declining a knighthood, which he felt he could not accept on account of this ideology and he did make the Dublin United Tramways Company a world leader.

George Marshall Harriss MIEE (1865-1947) succeeded C W Gordon as General Manager of the DUTC in 1916. Like many of his contemporaries, he had worked abroad, acquiring wide experience in railway engineering. He was prominently involved in the urban electrification of Bray and Carlow, and was engineer to the Irish International Exhibition in 1907. Here he became associated with William Martin Murphy for whom he subsequently worked in Africa. An expert on electric traction, he was appointed, on his return to Ireland, as Electrical Engineer to the DUTC and Lecturer on the same subject at Trinity College Dublin. A skilled and thrifty administrator, Harriss's appointment as General Manager ensured the continuity of the DUTC's unique ethos for more than

another decade and a half during which he was largely responsible for maintaining its pre-eminent position as a tramway operator.

Route Numbers Replace Symbols

Tramway reconstruction and renewal began before the end of the troubled years. To a casual observer, the first indication of the new era would have been the replacement, in the Spring of 1918, of the route symbols by service numbers. The distinctive coloured destination boards, symbols and light codes displayed on the various Dublin tram routes from 1903 were rarely, if ever, referred to in the press. A table showing the symbols, but not the lamp code, appeared in the timetable and were well known to regular travellers. They were simply an accepted fact of Dublin life.

Because route numbers or letters were in almost universal use elsewhere, the symbols became increasingly anachronistic as literacy rates improved. At the DUTC general meeting on 6th February 1917, William Martin Murphy said that the subject of signs versus route numbers had been frequently considered and 'that there was a great deal to be said on both sides.' The company was keeping the matter in view and it would appear that Murphy had an open mind on it.

Replacement had clearly been decided on by March 1918, but any official reports or proposals about the change were lost in the destruction of 9 Upper Sackville Street in 1922. As when the symbols were introduced 15 years earlier, the supplanting numbers appear to have been introduced gradually. Some historians believe that the first route number may have appeared on trams working the short-lived cross-city route from St Lawrence's Road. Before its extension at both ends on 17th February 1918, the symbol for this service was a white square with a red diagonal bar. Allocated the route number 13, it may actually have carried this identification before its untimely exit in March 1918. The only public notice from that period mentioning a route number so far discovered by the author relates to the Clonskea service via Leeson Street. The notice announcing this route in April 1918 stated that the cars would carry the service number 11.

The scheme adopted was simple, the numbers starting with 1 at Ringsend and following the outer termini clockwise until Howth was reached, this receiving the number 31. Services 1, 2 and 3 comprised the Sandymount group, while 5, 6, 7 and 8 were on the Dalkey line. The first of these, 5, was given as Pembroke, the name then used for the district known to-day as Ballsbridge. At one time it designated trams running to Merrion Gates. The original No 5 ran across town to Phoenix Park and was one of several services experimented with up to about 1930.

Apart from trying to see which services attracted most custom the DUTC was also dealing with the problem of having twice as many termini on the south side as it served north of the river. Cross-city connections thus became a process of trial and error. Several routes came and went as different destinations on either side of the Liffey were joined by a variety of routes until the system assumed its final shape in the early thirties.

Routes 9 and 10 had Donnybrook as their southern terminus. No 9 trams originally went to Phoenix Park via Merrion Square and the North Circular Road, while 10s ran to Finglas Road (Hart's Corner). Clonskea, connected at different times to Phoenix Park or Drumcondra, was numbered 11. The 12 was Nelson Pillar to Palmerston Park. No 14 was Nelson Pillar to Dartry (Upper Rathmines) and 15 ran from the Pillar to Terenure via Rathmines.

Together, Nos 16 and 17 were the Rathfarnham to Drumcondra and Whitehall services, 16s usually going only to Botanic Avenue. No 18 was the 'cross tram' from Kenilworth Square to Ballsbridge. Rialto to Glasnevin became 19 and 20 was used for a time on cars operating between the same termini but via Harcourt Street. Route No 21 was allocated to the Inchicore line on which some cars terminated in College Green, while others ran on to Westland Row, going from College Green through Great Brunswick Street and returning via Lincoln Place and Nassau Street. When restored, the Kingsbridge to Hatch Street line took the number 22 and was extended to Rathmines. Across the river, 23 was Parkgate Street to Ballybough, while the 24 worked between O'Connell Bridge and Parkgate Street. Nos 25 and 26 were not immediately issued.

A complication of the numbering system was that cross-city services taking their numbers from southern termini resulted in the sequence becoming meaningless on the north side. In addition, some numbers were omitted to allow for new services in the future. Following the pattern adopted, 27 would logically apply to a north side route. It may have been reserved for the College Green service to Drumcondra via Capel Street, closed just as the new system was being introduced. Trams operating

between St Lawrence's Road and James's Street via Abbey Street showed the number 28. No 29 covered short workings on the 30 (Nelson Pillar to Dollymount) and 31 was Nelson Pillar to Howth.

The numbers were painted white on black plates and mounted on the same prongs as the symbols they replaced. Later, they were placed further back on the top of the destination box which had a glass panel set in its top, thus enabling the bulbs in the box to illuminate the plate. The Dalkey expresses were distinguished from trams on ordinary service by having red numbers on a white ground. Quickly accepted by the travelling public, the demise of the symbols did not feature in newspaper reports of the next DUTC shareholders' meeting. Of far more interest was the 1918 increase in passenger numbers, up by 4.38m to over 71 million.

Fares and Tickets
Always a source of friction with passengers and the Corporation, fares were increased by the DUTC in the Spring of 1918 to cover increased operating costs and maintain profitability. There was also some pressure in the opposite direction, firmly resisted by the company. On several occasions over the years, there had been proposals for a ½d fare. Offered in other cities for workmen and school children, it had previously been suggested in Dublin for similar categories of passenger. In 1917, it was unsuccessfully requested for poor city centre residents who had taken vegetable plots in Drumcondra.

In July 1919 the through fares to Dalkey and Howth were 7d, children were carried free and bicycles could be stored at the depots for 1d per day. In 1920, the highest cross-city fare was 5d from Rathfarnham to Whitehall, Donnybrook or Pembroke to Phoenix Park and Rialto to Glasnevin were 4d. All other cross-city full distance rides were 3d. Except for Dollymount and Rathfarnham, both 3d from Nelson Pillar, all other termini were 2d from town. This was also the fare for the full journey on the 23 between Parkgate and Ballybough or the 18 from Kenilworth Square and Lansdowne Road. For one penny a passenger could travel the length of the 24 from O'Connell Bridge to Parkgate Street.

Another post-war change involved the format of the ticket. From horsecar days, the DUTC had used geographical tickets, with separate issues for each service. These tickets listed the names of the various stages in which a passenger could travel for the fare value shown. A new style of ticket was introduced in April 1918 with one issue common to all routes. The colour coding for the 1d and 2d issues was now reversed, the 1d becoming white and the 2d blue. The 3d pink, 4d green and 5d yellow remained as before, while the new 1½d ticket was orange. Instead of the stage names, down

each side of the ticket was a series of numbers representing stage points. One side represented journeys into town, the other outward trips. The locations to which the numbers referred were displayed on a fare list in the tram, as was later the practice on the buses.

Because fare increases had co-incided with the introduction of the new tickets, passengers were confused about the distance they could travel without the familiar stage listings. Replying to criticism at the DUTC shareholders' meeting on 11th February 1919, the Chairman explained that a grave shortage of paper was a major influence in the decision to change.

If at all possible, the DUTC would never source abroad anything that could be produced in Ireland. In June 1918, Michael O'Flanagan, secretary of the Dublin Typographical Society, asked publicly why the DUTC could not have its tickets printed in Dublin. William Martin Murphy replied in a letter to the *Irish Independent* on 24th June, pointing out that the company needed 66 million tickets per year and that half of these were printed by the Dublin firm of Falconers - this was as much as they could handle. The DUTC had recently bought £1,000 worth of material from the Clondalkin Paper Mills and kept this available for Falconers. He also queried the DTS use of a letter heading made in England and enquired if this could not be produced in Dublin.

In 1920 children under three years of age were carried free. School tickets and fare tickets (pre-paid tokens which could be exchanged for travel tickets) were offered at a discount of 25%, and bicycles or bassinets (prams) could be carried on the motorman's platform of a tram if there was room, at a charge of 3d each. The DUTC Parcels Express was as extensive as ever, with through bookings accepted for as far away as Greystones on the Dublin & South Eastern Railway, or any points on the Dublin & Blessington or Dublin & Lucan systems.

In addition to the head offices, eight of the depots were advertised as having telephones. The highest DUTC phone number in the city area was 1750 at Kingsbridge. Dartry and Terenure depots were on Rathmines exchange, Cabra was on the Drumcondra one, while Clontarf and Ballsbridge were on their own area exchanges. The company gave notice that it was prepared to carry freight from any one point on its system to any other at any time outside traffic hours and at very reasonable rates. Finally, it invited enquiries for special cars for private parties or bulk goods haulage.

New Trams
A replacement for one of the two trams destroyed during Easter Week 1916, the unvestibuled former horsecar No 72, appeared in 1917. This car, a Dalkey Balcony

No 129 dating from 1923 was one of the 33
Standard Balcony trams built between 1922
and 1924 and fitted with totally enclosed
top covers in 1927-30. No 129 became a
Standard Saloon in 1929. The car is seen in
the elaborately lined Prussian blue and
ivory livery carried until 1929 and has a
destination box with bulls-eye lights which
was obviously recycled from an older
vehicle. The tramwaymens' caps are of the
cheese-cutter style introduced after the
First World War , the detachable white tops
being worn in summer. Birney collection

Bogie vehicle, was the first new tram built at Spa Road for five years. It differed in several details from its predecessors of 1912 and was the last Windjammer to have wind-down windows on the upper deck. In the following year there appeared another new Dalkey tram, No 221, which was again different in many respects, most notably in having fixed windows on the upper deck with two hinged ventilators above each one. During the early 1920s a programme was begun to extend the roofs on short-canopied Windjammers to cover the entire area over the balconies. This continued spasmodically up to 1930 but not all cars were modified and a handful of short-canopied bogie vehicles continued in service up to 1938.

The year 1918 also marked the start of an intensive programme to replace older cars dating from the 1896 to 1903 period. Around 1918, there were 276 four-wheeled cars in the fleet of which about half were vestibuled. Replacement was based on two main considerations, the condition of the bodywork and whether a car was vestibuled. Decrepit unvestibuled cars were shown little mercy, their replacements having three main attractions, a new image, weather protection for the crews and four extra seats, very useful on a system with loadings increasing constantly.

Sixteen new four-wheeled open-toppers were built in 1918. Some of these vehicles incorporated parts of those they replaced. For example No 25 was described as a new open top car retaining five rounded body windows. A handful of open fronted cars, found to be in good condition were fitted with vestibules and soldiered on for a few more years. Trams thus treated included Nos 46, 104 and, as late as 1923, No 189. Because the DUTC always had more trams than they needed for ordinary traffic, fleet

numbers sometimes lay vacant for years. No 36 was withdrawn by 1910 but was not replaced until 1923, whilst No 188 was removed to Inchicore in April 1914 but its successor did not appear until 1921.

While the majority of the new cars were on Peckham trucks, No 63 at least was on a Brill 21E. This type of truck, eventually to be found under more than half the fleet, was partly manufactured or at least assembled, in Ballsbridge. One of the new open-top cars, No 234, took the identity of a Sandymount single-decker which was scrapped. This was replaced by No 246, another former ex-horse double-decker suitably cut down. The most notable withdrawal in 1918 was No 191, 'The Coffin', the prototype vestibuled car of 1899.

Three single-truck Balcony cars were also built in 1918, and a fourth probably dates from the same year. Nos 257 and 259 replaced two of the original top-covered cars bearing the same numbers, while Nos 266 and 268 took the identities of former open-toppers. While there is no doubt that No 268 was built in 1918 the date for 266 is less certain but the two cars were probably built at the same time. These two trams were noteworthy in having short upstairs saloon sections with only two full-sized windows, plus a half length unit with a single louvre above it at either end. The roof extended the full length of the balconies. Aesthetically, these two trams fell far short of the DUTC's normal standards, they looked like a botched attempt at copying the very elegant Belfast Balcony cars.

The unusual appearance of Nos 266 and 268 was heightened by the use of boards instead of wire netting around the balconies. In view of the high profile of such vehicles at the time, it is not surprising that they came to be called the 'Armoured Cars'. They were also irreverently referred to as

the Isle of Man boats. No further cars with this type of top cover were built. Nos 266 and 268 were mounted on Peckham trucks and reputed to be rough-riding, but this allegation may have been due to prejudice caused by their unhappy appearance.

The tramcar renewal programme continued with a vengeance in 1919, no fewer than 51 vehicles, all four-wheelers, being built, of which seven were Balcony type. A further 37 new four-wheeled trams were turned out in 1920, including seven Balcony cars. A new Howth car, No 308 was also built, replacing the vehicle lost in 1916. In 1921 35 single-truck cars were built, of which 16 were top-covered. Four of these, Nos 258, 261, 262 and 286, replaced earlier Balcony cars with the same numbers.

During 1922 15 new single truck trams emerged. Eleven were open-toppers and three, Nos 65, 186 and 190, were single-truck Balcony cars of the same type as previous deliveries. The other new tram from the year 1922, No 8, properly belongs to a later era and will be discussed later. Finally in April 1922 the conversion took place, of a Dalkey bogie car, No 294, to a single-decker for the Bath Avenue service, the forerunner of several such conversions.

Changing The Make Up Of The Fleet
Towards the end of 1922, the DUTC fleet of 330 passenger trams included 54 bogie cars, 41 of them top-covered. Among the 276 four-wheelers there were 239 open-toppers and only 45 top-covered cars. While railway bridges on some routes, especially that to Clontarf and Howth, were an impediment to top-covered trams, other lines could accommodate such vehicles but greater numbers of Balcony cars would inhibit overall route availability. Again, this would be felt most keenly on the Howth line, where large numbers of extras operated on summer days and in connection with events like Baldoyle races. Ignoring the important matter of route accessibility, passengers were quick to point out that some services were more favourably treated than others in having top-covered cars, curiously referred to as double-deckers, open-toppers being regarded as single-deckers with seats on top and the Bath Avenue cars as 'bald' trams.

Unfavourable comparisons were made with other cities, especially Belfast where top-covers had been fitted to all but a few cars before the outbreak of war in 1914. In December 1920 Belfast received the first of 50 new trams known as the Moffett class. Like subsequent types of Belfast tram, their class name was that of the General Manager under whose auspices they were introduced. The Moffetts, totally enclosed top covered cars setting a new standard in weather protection for passengers and crews, could not be ignored. Such was part of the thinking behind the appearance of No 8, the DUTC's 1922 car referred to earlier. Because No 8 was still a Balcony car, but built lower than its predecessors, it therefore had greatly enhanced route availability.

Standard Balcony Cars
Sixteen more similar cars, on Brill 6ft 6in wheelbase trucks and known as Standards, appeared in 1923, in which year were also built the last two open-top four-wheelers, Nos 94 and 142. Another 16 Balcony Standards were built in the following year. Most of these trams had BTH 200KK motors.

References to the DUTC tram fleet and its composition were made from time to time at company meetings. Some of the details cannot be reconciled with the record books, probably due to misunderstandings about data periods. One fact that comes through is that trams which included major components from older vehicles were officially regarded as rebuilds by the company. This was stated clearly at the annual general meeting on 8th February 1921 by the Hon L A Waldron, the DUTC Chairman, who also reported that indigenous timber was now being used in the construction of four-wheeled cars.

Speaking at the 1923 annual general meeting, Waldron's successor, Joseph Mooney, informed his listeners that the company would like to replace open cars with top-covered cars of standard size - a clear reference to car No 8. A year later, Mooney said that the extra top-covered cars commissioned in 1923 had proved satisfactory to passengers, who were demanding more of the same. In this respect, the company complied with commendable speed. Apart from projecting a more modern image, covered trams attracted more passengers, especially in wet weather.

Standard Saloons
A further refinement of the Standard design was introduced in 1924 with the appearance of No 111, known as the 'Sergeant', the three stripe-like digits being reminiscent of the eponymous rank markings. This was a totally enclosed 62-seater which was exhibited at the Royal Dublin Society Show at Ballsbridge in July of that year and entered service on the Terenure (15) route in

August. No 111 initially had its route number on the traditional metal plates above the destination boxes. All later cars had number boxes with the scrolls illuminated from behind, No 111 soon being similarly equipped.

Unlike totally enclosed cars elsewhere, the Standard Saloons had one design feature reminiscent of much older trams. This was the upper deck dash panelling, the bottom edge of which reverted to the arched shape to follow the curved roof of the lower deck. In fact, this was necessitated by the upper and lower saloons being separate structures. Being deeper than earlier dashes with curved lower edges, however, those on the Standard Saloons were capable of displaying full-size advertisements.

No 111 was the precursor of 57 similar cars built over the following five years. Like their Balcony companions, the Standard Saloons had excellent route availability. They could safely pass under all bridges except Bath Avenue and, briefly, two at Ranelagh. Most of the Standard Saloons accommodated 24 passengers on longitudinal seating inside, upstairs there were double transverse seats for 32 people, with room for three more on a longitudinal bench opposite the stairhead at each end of the car. This gave a total seating capacity of 38 'outside', to quote the notice on each platform of the cars. Three trams of 1926 vintage, Nos 10, 11 and 47, had transverse seating on the lower deck, with double seats on one side of the aisle and singles on the other.

The demand for all-weather cars was virtually unanimous, most people seeing no reason why their own particular line could not be served by such vehicles. The trams were crowded for most of the day and grossly overloaded at peak hours. Disgruntled passengers forced to travel on open upper decks in bad weather frequently aired their grievances in the newspapers. They also enlisted the help of their local public representatives in pleading for relief. In November 1925, Pembroke UDC passed a resolution calling on the DUTC to provide covered cars for their patrons on routes 2 and 3, 'in the interests of public health in view of the exposed route from Nelson Pillar to the Tower at Sandymount via Ringsend.' Here were echoes, 21 years later, of the death trap identified by the *Irish Builder and Engineer* in October 1904.

Serious Problem, Simple Solution
Excepting the Standard Saloons, the DUTC now had a total of 78 top-covered single truck tramcars having two different heights and ranges of route availability. These also had numbers scattered between 8 and 291, intermixed in such a way as to guarantee that sooner or later an embarrassing incident would occur. There are at least two

known instances of tall Balcony trams getting stuck under the same bridge, at Westland Row.

The late Ned Smith of Donnybrook garage who in the mid-1920s was just beginning his career as a fitter in the DUTC gave a graphic account of the second incident. When the tram involved got so very publicly stuck two men were sent to extricate it but found it to be securely jammed. After lengthy slaving and sweating in an impossible situation, and goaded on by the wisecracks of those who invariably gather at the scene of such embarrassments they eventually, in despair, resorted to drastic methods.

Meanwhile, the anxious depot superintendent and other officials heard nothing from the rescuers for hours but much from the railway company, the police and sundry annoyed citizens. On going to investigate, they found the rescue team purposefully working their way through the upper deck pillars of the tram with a crosscut. The damaged tram was eventually pulled from under the bridge by another car, with several men jumping up and down in the trapped vehicle to depress its suspension, thus easing its trolleybase from under the bridge. The two alleged miscreants received a communal tongue lashing from the assembled officials but as Ned Smith pointed out, nobody else could think of an alternative way of moving the tram until the jumpers took over.

Visions of trams stuck under bridges had probably haunted DUTC managers since the beginning of the Standard era. Something would clearly have to be done, especially following the Westland Row debacle. The solution proved simple, practical and effective, easing several problems at once. A Standard Balcony car, No 74, was brought into the works in November 1926 and had its top replaced by a new, totally enclosed upper deck structure, converting it into a Standard Saloon. It returned to service in May 1927.

No 74's original balcony top-cover was transferred to an open-top car, No 107, in the second stage of a highly successful operation repeated with the other 32 Standard Balcony cars and an equal number of open-toppers over the following three years. Among the converted Standard Balcony cars was No 222, another of the few Dublin trams having an unofficial title, in this case the 'Three Swans', the title being inspired by the particular style of numeral used in DUTC fleet numbers.

The programme just described eventually increased the total number of Standard Saloons to 91, making them the most numerous class on the system. An added bonus was the unequivocal height distinction between Standard and Balcony cars. The reduction by 33 in the number of open-top cars was happily balanced by a similar increase in top-covered vehicles, which further encouraged the company to build 15 more top covers for existing open-toppers, and to transfer another two from withdrawn cars.

The Standard cars were often referred to as 'All bridges' trams - they could go anywhere an open-topper could except, initially, under two railway bridges at Ranelagh. After the roadway was lowered under the Ranelagh Road bridge and the one at Charleston Road was raised, Standards were unrestricted, but a small enamelled plate on the sill under the windscreen at each end still said 'All bridges except Ranelagh'. This plate remained on Standard Saloon No 44, originally a Balcony car, until it was scrapped in 1948. Only one insoluble obstacle to double-deckers now remained, its existence marked by a plate warning, 'All Bridges except Bath Avenue', affixed to several trams.

Trams built prior to the first Standard Saloon had metal route number plates. Open-top cars receiving top covers from Balcony Standards exchanged these for scroll boxes on conversion. The new top covers fitted to 15 open-toppers up to 1931 were also fitted with scrolls and during the 1930s 27 older Balcony cars were similarly equipped. As a result, less than ten Balcony trams remained with metal route number plates by the end of their working lives.

Dalkey Bogie Car Evolution
Four new Dalkey bogie Balcony cars were built in 1924, Nos 82, 112, 214 and 228. These can best be described as a handsome 'Balcony Standard' stage in the evolution of the DUTC Windjammer into a bogie version of the Standard Saloon. While retaining the open balconies, they had distinctive Standard features such as slightly flattened roofs and louvred ventilator windows on the upper deck. Other details, such as number blinds instead of plates, added to the effect. Two totally enclosed vehicles followed them, No 224 in 1925 and 218 in 1926. Nos 218 and 224 were the precursors of a numerically small class of cars, but which played an important role in the penultimate major development on the Dublin tramways. Their great distinction was to take over the operation of the Lucan line following its reconstruction and re-opening in 1928.

Improved - and More - Motor Vehicles
Prior to 1896, road motor transport was crippled by the Locomotives on Highways Act, the notorious legislation requiring a man with a red flag to walk in front of every mechanically propelled vehicle. Following the abolition of this folly by the 1896 Highway Act, vehicle development thrived, hand in hand with increased usage. During the next decade the primitive and temperamental technology of 1896 improved considerably, producing several design features which have stood the test of time. Commer-

cial vehicles developed alongside, and often ahead of, private cars. In time, petrol-engined commercials, including buses, became a practicable proposition, but road transport was not initially seen as a threat to the railways or tramways. Roads were atrocious, the commercial motor vehicle was not yet sufficiently reliable to mount a realistic challenge and there were countless problems with everything from tyres to fuel supplies.

While commercial road transport was more problematic than private motoring, there were several pioneers in the manufacturing sector whose ingenuity, perseverance and good workmanship began, inevitably, to produce superior vehicles. London saw motor bus services becoming a well-established and vital part of its urban transport network from 1905 onwards. In the Dublin area, also in 1905, an Albion charabanc began working between Kingstown and Bray. This, however, did not compete with the trams, which encountered little real opposition before the war.

Before its potentially devastating impact on tramway services became clear, the DUTC embraced motor transport enthusiastically, but as a support to the tramway system. A motor tower wagon was placed in service as early as 1911 and three years later, a fleet of Commer vans was bought for Parcels Express and maintenance work. Ironically, also in 1914, a portent of things to come went almost unrecorded. This was the apparently successful test of a double-deck bus between O'Connell Bridge and North Wall on Saturday 25th July. That was the day before the Howth gun running which virtually monopolised press coverage on the following Monday.

The First World War changed the motor vehicle beyond belief. Four years in the toughest possible conditions had further improved the reliable subsidy models available in 1914. By 1918, what had been an object of some ridicule four years earlier had become a trusted and dependable workhorse. In earning their spurs, these vehicles effectively saw off the horse in military service.

Thousands of ex-servicemen who had worked with motor vehicles during the conflict were well qualified to drive and service such machines. Many of them were looking for business openings on which to lay out their Army gratuities. The skills and capital invested in the almost unlimited supply of affordable ex-military lorries then available greatly expanded the embryonic road transport industry.

Motor vehicle numbers can be gauged by looking at the Dublin City and County registrations from 1st January 1904, the date from which the 1903 Motor Car Act decreed the registration of all self-propelled road vehicles. In the six years to December 1909

there were just 1,100 motor vehicles (including a high proportion of motor cycles) registered in the City, but this number almost doubled in the three years to 1912. From 1912 to 1921, including the four war years, there were five times as many registrations as in the previous nine years. Ten thousand vehicles were registered in the 18 years up to 1921, but as many numbers again would be issued in the following six years. While not as spectacular, the growth in County Dublin, which included the Urban Districts, was also steady. There were less than a thousand vehicles registered by 1912 but over 4,000 in 1921 and 10,000 by 1927.

Lorries and the Freight Service
The DUTC's lucrative parcels and other non-passenger traffic was featured in the *Railway and Tramway World* in January 1918. Regretting the general failure of so many tramway undertakings throughout the United Kingdom to develop this type of business, the journal praised the Dublin operation. 'One of the earliest systems in the country to introduce a parcel service was the Dublin United Tramways Company, and it has been an unqualified success. The arrangements are as follows:- A chief depot is situated at the rear of the general offices in Sackville Street, where parcels are received and dispatched to depots in the outlying districts, whence they are distributed either by vans or messengers to the consignees. In connection with this system the company also control and manage the whole of the parcel traffic of the Dublin and South Eastern Railway Company to all that company's stations as far as Greystones, 17½ miles from Dublin, and also deliver in the suburbs all the parcels of the London and North Western Railway Company. The growth of the system may be seen from the fact that in 1883, shortly after the inception of the scheme, the receipts were only £359, while for 1916 they had increased to £9,178…the facilities…extend to Howth in the north-east and to Dalkey in the south-east. The company carry their own mails by special motors and goods trains.'

Competition from lorries after the First World War introduced several new elements to the concept of carrying certain types of freight by tram. Dumping a load of sand from a tramway wagon at the Drumcondra/Clonliffe Road junction as described on page 79, was unacceptable even in the 1920s, when this delivery was made.

Although much of it took place at night, the movement of tramway wagon trains interfered with other traffic. There were interminable disputes with car owners, while inconsiderate driving and careless parking led to several altercations. Representations were made to the DUTC by Rathmines Urban District Council about the nocturnal movement of goods traffic, which disturbed sleeping residents. Moreover, apart from parcels traffic, the DUTC was increasingly seen as solely a carrier of passengers, whose numbers grew continuously.

The DUTC had no answer to the obvious advantages of getting a motor lorry to collect the sand at the quarry and take it direct to the building site. The same arguments applied to most of the other bulk loads they carried and, as might be expected, such traffic declined sharply. Finally, on 1st July 1927, the freight service closed down. Some of the redundant locomotives and wagons found further employment in maintenance, permanent way and stores work.

Incipient Bus Competiton

The rapid expansion of commercial motor traffic following the end of the war is best illustrated by the fact that advertising for lorries was almost non-existent in newspapers up to the end of 1918 but during the first four months of 1919, no less than nine premium petrol chassis marques were advertised in the Dublin papers, plus at least four makes of steam wagon. An insidious threat to the DUTC and the railway companies, which was possibly not realised at first, was the statement in several of the advertisements that the chassis on offer were suitable as the basis of charabancs. Their use as buses would inevitably follow. By the summer of 1919 at least three charabanc operators were offering tours in the Dublin area.

At first, the DUTC did not take buses too seriously, even as these became more reliable and competitive. This was because, apart from the company's belief in the invincibility of its trams, it had friends in the Dublin Metropolitan Police, which had looked after the its interests during the 1913 labour troubles. The DMP operated the Carriage Office, responsible for licensing public service vehicles and so, for the time being at least, a discreet word in the appropriate ear eased any problems buses might create.

The first of several bus operations, all destined to dictate the future pattern of public transport in Dublin, began in 1918. The route of the 1914 North Wall experiment was now covered by a regular if transient service, which did not compete with the trams but traversed streets partially intended for horse tram operation in the 1870s. The first serious threat to the tramways arose in 1923, when the Tower Bus Company began its operations (see page 97).

Encroachments by the ever increasing number of private cars during the 1920s caused serious problems for traffic everywhere. Dublin was no exception, and this picture of parking on both sides of the island on O'Connell Bridge shows how every one of us, given the chance, will park where it is most convenient for ourselves. Preceded by a Palmerston Park open-topper, Balcony car No 212 is en route to Whitehall, while a Dalkey Windjammer and a Sandymount Standard Saloon are at either side of the O'Connell Monument.
Valentine collection, National Library

Higher Speeds – A New Rule Book

Commercial vehicles on solid tyres were restricted to a maximum speed of 12 miles per hour. The rapidly increasing numbers of those on pneumatic tyres were permitted to travel at 20 miles per hour. Faster motor vehicles led to the realisation that trams, already exceeding the limits imposed in the early years of the century by the DUTC and the Board of Trade, should conform officially to the increased speeds required by changed traffic conditions.

Motors in the first generation of Dublin trams were rated at 27hp, but those fitted to the least powerful of post-war cars were rated at least 50 per cent higher. Ability to achieve greater speeds and keep pace with the increased level of faster motor traffic was recognised in the DUTC's 1925 Rule Book. A maximum speed of 16 miles per hour was prescribed for some sections of the Dalkey line, and in the case of the Howth route, only one speed restriction was laid down, 10 miles per hour from the Claremont level crossing to East Pier.

Other routes had stricter limits, but it was tacitly accepted by crews and supervisors that the speeds were intended to be average and include stops, so a respectable pace could in fact be achieved. Faster journeys were also facilitated by the widespread use of electric points, about which detailed directions were given in the section entitled 'Special Instructions to Motormen'.

Compulsory stops were listed for each route in the 1925 Rule Book, and rights of precedence set out in detail. At the beginning of the list, certain universal instructions were given in Motormen's' Rule No 2; '…cars must not pass on curves. When both reach the curve at the same time, the car on the outside track has the right of way. When two cars arrive at the junction at the same time, the car on the main or straight line will

have the right of way. If the leading car is behind time, do not run close up to it unnecessarily; hold back a hundred yards, till it regains its proper place.'

There followed a comprehensive list of priorities at junctions. For example, at Doyle's Corner in Phibsboro, cars travelling in from Glasnevin had to give way to those coming from Phoenix Park. At the Dorset Street junction, trams travelling from Drumcondra yielded to those going from Blessington Street on to North Frederick Street. Every important junction was dealt with similarly, a rather surprising stipulation, at first glance, being that trams coming from Dartry took precedence over Terenure cars at Rathmines. The list ends with a further general instruction that, 'all cars proceeding citywards are to have the Right of Way up to two o'clock in the event of two cars meeting where there is a single line. All cars proceeding from the city are to have the Right of Way after two o'clock.'

Improvements in Difficult Times

Ireland in the early 1920s was in a very impoverished state. The First World War, the 1916 Rising, the War of Independence, the Civil War, partition, any of these on its own was a devastating blow. Their combined sequential effect on Dublin, a decaying city long relegated from its once proud status, and one in which so much destruction had taken place, was a disaster compounded by the lack of official recognition accorded the capital by early Free State governments. However, work did begin on the reconstruction or replacement of the many buildings destroyed in the 1916-1922 period. Business and commerce enjoyed some success and a modicum of private building development took place during the 1920s.

Public services, including transport, continued to function surprisingly well, the versatility of the tramway system proving a

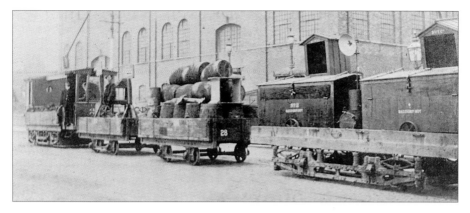

A materials train outside the generating station in Ringsend Road in the second decade of the twentieth century. The distinctive DUTC haulage locomotive has three wagons in tow, the one nearest the camera being based on a redundant tramcar truck. *Tramway and Railway World*

major asset. During the monster political gatherings of the period, usually held in College Green or other places equally awkward for the travelling public, services could be diverted because of the various alternative routes afforded by the track network in the city centre. For instance, trams working between north and southside termini could, in the event of College Green being blocked, run via D'Olier Street, Pearse Street and Westland Row to Merrion Square or St Stephen's Green and by a variety of other detours eventually reach their southern destinations. Rarely used crossovers and junctions came into use as required and the advertised services were usually maintained.

Despite the uncertainties, the DUTC undertook extensive permanent way improvement works from the mid-twenties onwards, the Drumcondra line being a good example. To facilitate growing traffic, both local and long distance, Drumcondra Road was widened around 1930. The previously single track tramway from Botanic Avenue outwards was doubled except for two short sections north of Wellpark Avenue and through the narrow section of roadway which still exists in front of the Cat and Cage public house.

An interesting feature here was the junction at the northern end of the single-line section, laid with a turnout rather than a bifurcation to make doubling easier when the road would be widened. The tramway planners were too far ahead of their time, because the road has never been improved at this point. From Botanic Avenue to Ormond Road, the rails were laid in asphalt, used increasingly from 1925 onwards. In time, College Green, O'Connell Bridge and the Dartry Road line were among locations which also received this treatment.

An interesting feature of some streets at this time was the continuing use of wooden paving blocks. These were intended to provide a more silent and resilient surface in streets passing hotels, hospitals and similar locations where the clatter of horses' hooves and steel-shod or solid rubber-tyred wheels on traditional stone setts was undesirable. While wooden surfaces succeeded

to a degree, they were a menace in wet weather, causing many severe skids for unwary car drivers and motorcyclists. For pedal cyclists they were an unmitigated disaster where they were laid beside or between tram rails, because cyclists had to cross grooved rails at an angle to avoid being caught in the rail and thrown off. With the added hazard of wet wooden paving blocks, lethal situations could arise and caused some serious accidents. These blocks had largely been replaced by the early fifties.

Traffic and Engineering Work
Cyclists had a love-hate relationship with the trams, much of the hate being caused by the rails and paving blocks. They loved trams on windy days when they could get behind them and use the cars as windbreaks to work up a respectable speed, stopping when the tram did and racing on after it as it took off from a stop. This however had one major trap into which cyclists could, literally, fall if they failed to read the road ahead. Trams were rarely affected by roadworks, holes being dug between or around the rails, while the cars proceeded cautiously past the scene under the direction of a flagman. One unwary cyclist recalled speeding along behind a tram in Harcourt Street, stopping and accelerating as necessary. Then the tram slowed down and took off again rapidly as only electric vehicles can. Too late the unfortunate cyclist saw the flagman beside him and his next recollection was of being pulled, with nasty injuries, from a deep excavation between the rails.

While trams were not affected by roadworks where the rails could be left in position there was one operation which certainly interfered with their smooth passage – work on the track itself. A very important section of any tramway undertaking is the Permanent Way Department which looks after the track, its foundations and paving. It is essential for this department to carry out its work quickly and efficiently, causing as little interference as possible to traffic, not least on the tramway itself. Where track has to be replaced, realigned or relaid, and it becomes necessary to restrict running to

one line while work proceeds on the other one, there are at least three alternative methods of dealing with tramway traffic.

A long single-track section between two existing crossovers at either side of the working area can be utilised, leading to protracted and frustrating delays. This is theoretically cheap but very inconvenient for passengers. At the other end of the expense scale is the practice in some places of laying two fully paved crossovers at the approaches to the operation. These may have to be moved as work progresses. The DUTC liked the third alternative of putting down sets of Kletterweiche portable crossovers, laid on the road surface and requiring trams using them to rise up out of the normal rail grooves to negotiate the obstruction. This was always a fascinating spectacle, well recounted by Fitzgibbon in his reminiscences of the Dublin tramway system.

Work on the rails necessitated the use of welding equipment and power tools. In earlier days these items were carried on special Permanent Way Engineer's trams, some of which also hauled trains of wagons bearing materials. Power for the electric welding equipment was drawn from the overhead through the powered vehicle's trolley but in the thirties redundant buses were adapted to house and carry the equipment. These had a pole to which a power cable was lashed and this was carried horizontally at cantrail level while travelling, being erected in brackets on the side of the bus at the work scene. The bus stood at the side of the road and a special connection was made from the cable at the top of the pole to the running wire over the track to collect current. This connection was fixed above the wire in such a manner as not to obstruct the passage of a tramcar's trolley underneath.

Some years before the use of withdrawn buses for permanent way work, commercial motor vehicles had begun causing changes in other areas of tramway operation. As noted earlier, the company's first motor tower wagon joined the DUTC Overhead Lines Department around 1911, heralding the gradual disappearance of horses for this type of work. Further motor tower wagons were bought over the years, including Orwell battery electrics (a brand name used by Ransomes, Sims and Jeffries) and a Commer, registration number YI 7571, in 1925.

In the same year, another erosion of tramway usage occurred when Dublin Corporation awarded the cleansing contract for the city to Franco-Irish Enterprises. This company brought in a fleet of de Dion freighters which took refuse direct to the tipheads, thus bringing to an end the regular operation of the municipal trains between Stanley Street and Fairview. In any event, the sloblands were almost completely filled and ready for development as a park by 1930. As a reminder of an earlier era, at least one of the turnouts from the tramlines near Fairview Strand remained in position until the tracks were finally lifted in the early sixties.

Limitations
There have been several allusions in earlier chapters to the Dublin trams being essentially a middle class preserve. This contrasted with the situation in Belfast, where the system was an integral part of the municipal services available to people in all parts of that city. Back in the 1870s, the pioneering William Barrington had a vision of trams serving every part of Dublin and, as recorded in Chapter One, similar aspirations were widely expressed in the great public debate that preceded electrification. However, apart from a few tangential encounters, the tracks did not penetrate less affluent areas. such as East Wall/Sheriff Street, the Liberties, Lower Clanbrassil Street, Patrick Street and the Coombe.

That passengers from these areas or the lower social orders were not exactly welcome on the trams was well demonstrated by Jimmy O'Dea and Harry O'Donovan in their short comic sketch 'Mrs Mulligan on the Rathmines Tram'. In the script, the inimitable heroine of the Coombe got into an argument about whether a window should be open or closed. This was a frequent source of disagreements between passengers, but in this instance the clash of an upper crust Rathmines accent with a more colourful one from the Liberties pointed up the exclusivity of the Dublin trams very effectively. Unfortunately this image, exploited by those promoting buses as more egalitarian, did the Dublin trams no favours.

During the twenties housing development, much of it capable of providing extra traffic for the trams, resumed. Dublin Corporation began a gigantic housing programme, and the relationship of some early estates to the tram service is interesting, the circumstances of the potential clientele being an important consideration. Many of the residents in the new estates had moved from appalling inner city living conditions, were anything but affluent, and more likely to walk or cycle than use public transport. Because of their perception of the trams as being for the middle classes, their natural public transport preference would have been for the bus. Fairbrother's Fields, between Blackpitts and the South Circular Road, generated some extra revenue for cars working the Rialto route because it was built just before the onslaught of the mid-twenties. Marino was slightly later and although its southern end at least was within convenient walking distance of the Dollymount line, it was served by buses at an early stage.

Contemptible Challenge: DUTC Buses
During 1923 and 1924, the tram company became increasingly convinced that they should become bus operators, the original intention being to use buses in outlying areas or as feeders to the tramway system. It was apparently envisaged that when usage built up sufficiently, new or extended tram routes would be built to cater for the traffic. Under its 1905 Act, the DUTC did not have bus operating powers and when it sought to remedy this deficiency, there was opposition from Dublin Corporation. This was based principally on a fear that if the company obtained bus operating powers, they would begin abandoning the tramway system, thus abolishing the municipal income from wayleaves.

In 1925, an all-round agreement was reached under the terms of which the wayleaves dispute was finally settled. The way was cleared for the DUTC to run buses and it would also, as we shall see in the next chapter, shortly extend its tramway operations quite dramatically. In the meantime, the most immediate and critical test for the DUTC centred on an extensive estate built between the years 1923-26 by the Irish Soldiers' and Sailors' Land Trust. This was located beside the inland Howth Road at Killester, about a mile from the Dollymount line.

Mrs Gilbert's 'Contemptible' buses began working to Killester as soon as the traffic warranted a service. The 'Contemptible' was a pioneering independent operator in the city area, serving a suburb to which the DUTC would like to run trams, but only when revenue would justify the capital expenditure. On obtaining the necessary authority to run buses, the DUTC lost no time in putting them on the road. The first DUTC buses began working between Eden Quay and Killester, route 43, in July 1925 eventually beating off the competition from Mrs Gilbert.

Clontarf Floods: The Storm Car
Clontarf had benefited greatly from its inclusion in the city from 1900, water and drainage services being provided within a few years to facilitate its development. While the growing population led to increased loadings on the Dollymount line, there remained a serious problem with flooding, leading to periodic suspensions of the tram service. The reason lay between Clontarf railway bridge and the Bull Wall, where the sea came very close to the road, which was flooded at intervals. The worst flooding took place during periods when heavy rain, a high tide and a south-easterly wind came

No 82 was one of the four Balcony Bogie cars built in 1924 which formed the penultimate link in the evolution of the traditional Dalkey Balcony tram into the Bogie Standard. The last of the original Dalkey bogie fleet, Nos 3, 91 and 185, were built in 1912, five years elapsing before No 71, a replacement for a four-wheeler destroyed in 1916, appeared. This was generally similar to the older cars, but its successor, No 221 of 1918, incorporated new features, most noticeable being the ventilator windows on the upper deck. Nos 82, 112, 214 and 228, all of which lasted until 1949, were followed in 1925 by the first of the Bogie Standard Saloons, No 224.
Burrowes collection, East Ham Public Libraries

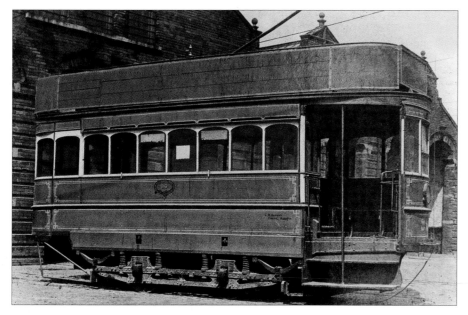

No 80 was the famous Storm Car or Submarine that operated along Clontarf seafront between the GNR railway bridge and the Bull Wall from 1926 until the implementation of flood control measures by Dublin Corporation ten years later. This tram had a convoluted history, beginning its career as horse car No 17 in 1890. In December 1900 it was rebuilt as single decker No 254 for the Bath Avenue line. For some unknown reason, it was not vestibuled at first, gaining this amenity in 1905. It had several truck changes during its working life, ending with the specially modified Peckham truck seen here at Clontarf depot in 1938, by which time No 80 was officially withdrawn. Fayle collection, Irish Railway Record Society

No 218, built in 1928, one of the first two Bogie Standards, is seen at the Lucan terminus. This tram and No 224, built the previous year, were fitted with longitudinal seating on the lower deck and were described by the late Frank Murphy as a conductor's dream so easy was it to collect fares in the lower saloon. Transferred to the Dalkey line in 1940, No 218 lasted until the final abandonment of the system in 1949. Author's collection

together, a synergy still capable of causing alarm. The DUTC was severely embarrassed at having to interrupt the tram service on Clontarf Road at unpredictable intervals but always when they were needed most. A somewhat crude but effective solution was applied in 1926.

In October 1926 Sandymount single-decker No 254, recently replaced by a bogie car with a higher seating capacity, was taken into the works and its body, which had begun life in 1894 as horsecar 161, was mounted on a special truck. This was a Peckham with motors carried above rather than level with the axles, thus giving it greater freeboard in flood conditions, when water could cause havoc to traction motors. Extra steps were provided to the platforms and the vehicle, given the fleet number 80, was sent to Clontarf depot.

Used only in the most extreme circumstances, No 80 could carry only 27 seated passengers, as compared to the 62 of a stan-

dard four-wheeler or the 75 plus of a Howth bogie car. In addition to carrying passengers, it could also rescue disabled trams and was always ready for use. This unique tram was known as the Storm Car or, more popularly, the Submarine. During the mid-thirties the Corporation undertook a programme of work which in time created the present promenade and prevented all except the worst flooding, but No 80 remained at Clontarf up to the late 1930s.

Continued Faith in the Tram

A positive indication of the DUTC's intention to further develop the tramway network is provided by the numbering of early bus routes, and the vehicles themselves. No 31 was the highest allocated to a tram service under the route numbering system introduced in 1918. When bus services began in 1925, route numbers for the new vehicles ran from 40 upwards. While lower ones were afterwards used, bus route num-

bers below 37 were not issued until after the trams had gone. Moreover, the first buses had fleet numbers from 380 upwards, leaving 50 blanks above 330 for possible additions to the tramcar stock. By the time bus fleet numbers reached 430 it was realised that even with new services, 330 trams would be adequate, and so additional buses were given numbers from 331 upwards.

Like the DUTC, the railways saw buses as a danger in the hands of competitors, but potentially beneficial if under their own control. The Great Southern Railways, formed in 1924 by amalgamation of all the principal railways operating entirely within the Irish Free State, initially operated through the Irish Omnibus Company. From its establishment in 1926 this front for GSR interests bought up as much as possible of the opposition. The Great Northern Railway entered the bus business directly in 1929 and while both railway companies had services competing with those of the DUTC, there was a degree of co-operation between them. The real threat came from the independents who waged war on the trams, the trains and one another from 1925 onwards.

Chapter Five

RENAISSANCE AND DECLINE

Early Bus Competition: The Tower

An early city bus service in Dublin, although not competing directly with the trams, was the one, already mentioned, that worked to the North Wall in 1918 using an open-top double-decker, probably obtained second-hand from London. Over the next three years small independent operators appeared spasmodically, but the first really serious threat to a tramway service occurred with the arrival on the scene in 1923 of the Tower Bus Company run by the Spendlove brothers. They used various vehicles, ranging from small 14-seaters on ex-military Crossley chassis to heavier Karriers having up to 26 seats and in 1924 tried an open top double-decker. This however failed to win the approval of the Dublin Metropolitan Police Carriage Officer.

The End of the Dublin & Lucan Electric Railway

In the Dublin area, one of the tramways outside the control of the DUTC was the Dublin & Lucan. This had commenced operation in 1881 as a steam operated line on the 3ft gauge, as outlined in Chapter One. It was reconstructed and electrified in 1900, when the gauge was increased to 3ft 6in. A fear of being taken over by the DUTC was cited as one of the reasons for not adopting the 5ft 3in of the city system.

The Dublin & Lucan Electric Railway, as it was now called, worked between Conyngham Road and the Spa Hotel at Lucan. The fleet eventually totalled eight motor trams, including six bogie open-toppers and some trailers. There was a reasonable level of goods traffic. The company had a power station at Fonthill from which it additionally supplied current to customers in the Lucan area. The D&LER was also a contractor to the Post Office, having a special tram for the carriage of mails. Despite its apparent arm's length policy, the Lucan company's timetable appeared, although not consis-

tently, in the DUTC's booklet. Through tickets were also available between O'Connell Bridge and Lucan.

The 1914-1918 War was difficult for all transport undertakings, more so for smaller concerns like the Dublin & Lucan. Legally a railway, it was taken over by the government during the war under the Defence of the Realm Act, thus guaranteeing continuation of operation at a time when receipts did not match expenditure. As with the DUTC, coal consumption had to be reduced, resulting in a curtailment of services from April 1918. Wages and fares both went up, the latter by 50 per cent and the directors were fearful of what would happen when government control ended.

When this occurred in August 1921 the company was in dire financial straits, despite the fare and rates increases of the previous year, which had adversely affected traffic. Wear and tear on track and rolling stock, damage caused during the War of Independence and the Civil War, arrears of maintenance and finally the onslaught of bus competition, brought the Dublin & Lucan ever lower.

It is paradoxical that, in the Dublin area, the infamous bus wars in which every tactic was deemed fair began with a battle where one of the combatants was a tram. Competi-

tion for passengers was savage, leading to numerous fierce confrontations between Lucan trams and Tower buses. Further embellished with every telling, some incidents passed into folklore, but the fact is that the Tower buses damaged the local roads seriously and dealt a mortal blow to the tramway, encouraging others to do likewise elsewhere. So dreadful were the consequences for the D&LER that, when arrangements were being made in 1924 for railway amalgamations, the company unsuccessfully sought to be included.

In April 1924, the Dublin & Lucan was forced into reluctant negotiations with the DUTC, not that the latter was enthusiastic about a take-over. From 18th April 1924 the timetable, as published in the DUTC's booklet, showed the first weekday trams leaving Conyngham Road and Lucan Spa at 7.45am and 7.55am respectively. Last trams were at 10.00pm outwards, 9.55pm in the opposite direction. During much of the day, even on Sundays, a half-hourly headway was maintained, and the services were advertised as being, 'all one class.' This was a reference to the railway class system with differential fares found on the Lucan line in earlier times.

The Dublin United looked on the Lucan concern as a possible millstone, probably

No 17 was one of several unusual vehicles that worked on the Dublin & Lucan line in its second reincarnation as a 3ft 6in gauge electric railway. The locomotive was used on the line's freight traffic.
Author's collection

The lower deck of Bogie Standard No 181, a Lucan car turned out from Spa Road on 17th May 1929 and transferred to the Dalkey route in April 1940. Nine of the Bogie Standards had a two and one seating arrangement downstairs, with six single seats as against five doubles, the wider spacing of the latter facilitating access to the window seats. There were longitudinal seats for three passengers at each corner of the saloon, and the famous piano stool can be seen in front of the bulkhead. The wide gangway and 46 seats upstairs allowed these huge trams to carry 100 passengers with ease. Fayle collection, Irish Railway Record Society

needing up to £70,000 of expenditure to bring it up to acceptable standards. On 29th January 1925, while the government was in discussions with the DUTC on a possible acquisition of the Lucan line, notices in the Dublin papers announced the end of all passenger services from close of traffic that evening. The company had gone bankrupt, but Post Office traffic was continued pending new arrangements.

This was the first tramway in the Dublin area to succumb to bus competition, with serious results. Sixty tramway staff lost their employment and many electricity consumers in the Lucan area, served from the generating station at Fonthill, retained current only through an arrangement made with the DUTC. The County Council was deeply concerned about expensive damage caused to the Lucan road by the buses and former tramway passengers demanded that the service be restored. Not surprisingly, a group was established to achieve this and included Lorcan Sherlock, a prominent public figure. He was very close to the centre of power following the appointment of Commissioners to administer the affairs of Dublin Corporation, abolished by the Minister for Local Government in May 1924.

DUTC Buses and the Lucan Takeover
As we have already seen, the DUTC had been considering for some time operating motorbuses as feeders to the trams or on new routes which would not initially justify a tram line. The matter became more urgent as competition increased and there was a strategic imperative to pre-empt the private operators in new residential areas. But to begin bus operation, the company needed legislation and the City Commissioners pressed them, in return for not opposing DUTC bus operating powers, to acquire and re-open the Dublin & Lucan.

While negotiations continued about the Lucan line and other outstanding matters, DUTC buses began running between Eden Quay and Killester on 7th July 1925. On the same date, the DUTC paid £12,500 for the assets of the Dublin & Lucan Electric Railway. Final agreement was reached in the long-running wayleaves dispute with the Corporation, with a bonus for the DUTC in a guarantee that the Corporation would not consider taking over the tramway system for another 40 years. The Dublin United Tramways Company (Lucan Electric Railway) Bill finally passed into law in 1927.

Reconstruction
Reconstruction of the Lucan tramway commenced in September 1927, for the most part on the original trackbed. The line ran on a roadside reservation from Conyngham Road and even today the public lighting pillars, most of them former traction poles, show which side was used. The DUTC provided additional passing loops and made one alteration to the alignment, changing a section from the north to the south side of the road between the Chapelizod gate of the Phoenix Park and the village, where it crossed the bridge on the east side of the road. During resurfacing in the 1990s, the rails across the bridge were found to be still in position.

There were loops, referred to in the timetable as sidings, at Islandbridge, Neptune Rowing Club, Chapelizod Gate and Mullingar House. Immediately across the river, where the road turns westwards, was the next loop, followed by Belgrove, another at the top of the hill entering Palmerstown and one in the Main Street. Riversdale, Quarryvale, Cursis Stream and Larkhill were passed before coming to Fonthill power station. Loops at Hermitage Golf Club, Langan's Licensed Premises, Esker

Lane, Ballydowd, Lucan Convent and Lucan Village terminus completed the list.

The original Dublin & Lucan Electric Railway ran as far as the Spa Hotel at Dodsboro but the DUTC did not reconstruct the half-mile section beyond Lucan, probably because of differences with the County Council. The new terminus was located at the former tramway depot in Lucan which was disposed of by the DUTC, all the cars being concentrated at Conyngham Road depot. This, the former main depot and registered offices of the Dublin & Lucan, was reconstructed and enlarged and a new bus garage was later built alongside it.

The depot at Kingsbridge (Victoria Quay) was closed and sold off, the displaced trams from the 22, 23 and 24 routes being henceforth shedded at Conyngham Road. The track layout in Conyngham Road was also altered, the double line from Parkgate Street being continued past the depot, but leaving a terminal stub for cars operating from the Phoenix Park gate. As reconstructed, the Lucan line had three-aspect automatic colour light signalling, operated from the overhead. On reaching a loop, a motorman knew that the line ahead was clear if a green light was showing, white indicated that another tram was running ahead of him, and red gave warning of a car coming in the opposite direction.

Re-Opening
Re-opening of the Lucan line as far as Chapelizod took place on 14th May 1928 with a through service from O'Connell Bridge, the fare being 2d. On 27th May the line was fully operational to Lucan, at a single fare of 5d all the way or 8d for a return ticket. The route numbers were 25 to Lucan and 26 to Chapelizod. Frequencies were 25-30 minutes throughout the day from Monday to Friday with 20 minute headways at peak hours. Saturday services were at 18 minute intervals, increasing to 13 minutes at busy times. Sundays, when a heavy leisure traffic was carried, called for 15-minute headways. On weekdays, the first car to Lucan left O'Connell Bridge at 7.45am, the first in the opposite direction departing

from Lucan at 7.20. Forty minutes were allowed for the whole journey and the timetable pointed out that cars arrived at Chapelizod 20 minutes after leaving either Lucan or O'Connell Bridge. Bank holidays also saw heavy loadings, Lucan proving to be a popular destination for day-trippers.

Another result of the Lucan line being rebuilt was the maintenance of direct current electricity supplies to the consumers in the area until such time as this service was taken over by the Electricity Supply Board. Electricity generation at Fonthill was not resumed, however; this became a substation supplied by a high-tension cable laid from the DUTC station at Ringsend. Also around this time what appears to have been the last of many additions and improvements to the Ringsend generating station was made with the installation of a 3,000kw turbine. The Fonthill premises was retained and some departmental vehicles were based there. The Dublin & Lucan rolling stock was scrapped, some of the tram bodies being sold off for other purposes. A few electrical and mechanical spares are said to have been acquired by the DUTC. The D&L rail-borne tower wagon, essential on reserved track, survived It was mounted on a standard gauge truck by the DUTC and numbered 75.

New Trams

The evolution of the Dalkey bogie car or Windjammer into an elegant eight-wheeled version of the Standard Saloon has been described earlier. The first two totally enclosed eight-wheeled cars, known as Bogie Standards, Nos 224 and 218, appeared in 1925 and 1926 respectively. For the Lucan line, nine similar cars were built, but in fact only four, Nos 254, 255, 278 and 284), were ready for the re-opening of the Chapelizod section, with No 314 making it for the Lucan re-opening on 27th May. Nos 252 and 253 followed in December but cars 181 and 184 did not enter service until 1929, Nos 218 and 224 having meanwhile been transferred from the Dalkey line. Several of the Bogie Standards took the numbers of the last surviving unvestibuled trams, although these had in fact been out of service for some time, their fleet numbers being effectively, vacant.

Dublin-bound Bogie Standard No 284, one of nine similar cars built for the reconstructed Lucan line, climbs out of Lucan in 1938. There were only twelve Bogie Standards, including No 313, the 1906 Balcony car rebuilt in 1929. Following closure of the Lucan route in 1940, all the Bogie Standards except No 313 (scrapped in 1944) served on the Dalkey line until July 1949. No 284, which became a seaside home at Malahide, was presented to the Howth Transport Museum by Dublin County Council in 1975 and has since been in storage awaiting restoration. H B Priestley

Nos 218 and 224 had longitudinal seats downstairs and were officially 76-seaters, but the other nine new Bogie Standards had transverse seating on the lower deck with singles on one side of the aisle and doubles on the other. Including the movable seat or piano stool 29 passengers could be seated downstairs and 46 upstairs, a total of 75. There was also standing room for up to 20 below. The Bogie Standards with transverse seats were referred to as Lucan cars. With their 45hp motors, all these trams were capable of maintaining satisfactory timings on the Lucan line.

There was a twelfth Bogie Standard which was anything but standard. This was No 313, a rebuild of the oldest Bogie Balcony car in the fleet. It appeared in its new guise in May 1929 but does not seem to have been permanently allocated to the Lucan service. Eight or nine trams were needed to work the basic Lucan timetable, so three or four of the 12 Bogie Standards were not to be found regularly on the line. These cars are listed in Section Two of the Rolling Stock Catalogue.

Local People's Reminiscences

People living in the catchment area of the Lucan line welcomed their new tramway enthusiastically. Within a short time of its introduction, season tickets were offered and Chapelizod, 20 minutes' running time from O'Connell Bridge, had a tram every seven and a half minutes on weekdays and for most of the day on Sundays.

An amusing way of remembering the numbers of the Lucan trams was recounted by Mr Kennedy of Lucan many years later. He related how he and his classmates at Palmerstown National School in the late

twenties were so impressed by the magnificent new trams passing their school that they used to play at being trams during lunch breaks. They held sticks on their heads to simulate trolleys and ran around the schoolyard, each of them assuming the number of one of the cars. His number was 314 and in later years he often remembered his school friends by their numbers, retaining an interest in the vehicles which had given them so much childish fun. In the 1990s, aboard No 253 in the Transport Museum at Howth, he recalled wistfully by number his young friends of long ago who played this innocent tram game and in the process verified some points of historical fact.

Recalling childhood journeys on the reopened Lucan line, the late C L (Clair) Sweeney of Palmerstown, and author of *The Rivers of Dublin*, said he marvelled at how the DUTC managed to get the trams to sway in such a way that they seemed to waltz between the poles, missing each one by what looked like a hair's breadth. The possible dangers arising from this obviously worried the company, because several Dalkey Windjammers were used on the route, both as regular service cars before the full complement of Standards was available and later as extras, of which there were large numbers on Sundays and holidays.

Several Windjammers had special wire netting frames placed at the sides of their balconies to prevent injuries to passengers from external objects such as trees or poles, to which they came too close for comfort. Trams listed as having wire netting panels fitted are 64, 91, 117, 183, 315, 319, 325, 329 and 330, but there may have been others and some further cars are known to have worked the line without modification. As an

extra precaution, No 319 even had its upper deck opening windows on one side fixed in the closed position. There were also many journeys performed by single-truck cars, which reputedly suffered derailments from time to time.

Bibulous Adventurers

A popular practice among bibulous Dubliners in times past was known as 'doing the *bona-fide*'. This arose from the licensing laws which allowed persons who could prove that they had travelled more than three miles out from the city to drink for periods longer than those who stayed inside the boundary, in other words, *bona-fide* travellers enjoyed privileges exploited zealously by thirsty citizens.

A favoured destination was the Deadman Murray's beyond Palmerstown to which the DUTC sent special trams to bring Sunday tipplers back to the city. This arrangement kept regular cars comparatively uncrowded for ordinary passengers, who complained regularly about the antics of some *bona-fide* travellers. The behaviour of well tanked up *bona-fide* travellers had been noted as far back as July 1900 by DUTC shareholder Dr Delahoyde who suggested the employment of a second conductor on trams catering for *bona-fide* traffic to prevent insults to ordinary passengers.

The *bona-fide* duty was unpopular with crews, particularly the conductors who were instructed to collect fares before allowing the boisterous revellers aboard. Because the majority were smokers and therefore not allowed to travel inside, the lower deck remained almost empty on these specials. The relative cleanliness downstairs was often more than counterbalanced by what the drinkers left behind on the upper deck.

Joe Greally recalled one exceptionally stressful journey when most of his paid-up customers went aloft, as was normal. Descending the steep hill in Chapelizod, they sounded unusually noisy. As the tram approached the sharp left-hand turn on to the bridge, where the rails ran beside the parapet, it assumed a dangerous list to the right. Alarmed, he rang the emergency stop signal and on going upstairs found all the passengers on the right-hand side of the car cheerfully shouting 'heave' in their enthusiasm to see if it would topple over. They were so sozzled and oblivious to what could happen that he simply refused to go any further until they resumed their seats.

Unrealised Potential

The re-opening of the Lucan line, which many people hoped would be the first of several new DUTC tram routes, brought the route mileage to its maximum of about 61 and was the last extension of the network. It was also the last major tramway project undertaken in Ireland prior to the inauguration of work on the new Tallaght line in 1999. Unfortunately it did not last: the rebuilt Lucan line had an incredibly short working life of 12 years. Of the three long lines, it is the one which would have most readily fitted in with plans to re-introduce trams in Dublin, the DART having so effectively taken over the function of the other two, to Howth and Dalkey.

Joe Greally, who had worked on several other lines before taking up duty on the Lucan route, said that the experience of running flat out with new cars on new reserved track, protected by colour light signalling, was exhilarating for any tram crew.

When the DUTC assumed responsibility for the Lucan tramway in 1925, a prolifera-

tion of competing bus services was expected. By the time the line re-opened three years later, that competition had become a reality. Nevertheless, the outlook for the future of the tramways was bright and the DUTC had at the same time expanded its own bus operations. By December 1926 the company had 34 buses working on 13 routes. Three years later the fleet had almost doubled and 20 routes were in operation.

Tram and Ship Collide

Adjacent to the site of the Ringsend Road power station is the Grand Canal Dock, the entrance to which is crossed by McMahon Bridge, a modern lifting structure erected in the early 1960s. This replaced Victoria Bridge, the 1900 opening structure described on page 48. This had two separate, narrow carriageways, in each of which was a tram track. On the evening of Sunday 12th February 1928, at this location, there occurred one of the most bizarre incidents in transport history. The sailing vessel *Cymric*, owned by the famous Tyrrell family of Arklow, was waiting to enter the dock, when a gust of wind caught it just as Standard Saloon tramcar No 223, bound for Sandymount, was crossing the bridge.

The bowsprit of the *Cymric* struck the tram, breaking some glass but, fortunately, nobody was injured. On any scale of gravity, this was not a really serious accident, but its very nature has invested it with such an aura that it is frequently recalled, and habitually exaggerated. So minuscule was the damage that there is no record of No 223 undergoing any repairs, and the *Cymric* continued to sail until its tragic loss with all hands in 1944.

Livery Change

For over 30 years from the introduction of electric cars the DUTC livery remained unchanged. Waist panels were a very rich ultramarine blue, sometimes called Prussian blue. The rocker panels and upper works were ivory, all enhanced by intricate red, gold and blue lining out, trucks were painted red and lined out. Some open-top cars had a brick-red finish on the upper deck panelling. Towards the end of the Standard car building programme in 1928 a change was made, the new livery being French grey and off-white, less elaborately lined out than before.

No 278, one of the Lucan Bogie Standards, outside Conyngham Road depot, a combined tram and bus facility on the site of the former Lucan company's headquarters. This tram, which lasted until closure of the Dalkey line in 1949, has for company only a Ford car and a Bedford commercial vehicle. When the picture was taken in 1938, Conyngham Road was still lit by gas. H B Priestley

One of the Howth open-toppers is included in this view of the East Pier at Howth. This was the terminus of the DUTC's 31 route from the city centre to Howth via Clontarf. This route number, like several other tramway route numbers elsewhere in the city, is perpetuated by today's Dublin Bus services. The 31 bus route however no longer goes to Howth via Clontarf but takes the inland road through Killester and Raheny. Author's collection

The earliest tram recorded as having this colour scheme was No 40, which appeared on 30th August 1928, but the new livery was not universally applied at first. No 170 emerged in blue in October and as late as December, Howth car No 302 was also turned out in blue. A further change occurred in January 1929 when Balcony car No 281 was painted grey but left unlined. This change was not, however, perpetuated and subsequent trams received lined grey livery up to 1935. Dublin trams were painted at approximately two-yearly intervals so there were several blue and cream ones up to 1932 and a few may have lasted even longer.

The grey livery brought a strong reaction from an *Irish Times* reader whose letter appeared on 23rd October 1928. 'Dublin is, on the whole, a grey city; grey buildings and grey skies; and when the sun fails to shine the streets can look exceedingly drab and dull. So any little touch of colour is to be welcomed. What little colour there was used to be supplied by the tramcars; but, now that these are assuming the civic colour, that little splash of colour will be removed…The old-time blue and cream of the tramcars gave to Dublin's trams an appearance which made them, in my opinion, the most handsome trams in Europe…Our grey trams will now look like battleships coloured for war, without any variant to relieve their dull monotony…Only the advertisements on the trams will keep their one-time splendour, and it may be that advertisements will cover completely the body of the car.'

The *Irish Times* correspondent was right. The grey livery was hard to keep clean and proved unpopular, drawing unfavourable comment during its period of use. In retrospect, its choice was unfortunate, especially at a time when the trams needed to present the most cheerful image possible.

A New Energy Source

The first major infrastructural investment by the government of the Irish Free State was the Shannon hydro-electric scheme. It was operated by the Electricity Supply Board, a public monopoly that would take over all existing electricity providers in the state. Industries which up to then had produced their own electricity were also expected to change over to the new system when it came into operation. The DUTC reckoned that its current could be more cheaply and efficiently delivered by the ESB, so the power station at Ringsend Road would have closed even if there was freedom to choose.

A new transformer station was erected beside the old generating station at Ringsend Road. From here ESB current, transformed and stepped down, was distributed as before through the underground feeders to the various parts of the system. Appropriate changes were made to the substations at Clontarf, Blackrock and Dalkey.

The effects of the changeover from generating its own current to taking an ESB supply were dealt with at some length by the Chairman, Mr Hewat, addressing the company's annual general meeting in 1932. They had now had the experience of a full year's working of the trams with supply of current from the Shannon Scheme. There were no complaints about the change over, there was an ample supply of current with no serious interruptions. The new substation which had been commissioned at Hatch Street in November 1930, had proved very useful and another one being fitted out at Phibsboro was expected to be equally successful in improving pressure on the lines serving the North side.

While the overall effect of the change to ESB current was beneficial, the DUTC now had on its books the redundant power station at Ringsend Road, containing plant, which had no commercial value. The company's finances had benefited by reductions in charges and other changes in the balance sheet. The derelict Ringsend building would remain on the company's hands until an alternative use was found for it. The Ringsend plant was dismantled shortly afterwards, the building then being used for some years as a bus garage. Demolition of the chimneys, the 224-feet high 'Heavenly Twins', turned out to be a difficult and costly part of the operation. Later, in 1941, a new bus garage was built on the site of the former permanent way yard and depot, which had been transferred to Donnybrook. The power station building was subsequently used as a motor assembly plant and demolished in the early seventies to provide additional parking space for buses operating out of the adjoining garage. The ESB era substation, which had later passed to the Bovril company, became a listed building.

Boundary and Other Changes

The Electricity Supply Board also took over Dublin Corporation's Electricity Department in 1930. In the same year the existing pattern of local government for the Dublin area, which had been established around the turn of the century, changed drastically. The Urban Districts of Rathmines, Pembroke, Blackrock, Kingstown, Dalkey and Killiney/Ballybrack had been established in 1898, Howth following in 1917. A massive city boundary extension in 1900 had taken in the short-lived Urban Districts of Clontarf, Drumcondra/Glasnevin and New Kilmainham plus areas of the county. In September 1930 more sweeping changes took place, when the hitherto independent Rathmines and Pembroke Urban Districts were incorporated into the city, together with some further areas of the county.

At the same time, the Urban Districts of Dun Laoghaire, Blackrock, Dalkey and Killiney and Ballybrack were combined to form the new Dun Laoghaire Borough Corporation. Kingstown had changed its title to Dun Laoghaire Urban District Council in 1920. Despite the official change of name, several years passed before Kingstown gave way totally to Dun Laoghaire, many of the residents of that borough preferring to retain the original appellation. This was reflected for some time in the destination

Independent buses became a serious threat to the trams in the 1920s, this situation continuing until 1934 when legislation facilitated wholesale acquisition of these concerns by the DUTC. In this c1933 postcard view, Standard Saloon No 240, operating on route 14 to Dartry, picks up passengers at St Stephen's Green while an independent International bus bound for Crumlin comes up behind. The picture points up a serious disadvantage of traditionally laid-out tramways in the increasingly cluttered streets of the period when passengers had to board or alight in the centre of the roadway. Valentine collection, National Library

boards on the sides of the trams, which read 'Dun Laoghaire (late Kingstown)'.

Another name change which caused both trouble and confusion for many years was that of Sackville Street to O'Connell Street. An official change was proposed in 1884 but was dropped following legal action by the local ratepayers who wanted to keep the old name. For nearly 40 years after that, the street had two names, its official one and the more popular widely used one commemorating Daniel O'Connell. Finally, on 5th May 1924 the name O'Connell Street became official. Curiously neither this title nor its predecessor ever appeared among the destinations on DUTC trams.

Only two further changes were made in the local government boundaries in the Dublin area before the disappearance of the trams. Parts of Crumlin were taken into the city in 1941, followed by the Howth Urban District in 1942. The next major boundary changes did not take place until April 1953.

Coming to Terms with the Bus
The growth of commercial vehicles, both in size and numbers, was significant during the 1920s; but this was not the full story. While early post-war chassis were merely improvements of older types, after 1925 a succession of more advanced designs became available. The new ranges included models designed specifically as bus chassis, built lower than their predecessors. They were safer and offered better accessibility, further enhanced on double-deckers by single step dropped frame platforms. Greater reliability, totally enclosed bodywork of modern appearance, pneumatic tyres, more powerful engines and higher carrying capacities all combined to make buses more attractive than they had been previously.

Following its first service to Killester in 1925, the DUTC steadily expanded its bus operations. Within five years the company had more than 60 buses working about 20 services. Some of the routes were long radials serving villages up to 15 miles from the city. In suburban areas, they intended to develop traffic on routes that could be served by tramway extensions when loadings reached the necessary levels. This was especially critical on the north side of the city where the tramway system would need considerable improvement and extension to cater for new developments. Apart from the Howth line, there were only four comparatively short radial routes north of the Liffey. In contrast, the more developed south side had numerous lines, with extensive linking and some termini capable of being served by alternative routes.

Lethal Competition
The effect of aggressive bus competition, even with primitive vehicles, was debilitating for any tramway system already experiencing difficulties. While in nothing like the same financial or structural straits as the Dublin & Lucan Electric Railway, the DUTC was nevertheless very worried. It dithered about whether to extend the tramways into new housing areas such as Killester which already existed or Cabra and Crumlin which were shortly to be developed, or use buses instead. The directors perceived the developing situation largely in terms of profit and loss, and while still nominally committed to trams, were ever more impressed by what buses could do. Buses also cost less in capital investment than tramway extensions.

On the other hand the DUTC General Manager, George Marshall Harriss, while recognising the contribution buses could make to the public transport scene, was a dedicated proponent of the tramways. Addressing the Institute of Engineers in February 1925, he unequivocally stated his belief that while, 'buses are suitable as feeders to the tramway system or in outlying areas…no vehicle yet is considered capable of moving people en masse as the tram.' There was some unease about estates being served by DUTC buses which might divert passengers from the nearest tram line but its competitors had no such reservations and the vehicles available to them were getting better with each successive purchase.

Arguments about trams versus virtually every other type of vehicle were very prevalent, the subject being well aired at the Greater Dublin Commission in 1925. Giving evidence on 6th May, Harriss expressed the opinion that trams caused the least congestion on busy thoroughfares. If a tramcar carried 76 passengers, the space occupied by each passenger would be 0.3 of a square yard, while each passenger in a single-deck omnibus would occupy 1.8 of a square yard. A man would occupy 1.21 square yards and a bicycle, 2.5 square yards. He thought that there should be some regulation to prevent bicycles coming into thickly populated parts of the city.

Standing Up for the Tram
Harriss reiterated that he favoured tramcars in the city and buses in the outside areas. Mr D Brophy, the DUTC's Traffic Manager, pointed out that tramway movements in the congested areas formed only a small proportion, estimated at not more than 16% of vehicular traffic. He contended that up to that time, except for the London Underground, no better system of transport had been devised that would transport as quickly and economically the same number of passengers as tramways. He also contended that if buses replaced trams twice as many vehicles would be needed. The greatest number of trams operated by the DUTC was each evening between 5 and 6pm when 118 cars were dispatched southwards from Nelson Pillar. The average time taken to load and unload passengers was 26 seconds. The average number of passengers for a given date alighting from and boarding cars was 16,670 per hour. There were, however, recently developed districts where a bus

service would be useful because the population was insufficient to warrant the expense of laying down a tramway. He believed that it would pay the DUTC to introduce feeder buses from the tramway routes to new estates.

The number of tram passengers declined in the mid-twenties, a period during which business was generally depressed. In Dublin, the situation was exacerbated in the aftermath of the successive and debilitating conflicts the city and its transport system had suffered for more than a decade. A promised Utopia had failed to materialise, leaving people unsettled and uncertain about the future. They spent only what they needed to, the decrease in consumption being highlighted at the DUTC's annual general meeting on 9th February 1926. The need to economise understandably made the cheaper fares offered on the competing buses more attractive than those of the DUTC.

The Opposition
A classic example of the damage done by uncontrolled bus operation to tramway systems generally and to Dublin's in particular can be cited from this period. Around 1928, an estate of over 500 houses was built in the Walsh Road/Ferguson Road area of Drumcondra. The most remote part of the development was about half a mile from the tram route, for which it was a potentially valuable source of revenue. The estate was quickly invaded by a horde of private bus operators, one of whom introduced double deckers for a short time in 1929, until they were banished by the Carriage Office. The DUTC also served the area with two bus routes, one of which traversed the same streets as the former tramway connecting Drumcondra with College Green but abandoned in 1918.

The arrival of the double deckers, top-covered London-style NS type AECs, coincided with a tram strike, a circumstance enthusiastically exploited by all the bus owners to the eventual detriment of the tramways. The increasingly combative bus operators, whose antipathy to trams was shared by the growing number of motorists, seized upon every potential defect in the

system or its organisation. The sensible position, that both trams and buses had complementary not mutually exclusive, roles to play in public transport, was signally avoided at the time and for many years afterwards.

Most bus operators were well organised and efficient, but some were extremely irresponsible, showing little regard for their passengers or other road users. There are dire tales of chasers, buses that cut in front of trams or competitors' vehicles just as they were coming to a stopping place, to grab as much traffic as possible. Typically this type of operator often had buses that were badly driven, mechanically deficient and uninsured. He had little concept of the need to carry out maintenance or provide a reliable service. Such operators frequently failed to show up at advertised times, due to financial difficulties, mechanical failure or the prospect of richer pickings elsewhere. These people earned the title pirate, a pejorative term applied almost universally, and often unfairly, to all the private bus operators of the day.

Where the enterprising independents really shone was in their ability to go off the main roads into housing estates, providing a veritable door-to-door service. The level of fares they charged was hopelessly uneconomic, some 14-seaters on routes less than two miles long having a two man crew. Carriage Office Inspectors who were hard pressed to try and regulate matters frequently put them off the road. Indeed, experience with the pirates was used some years later as an excuse for outrageous behaviour by one individual carriage examiner who caused great grief to even the most responsible operators, including the DUTC. While

passengers were naturally delighted to avail of the facilities offered by the independents, they must nevertheless have had nagging doubts about how long the situation could continue. People who remember the period recall hearing of concerns about accidents and what would happen if the trams continued to lose custom.

Enter the Titan: Cork Succumbs
We have seen the inevitable consequences of motorbus competition for tramway concerns, big and small. In this context, it is easy to appreciate the difficulties of the many tramway systems throughout Britain, which had soldiered through the 1914-1918 War with almost no maintenance. Some were now in a truly dreadful situation, with track and rolling stock in dire need of renewal but often there was not enough money to replace worn out equipment, the capital cost of which would far exceed that of the buses by then available.

Thus there began an inexorable decline of tramway systems, the smaller ones being most vulnerable. In some instances, trams were replaced by buses of doubtful quality or durability that had themselves to be replaced within a fairly short time. Then in 1927, the Leyland Titan burst upon the market. This radically new double deck bus set standards for years to come and was the nemesis of many tramway systems. Although it was very unfair to compare 25-year-old trams with new buses Leyland Motors worked on this theme for all it was worth, with its slogan 'When you bury a tram mark the spot with a Titan'.

Ireland, with smaller cities and only three urban tramway systems, nevertheless provided a copybook example of this scenario.

In this mid-twenties view of No 297 crossing O'Connell Bridge, increasing traffic is already becoming a problem. The two-ton dray in the background had been part of the streetscape for a long time but the two motor cars provide a foretaste of what will in time overwhelm the efforts of the pointsman. No 297 was one of the nine six-window cars purchased in 1906 from the Electric Railway and Tramway Carriage Works of Preston and fitted with DUTC built top covers. All nine Preston cars were later replaced by Luxury Saloons, No 297's successor appearing in February 1932.
Birney collection

The problem alluded to below, the positioning of tram tracks in the streets, is graphically illustrated in this view of single truck Luxury car No 205, one of the last four such trams to be built in 1936, on a service on the Dartry line. The layout of the tracks away from the kerbs was unchanged since the days of horse traction. Passengers had to walk out into the middle of the road to board and leave the trams. When there was little traffic on the roads this was not a problem but with the rapid increase in the numbers of cars and other internal combustion engined vehicles in the years following the First World War, tram passengers were increasingly vulnerable to other road traffic. G S Hearse

Cork's brave little tramway system, not extended since 1902 and with its original Victorian and Edwardian rolling stock, had somehow survived the horrors of the city's virtual destruction in 1920. From the mid-twenties it was subjected to fierce bus competition and its inexorable fate was precipitated when its electricity supply function was assumed by the recently established Electricity Supply Board, which had no desire to become involved in public transport. Reluctantly, the Irish Omnibus Company took over operation of the trams until their replacement in September 1931 by Leyland Titans.

Fighting Back

Far from surrendering, some eminent engineers, while recognising the difficulties faced by tramway systems, were still extremely positive. In a paper entitled, 'Electrical Progress', prepared for the Institution of Municipal and County Engineers in May 1931, Mechanical and Electrical Engineer Laurence Kettle said that, '...tramways are...closely connected with the making and the use of streets and roads. It must be admitted that tramcars interfere to a considerable extent with the use of streets in an efficient way by the more flexible modern traffic', but then contended that '...a considerable amount of this obstruction might be got rid of by more intelligent regulations regarding stopping places, and by altering the position of the rails to suit the new traffic conditions. Electric tramways have adapted themselves to the modern requirements by using larger cars and by increasing the average speed of handling the traffic.'

Kettle also dealt with the economics and future of trams. He noted the constant growth in electricity generation and its improving cost effectiveness. In 1920, 3.4lbs of coal were needed to produce one unit of electricity. Only 2.05lbs of coal were

required eight years later. At the same time, the cost of generating plant in 1931 was only a third of what it had been ten years earlier. The paper looked at other transport options, giving details of the costs involved in operating trams, trolleybuses and motor buses. However, if motor buses were used, he emphasised that, 'the use of the omnibus means that the money leaves the country for petrol to replace the electric traction load at present being carried by the Shannon Scheme.' The ESB system was widely known as the Shannon Scheme in the thirties.

A table in the paper compared the average number of units used per car mile on eight systems. In Dublin, consumption was one unit per car mile in 1901, when the largest trams carried 54 passengers. By 1918, 318 trams used 1.5 units per car mile, the year's total being 12,620,000 units to move 71,008,655 passengers. In 1930, 321 cars, using 2.34 units per car mile, consumed 20,789,853 units to carry 88,959,343 passengers. By 1918, tramcar seating capacities had increased, the smallest double-deckers accommodating 58 people, bogie cars carrying 71. Four-wheeled and bogie cars built after 1923 seated 62 and 75 passengers respectively and their productivity was greatly enhanced by the higher speeds at which they operated. To distribute the additional current required by these improved vehicles, new substations were provided at College Street in 1918 and at Hatch Street in 1930. A new installation followed at Cabra (Phibsboro) in 1932.

Competition for Road Space

As the area used by public transport was increasingly encroached upon by other motor vehicles, there was less road space on which to move. The layout of tram tracks in most streets, unchanged since the days of horse traction, was awkward for everybody. Passengers had to walk to the middle of the

street to board a tram, and do the reverse when alighting. There were no traffic islands or refuges, thus making life even more difficult. Motor vehicle drivers found trams difficult to overtake and accidents were commonplace.

Traffic management was as yet unknown, and with motorists relatively free to do as they wished and uncontrolled parking the order of the day a fraction of the vehicles in use were capable of creating chaos. For example, contemporary photographs show cars parked herringbone fashion at both sides of the island on O'Connell Bridge in the late twenties. On Bachelor's Walk, the terminus for the Lucan trams, just beside the bridge, had a taxi rank between it and the river wall, while buses turned off between the two from O'Connell Bridge, and in those days the quays carried two-way traffic.

The majority of motorists in the years between the two World Wars were people of some influence which they used unhesitatingly. For instance, in the 1920s the tram tracks in Lower Grafton Street were realigned to suit the motor car, bringing the southbound line right alongside the footpath. The trams were constantly under fire, breakdowns providing so much ammunition for the motor lobby that the DUTC directors demanded regular reports, with statistics, from the Traffic Manager and the Chief Engineer. The commonest causes of these were broken trolley wires or defective trolley heads and the staff was constantly exhorted to improve matters.

Updating Trams

When the golden age of the motorbus dawned in the late twenties it posed an increasingly serious threat, not just to the immediate competitive capability of the tram; its long-term future was also very much in doubt. Many undertakings still believed in the tram, at least in the short term, and fought back, meeting the challenge with improved vehicles. In certain instances, these were existing cars suitably rebuilt or modernised; the conversion of

Dublin Balcony cars to Saloons is an example. Although an archaic appearance was often the downside of the tram's legendary longevity, sturdy construction meant that it could stand an extensive rebuild, its image being partially updated in the process.

Some large operators did not even bother to take this first step in upgrading their trams, feeling unable to justify heavy investment in refurbished, much less new rolling stock and opted for buses. Except for London United Tramways and London Metropolitan Electric Tramways company systems around this period were changing over to motorbuses or in some cases trolleybuses. It was the great British municipal systems, about 15 in all, that began building modern trams, proving beyond doubt that such vehicles were the answer to traffic and transport problems on heavily used routes.

Despite some extensions to its network in the twenties and the introduction of new cars, Belfast Corporation Tramways nevertheless endured severe bus competition. The Corporation became a bus operator in 1926, but still saw the tram as the mainstay of city transport. The 50 new Moffett class cars had appeared in 1920 and older vehicles were rebuilt, but there was still speculation, at the height of the bus war in 1928, as to the future of the trams. The appointment of William Chamberlain as General Manager, a dedicated tramway man who believed that trams had to be given a new image, put the issue beyond doubt. He set about further modernisation of the fleet and in 1930 brought out 50 new 66 seater trams with sprung leather upholstery and 50hp motors. A new livery was also introduced on the Chamberlain cars.

Modernising the Dublin Tram Fleet
Meanwhile, in 1929 the DUTC placed an experimental Standard Saloon top on No 313, the original Spa Road Balcony Bogie car of 1906. Praiseworthy as this was, the Standard design now looked decidedly dated, the upper deck structure of the Standard Saloons was a readily recognisable development of No 313's original balcony top cover. Paradoxically, this image predicament was compounded by the fact that 249 four-wheelers, open top, Balcony and Standard Saloon, were comparatively young in tramcar terms, dating from 1918 or later.

Between 1918 and 1923, 121 new open-top cars were built, and 48 of these received top covers from 1927 onwards, the last five being so fitted as late as 1931. Thirty-seven new Balcony cars were built between 1918 and 1922, followed by 91 Standards in the years 1924-1929. Of these, 33 had entered service as balcony vehicles, their top covers being transferred to some of the open-toppers when it was decided that all Standards should have saloon tops. Also noteworthy is the fact that while there had been only ten

top-covered four-wheelers in 1918, there were 178 by 1931.

The Luxury Tram Concept
Realising that they faced the same stark choice as Belfast Corporation and other major operators in Britain, the DUTC now took radical action and made a clean break with all previously accepted concepts of tramcar design. Bus bodywork, which had hitherto resembled that of trams in many respects, had taken off in a new direction in the mid-twenties. Vehicles like the Leyland Lion single decker or Titan double decker had set new standards in appearance and passenger comfort. All of this made contemporary tramcars, no matter how well constructed or fitted out, look very old fashioned in a world where a modern image was all important and the bus was the tram's deadly rival. This scenario, together with the DUTC's, or, more accurately, G Marshall Harriss's, commitment to continued tramway development, prompted the concept of Dublin's Luxury tramcars, the bodywork of which clearly owed more to bus design than the traditional tramcar.

While, as described earlier, all previous Dublin trams, beginning with open-fronted cars and progressing through vestibuled open-toppers to balcony types and finally Standard Saloons, showed a clear line of evolution, the new design broke radically with all of this. The shape was different, gone was the time-honoured lower deck structure with slightly recessed rocker panels, heavy mouldings and ventilator windows, up to now visually the same for all Dublin trams.

Also ousted were the three alternative upper-deck structures, open-top, covered top with end balconies or totally enclosed saloon, each capable of being removed and replaced by either of the others. The new vehicles presented a smooth outline, with both decks obviously designed as a unit. This was literally true. The body pillars of the Luxury cars ran the full depth of both decks, a complete break with normal practice. With the exception of the Luxury cars, up to the mid-sixties the upper and lower decks of all Dublin trams and buses were constructed separately before being united.

Design Details
Featuring five bay construction for four-wheelers and six bays for bogie vehicles, the new design utilised hardwood body framing and pillars on a welded steel underframe. The platforms were level with the lower saloon floor, thus eliminating a step at that point but necessitating two or three steps to board the car. Externally, the rocker panels were gently curved inwards towards the bottom and a half-round moulding marked the division with the waist panel. This was carried around the dashes in traditional DUTC

fashion, thus subtly retaining a characteristic design feature that was a hallmark of Dublin trams.

The pillars assumed a gentle tumblehome or inward slope at upper deck waist level, topped by a curved roof with flattened peaks at either end, in clear deference to bus design. The lower deck panelling was in aluminium but treatment of the upper deck cladding varied. While most of the cars had aluminium panelling others had planking, some narrow, some deeper. Taken with other differences in detail between these trams, such features gave the Luxury cars a greater degree of individuality than their Standard Saloon predecessors.

Half-drop windows were fitted to the Luxury cars, slight variations in the positions of opening windows conferring further distinction on many of them. The stairs at either end were a complete change from previous Dublin practice, being direct, that is, ascending from the trailing platform in the direction of travel. The stairs were coachbuilt and had a 90 degree left turn at the bottom before going straight up in a narrow stairwell. This had a full height partition to the left and a hinged door at the top, which clipped back so as to eliminate any obstruction to passengers at the head of the stairs.

Unlike previous trams, the resistances (devices that dissipate surplus current as heat) on the Luxury trams suffered from a lack of ventilation in their totally enclosed compartments under the stairs. Neat unobtrusive ventilators were fitted in the lower nearside corners of the lower dash panels to overcome this but were never completely satisfactory. The white ceilings were coved on both decks, the lighting being provided by bulbs with reflectors in neat recessed fittings above the windows. The window surrounds were in varnished grained timber.

There were double transverse seats on both decks, those in the earlier cars had ball-type stainless steel grabs at the outer corners of the reversible seat backs, some later four-wheelers being fitted with grooved timber top rails. Over the sandboxes in each corner of the lower saloon there were single and double seats in opposite corners with their backs to the windows. The arrangement of these varied slightly in some cars, and as with earlier vehicles having transverse seating, the layout provided room for up to 20 standing passengers.

Seating arrangements at the ends of the upper deck were easily the most unsatisfactory design feature of the Luxury cars. Behind the partition at the side of the stairs there was a U-shaped seat for, theoretically, up to eight people who had to struggle in and out when the tram was crowded. But in contrast, passengers on the transverse seats enjoyed a standard of comfort completely justifying the company's description of

This compares more than favourably with
the seating capacity of double deck buses at
that time. These usually offered 48 to 56
seats with standing room for eight people,
the full complement putting the bus under
severe mechanical strain.

The DUTC's fully justified faith in the Luxury trams was evidenced by remarks made at
the 1932 annual general meeting by the
Chairman, Mr William Hewat. He stated that
trams should be made as attractive as possible and it was with this in mind that the company had embarked on the building programme. He stressed, with obvious pride,
that the new trams now running were
designed and built by their own people at
their own works. Ten had been placed in
service during 1931, a further five had been
finished by the date of the meeting, held on
1st March, and 14 more were at various
stages of construction. While the investment
had been heavy, the new trams seemed to
have met with general approval and had certainly helped the Traffic Department's
efforts to increase the number of passengers
carried.

Thirty-five four-wheeled Luxury cars were
built on Maley and Taunton trucks, a make
new to the DUTC. These had 32in diameter
wheels, with two 40hp BTH motors. Thirty-
two of these trams had B49 controllers,
while the other three, Nos 12, 167 and 205,
had B13s. At seven feet, the trucks had a
wheelbase six inches longer than the Brills
under the Standard cars. They were of the
swing-link type, the axles being allowed a
slight degree of articulation when negotiating sharp curves but at speed on straight
track, this led to severe pitching and rolling,
known as jazzing.

Jazz had crossed the Atlantic a few years
earlier and was an extremely popular form
of music and dance. This was frowned on by
conservative clergy who fulminated from
the pulpit against jazz and led a movement
to have 'the Devil's Music' banned. When a
mechanism was devised to help steady the
four wheeled Luxury cars, it was, not unsur-
prisingly, known to tramwaymen as anti-jazz
gear, parodying the campaign of the religious purists. While it improved their riding
qualities, the anti-jazz gear made Luxury
four wheelers less amenable on sharp
curves, an abiding memory being their

these trams and arguably not equalled in
any subsequent Dublin stage carriage vehicle until the arrival of the City Swift
Olympian buses nearly 60 years later. The
seats had deep sprung cushions and backs
covered in moquette, at least three different
patterns being used in various trams. All
handrails and fittings were in stainless steel
or chrome and the entire decor of the vehicles was of a style still found in quality bus
designs 30 years later.

From the crew's point of view, the Luxury
cars lacked some amenities then becoming
standard on modern trams elsewhere. One
deficiency in the design was the lack of platform doors: if fitted, these would have
afforded the motorman a completely weath-
erproof working environment. The fitting of
these doors would have been a fairly simple
modification, as would the provision of a
motorman's seat, which would have
reduced fatigue considerably. Driver's mir-
rors and windscreen wipers would also have
highly desirable. Wipers were probably considered but not fitted, this may have been as
a result of experiments said to have been
carried out on Windjammer No 71.

The First Luxury Bogie Car
Construction of the first Luxury tram, bogie
car No 280, began on 6th October 1930, the
new vehicle being shown in the fleet records
as leaving Spa Road on Sunday 12th April
1931. Eight months was a creditable time in
which to build a prototype. A few days
before, on Wednesday 8th April, the *Irish
Independent*, in a report headed **DUBLIN
LUXURY TRAMS – MANY ATTRACTIVE FEATURES**
informed its readers that, 'The first of the new luxury tramcars built for the DUT Co had a trial run on Sunday, when it was driven from Inchicore to Dalkey and
back. Amongst the passengers was Mr W Kirwan, Rolling
Stock Supt., Ballsbridge; Mr J Malone, Works Foreman,
Inchicore, and a number of other officials of the company.'

The report, which got some details slightly
askew, especially recorded the fact that
when the seat backs were reversed, the
cushions tilted slightly, enabling passengers
to settle back into their seats.

Because its own running gear was not
ready in time, for its trials No 280 borrowed
the Hurst Nelson bogies of Balcony car 72
which was off the road at the time. While the
building of No 280 was nearing completion,
work was put in hand on two more cars, Nos
282 and 316. These left the works on 14th
August and 30th July respectively, fast times
in DUTC terms. All three trams were allocated to the Dalkey line, being joined later in
1931 by Nos 178 and 273. Over the succeeding five years, 15 more Bogie Luxury
cars followed, the years in which they
entered service are set out in Section Two of
the Rolling Stock Catalogue.

These trams were 74 or 76 seaters, with
capacity for a further 20 standing passengers, the discrepancy being due to slightly
differing arrangements on the lower deck,
which in some cases had 30 seats, in others
32 though all seated 44 upstairs. The Bogie
Luxury cars were all on Hurst Nelson maximum traction bogies and had two BTH
509C 50hp motors. No 280 had B13 controllers, as had most of the new trams, but
Nos 295, 299 and a few later cars had B510s.

Four-Wheelers
While No 280 was being built, work was also
put in hand on 14th March 1931 on the first
single-truck Luxury car, No 131. This tram
left Spa Road on 18th September and was
one of six to enter service in 1931. A total of
37 four wheeled Luxury cars was built up to
1936, as listed in Section 4 of the Rolling
Stock Catalogue. No 131 was a 60 seater,
accommodating 38 passengers upstairs and
22 below on seating similar to that in the larger vehicles and with standing room for 12.

screeching progress from Lower Grafton Street into Nassau Street.

Two Luxury four-wheelers laid down in January 1934 and emerging in July of that year were Nos 266 and 268, replacing the two notorious Balcony cars, the so-called Armoured Cars or Isle of Man Boats, bearing the same numbers. The two new vehicles did not have Maley and Taunton trucks, being mounted instead on Brill running gear. The trucks were of 6ft 6in wheelbase, with 35hp motors and B49 controllers. A noteworthy design feature of these trams was the recessing of the destination and number scrolls behind the windscreens of the upper deck, adding to the sleekness of the general design. This detail was included in the remaining 12 cars turned out up to October 1936.

Experiments: Pride
One feature incorporated in some Luxury cars which was not successful was the high roof domes that appeared on buses in the early thirties and was copied on some six of the DUTC trams built in 1933, single truck cars 13, 43, 135, 140, 148 and bogie 294. These were found to be liable to damage from trolley booms being pulled down hard and one car, No 43, is recorded as having its 'roof curves altered' in 1936. However, the remainder of the batch, including Nos 140 and 294 retained this feature. Another noteworthy member of this group was No 13, one of those cars destined to have a very short working life. Some sources stated that No 13 was fitted with longitudinal seating on the lower deck some time after entering service and this was confirmed as a result of photographic research carried out years later by Clifton Flewitt.

The late Gerry O'Toole, last in charge of the coachbuilding department at Bolton Street College of Technology, served his apprenticeship at Spa Road during the construction of the Luxury trams. It was company policy to employ as few permanent craftsmen as possible, the construction of a tramcar frequently taking up to two years. No 140 is an example, being laid down in November 1931 but not emerging until November 1933. Men were often engaged to work on a particular tram but diverted to carry out repairs at intervals during which no progress was made on their vehicle. As

soon as the frequently delayed tram was completed, they were let go and re-employed to work on another. Despite this they took an intense pride in their work and Gerry O'Toole recalled cycling out on a Sunday morning to follow, on its first day in service, a tram on which he had worked, excitedly pointing it out to anybody who would pay him any attention.

That modern trams could compete with any bus was amply demonstrated by the Luxury cars and the DUTC deployed them so as to have at least one or two on most routes. While always in a minority, finally totalling 57 in a nominal fleet of 330, their increasing numbers over a five-year period, and their widespread utilisation without any route restrictions seemed to proclaim unequivocally that trams were here to stay. Even the Howth line, from which the bridges had hitherto excluded top-covered bogie cars, received an allocation of eight-wheeled Luxury trams. Following successful trials in February 1933, five cars of this type, Nos 93, 294, 300, 329 and 330, were assigned to Clontarf for basic timetable duties. These were occasionally replaced or augmented by temporary exchanges with Dalkey line stock.

The excellence of the new trams was widely recognised and they were the recipients of many compliments from experienced writers on tramway matters. The tramway historian H Fayle, writing in *Modern Tramway* in December 1940, described them as extremely comfortable. In *'Great British Tramway Networks'*, the biblical reference work by W H Bett and John C Gillham, they are 'wide and handsome...a magnificent fleet...very fast and smooth-running, and with outstandingly comfortable seating'. While invariably called Luxury trams in Dublin, these last Spa Road trams

were frequently called Pullman cars by British writers, yet another tribute to their attractiveness.

Make-Up and Allocation of the Fleet
In the mid-thirties the DUTC fleet of 330 trams contained 75 bogie vehicles, used on the three long routes to Dalkey, Lucan and Howth. There were 15 open-toppers, all allocated to Clontarf for the Howth service and despite their somewhat old-fashioned design, these cars were extremely popular in summer, carrying great numbers of passengers. Chronologically they were quite modern in tramway terms, their bodywork dating from the 1920-1926 period. No 311 was the last new open-top tram built at Spa Road. A curious aspect of open-toppers, both trams and buses, is that passengers rarely expect them to be as modern as their roofed stablemates.

The 28 Balcony Bogie cars, dating from between 1908 and 1924, worked mainly on the Dalkey line, being transferred to the Lucan route as required. Here they supplemented the nine Bogie Standards that formed the core allocation, the hybrid rebuild No 313 and two other Bogie Standards normally being found on Dalkey duties. Although five of the 20 Luxury cars ran on the Howth line, the other 15 on Dalkey, these too sometimes strayed. One regular interloper north of the Pillar was No 159 which worked a special through service from Dalkey to the North Circular Road every Thursday, cattle market day. Bogie cars were rare visitors on the short northside lines. This Thursday working was an extension of the daily 5.45am service to Nelson Pillar.

In the last days of the nominally complete tram fleet, the 275 four-wheelers included one single-decker (No 80, the Clontarf

Luxury cars 266 and 268 under construction at Spa Road. Work on both vehicles began on 17th January 1934 and both left the works in July, No 266 on the 11th and No 268 on the 20th. These were the only Luxury four-wheelers mounted on Brill trucks, and both replaced two somewhat inelegant Balcony cars dating from 1918. The two Luxury cars survived until 1949. DUTC, Transport Museum Society of Ireland collection

Storm Car) and 39 open-toppers. Many of these were unserviceable, transferred to departmental duties or used only when absolutely necessary. After one important match at Croke Park in 1938, there was at least one rather decrepit open-topper in a long line of trams waiting for passengers in Drumcondra Road.

While they could turn up, if required, on almost any service with adequate clearances, the 87 Balcony cars were mainly concentrated at Terenure and Cabra depots, working intensively on the Whitehall, Glasnevin, Rathfarnham and Rialto lines. The 91 Standards were truly universal, but had a number of routes almost exclusively to themselves, notably Sandymount, Donnybrook-Phoenix Park, Clonskea-Whitehall, Ballybough, Inchicore and Dollymount. On Sundays when fewer trams were required on some routes, they also took over from Balcony cars.

As already suggested, allocation of the 37 Luxury cars was a delicate matter, passengers along each route believing in their absolute right to a full service of these hedonistic vehicles. Charles Ross remarked that there were a lot of people who expected open-toppers on warm summer days and Luxury cars at other times. Nevertheless, while Luxury trams were distributed with a degree of fairness, preference was given to routes on which Balcony cars rather than Standards predominated. Also, in a conscious attempt to retain patronage and challenge the growing trend to use private cars for commuting, proportionately more Luxury trams were allocated to lines serving areas with high car ownership. As a result, the Palmerston Park and Dartry routes saw more of these vehicles than did Drumcondra or Glasnevin.

Contrasts: Belfast and Bristol
With the decline of tramway systems in these islands during the 1930s, deliveries of new trams dwindled. As demand decreased, trams and component parts became more expensive, causing a spiral of attrition. Only about a dozen of the great municipal strongholds placed further new vehicles in service. Belfast was among these, with the 50 celebrated McCreary streamlined 64-seaters of 1935. Well ahead of their time in appearance and specification, these trams looked set to guarantee the future of tramcar operation. In short, the McCreary cars manifested clearly the approach of a progressive municipal transport undertaking to mass transport but were intended to have only a ten year life.

In contrast to Belfast, a commercial company owned the trams in Dublin, one of only two large cities in these islands where this position existed. The other company-owned monopoly was in Bristol. There, electrification began in 1895, a year before Dublin, and was complete by 1900. There was however an important difference between the two cities. The possibility, every seven years, of compulsory acquisition by the local authority, discouraged the Bristol Tramways and Carriage Company from modernising its fleet. The result was, that right up to 1940 the city was served by a magnificently maintained fleet of 237 open-top unvestibuled cars; the comparison with Dublin could not have been more striking.

Trams and Buses: Complimentary Roles
That modern trams were capable of keeping competing buses at bay was proved conclusively by the DUTC Luxury Saloons. Despite this, by 1931 even the most ardent tramway protagonist would have to recognise certain realities. Among these was that the DUTC was now a successful bus operator and had

some tram routes that could be served better by buses. While staying loyal to the trams, G Marshall Harriss readily accepted this, even if his directors were showing some signs of dithering. For them and a minority of shareholders, buses offered the prospect of bigger profits, in the short term at least. The Leyland Titan and its role in replacing the Cork trams had been impressive, as shown by comments made at DUTC shareholders' meetings.

Before the company began operating buses, the sole reduction of the DUTC tramway system had been the stretch of track from the Capel Street/Parnell Street junction via Bolton Street and Upper Dorset Street to North Frederick Street. When this closed in 1918, the only service affected was the then rather poorly patronised one from College Green to Whitehall. Seen in a wider context, the loss of this link was the first blow to the concept of a tramway network, never seriously developed on the north side of the river, where the routes were largely unconnected radials.

Closure of the South Quays Line
Several important links were lost with the closure on 30th March 1929 of the No 22 route, connecting the railway stations at Kingsbridge, Westland Row and Harcourt Street, the associated tracks in Lincoln Place were by then also disused. However, from 1927 train travellers using Kingsbridge were briefly served better than before when rails were laid right into the north side of the station, connecting with the South Quays line.

Following closure of the 22 route, considerable changes were made to the track layout on and around O'Connell Bridge. Several connections were taken out and the tracks on the bridge were realigned to allow for better use of all available road space. At the same time traction poles on the bridge were relocated to the footpaths and for the first time in the city centre some of these lacked arms and scrollwork, the span wires being fixed direct to the poles. During the mid-thirties, the track layout both north and south of Nelson Pillar was also modified.

The disconnected tracks on Aston Quay and westwards towards Kingsbridge remained in position for some time after the

Luxury four-wheeler No 13 at Shelbourne Road. This car, which entered service in October 1933, was one of a small batch to have high end domes. No 13 had a comparatively short working life, being withdrawn by 1942 and stored until scrapped following the Terenure line closure on 31st October 1948. The paper advertisement for the Theatre Royal had to be replaced with every change of cine variety programme in this famous Dublin institution. Fayle collection, Irish Railway Record Society

Bogie cars 79 and 278 at Nelson Pillar in CIE days. No 79, built in 1910 at a cost of £862 7s 5d and with short canopies over its balconies, was one of the pre-First World War Dalkey expresses. It had its roof extended to full length in 1930 and was fitted with balcony side netting, making it suitable for running to Lucan. No 278 dating from 1928 was one of the nine Bogie Standards built for the reconstructed Lucan line. Both trams lasted to the end in July 1949. Burrows Bros

line's closure. They were referred to at some length by the DUTC Chairman, Mr William Hewat, at the company's annual general meeting on 1st March 1932. He told the meeting that the Corporation had been pressing for the reconstruction of the roadway on the South Quays, involving the altering of levels and relaying of track, an expense the company could not justify. The route had never been remunerative and was, in its later years, very little used. Moreover, traffic conditions had never justified two sets of tramway lines on the North and South Quays. Hewat confidently predicted that this closure, instead of causing the company any hardship, would in reality improve its financial position.

Buses, Passengers and Statistics

Statistics presented at that same meeting revealed increased traffic during 1931, when the total number of passengers carried on DUTC trams and buses reached a total 106,486,659, an improvement of 2,920,764 on 1930. The receipts from tramway passengers, at £530,494, were up by £11,772. However, on the debit side, there was an increase of £29,442 in working expenses, mainly explained by extra running, 446,550 extra car miles had consumed an additional 732,760 units of electricity. The increased mileage had reduced the receipts per car mile from 14.005d per mile the previous year to 13.684d in 1931, while working expenses had increased from 10.297d to 10.544d. Track maintenance costs and increased wages played a part in these results.

Hewat was very positive about the future of the tramways. The directors, he said, had never lost faith in the efficiency of the system and its suitability to meet the requirements of the public as the safest and best form of transport for the city. New rails were on order and within a few days work would begin on relaying the section from North Frederick Street to Nelson Pillar. This was also seen as a contribution to reducing the worryingly high rate of unemployment. Here Hewat was able to point out that the DUTC had 2,330 staff, with a weekly payroll of over £7,000.

Buses were playing an increasing part in the activities of the DUTC and were at least, profitable, despite the intense competition offered by private operators. Reductions in the cost of tyres and petrol had helped to turn in a profit and a new garage was being built beside Conyngham Road tram depot. There was still some uncertainty, which he hoped would be resolved when the new Transport Act took effect, but the results for the traffic problems of the city and country generally depended on how it was administered. While regretting the continuing world wide depression in trade, Mr Hewat was optimistic about the DUTC's prospects.

In the immediate future, the DUTC Chairman expected that the Eucharistic Congress to be held in Dublin in June 1932 would bring large numbers of visitors to Dublin, and extra traffic for the DUTC. His highest hopes for traffic during the week of the Congress were more than realised, 3,909,676 people being carried. This was the greatest number of DUTC passengers in any week in the company's history, exceeding the previous best by 1,477,878.

Traffic during the period 22nd to 26th June required the use of every available DUTC vehicle, tram and bus. The late William Birney suggested that the demand for trams was so great as to create the only instances of two DUTC trams with the same fleet number running simultaneously at that time. A new Luxury car, No 245, entered service on 17th June but the open-top tram it rendered due for replacement was available and is believed to have been used on Congress traffic. Subsequent research by Clifton Flewitt suggests that as many as five pairs of cars with the same number may have been in service simultaneously during the Congress.

Closure of the Bath Avenue Line

Route 4, Nelson Pillar to Sandymount via Bath Avenue, had always been a difficult one for the DUTC. The last service to be converted from horse traction, in January 1901, it was the only one on the system worked by single-deck cars, which were always cut-down double deckers. Four-wheelers had been used up to 1922, bogie cars after that. The eight-wheelers were brought into use on the Bath Avenue line for several reasons, the most important being that they had a higher seating capacity than four-wheelers.

The number of eight-wheeled vehicles had increased over the years and with the more strategic deployment of trams and latterly a greater use of buses, a few bogie cars could be released for conversion to single-deckers. The Bath Avenue bogie trams eventually totalled seven, the last two, Nos 320 and 321, being altered as late as 1931 and 1932 respectively. But they were a more expensive type to run and maintain than the earlier four-wheelers and the route operated only on weekdays, the first departure from Sandymount being at 8.35am and the last from the Pillar at 7.30pm; there was no Sunday service.

Bus competition had been very severe on the Bath Avenue route for some years, Mrs Clerkin's Carmel fleet providing the principal opposition. Faced with this situation, the DUTC decided to replace the trams and so the No 4 service closed on 30th July 1932, bus route No 44A (later 52) taking over the next day. Of the seven single-deck trams, four (Nos 294, 288, 299 and 300) were replaced within 18 months by new Luxury cars. The other three, Nos 320, 321 and 324, were rebuilt as open-top double-deckers for the Howth line. The first two of these had previously been Balcony cars, while No 324 was merely reverting to its original open-top state. No 321 had a notably short career of less than six months as a single-decker, having emerged from Spa Road in this guise as recently as 5th February 1932.

The Sandymount single-deckers were assured of a place in literary history by Flann O'Brien (Myles na Gopaleen) who commented that, 'anybody upstairs on the No 4 tram cannot fail to be struck by the beautiful stonework of Bath Avenue railway arch.'

The DUTC and the Railways:
Area Agreements
Buses, seen as a serious threat to both the DUTC and the railways in 1925, were part of all these companies' operations five years later. In 1932, by which time the bus networks had become well established, an agreement was concluded between the Great Northern Railway, the Irish Omnibus Company (agent for the Great Southern Railways) and the DUTC. Eliminating wasteful competition between the three, the agreement effectively recognised a DUTC area of influence, but could not do anything to restrict private operators. Under the 1932 agreement, the DUTC and GNR paid particular attention to eliminating unnecessary competition in so far as was possible in the north eastern suburbs.

Howth was now in a unique situation, being served by GNR trains from Amiens Street and DUTC trams from Nelson Pillar. There was also a GNR bus service from Eden Quay, operating via Killester and Raheny, with some interavailability of return tickets between the three types of service. While development was proceeding in the Killester and Clontarf areas, there was very little new building beyond Dollymount where there were some large estates like St Anne's and Betty Glen. Small groups of local authority houses and ribbon development along main roads were the only source of regular intermediate traffic but in fine summer weather the 15 open-top bogie cars of the Howth line were kept busy, backed up by vehicles from other parts of the system. Baldoyle races also encouraged heavy traffic, racegoers walking from the long loop at Baldoyle Road nearly a mile to the course.

Legislation: Monopoly Once Again
It had been obvious for a long time that some measure of regulation would have to be imposed on the road transport industry as it existed in the early 1930s. Based on recent British legislation, the freedom of private passenger and freight operators was severely circumscribed by the Road Traffic Act of 1933 and the Road Transport Acts of 1932 and 1934.

By 1933 most of the real pirate bus operators had disappeared, and several owners had either merged into bigger companies or formed co-operatives. Fewer in number, their improved organisation, expertise and confidence now posed a more serious threat than before to the railway and tramway companies. They were glad to comply with the obligation to obtain service licences and have vehicles satisfying the new stringent Construction and Use Regulations. However, their further development was stopped peremptorily by the powers conferred on statutory operators to buy competitors out compulsorily. Some companies sold out voluntarily, others resisted all the way, but in the end the DUTC obtained almost the monopoly it sought.

G Marshall Harriss's Last Stand
On 14th March 1935, in a profile of General Manager George Marshall Harriss, *Transport World* pointed out that, until recently, the DUTC '...operated 300 tramcars and about 100 omnibuses (carrying approximately 120 million passengers yearly) and that Dublin was also served by a number of rival omnibus undertakings whose passengers numbered between 30 and 40 millions annually. The article went on to state that, 'To-day, as the result of recent legislation, independent competition has disappeared, and the Dublin Tramways Company – now operating 300 tramcars and 300 omnibuses – is faced with the problem of how to serve the interests of shareholders, who have invested more than £2,000,000 in their undertaking, and the local transport needs of more than over 500,000 citizens who are distributed over urban and semi-rural suburbs which lie within a radius of about 12 miles from the city centre…an unrepentant believer in the tramcar as the most economic means of street transport, Mr Harriss, like other transport administrators, realises that there is a big and growing sphere for the omnibus…'

The General Omnibus Company: End of the Blessington Tramway
The most successful of the private passenger carriers was undoubtedly the General Omnibus Company, which began business in 1927 and established for itself a generally favourable public image. This company, which was managed very professionally, put the Tower Bus Company, the concern that had forced the closure of the Dublin & Lucan Electric Railway three years earlier, out of business in 1928. The General was in direct competition with the DUTC trams working the Lucan line, beyond where it operated to Maynooth and Celbridge. Another General acquisition was the Paragon Bus Company which operated to Blessington.

Blessington, 20 miles from Dublin and 17 from Terenure, was served by the Dublin & Blessington Steam Tramway Company since August 1888. The hour and a quarter allowed for a journey from Terenure in 1912 was 15 minutes longer by 1930, the number of weekday through services in those years numbering six and three respectively. There had been a proposal, before the First World War, to electrify the line as far as Jobstown, but the only outcome was the purchase of two somewhat unreliable petrol-electric tramcars. Later, two Ford railbuses and a Drewry railcar were also bought, but the tramway's decline was terminal.

Standard Saloons Nos 168, 293 and 283 at Sandymount depot in 1938. No 168, built as a Balcony car in 1924, became a Standard Saloon in 1927, its original top cover going to No 151. No 293 was new in 1925, while No 283, the most recent of the trio, emerged from Spa Road in June 1926. The tramcar repair books record that No 283 was spray painted in 1936. There were two depots on this site. The older, dating from 1872 later housed the Bath Avenue line single deckers, while the structure in which the trams are seen here was built for the double deckers that began operating on the new route via Ringsend in 1900.
Camwell collection, Tramway Museum Society

The Civil War and the onslaught of motor vehicles damaged the Blessington line terribly, lorries taking over most of the freight traffic in the twenties. Like the Dublin & Lucan, the Blessington Company applied for, but was refused, inclusion in the railway amalgamations of 1924. Bus competition, especially from the Paragon, increased in severity, passengers being able to travel all the way from Blessington to the city centre by bus in about one hour. Not surprisingly, the extension to Poulaphouca, served by five trains on weekdays in 1912, closed in 1928.

Sustained by its Baronial Guarantee, the main line struggled on for another four years. The guarantee was included in several Irish railway Acts authorising lines in sparsely populated areas. This provision ensured that any shortfall in servicing Treasury loans were covered by the ratepayers of the districts the railway or tramway served. Eventually, the Blessington line, the last roadside tramway in these islands using double-deck trailers, succumbed on 31st December 1932. The baronial levies continued for nearly 30 more years, latterly contributing to the pensions of former staff.

The DUTC and the General
While legally and commercially acquired by the DUTC in 1934, what effectively occurred was a reverse take-over by the General's management. Following a long period of sick leave, G Marshall Harriss, the long serving DUTC General Manager, retired in August 1935. Several of the most senior posts in the company went to former General Omnibus Company executives, A P Reynolds becoming General Manager in January 1936 and later advancing to Managing Director.

Like all the erstwhile private bus operators, Reynolds had experienced considerable hostility from the DUTC and had an ingrained dislike, not only for the company, but also for trams. He was certainly determined to provide a good service, but he was an accountant by profession and therefore inclined to maximise short-term profits, an option notably associated with bus operation. The future of the tram as the mainstay of Dublin's transport system was therefore henceforth in serious doubt.

Despite Reynolds's arrival, everything in the tramway section of the DUTC appeared to be normal, for the time being. Six new Luxury trams were built in 1935, followed by another half dozen in 1936. From the end of 1935, the Dublin United adopted a cheerful new tram livery, broadly seen as a great improvement on the somewhat drab and dingy grey. The new colour scheme had Audley green lower panels, upper deck panelling and the window surrounds on both decks were cream, with a band of olive green between decks. Lining was cream on

green, olive on cream, this being simplified at a later date by eliminating frets at the corners of upper deck panels.

Bogie Luxury car No 300 was the first tram in the new colours, leaving the works on 31st December 1935. Over the next two years the entire fleet was dealt with, the only exceptions being the 40 or so remaining four-wheeled open-toppers and possibly one or two single-truck Balcony cars. A few trams subsequently received a somewhat sombre variation of this livery, the olive band above the lower deck windows being dispensed with and the upper deck panelling painted olive all round. Cars so turned out included Nos 157, 197, 209, 185, 220 and 231. While these retained the non-standard colours in later repaints other trams continued in the normal green and cream.

Tower Wagon Fatality
In 1935 there also occurred the last fatal accident to be included in this book because it was specifically related to tramway operation. This tragic mischance occurred at Dollymount on the morning of Tuesday 12th February. A 34-year old overhead linesman named Michael Scanlon fell from the platform of a tower wagon, suffering fatal injuries. At the subsequent inquest, the jury found that there was insufficient protection to ensure the safety of staff working on the platform.

Bus Developments
The DUTC's first bus service to Killester in 1925 was intended to be replaced with a tramway extension from Fairview at a later date, but this did not materialise. Further bus services were inaugurated quite rapidly, the bus fleet totalling 12 at the end of 1925. Their numbers had increased to more than 60 by 1930 and in 1933 the company had over 100 buses. The 12 buses of 1925 produced £6,510 in revenue, the much-expanded fleet of 1933 earning £198,214. In the latter year, 318 trams produced £534,633, carrying 91.476m passengers over 9.876m miles. By 1937 tram passengers had declined to 88.530m, up by over a million on the previous year, but being hotly pursued by an increase of nearly 2.5m bus passengers who totalled 62.829m in 1936 and 65.350m in 1937. These statistics well indicate the growth in the company's bus operations.

Prior to 1933, all buses placed in service by the Dublin United were petrol-engined, and except for the first 12, had bodywork designed and built at Spa Road. They were relatively expensive to run and maintain but there was a growing body of opinion in their favour, especially among the motor lobby and on the DUTC board. There were also a great wealth of very solid arguments in favour of trams, particularly on heavily traf-

ficked routes. Their initial cost was admittedly higher and there was the expense of track, overhead, power supply and distribution; to this could be added their inflexibility when compared to buses. The tram's great strengths lay in lower operating costs and superior carrying capacity, with a tremendous overload facility. Their reliability was vastly superior to that of buses, their maintenance costs much lower. The trams' use of locally produced fuel and freedom from pollution were among their other advantages not fully pressed home at the time. The ability to keep going in the most adverse weather conditions was also a considerable plus for the tram.

Buses were comparatively cheap to buy and did not require expensive fixed plant like track, overhead gear or a power distribution system. They were, however, unable to endure the same daily punishment as trams, requiring more frequent maintenance and having a lifespan considerably less than that of a tramcar. In the late 1930s, seven years was regarded as a reasonable working life for a bus, as against more than 20 for a tram.

A double deck four-wheeled tram could carry 60 seated and 12 standing passengers, while a bogie car could manage 76 plus 20 standees with no appreciable diminution in acceleration or performance. The acceleration curve is one of the tram's great strengths. Electric vehicles generally enjoy a sharper rise in speed from stop to around 20mph than those fitted with internal combustion engines. This is a decided advantage in urban conditions with frequent stops and relatively low maximum speeds.

Up to 1937, the largest modern single-deck buses seated 36 passengers, and double deckers, of which there were as yet none in Dublin, could seat up to 56, with eight standing passengers. The buses would also make heavy work of such a burden, while frequent stops and heavy loads played havoc with fuel consumption. Another fact to be borne in mind is the number of stops. Up to 1960s, there were about eight per mile on Dublin tram and bus routes, twice the number encountered today.

During the early thirties development of the automotive diesel engine made the motor bus a more attractive alternative to the tram than it had been previously. For the operator, it certainly created an expectation of greater profits, at least in the short term. The prospects of better fuel consumption encouraged many transport companies to experiment with diesel engines. The DUTC put their first diesel engined bus, a Dennis Lancet 32-seater, to work in September 1933 and as a result, only diesel-engined vehicles were bought subsequently.

When Leyland Motors offered a 56 seater diesel version of the Titan double decker with very advanced body styling the DUTC decided not only to operate such vehicles but also to build them under licence at Spa Road. The method of construction also changed from timber to metal framing for the bodywork, thus giving the vehicles a longer life expectancy. With the DUTC under pressure from various lobbies, discounts available to large operators buying buses in quantity, and most particularly the philosophy of the Reynolds management, the fate of the tramway system was now all but sealed.

Moving Towards a Better Society

Between the two World Wars, working people strove to achieve a more liberal and equitable society. Mindful of what had happened in 1913 and afterwards most citizens had a renewed sense of their own worth. While discouraged and slowed down by the Civil and Economic Wars, this spirit had begun a long drawn out process that would, many years later, greatly raise the status and living standards of workers.

After 1913 the tramwaymen had resolved that they would never again be left unprotected, but one of the conditions under which they had been taken back in 1914 was that they signed an undertaking - 'the Document' - as it was called, never to belong to the Irish Transport and General Workers' Union. They therefore joined a British union, which in time became part of the Transport and General Workers' Union, the word 'Amalgamated' being prefixed to the Irish section at a later date. Imperfect though the situation was in the eyes of many, the right to belong to a trade union had at least been vindicated.

DUTC management appears to have read the trends imperfectly, if at all, as the age of autocracy slowly yielded to one of egalitarianism. They failed to recognise that ordinary people were becoming increasingly less amenable to the master/servant rela-

tionship with their employers as set out in Tramway Company Rule Books. For many, William Martin Murphy's death in 1919 had been a milestone in the extinction of that oppressive era, its ethos and social structures, but its legacy remained long afterwards.

The DUTC's recognition of a changing world does not appear to have grasped the need to tackle the poor industrial relations that had been a regular source of trouble since the earliest days of the Dublin tramways. The result was that a sorry raft of unresolved problems spanned the transition from the old to the new DUTC regimes. Despite all that had happened in the years between, the 1925 'Standard Rules and Regulations for the Guidance and Government of Officials and Employees' had the same title as its 1902 predecessor. Traffic rules were re-arranged or expressed differently, but the general thrust of employer/staff relationships had not changed.

Among other things,tramwaymens' continuing antagonism towards DUTC management arose from a belief that promotion would always go to those who had been loyal to the company at the expense of their colleagues. During the 1920s, hostility between staff and management had effectively become institutionalised in the DUTC. Real or imagined slights were not taken lightly and petty misunderstandings could escalate quickly into major confrontations. Several strikes took place during the twenties, particularly strong reactions being caused by wage cuts in 1927 and 1929. As time went by several new elements compounded existing difficulties even further.

Living Costs, Wages, Fares and Profits

The 1914 cost-of-living base figure of 100, which peaked at 249 in 1920, thereafter fell dramatically, and bottomed out at 151 in 1933. A wave of industrial disputes arising

from pay reductions related to the falling cost of living in the United Kingdom during the twenties inevitably had repercussions in the new Irish Free State. Employees in most companies suffered reductions in pay during this period, some of the clawbacks being accounted for by the withdrawal of temporary rises to meet the increased cost of living during the war.

Joseph Mooney, the Chairman, complained at the DUTC's annual general meeting on 11th February 1924 that the company had only succeeded in getting back 4/- per week off the war bonus of the traffic and permanent way men's wages. This compared with 15/- per week on English tramways, the war bonus in each case being £2.3s. per week. The company was negotiating with the staff, claiming that alterations in the conditions of work had wiped any advantage they hoped for from the reduction of 4s. per week in wages.

Fares, costs, (especially wages) and profits were inextricably linked in such a way that at least one of three groups, passengers, workers or shareholders, was always bound to be aggrieved. If wages fell, so did fares and, usually, profits. Government policy and decisions could affect matters directly, as when the Minister for Industry and Commerce made an order reducing fares in August 1923. Mooney stated that as a result, receipts for the 18 weeks from the date of the order to the end of the year were £11,000 less than in the corresponding period for the previous year, but passenger numbers increased by 3,189,035, requiring additional cars.

The 1929 Strike

A protracted strike was sparked off by the wage reductions that accompanied the 1929 decline in living costs. In its fall from the 1920 apex of 249, the cost of living index had reached 174 by July 1929. Wages were cut by 10%, the tramwaymen being asked to accept a reduction of 6/- per week. Negotiations failed and the men struck on 15th August, staying out until 20th September when they returned to work after conceding a 1/- drop in pay. The buses were back a day before the trams because permanent way and overhead line staff had to check all installations before services could resume.

Luxury four-wheelers 12 (1935) and 176 (1932) at Terenure depot in 1938, with Balcony trams 226 and 227. No 226 was built as an open-topper in 1921, receiving its top cover from No 170 in 1928, while No 227 was built as a Balcony tram in 1921. Both vehicles were fitted with numeral scrolls in 1938. No 12 was withdrawn by 1942 but No 176 survived until the closure of the Dalkey line in 1949.
Camwell collection, Tramway Museum Society

Standard Saloon No 40 at Pembroke Road in the late 1930s. It is working on route 18, known as the cross-route because of the number of other services it crossed or met between Ballsbridge and Kenilworth Square. By the time this photograph was taken, street lamps were being placed on top of the traction poles. Camwell collection, Tramway Museum Society

This strike was more serious for the company than any previous one because the independent bus operators were now on the streets in great numbers. They wrung every possible advantage from the situation, the more responsible ones carefully wooing former tram passengers, some of whom became converts to the bus. There were also the real pirates who behaved in ways that did the image of the public transport industry in general and the bus business in particular much long-term damage. The settlement of the 1929 strike simply dealt with its immediate causes, doing nothing to eliminate the long-standing complaints at the root of labour relations in the DUTC. However distressing for the participants, it was nothing in comparison with what was to follow, in scale, bitterness and complication.

The 1935 Strike
Completion of the virtual transport monopoly in 1934 brought in from the acquired bus companies a large body of men ill disposed to the DUTC. They saw the company not as their employer but an enemy, the atmosphere being further poisoned by an inability or unwillingness to get along with existing DUTC staff. An undercurrent of tram versus bus rivalries that already existed within the DUTC became more palpable with the arrival of the new staff. Seniority and levels of skill threw up additional problems that management failed to identify and resolve. While seniority disputes among DUTC staff were fairly straightforward, the rights of the men who came in with the acquired companies led to more sensitive situations.

Spilling over from the core tramway staff of the DUTC were all of the long-standing grievances left over from 1913. These worsened an accumulation of more normal industrial relations issues concerning spread-over duties, overtime, holidays and pensions. The question of pay, central in most disputes, was exacerbated not only by the recent pay cuts but also by the operation of what was known as the subsistence wage principle. Using this widely applied yardstick of the thirties. Employers, wherever possible, paid slightly more per week than the minimum a worker in a particular employment was thought to merit in the struggle to keep body and soul together.

The unproductive negotiations which had been dragging on over several months were dramatically overtaken by events in February 1935 when a bus driver was dismissed in highly questionable circumstances. The resulting strike began on 3rd March and continued for eleven weeks. Several attempts were made to settle the dispute, but infighting, external interference and inter-union rivalry made agreement more difficult by the day.

Added complications were rivalry and poaching between the two transport unions, the stirring up of national feeling by charge and counter charge about foreign unions and the latent possibility of pseudo-military involvement. The atmosphere was made more volatile by the revolutionary feelings prevalent at the time, some DUTC employees seeing the situation as a re-run of 1913, but one in which they would be the victors.

Bill McCamley, in *The Role of the Rank and File in the 1935 Tram and Bus Strike* (Labour History Workshop, 1981), points out that between them, for the four DUTC directors, Chairman William Hewat, Dr William Lombard Murphy, James McCann and Hon James McMahon, their many and varied business connections represented a substantial interest '…in all the most capitalist concerns in the country'.

The alternative services which had been provided by the independent bus companies during the 1929 strike no longer existed in 1935 and there was a widely held view that the creation of a new monopoly had led to the long-drawn out hardship now being suffered. Frustrated citizens made their feelings known to the politicians in very direct terms. Exasperated by growing criticism and the failure of attempts to settle the dispute, the government put military lorries on the streets to minimise the worst effects of the dispute, thereby setting a precedent for future strikes.

Comparing 1937 with 1872 and 1904
For 1872, the year in which trams first ran in Dublin, the public services then available in the city were outlined in Chapter One. Thirty-two years later, the state of these services in 1904, a year important in both tramway and literary terms, is outlined on pages 66 and 67 of Chapter Three. Just one year further forward from 1904 than 1872 was behind it, 1937 was also important in that it was the last year in which the tramway system was more or less complete. It is therefore worth while to set the DUTC's operations in the context of the other public services of the mid-thirties and 1937 in particular. All that happened at that time, took place in a much changed political environment where social relationships were also moving away, albeit slowly, from the old patterns.

In Context: Public Services in 1937
As in both of the earlier years referred to, gas supply was still in the hands of the Alliance and Dublin Consumers' Gas Company whose customers were divided between those on penny-in-the-slot meters and people paying quarterly bills. There were still numerous houses lit by gas, some on the ground floor only. The Gas Company's fleet of orange vans toured the city, their sirens letting the meter cash collectors know that they were in the vicinity to gather the takings. Gas Company work gangs pushed handcarts containing their tools and equipment to work sites.

The Electricity Supply Board, now responsible for power supplies and most electric public lighting in Dublin, was in the process of installing overhead distribution lines in side roads where houses had hitherto been lit by gas, if at all. In contrast to the furore caused by the DUTC's proposed installation 40 years earlier, the use of overhead wiring by the ESB was accepted as an economic necessity by the Corporation. Lamplighters were still in business, while the uniformed men responsible for maintaining lamps and winding the clocks controlling time switches, travelled around on bicycles, carrying extension ladders attached to the crossbars. Gas lighting was being replaced on some main routes, the electric lamps being mounted on traction poles in streets served by trams. The principal streets were still lit by arc lamps, carried on the Arc, Scotch and Hammond Lane columns still in use to-day. Most of the electricity generated in the state, including that used to drive the trams, came from either the Pigeon House or the Shannon Scheme at Ardnacrusha.

Telephones and the telegraph service were both under the direct control of the Department of Posts and Telegraphs. Telegrams could be transmitted from any telegraph office, incoming telegrams were delivered by messengers, using motor or pedal cycles. Automatic or dial telephones were general in the city area, having been introduced in 1927 but several suburbs still relied on manual exchanges. Ballsbridge, Blackrock, Dalkey, Donnybrook, Drumcondra and Howth were among places still not linked to the automatic system. Making a phone call in those areas began with turning a handle to alert the operator who then connected the caller to the requested number.

Telephones were to be found only in business premises or the homes of the well to do. Local calls from coin boxes cost 2d for five minutes. The paucity of telephones can be gauged from one simple fact of history. In 1937, contagious diseases now almost forgotten or treated differently from today were still widespread. Patients were isolated to Cork Street Fever Hospital and its convalescent home Beneavin, between Glasnevin and Finglas. To save relatives the expense of phoning, lists of patients' numbers were published daily in the evening papers,

appearing under categories that included 'Progressing' and 'Not so well'.

Refuse collection in the city area was largely by the solid-tyred de Dion freighters introduced in 1925 and owned by Franco-Irish Enterprises, contractors to the Corporation. This arrangement had replaced the haulage of material from the Stanley Street destructor to Fairview which was now almost fully developed as a park. The refuse was brought to various landfill tips including Ringsend, while filling in of many old quarries had begun and would continue for several years. In Rathmines, the Corporation had taken over refuse collection from the former Urban District Council, using side-engined Shelvoke and Drewry freighters, known to staff as 'tillers'. Later the Corporation assumed control of Franco-Irish Enterprises.

The main drainage system had changed little since 1906, but expanding areas, especially in the north eastern suburbs, still had septic tanks or direct untreated sea outfalls. Development of the Liffey hydro-electric scheme at Poulaphouca, a joint operation between the Corporation and the ESB, was getting under way; other sources of water were Bohernabreena and Roundwood. For much of its transport requirements, the Corporation still relied on horse-drawn vehicles, some of which were supplied by private contractors, known as hackers.

Fire Brigade stations were at Tara Street, Buckingham Street, Thomas Street and Dorset Street. The Brigade had six motor pumps and three turntable ladders and at least one fire appliance still awaited conversion to pneumatic tyres. The street fire alarm network had been extended to several new areas, the person breaking the glass and ringing the bell to summon help being expected to remain at the spot until the Brigade arrived to ascertain the location of the fire. The Fire Brigade also operated the

accident and emergency ambulance service.

The Dublin Metropolitan Police, which had become the Dublin Metropolitan Area of the Garda Siochana in 1925, was responsible for policing. It was organised in districts clearly recognisable as enlarged versions of those existing in 1872 and 1904. There were still the A, C, E and F divisions south of the Liffey, B and D being on the north side. Enlarged areas of jurisdiction and new stations had followed the growth of the city. Motor transport was available but the notion of the patrol car as we know it had not yet arrived. Patrolling was carried out either on foot or bicycle. In Dublin, the policemen's helmets were similar to those worn by many forces in Britain.

The streets were filled with a great variety of horse-drawn and petrol-engined vehicles, plus a smattering of steamers. Laundries, bakeries and dairies still relied almost exclusively on horses for delivery work, although one bakery, Rourke's, had already invested in at least one battery-electric van, while Johnston, Mooney & O'Brien were just about to embark on replacing all their horse-cars with electrics. Horses were still the mainstay for much commercial traffic for loads up to two tons, with petrol-engined lorries, principally Fords, Bedfords and Morris-Commercials dominating in the 2-5-ton sector. Above that, there were some larger lorries, especially Leylands, but the heaviest loads were entrusted to steam. The Gas Company, which had a sizeable fleet, had bought their last new Sentinel steam wagons in 1936.

To understand just how motor vehicle numbers had increased can be gleaned from the progress of registration marks. It had taken 18 years to exhaust the 9,999 numbers contained in the original Dublin RI issue, first used in January 1904. Its successor, YI, lasted only until 1927, to be followed by ZI which ran out in 1930. By 1937, the next mark ZA, was finished and ZC had taken over. In County Dublin, IK, used from 1904 to 1927, had been replaced by Z and this had run about three quarters of its course by 1937. In those times, many cars remained in use for much longer than they did in later years and the number of vehicles was further augmented by imports, which did not have to be re-registered if they came from the United Kingdom.

A splendid shot of Standard Saloons in Cabra (Phibsboro) depot around 1938. The readily identifiable vehicles are Nos 171, 249 and 264, displaying a wonderful array of advertising panels which were such a distinctive feature of Dublin trams. Cabra was one of the two depots equipped with a traverser, which can be seen in the foreground. Camwell collection, Tramway Museum Society

Public Transport

All the railways operating entirely within the Irish Free State were amalgamated on 1st January 1925 to form the Great Southern Railways. This company had its headquarters at Kingsbridge, the former GSWR Dublin terminus for services to the south and southwest. GSR trains for Wicklow and Wexford ran from Westland Row, while Broadstone was being phased out as the terminus for those to the west, finally closing to passengers in December 1937. Suburban services operated to Bray on the coastal line from Westland Row and the inland one from Harcourt Street. The Great Northern Railway operated both long-distance and suburban services from Amiens Street.

Railway Road Services

The two big railway companies were heavily involved in road transport. South of a line between Dublin and Sligo, provincial bus services were run by the Great Southern Railways, which had absorbed the Irish Omnibus Company in 1934. Broadstone railway works had become the road vehicle workshops of the GSR, which also used part of Broadstone station as a bus and lorry garage. The GSR's Dublin bus terminus was at Aston Quay. Both the GSR and GNR operated large road freight fleets, having achieved a near-monopoly in that business under the road transport and traffic legislation of 1932 and 1933.

The GNR had its garage on the north side of Upper Sheriff Street, adjoining Amiens Street station. The GNR, which built and overhauled its buses at its Dundalk works, operated both provincial and suburban services in north Dublin, the principal city-centre terminus being at Eden Quay. The city's first modern double-deck bus appeared in October when the GNR's AEC Regent double-deckers Nos 62 and 63 began operating on the Eden Quay to Howth inland route via Killester and Raheny. The only privately owned bus route still operating into Dublin was that of St Kevin's Bus Service between St Stephen's Green and Glendalough. Coach tours were offered by the railway companies and at least one private concern. The remaining areas of private operation were shared by taxis, hansom cabs and a dwindling number of outside cars.

Serving Expanding Suburbs

Following the 1930 city boundary extension the Corporation began to build large housing estates at various locations including Cabra, Crumlin and Kimmage. These, combined with a slightly quicker rate of private development, created several new suburbs, all requiring public transport. By the mid-1930s tramway routes could have been justified on a number of roads leading to new residential areas such as the Kimmage and Crumlin Roads on the south side and Cabra Road and Malahide Road on the north side. All these carried growing traffic to rapidly developing districts, served only by single-deck buses.

There were also estates newly built or in course of construction short distances beyond existing tram termini, as for example at Whitehall on the north side or Terenure Road West on the opposite side of the city. Extension of the lines in these instances would have greatly enhanced the network, as would the provision of some short links, like that proposed many years earlier connecting the Ballybough and Dollymount lines via Fairview Strand.

The Tramways in 1937

The tramway network was still almost complete in 1937. The only track closures so far had been in Capel Street and Bolton Street in 1918, revived briefly in 1922, the superfluous South Quays line in 1929, Lincoln Place and from Beggar's Bush to Irishtown Road in 1932. Some rationalisation was obviously inevitable, but failure to extend into expanding suburbs was an ominous sign. This was particularly so after the resignation of G Marshall Harriss, the pro-tram General Manager. His successor, A P Reynolds, was ambivalent about the future, but most of the lines and principal services appeared set to survive for several years.

More fully described in the Route Summary (see page 140), the routes as they existed in 1937 can be listed as follows:

No	Route
1	Nelson Pillar - Ringsend
2	Nelson Pillar - Sandymount Green
3	Nelson Pillar - Sandymount Tower
6	Nelson Pillar - Blackrock
7	Nelson Pillar - Dun Laoghaire (Marine Road)
8	Nelson Pillar - Dalkey
9	Donnybrook - Phoenix Pk via Merrion Square
10	Donnybrook - Phoenix Park via Dawson St
11	Clonskea - Whitehall
12	Nelson Pillar - Palmerston Park
14	Nelson Pillar - Dartry
15	Nelson Pillar - Terenure
16	Rathfarnham - Whitehall
17	Terenure (or Harold's Cross) - Whitehall
18	Lansdowne Road - Kenilworth Square
19	Rialto - Glasnevin via South Great George's St
20	Rialto - Glasnevin via Harcourt Street
21	Inchicore - Westland Row
23	Ballybough - Parkgate Street
24	O'Connell Bridge - Parkgate Street
25	O'Connell Bridge - Lucan
26	O'Connell Bridge - Chapelizod
30	Nelson Pillar - Dollymount
31	Nelson Pillar - Howth

The route number 17 was often used for short workings on the Rathfarnham to Whitehall line, such as Harold's Cross to Drumcondra or Terenure to Whitehall. During 1937, Harold's Cross (Robert Emmet) bridge was rebuilt, trams terminating at either side of the bridge while work was in progress. Passengers had to walk across to board the tram in which they would continue their journeys.

By 1937, growth adjacent to the Whitehall extension was a copybook instance of a tramway facilitating suburban development. When the Drumcondra route was extended in 1903, the outer section of the line served a sparsely inhabited area, the terminus being a lonely rural outpost. Thirty-four years later, there was extensive building right out to the end of the line, upper Drumcondra and Griffith Avenue being highly regarded residential areas. The extended line fronted two important shopping precincts and right beside the terminus was Whitehall Garda station, built in 1934 to serve the much expanded D District referred to earlier. But there was also a classic missed opportunity for the tramways as half a mile beyond the terminus further new development had taken place at Gaeltacht Park, while even more building was imminent at Ellenfield and Larkhill. In between lay that other great bugbear of public transport in Dublin, vast tracts of institutional land on both sides of the road, still undeveloped 60 years later.

A very simple system was used in the thirties to determine the diversions on the Donnybrook to Phoenix Park routes. Every alternate tram worked via Merrion Square (9) or Stephen's Green (10). The number 9P was used on Nelson Pillar to Phoenix Park cars, very frequent on Sundays and public holidays. The other two termini connected by diverging routes, Glasnevin to Rialto via South Great George's Street (19) or Harcourt Street (20), used an alternating system similar to the Donnybrook line.

The letter S also appeared on numeral scrolls during the 1930s. This was used to denote short workings, specials and trams serving the Spring and Horse Shows at Ballsbridge. It was sometimes displayed on trams out of service or going to the depot, but a more usual practice here was to turn the scroll so that it showed the upper and lower halves of two numbers.

Travel Patterns And Events Promotion

Most tram lines had their first weekday services between 7 and 8am, while some, for example Dalkey and Sandymount, had special early cars to suit particular circumstances. A frequent service was provided during the day, last cars leaving Nelson Pillar at 11.30pm. In the thirties, very few people who lived within two or three miles of their employment and could travel home in the middle of the day, had lunch in town. Staff canteens were extremely rare and there were far fewer restaurants than exist today. The result was a traffic surge for about two hours between 12.30 and 2.30pm.

People employed in shops and offices generally worked a five and a half-day week. While most office workers had their half-day on Saturdays, some shops closed on Wednesday afternoons, other trades doing so on different days. In the evenings, there were further peaks from around 7 to 8.00 pm inwards and 10.30 to 11.00pm outwards to cater for people attending theatres and cinemas in the city centre. Sunday tram and bus services normally started around 10.00am, and according to the time of year, prevailing weather conditions or to serve special events, extra trams operated as required.

The fare from most suburban termini to Nelson Pillar was 2d. The three longest routes, to Dalkey, Lucan or Howth, each about nine miles long, had adult single fares of 5d or 8d return. A child's single fare was 2d. Childrens' fares were limited to those under 12 years of age, but during school hours, 8.30am to 5.30pm on weekdays, the qualifying age was raised to 15 for those attending school; children under three years of age were carried free. A further service offered to passengers was the carriage of bicycles and prams at the owner's risk on the motorman's platform, if there was room, at a charge of 3d. Bicycles could be stored at the Blackrock or Dalkey depots for 2d per day. Season tickets were offered on the Lucan line and passengers on the Howth route could use their return tickets on GNR trains or buses, and vice versa.

The DUTC frequently collaborated with the managements of public institutions or the organisers of special events to issue all-in tickets. The best-remembered and most permanent arrangement was probably that with Dublin Zoo. Notices in the timetables and fare lists were headed **VISIT THE ZOO** and read, 'Combined Tickets can be obtained from all Tram Conductors. Return Fares including admission to the Zoo: From within City (Old Boundary): Adults 8d, Children 6d. From Suburbs, including Howth, Dalkey: Adults 1/-, Children 8d.' The 'Old Boundary' referred to was that which existed prior to September 1930. The combined tram return fare and zoo admission was 1/- and 8d for a child. Blackrock and Clontarf baths were also destinations for all-in return tickets. For 7d and entry to Clontarf Baths, swimmers could travel to and from Nelson Pillar, the children's rate being 4d.

The Tram Fleet in 1937

The last six new DUTC Luxury trams entered service in 1936. There were four single-truck cars, Nos 102, 103, 167 and 205, and two bogie vehicles, Nos 326 and 327. These two 76-seaters which left Spa Road on 3rd and 17th October, respectively, were the last to be completed. Thus, the tram fleet was in its final form at the beginning of 1937. (see Section Five of the Rolling Stock Catalogue)

The remaining 39 four-wheel open-toppers had effectively been withdrawn, as had one or two Balcony cars. Allowing for a ten per cent float to cover overhauls and spares, there were therefore about 255 operational trams. The official lists (Section Six of the Rolling Stock Catalogue) show five trams as withdrawn by 1937, with a further six being taken out of service in that year.

One tram, which had been out of the limelight for several years, usually working as an instruction vehicle, was the Directors' Car. It made a brief but spectacular return to service in May for the Whitehall Carnival, one of a series of church fund-raisers run over several years. It operated every evening as an illuminated car and is probably the only example of such a vehicle running in Dublin.

The Glasnevin Accident

On 1st November the second and last instance of a tram overturning on the Dublin system occurred at Washerwoman's Hill, Glasnevin. Around mid-day Balcony car No 76, working the 19A service with Motorman J Hartnett and Conductor Thomas Scott, left the terminus outside the Holy Faith Convent gates for Rialto. At the steeply inclined right hand curve outside the present main gates of the Bon Secours Hospital, it became derailed. It struck a pole, crashed into a wall and fell on its side at a traction standard still in use as a lighting pillar at the time of writing.

Five people, including the crew, were taken to hospital; fortunately none of them was seriously injured. A boy who was on the tram jumped clear and ran away, but No 76 did not fare so well; its roof was ripped off and it sustained much other damage. Tramway traffic was not disrupted as the car fell clear of the tracks. Late in the evening the tram was righted and towed away but it did not re-enter service.

DUTC Buses

In 1937 the DUTC had about 180 single-deck buses, mainly AEC, Albion, Dennis and Leyland. Following its 1933 experiment, the company had bought only diesel-engined buses, starting with 46 A class AEC Regals and an equal number of N class Leyland Lions. These had largely replaced first generation DUTC vehicles and some of the motley collection taken over from the independents. However, some acquired buses, including 19 ex-General Albions, remained in service pending new deliveries. By 1937 a further 55 Leyland Lions, this time with metal-framed bodies, began ousting these survivors.

In 1937, there were some 55 DUTC bus routes, including a number of split-tails. The furthest points served were Portrane on the north side, Celbridge to the west, Poulaphouca and Kilcoole to the south. The DUTC's bus garages were at Summerhill, Lime Street, Conyngham Road and Donnybrook. The former generating station in Ringsend was also partially used as a garage. Mechanical overhauls were carried out at Summerhill while Spa Road looked after

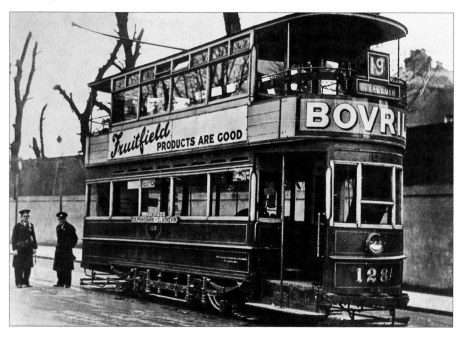

The crew of No 128 pose at Glasnevin terminus in 1938. To the left, out of the picture, is the descent and sharp right-hand turn where No 76 overturned in November 1937. The Glasnevin to Dolphin's Barn route closed on 5th March 1939, being the first cross-city service taken over by buses. No 128, built as an open-topper in 1919, received its balcony top from No 58 ten years later. Withdrawn in 1939, it was one of several trams that languished on the scrap line until 1942, when its truck went to Standard Saloon No 54. Birney Collection

bodywork on both buses and trams. On 20th December, the DUTC's first two double-deckers, Leylands R1 and R2, began work on the Crumlin (50) route.

A New Breed of Tramwaymen

After 1920, DUTC recruitment policy changed somewhat. William Martin Murphy had favoured candidates from rural areas, but Dubliners now became more numerous, many new employees being sons of DUTC staff. This new generation of tramway men were less subservient then their predecessors, showing flashes of independence not previously encountered. They were often known for their sharp wit, expressions of which would have led to severe disciplinary action a few years earlier.

One noted character of the period was 'Sheriff' Gallagher of the Dollymount line whose less than sycophantic attitude is recalled by his stage point call at St Lawrence's Road, off the Clontarf seafront. The houses there were probably a little beyond the means of some residents who tried to display the outward manifestations expected of people with such upmarket addresses. In an age when home music making was an important part of socialising the Sheriff would call out, 'St Lawrence's Road - pride, poverty and pianos!' This could have resulted in severe disciplinary before 1914, but complaints do not seem to have had the same effect a few short years later.

Both the Sheriff's name and his stage point call show up yet two more aspects of transport lore that have never been even sketchily recorded. Here it is also worth mentioning that several tramway stories are very much in the tradition of urban myths, the same narrative turning up in several different cities and towns. Some conductors' wisecracks and their descriptions of stage points, ranging from funny to cynical, can be positively located, as for the example of the South Dublin Union in James's Street being called out as 'St James's Hotel'. Nicknames were legion and while a few were malicious, identifying some less than popular individuals, the majority were benign. Most were funny, some hilariously so, and many men who knew and answered readily to their nicknames were highly regarded.

Despite their more independent demeanour, DUTC staff still displayed a very strong sense of public service. This had been well demonstrated by their efforts under extremely adverse conditions in February 1933. From the night of Thursday 23rd and the next day, Dublin was almost overwhelmed by a blizzard, gales and thunderstorms. Most transport services were brought to a standstill, but the DUTC Traffic Manager was able to report afterwards: 'We carried on our tram service, with interruptions due to the storm and shortage of current.'

Tact was a hallmark of most conductors, who sometimes had to avoid taking sides in delicate situations. Although said to be original, the scenario set by Jimmy O'Dea and Harry O'Donovan in their recorded sketch of Mrs Mulligan on the Rathmines tram had plenty of precedent. It has echoes of the 1878 comments of the Dublin Tramway Company's shareholders about a proposed tramline connecting Rathmines with Kingsbridge via the Liberties. On the recording, the Coombe's most famous if fictional denizen engaged in an argument, through the conductor, with an upper-crust passenger about whether the windows of the tram should be open or shut. Yet again, and not too subtly, the point was made that the Dublin trams were for the genteel rather than the artisans, mechanics and daily labourers of the Tramway Acts.

Uniforms and Pay Rates

Until recent times, clothing was a significant part of the emoluments in most public services and the wearing of a uniform was compulsory in many employments. Worn with pride, uniforms invested the staff with considerable authority, which was usually respected and would have been essential if the conductor of the Rathmines tram had to intervene between Mrs Mulligan and her opponent in the window dispute.

Prior to the First World War the distinctive uniforms of Dublin tramway men were modelled on American practice. The most notable feature was the kepi-style cap, discarded by conductors and inspectors in favour of straw boater hats during the summer. Soon after the war, more modern uniforms were introduced by the DUTC. Around that time, fashions had changed and there was a tendency to copy various details from army uniforms. This showed up most markedly in the cap, a military-style issue with a broad wired crown, topped in summer with a removable white elasticised cover. This was part of the tramway and later the bus scene for about 30 years.

Some time after the introduction of the new-style uniforms, the cap badge was also changed. The new badge was an attractive metal item, oval in shape and with laurel leaves surrounding the DUTC crest. The wearer's title, motorman, conductor or inspector, was inscribed below the crest. Badges for motormen and conductors were brass coloured, those for the inspectors being chrome or silver. Similar badges, appropriately lettered, were worn by bus drivers and conductors.

In June 1937, when the cost of living index stood at 170 in relation to 1914, the weekly pay rates for tram conductors ranged from £2 17s 0d to £3 5s 0d, motormen earning between £3 0s 0d and £3 7s 6d. Bus drivers got £3 6s 0d to £3 15s 0d, conductors £1 19s 0d to £2 12s 0. Pensions were

set at 13/- per week. Salaried staff, their income quoted in annual rather than weekly figures, included a draughtsman at Spa Road whose pay was increased to £364 in 1938, while the Works Manager was brought up to £468. The 1937 index figure of 170 compares with nearly 6900 in 1999.

Schoolboy Pranks

A former participant described a dangerous and cruel a game played regularly on Terenure motormen by schoolboys in the 1930s. Going from Rathmines, exuberant pupils would congregate at the rear of the upper deck of the tram. When it had notched up a good speed along Rathgar Road, they would lean out and pull the trolley rope so as to hold the wheel just below the wire and bring the car to a sudden stop. The next step was to await the appearance up the leading stairs of the angry motorman, then put the trolley back on the wire in the frequently fulfiled hope that he had neglected to turn off the power. His hasty departure back to the controls would be cheered lustily and while ejection of the boys from the tram usually ensued, they managed to repeat the procedure quite often.

'Scutting', riding illicitly on the backs of moving vehicles, has long been practised in Dublin. As far as the trams were concerned, this usually occurred at or near areas contributing few regular patrons to the DUTC. For children daring enough to jump on the rear fender or buffer rim of a tramcar it was essential to stand as far as possible to the right, away from the platform. This was so as to remain out of range of the knotted end of the trolley rope which a skilful conductor could use as a whip with devastating effect. In those days of summary justice, any other adult witnessing the practice was equally likely to react physically. Another form of 'scutting' was practised by cyclists who would attempt to grab a handrail on the platform of a passing tramcar to hitch a pull up a hill or against the wind.

Schoolboy's Revenge

Most young passengers accepted short shrift for excessive misbehaviour with little demur, but victimisation could, and did, lead to unorthodox retribution. An instance occurred one day when an intolerant conductor on the Lucan line unfairly put a schoolboy off his tram, forcing the hapless child to walk home, a distance of some miles. Because the lad could not tell his parents in those days when authority was invariably backed without question, a burning sense of injustice led to revenge by the enforced walker's friends.

A few days later, when a Lucan bound tram had just left O'Connell Bridge, a diversion was staged, causing the same conductor to alight momentarily. The starting signal was promptly given, and, conductorless,

Looking down the North Circular Road from the Phoenix Park gates in 1938, Standard Saloon No 229 is about to depart for Donnybrook on route 9, which travelled from Nassau Street via Merrion Square North and East to Baggot Street. Luxury Saloon No 235, waiting to reverse, is working Route 10, which diverged from the 9 at Nassau Street to go via Dawson Street and Merrion Row, the two services rejoining at the Merrion Square/Baggot Street junction. No 229 was new in December 1925 and withdrawn in 1942, while No 235, which left Spa Road works in February 1932, was one of several Luxury cars withdrawn in the early forties and scrapped at Terenure in 1948. Camwell collection, Tramway Museum Society

the tram travelled for several miles, with the schoolboys dutifully ringing the starting bell whenever it stopped to pick up or set down. Passengers' reactions are not recorded but they may have been cheered by avoiding payment of fares, which the conductor would have to explain. The avengers could not, of course, enquire about subsequent events, but nearly 60 years later the man who related the incident clearly enjoyed recalling it.

Zealotry
During the thirties, the trams became victims of an unhappy set of circumstances over which the DUTC had little control. Traditionally, the company's well-turned out cars had been a source of great pride; initially, its buses shared the same high standard, but as in any rapidly growing fleet they slipped somewhat within a few years. Trams and buses alike suffered visually when the grey livery was introduced in 1929 and got dirty very quickly. In 1933-34, the company's image was further tarnished by the intake of large numbers of acquired buses which were in a deplorable state and retained only until they could be replaced. Unfortunately, all of this coincided with the arrival on the scene of a notorious Garda Carriage Examiner who made life as difficult as possible for all transport companies.

This man caused havoc, grounding vehicles on the flimsiest pretext and, where possible, issuing summonses. In November 1935, the DUTC was fined 10/- in the District Court on each of several counts of not having its tramcars properly painted and varnished. So far as is known, the offence quoted did not exist and it is highly probable that the prosecuting Carriage Examiner would have been deeply embarrassed by a competent lawyer if the DUTC had elected to defend itself. On 17th December the Rolling Stock Engineer reported that in the preceding

weeks, 90 buses had been put off the road, 60 of them for trivial reasons, and a number of tramcars had been ordered off for painting, dented panels and damaged upholstery. This petty but costly harassment continued for several years. The Courts may have become tired of the process for on 24th May 1938 the Probation Act was applied in respect of three summonses.

Linguistic Pressure – Tickets
During the thirties, the company was subjected to other pressures. The increasingly influential Irish language lobby, operating through at least two government departments and the Gaelic League, began to harass the DUTC about the use of Irish on its vehicles, principally on destination displays, tickets and notices. Some time afterwards, the parliamentary lettering on the rolling stock appeared as, *Comhcomhlucht Aontaighte Trambhealach Atha Cliath (1896) Teo – A. P. Mac Raghnaill – Priomh Stiuirthoir*. This was a direct but awkward translation of *Dublin United Tramways Company (1896) Ltd – A. P. Reynolds – General Manager*. Similar lettering appeared on a small number of the garter belt insignia carried on trams and buses, and also on some internal notices.

It was government policy in the 1930s to persuade companies to source as much as possible of their goods and services within the Free State. One of these was the printing of tickets which, in March 1935, were being supplied by Auto Tickets of Birkenhead. However, following representations from the Department of Industry and Commerce, the DUTC agreed to split its next order for 40 million tickets equally between Auto Tickets and Flanagans of Distillery Road, a Dublin company which produced a wide range of numbered receipt blocks and similar stationery.

Bilingual tickets appeared before 1938, but space limitations meant that only the company's initials appeared in the Irish version. 'Issued subject to the Co's Bye-laws' was in both languages and was all that remained of the more traditional legend which had also contained the words 'This ticket must be punched in Section in which Passenger is entitled to travel.' Along the vertical bands inside the stage numbers at either side of the ticket there was a further compromise. The words 'Stages as per Fare Slip' which had previously appeared in both the 'To City' and 'From City' bands were now replaced on the 'To City' side with 'Cuig an Cathair', the Irish translation of the phrase. Otherwise, the general appearance and colour coding of the tickets remained unaltered.

During the early thirties, the DUTC purchased some TIMs (Ticket Issuing Machines); their number has been authoritatively put at 150, in at least three batches. They were apparently confined to one depot, Terenure, and did not win universal favour. These machines lasted well into CIE days, when TIMs became the standard equipment on city buses. They still displayed the DUTC's initials long after the company's disappearance.

Tramcar Advertisements
For many years, most exterior tramcar advertising had been on colourful enamelled plates. End (upper deck dash) advertisements were on single plates, the bottom plate in earlier times being frequently curved to match the panel profiles of the older cars. The longer side displays were made up of multiple sections. These were supplied by the advertisers or company-appointed contractors who looked after all the spaces in the fleet. Much of the enamel work for DUTC vehicles was by the Dublin Japan Works of Jervis Street, its name as the manufacturer, appearing in small letters at the bottom of the panel.

For some years, the DUTC looked after its own advertising space lettings, but later employed a contractor or agent. In October 1935, Frank Mason & Co Ltd, who rented all the advertising spaces on DUTC trams and buses, obtained permission to use paper for some displays. This was subject to advertisements being properly kept; paper was liable to get dirty or torn very easily. Increasing numbers of paper advertisements subsequently appeared, especially for advertisers requiring frequent changes. An example of this was the Theatre Royal, (see the photograph on page 108) which advertised its cine-variety shows on the trams, and these usually changed every week.

As at every period in the long history of public transport advertising, the displays carried by the Dublin trams in the 1930s identified many companies and services that are now gone. Several of these would be either redundant or politically very incorrect today, such as those for tobacco products.

Secret Preparations

With the appearance of the DUTC's new Leyland double deck buses in December 1937, any possible extension of the tramway system obviously became less likely than before. The new bus fleet would replace single-deckers on busy routes and would certainly take over on some of the less patronised tram lines. Meanwhile, it looked like business as usual for the most heavily used tram routes. Track and overhead maintenance continued as usual, as did tramcar overhauls and repaints.

Much planning seems to have taken place behind the scenes, most of it undocumented. Even in those distant times when public consultation was a lot less practised than it is today, there was a surprising lack of publicity about the DUTC's real plans. Anodyne or non-committal answers were given to any questions about the future of the trams, the usual line being that the company had an open mind on the matter and that the travelling public would have the final say.

The Announcement, Public Cynicism

The DUTC board met on 1st March 1938 and 'considered the replacement of trams by buses on certain routes and it was decided that the future policy of the board shall be the ultimate replacement of the tramcar by the bus and that the General Manager be

authorised to proceed on the lines of his memorandum'. The board's decision was warmly welcomed by the *Irish Times* on 5th March, 'We congratulate the Dublin United Tramways Company on its new policy, which is sketched in our columns this morning. The company, according to our information, had deferred to the inevitable, and is doing away with the trams. Already the number of trams on certain routes has been reduced, and their place has been taken by omnibuses, either of the single-decked, or of the double-decked, type. This process will continue until the last tram will have disappeared from Dublin – probably within another three years'.

Immediate and total disappearance of the trams would have been even more pleasing to DUTC management, despite A P Reynolds' disingenuous assertion to an *Irish Times* reporter that the company was neither pro-tram nor pro-bus. It has been said, probably accurately, that the directors simply did not care, being interested only in dividends. If buses yielded bigger profits than trams, so much the better.

Obviously suggestible to A P Reynolds' promises of greater profits, the directors had gone through a remarkable conversion in 12 months. At the 1937 shareholders' meeting, Chairman the Right Hon James McMahon cited Glasgow as a headline for tramway development, with its new cars and extended routes. He also pointed out that traffic congestion had worsened during the 1935 strike when the trams were off the streets for eleven weeks. He indulged in some sleight of woolly logic by saying that the case for trolleybuses had not been established and that two trams could do the work of three trolleybuses.

Generally speaking, the travelling public simply wanted a good service at economical fares. Nevertheless, there were some people who, for various reasons raised awkward but valid objections to the company's proposals. Many of the fears about replacing trams were succinctly put in a news item which appeared in the *Evening Mail* on 5th March. Headed **Higher Fares and Shorter Stages** it said: 'The citizens are likely to be made pay for the

change. Shorter distances at higher rates will be offered to passengers by the Company. The ratepayers generally, too, are likely to suffer – even perhaps by higher rates – since wayleaves now provide a big source of revenue to the Corporation and go towards the relief of rates. The Electricity Supply Board will also lose a big customer, unless steps are taken to see that oil, as at present, is not to be the only source of power used.'

Over the following weeks, DUTC spokesmen made conflicting statements about the company's intentions. People who wrote letters to the papers expressed serious concern at the prospects of higher fares and inferior service, but any answers wrung out of the DUTC, usually by intrepid reporters, were routinely ambiguous and never convincing.

Why Not Trolleybuses?

The last paragraph of the *Evening Mail* item quoted above clearly referred to trolleybuses. Seen in many cities as an attractive choice for public transport, they combined the best features of trams and motorbuses. They were mentioned spasmodically as a possible solution to Dublin's needs but were only briefly considered, if at all. The DUTC was definitely opposed to them. One correspondent in the *Evening Mail* had made positive suggestions for some routes, which could be operated by these vehicles, but his ideas were dismissed out of hand.

In his address to the shareholders at their general meeting on 15th March 1938, DUTC Chairman James McMahon said, 'If and when it may be deemed fitting to discontinue the use of tramcars on any of the routes, and such discontinuance on any of the routes must depend on the extent to which the public availed or did not avail of the tramway service on that route, they were definitely opposed to the idea of replacing them with trolleybuses, the main reason being the prohibitive capital cost of transformation of the system.'

Co-incidentally, Belfast Corporation was looking to the future of its operations around this time and experimentally con-

Seen in St Stephen's Green in the late 1940s, Standard Saloon No 129 is working the Terenure route. This car may have been used as a scrap yard shunter at Dartry in 1942 and was one of five similar vehicles reprieved for the Dalkey line after the Terenure abandonment in 1948. It was one of the three trams bought for preservation by the Tramway Museum Society after the Dalkey closure but all three vehicles were later lost. Burrows Bros

verted the Falls Road tram route to trolleybus operation on 28th March 1938. This proved so successful that it was decided in 1939 to replace all the Corporation's trams with trolleybuses by 1944. Although wartime conditions delayed the conversion, a further 88 trolleybuses were placed in service up to 1943. Following the virtual cessation of bus building at Spa Road during the war, some DUTC craftsmen were taken on by Harkness Coachworks to work on the Belfast trolleybuses.

Staff Problems

Much more sceptical than the public and potentially far more troublesome was the company's staff. DUTC bus operations now presented the company with additional problems that should have been foreseen and dealt with. Instead, they were added to the long litany of industrial troubles they had inherited or created, but made little serious effort to resolve.

There were pay differentials between tram and bus crews, the latter having further differences in the rates for double and single deckers. The DUTC had no one-man buses and the economics of small crew operated vehicles, even in the thirties, were anything but good. Seniority, always a delicate issue, was complicated by the position of men who had come over with the acquired companies. Many of these men would be natural candidates for double deck driving, thus forming one more issue capable of causing trouble, especially in the resentful environment prevailing after the 1935 strike.

Another source of friction existed in Spa Road, with the change from traditional timber coach building to the metal framed bodywork of the new buses. Higher productivity was expected and obtained, but at some cost and with the ever present danger

of demarcation disputes. Seventy five men were laid off, the *Evening Herald* reported on 11th March 1938, due, 'to an easing off in the building programme owing to the opposition to the replacement of trams by buses.'

All of these concerns were evident in the reports of the DUTC annual general meeting held on 15th March 1938. It was announced that some tram routes would go and, primly, that the company had no fixed attachment to trams. The routes mentioned were Nos 18 Kenilworth Road to Lansdowne Road and 23 Ballybough to Parkgate Street. It was also intended to cut the Rathfarnham service back to Terenure. Many observers, with good reason, saw this as a very serious reduction in the capacity and catchment of the cross-town line to Whitehall, which was regarded as the backbone of the city system.

More important was an announcement that some fares would be adjusted, or balanced. The next day, 16th March, saw new scales in operation, the main feature of which was the introduction for the first time of a 2½d fare. Adjustment or balancing was a euphemism for increases, a most injudicious act for a profitable company that had recently regained its previous monopoly status.

The First Closures

April 1938 saw the first closures under the general abandonment policy. The 19 route had already been shortened by the cessation, in February, of the 1905 extension from Dolphin's Barn to Rialto. This was originally announced as merely a suspension to facilitate a public works project, its later permanent closure being one of many similar exercises to be found in tramway history. Now the first withdrawal of a complete cross-city tram service under the new pro-

gramme took place. On 16th April, buses, initially six single-deckers, took over operation of route 23 between Parkgate Street and Ballybough. This change resulted in the abandonment of track from Capel Street Bridge to Parnell Street and from there through to Ballybough. The buses did not run beyond the termini at either end of the former tram route until after the Second World War, when the service reached Distillery Road and Drimnagh. The Ballybough buses, and all those subsequently taking over from trams, retained the route numbers of the tram lines they replaced.

On the same date, buses ousted trams on route 24, O'Connell Bridge to Parkgate Street. No track was closed by this substitution as the Lucan service continued to operate. The trams latterly used on route 24 were Balcony Bogie cars, there being several surplus eight-wheelers of this type after the arrival of the Luxury trams. Buses on route 24 ran initially from Parkgate Street to Marino, the service being extended to Bulfin Road shortly afterwards. This provided a new cross-city route replacing earlier separate radial bus services. Six double-deckers worked the new route.

Buses took over operation of the Dollymount route on 1st June 1938. There had been a DUTC bus service to Dollymount for some years, travelling through Cathal Brugha Street on the inward journey. Numbered 58 by the DUTC, this had been formerly an independent enterprise but on the closure of the tramway service the number 30 was allocated to the buses. Tramway protagonists were quick to point out that closure of the well-patronised Dollymount and Parkgate Street services weakened the longer workings to Howth and Lucan respectively, thus hastening their demise.

Clontarf depot became a bus garage on closure of the Dollymount service but for some time afterwards the five Luxury Bogie cars allocated to the Howth line remained there. The Nelson Pillar to Dollymount and Parkgate Street to Ballybough routes were the only ones on which buses replaced trams in 1938. By the end of the year the DUTC had 62 double-deck buses, but less than half of these were employed on tramway replacement work. All the buses involved in these first change-overs were Leyland Titan TD4s, numbered R1 to R50.

Apart from the two closures just described, there were few other noteworthy developments on the tramway system in the latter part of 1938, except for one accident. Bogie Luxury car No 327, the last new tram built in 1936, ran out of control at Royal Marine Road in Dun Laoghaire on 9th December. It came off the tracks and went through a railing into a grassy area outside the railway station. Fortunately, nobody was injured, only the crew being on board. Having suffered little damage, No 327 was re-railed and continued in service until final closure of the tramways in 1949.

1939: A Year of Major Closures

Palmerston Park (route 12) trams were replaced by buses on 1st January 1939. A considerable amount of track was abandoned with this closure, although other services ran over parts of the route in the Ranelagh area. For some years the DUTC had operated a radial bus service, the 54A, to Cabra. A new cross-city route 12 re-established a connection between Palmerston Park and a northern suburb for the first time since the short-lived link with Clontarf in 1899. It was the first of several new cross-city facilities to be developed by the DUTC and CIE over the following 15 years. The TD4 Leyland Titan double deck bus was improved with the emergence of the TD5 variant, easily recognisable by its rear dome which was noticeably less upright than that on the TD4. Nos R51-62 of this type entered service around this time.

Dublin Corporation's housing programme was pushed ahead vigorously during the late thirties. The suburbs of Cabra, Crumlin, Donnycarney and Drimnagh all took shape, while new estates of flats were built in the inner city. At the same time, private developers were also building in the suburbs and while some of the new housing was of an infill nature, most of it was beyond the tram termini. In fact, many of the lines ran along roads on which had poor catchment areas, because of the huge pockets of land owned by religious orders and other institutions. On some routes much of the housing was little more than ribbon development, the hinterland not being built upon even up to the time of writing.

On 5th March 1939 the entire 19/19A line between Glasnevin and Dolphin's Barn went over to buses. This was the first north-

south cross-city route to be converted involving a further significant loss of track. With it went the northern section of the 14 route from Dartry, which henceforth terminated at Nelson Pillar, robbing passengers of another cross-city tram service. The replacement buses on the 19 did not extend beyond the tram termini at first, but the split-tail 19A was introduced. This left the existing route at the Botanic Road/Mobhi Road junction, running initially to where Mobhi Road rejoins the original Ballymun Road. This was to be an important bus terminus for many years. Just prior to the abandonment of routes 19/19A, on 1st March, the records show buses R63 to R82 entering into service.

More Abandonments

Press coverage of closures was patchy, but in the case of the Glasnevin to Rialto route, it was reported that 18 tramcars were being replaced; this was one less than the number of new buses entering service. Immediately prior to this change-over, the *Irish Independent* published several photographs showing former tramway motormen being retrained as bus drivers. Curiously, in two of the pictures the training vehicles were ancient Dennis single deckers, a remarkable contrast to the new Leyland diesel double deckers. One long-retired motorman who learned bus driving on one of these Dennis buses swore that mastering the peculiarities of that ancient chariot rendered him fit to drive anything.

The fare increases introduced in March 1938 had caused both the DUTC and the government some worry. Both the abandonment and the fare increases had been handled clumsily and once politicians began to feel the heat action was bound to follow. On the day the buses replaced the Glasnevin trams, fare reductions came into

force all over the DUTC network, many 3d journeys being reduced by a halfpenny. Journeys which could be made at lower fares were also lengthened.

Spa Road works was now turning out buses at a rate of two a week, hastening the pace of tram replacement. The Whitehall to Rathfarnham trams (routes 16/17) were replaced from 1st May 1939, with them went the northern section of the 11, Clonskea to Whitehall service. The buses from Terenure and Rathfarnham ran half a mile beyond the former Whitehall tram terminus at Griffith Avenue to the junction of Collins Avenue. Here there was a large roundabout which they used as a terminus until the service was extended into Ellenfield.

Buses R83 to R101 were at work by 1st May, followed later in the month by R102 to R108. Bearing the number 11A, a replacement for the 11 tram service ran from Nelson Pillar to Griffith Avenue (Sherkin Gardens) until the southern part of the route was abandoned on 2nd July. Buses R109 to R121 began work on that day and Clonskea became the first tramway depot to be made redundant since the replacement of Kingsbridge (Victoria Quay) in 1928. Following the total displacement of trams on route 11, the replacing buses ran from Clonskea (Vergemount) to Mobhi Road via Drumcondra Road and Home Farm Road. Another closure in May 1939, but involving no abandonment of track, was route 1, Nelson Pillar to Ringsend; the number thereafter remained unused for several years.

Doubts, More Closures and Public Relations

Following a long period of deepening foreboding, the Second World War began on 3rd September 1939. Although it did not immediately affect the lives of people in Eire as the former Irish Free State was by then

Nos 266 and 268, built together in 1934, were the only two of the 37 single-truck Luxury Saloons to be mounted on Brill 21E rather than Maley and Taunton trucks. They were the first of the twelve four-wheelers to have their destination and number scrolls recessed behind the upper deck end windows. Both vehicles lasted until the end of the Dalkey line in 1949. Here, No 268 stands at Terenure terminus. A R Spencer

Howth line open-topper No 307, is seen in the yard at Clontarf depot in 1938. This car, new in May 1920 and overhauled as recently as 1938, was scrapped at Donnybrook in 1941. The internal partition dividing the smoking and non-smoking compartments is visible. Fayle collection, Irish Railway Record Society

known, it was obvious that this situation would change if the war continued for any length of time. There were many who felt that increasing dependence on fuel imported from beyond these islands could not be justified in the highly uncertain circumstances then prevailing and that abandonment of the Dublin tramway system, wrong at any time, was now an act of folly. Despite this, the DUTC still went ahead in the face of stiff and well-grounded criticism.

The Inchicore (21) tram route closed on 4th February 1940, the replacement bus service being extended to Ring Street at its outer end. Buses R171 to R180 are shown to have entered service in January 1940, followed by R181 to R194 on the date of the Inchicore change-over. While work on trams had already ceased at Spa Road, this closure isolated the works from the remainder of the tramway system. The running shed became part of the main Spa Road works, the older horse depot at the junction with Emmet Road probably being already in use as part of the bus building and overhaul complex. Shops now occupy the site.

Inchicore was connected to Sandymount Tower by bus No 52A which initially took over from the No 3 tram service on the section from College Street to the sea. However, following the replacement of the Nelson Pillar to Sandymount Green (2) trams on 26th March, the 3 reappeared as a cross-city bus service from Sandymount Tower. It ran via Drumcondra to the Whitehall Roundabout at the junction of Swords Road and Collins Avenue, sharing this terminus with the 17 until both routes were extended after the Second World War. Buses R195 to R209 are recorded as going on the road on the date of the route 2 change-over.

Despite a plethora of letters to the papers on the subject of tramway abandonment and the bus versus tram argument general-ly, the DUTC did not seem to understand the gravity of the situation or the strength of public opinion. At the shareholders' meeting held on the day of the Sandymount change-over, 26th March 1940, it was announced that tram replacement would continue despite wartime difficulties. It looked as if the company was completely impervious to the public opinion it had cited only two years previously as the arbiter of its programme.

An indication of the company's insensitivity to its passengers' needs was its refusal, in March 1939, to provide a bus shelter at Killester. The reason given was that if a shelter was erected here, everybody would look for one. Right through the tramway era, the DUTC had resolutely refused to provide shelters, although they had conceded the use of a staff shelter at Northumberland Road to waiting passengers, certainly by 1896.

Another long-established part of the tramway company's services to close down in 1940 was the Parcels Express. This had become less and less viable with the continuing decline of the tramway system. Tramway depots were closing, buses were unsuitable for the transport of parcels and alternative forms of delivery were being increasingly used. The parcels office at 62 Dawson Street was closed and the premises disposed of.

The DUTC was a progressive bus operator needing public goodwill and by now must have been wary of alienating existing or potential passengers. Conscious of the need to convince people that it was a responsible organisation providing a better service with buses instead of trams, it decided to appoint a public relations officer in 1940. A pioneering step for an Irish company at the time, the inspired choice was Mr L A (Leslie) Luke, whose department

became an essential part of the DUTC and later CIE structures. Leslie Luke's name became a household word within a very short time. Meanwhile, the most severe effects of the war were not yet being felt in this country.

Lucan Change-Over
On 13th April 1940, buses took over on the Lucan route which had been re-opened only 12 years previously. This was the first long route to close, more than 30 years before its catchment area developed. Only three buses, R210, 211 and R212, are shown to have been put to work on the day the Lucan tramway closed. Upon closure of the Lucan line, the Bogie Standards were transferred to the Dalkey service where they ran until 1949. The late Frank Murphy, author of the Old Dublin Society paper on Dublin's trams, who worked on the Dalkey trams in the 1940s, liked these cars. Motormen found them responsive and conductors appreciated their spaciousness. This was most noticeable in the lower decks of Nos 218 and 224 with their longitudinal seating, which also allowed standing passengers more room.

On 2nd June the entire No 10 route, Phoenix Park to Donnybrook via St Stephen's Green and Baggot Street, closed. With it went the northern end of the 9, which operated via Merrion Square, but this was completely withdrawn four days later. The fleet records show that buses R213 to R234 entered service on 2nd June. The final 1940 abandonment, on 1st December, was the No 18 between Kenilworth Square and Lansdowne Road, the seven points at which it connected with other tram services had by then been reduced to two. At that date, the DUTC had 236 double-deck buses, nearly twice the number of the remaining trams. Curiously, only one extra bus, R236, was licensed from 1st December, R235 having gone into service on 4th October. These two were the first of a small batch of Titan TD7s.

End of the Howth Line
As described in Chapter Three in 1907 the DUTC leased the tramway between Dollymount and Howth from the Clontarf & Hill of Howth Tramroad Company at an annual rental of £3,000. By 1940, the service was down to about 25 round trips on weekdays and 20 on Sundays. It was losing money and the company was anxious to terminate its agreement with the Clontarf Company and

close the line. Route 31 was the DUTC service most vulnerable to competition, but also offered passengers the widest possible range of choices. Howth was accessible by GNR trains and buses, the latter running through Killester and Raheny and there was interavailability of return tickets between train, tram, and bus.

Following lengthy negotiations with the Clontarf & Hill of Howth, agreement was reached to terminate the lease, the DUTC paying £42,000 or 14 years' rental to the Clontarf company. Negotiations also took place with the GNR which had been operating AEC Regent double deck buses on its Howth service since October 1937. As part of the resulting deal, the GNR withdrew its bus service to Malahide in favour of the DUTC.

The 31 tram service closed on 29th March 1941, the last tram from Howth at 11.45pm being Luxury car No 294, driven by Motorman Dick Ward. This was transferred to the Dalkey line the following day with its four companions, Nos 93, 300, 329 and 330. While the DUTC placed its last six Leyland Titan TD7s (R237-R242) in service between February and June 1941, no Dublin United buses were involved in replacing the Howth trams. The Dollymount to Howth track and overhead were removed very quickly after closure of the service, but that from Dollymount into the city remained in position for a long time, a curious event taking place two short months after the last tram came from Howth.

On 31st May 1941 there occurred the tragic North Strand bombing as a result of which 33 people lost their lives. Several buildings and public utility installations, including the tram tracks and overhead gear in North Strand, were destroyed or damaged. The permanent way and overhead were reinstated but never used again, and while both the track and the wiring have long disappeared, several traction poles remained in position, with shrapnel damage clearly visible, in the autumn of 1999.

The Howth closure was the last effected under the auspices of the DUTC. An interesting postscript is that when CIE took over the GNR in 1958 they allocated route number 31 to the former railway company's Howth bus service which does not follow the coastal route of the erstwhile Nelson Pillar-Howth trams. It goes instead via Killester and Raheny, the route originally proposed for the Howth tramway in the 1890s.

There are two other recorded bombing incidents on tram routes, one on the abandoned Dolphin's Barn line at South Circular Road. The second took place on the Dalkey line at Sandycove at 7.30pm on the evening of 20th December 1940. DUTC man Michael Callanan had a lucky escape here, having driven his tram past the critical location just before the bomb exploded.

The Dublin United Transport Company
Following the succession of tramway closures, the DUTC had become a major bus rather than tram operator. In recognition of this shift, the Dublin United Tramways Company changed its image and title in March 1941. It became the Dublin United Transport Company, thus retaining the original initials which carried considerable goodwill among the citizens of Dublin and in the transport world generally. At the same time, a new livery was adopted for the company's buses, the mainly Audley green and cream being replaced by a more sombre olive and eau-de-nil. The company also introduced a new symbol or logo.

Known officially as the 'Winged Wheel', this new device was a circle with five stylised horizontal bars arranged to suggest motion. The central bar, carried beyond either side of the circle as in the London Transport symbol was inscribed 'Iomchar Atha Cliath' (Dublin Transport) in Gaelic script. The symbol was in two versions, left-handed for the near side and right-handed for the off-

side of buses, the upper bars always pointing towards the front. This posed problems for any double ended vehicle like a tram; the initial solution was to have the upper bars pointing away from the entrance on each side but in time this system broke down, whatever was readily available being used. The 'Winged Wheel' became popularly known as the 'Flying Snail'.

The Diminishing Tramcar Fleet
Immediately prior to the tramway abandonment programme, the nominal fleet of 330 passenger cars included 75 bogie vehicles, 15 open-top, 28 Balcony, 12 Standard and 20 Luxury trams. The 255 four-wheelers were split as follows, 1 single-deck, 39 open-top, 87 Balcony, 91 Standard and 37 Luxury Saloons. The numbers of the cars in the various classes are set out in Section Five of the Rolling Stock Catalogue.

Starting with the four wheelers, withdrawal of open-top and Balcony vehicles began even before the general abandonment commenced. At first, this had no implications for the future, because the DUTC had always owned more trams than it needed to work the timetables. Only eleven trams had been officially withdrawn up to 1938 (see Section Six of the Rolling Stock Catalogue). Although the remaining four-wheeled open-toppers were officially in reserve, some (for example, No 30 which had the letter S suffixed to its fleet number) were in use by the Engineer's Department. Nos 77 and 99 were similarly employed, the latter losing its upper deck structure. Others, like Nos 4 and 33, in grey livery, stood on the long sidings at Donnybrook, yielding spares as needed for other vehicles still working.

There were also some redundant single-truck Balcony cars and it was obvious that

Luxury Saloon No 41 in O'Connell Street during the forties. New in December 1931, this car is carrying a Johnston, Mooney & O'Brien enamel advertisement intended for a bogie car on which it would fit neatly between the bulkhead pillars. McBirney's of Aston Quay advertised on the trams throughout the electric era, their later paper end displays carrying the slogan '40 Paces from O'Connell Bridge', in which the bridge title was in white letters on a black ground and shown immediately below the destination box, which it supplemented visually. Transport Museum Society of Ireland collection

Five Standard and eight Luxury single truck Saloons were transferred to the Dalkey route following the closure of the Dartry and Terenure lines on 31st October 1948, but their reprieve was to last a mere nine months. No 132 dating from 1935, is here seen on Merrion Road, its destination display 'S – Nelson Pillar', suggesting either an incomplete number scroll or a short working. This tram was one of three bought by enthusiasts but subsequently lost to the elements, vandals and official antipathy.
A R Spencer

these, and all other trams of this type, would logically be next for withdrawal as the replacement programme progressed. Despite this, some four-wheeled Balcony cars were modernised and overhauled right up to 1939. During 1936-38 no fewer than 27 of them had their destination number plates replaced by new illuminated number blind boxes. Surviving bogie cars of the same type had long been similarly equipped. In September 1938, by which time at least one Balcony four-wheeler with the new number boxes No 156 had been withdrawn, No 227 received similar new fittings. Such unnecessary expenditure on trams due for imminent withdrawal was by no means a Dublin phenomenon, there are many instances of similar happenings on other systems.

Repaints continued apace during 1938. Seat cushions from a withdrawn Dalkey car being fitted to No 248, while No 234 received the top cover previously carried by No 61. Two years later, all these refurbished cars were scrapped. Towards the end of 1938, the overall number of tram overhauls at Spa Road was drastically cut back. The meticulous Patrick Coleman, who was in charge of the Paint Shop, recorded every vehicle to leave the works for many years from November 1938 onwards.

Coleman's diary shows that three trams, all four-wheelers, were outshopped in November 1938: Standard 146 and Balcony cars 151 and 234. Two, Balcony car 119 and Standard 287, were repainted in December, and on 6th January 1939 the last tram to be overhauled at Spa Road left the works. This was the Balcony car No 110, which exchanged its truck with No 275 at the same time. Only 12 months later, No 110 was in the scrapyard. From January 1939 onwards, all overhaul work on trams was concentrated at Ballsbridge.

Disposals

By January 1939, 53 trams had been officially withdrawn. These included 35 four-wheel open-toppers. The last four similar cars still officially in stock, Nos 62, 139, 274 and 276, are shown as having their window glasses removed in January and February and being sent to Ringsend for scrapping, together with several similar vehicles taken out of service earlier. On 2nd May 1939, the board noted that 33 trams had been sold to J E Collins and Son, scrap merchants, for £430.

The DUTC intended to sell 20 more, but pending consideration by the General Manager, it was agreed that there would be no further sales. At the end of 1939, the operational tram fleet had dropped below 200 with 170 double-deck buses plus about 150 single deckers in service. The dates of entry into service for the 48 Titans R122 to R170, not recorded in the list of tram replacements, did not match any tramway abandonments, but their commissioning coincided with a similar reduction in the number of single-deck buses.

By 1940, several depots held considerable numbers of withdrawn trams. At Donnybrook, there was a large collection of Balcony cars, pushed off the rails and intermingled with redundant buses. Dartry depot ceased to be operational after the closure of the Palmerston Park (12) line in January 1939. The trams serving Dartry on route 14 were henceforth based at Terenure. For a time before being sold Dartry became a scrap yard, contractors being brought in to break up the trams. Bill Birney referred feelingly to it as an abattoir for trams. When work finished on the Balcony cars, 63 out of the fleet of 91 Standard Saloons were moved from the depots where they had been stored and broken up. A survivor from this time

was Standard No 129, originally built as a Balcony car in 1923 and totally enclosed six years later. It was used a scrapyard shunter at Dartry, after which it moved to Terenure depot for a further period in revenue-earning service. It eventually worked until the end of the tramways.

Bogie trams were treated somewhat differently. The saga of the 15 Howth open-toppers, Nos 301-312, 320, 321 and 324, is a sombre one and the fate of these vehicles was clearly a cause of some embarrassment to the DUTC. Twelve of the Howth cars were renewed or replaced from 1920 onwards, the newest, No 311 being of 1926 vintage. All were thoroughly overhauled and repainted in the late thirties. Displaced from Clontarf, they were kept at Conyngham Road from 1938.

The Howth open-toppers were moved to Donnybrook in 1940, when Conyngham Road closed to trams following the Lucan abandonment. At that time, the five Luxury cars for the Howth service are said to have been based at Blackrock. Meanwhile, the DUTC thought seriously about placing the open-toppers on other services and one car is said to have been tried out on the Terenure line. No 324 had certainly been over this route at an earlier date. There was, however an objection to working bogie cars on routes crossing hump-backed canal bridges and sadly the Howth cars were scrapped at Donnybrook during 1941.

A few redundant Windjammers appear to have been broken up at Spa Road in 1938 but only eleven out of a total of 28 were scrapped before 1945. This class included the oldest cars in the fleet, one (No 315), going back to 1906 and the four newest dating from 1924. All of the cars disposed of by 1945 had been built before 1913. Of the 17 remaining Windjammers, eleven were built before 1913 and one of these, No 328, deserves special mention. This car, built in 1908 and the last of its type in almost original condition, was set aside for preservation in January 1942. Seven years later it was to became the catalyst for transport preservation in the Irish Republic.

Twilight Refurbishment, and Brief Lives

During the war, the Dublin United Transport Company continued the tram services from Nelson Pillar to Dartry, route 14, and Terenure via Rathmines, route 15. Trams also ran to Blackrock, Dun Laoghaire and Dalkey on routes 6, 7, 8. At least 75 buses would be required to replace these trams, but during 1941 chassis deliveries ceased, 242 double-deckers being then in stock. Registrations had been booked in advance, as was DUTC practice, for another 75.

Urgent arrangements would now have to be made to keep the remainder of the tramway system and the surviving fleet in good order for at least the duration of the war, or the Emergency as it was euphemistically called in Eire. It was therefore decided, in April 1942, to overhaul 90 trams at a total cost of £15,000. The programme was put in hand immediately, and while few details of electrical, mechanical or coachbuilding repairs survive, Patrick Coleman kept scrupulous records of all repaints. Coach painters were sent from Spa Road to Ballsbridge where between May 1942 and March 1943 they dealt with a recorded total of 84 trams.

Patrick Coleman set out the date on which each car left the works and the amount spent on materials. Curiously, the lowest and highest expenditure was on two trams, which left Ballsbridge on the same date, 15th June 1942. Luxury car No 41 cost £3 11s 3d to refurbish. No 41 was the cheapest repaint, while Standard Saloon No 215 was the dearest, coming out at £5 17s. 11d. All other amounts fell somewhere between.

The breakdown, by type, of the trams dealt is as follows: seven of 22 surviving Bogie Balcony cars, 26 Standard four-wheelers out of the 28 then remaining; ten of the 12 Bogie Standards, 24 out of 37 Luxury four-wheelers and 17 of the 20 Bogie Luxury cars. To make the numbers up from 84 to 96, six were recently overhauled trams, including four bogie vehicles. Subsequent research by Clifton Flewitt and William Birney has identified the extra trams and also confirmed that some single truck Luxury Saloons had already been withdrawn.

During 1942, the number of Bogie Balcony cars was reduced by four, Nos 3, 85, 91 and 183 being scrapped. No 328, which, as mentioned elsewhere, was reprieved and stored as a candidate for eventual preservation, later re-entered service as a snow-plough. In 1944, No 64 was scrapped at Ballsbridge, with what was recorded to be No 323. In fact, the latter switched numbers with 113 which was broken up while the original No 323 survived, renumbered No 113. The non-standard Bogie Standard 313 was also broken up. This reduced the number of trams to that known to exist when CIE took over in January 1945.

Four-wheeled Luxury cars 153 and 176 were not among the vehicles refurbished in 1942-43, but they certainly remained operational, surviving until 1948 and 1949, respectively. The ten members of this class not accounted for and already written off were joined from 1942 onwards by others. Declining numbers of four wheelers were maintained in working order, most of the supernumeraries being shedded at Terenure with two or three in the remaining depots, where they could be cannibalised for parts as necessary. To give a three minute frequency on the Dalkey and Terenure lines and five minutes to Dartry at peak times, about 40, 17 and 13 cars were respectively needed for these routes. To provide extras for special events such as the Ballsbridge shows, a further 20 vehicles would be needed, thus the figure of 90 cars is about right.

Among the derelicts at Terenure depot on 30th October 1948, the second last day of tramcar operation on the 14 and 15 services, were Nos 12, 13, 22 and 56, thick with dust. They had obviously been out of service for at least seven years, still displaying on their sides the DUTC garter belt device, replaced on operational vehicles by the 'Winged Wheel' in 1941. The oldest of these cars, No 13, was built in 1933, No 56 a year later. Nos 12 and 22 dated from 1935 and were less than seven years old when withdrawn. Many people felt that these premature withdrawals, coupled with expenditure on Balcony cars so obviously due for scrapping, were clear indications of an accountancy based anti-tram programme. In reply to such allegations, the DUTC would have pointed out that they held a more comprehensive reserve of spares for the Standards and that these trams used less current than the Luxury cars.

Hard Times

During the Second World War the increasing isolation of the Irish Free State, especially from 1941 onwards, brought considerable hardship. While some Dubliners had seen an improvement in housing and welfare during the thirties there was still much poverty, exacerbated by harsh wartime shortages. Emigration to Britain provided an alternative, and virtually certain employment, for people who found themselves out of work as a result of the hostilities. For those who remained, it was an unpleasant period, although it was infinitely better than that endured by people in the United Kingdom.

In Dublin, on the very first night of the war, Corporation personnel began switching off most street lights individually, every lamp at that time had its own clockwork time switch and had to be manually wound at fixed intervals. Lamps were gradually switched on again as soon as cowls were fitted to direct the light downwards in concentrated circles. Although wattages were reduced, this relieved some of the gloom felt by many in those early, eerie days of the war.

Dark, badly lit streets were a potential cause of accidents, various methods of improving the visibility of vehicles being devised. On buses, life guard rails, rear bumpers and the leading edges of front wings were painted white, the fenders or buffer rims of the trams being treated similarly. Except for a reduced area of their front wings, buses retained the white trim after the war and tram fenders remained white until their final withdrawal.

Virtually everything was rationed, if it was available at all. Clothes and some foodstuffs could only be obtained on surrender of coupons from ration books. Coal disappeared from fireplaces to be replaced with turf that came from huge stockpiles, enormous ricks being built up along the roads in the Phoenix Park. Because it was frequently wet and hard to light, hard-pressed citizens often suggested that turf be sold by the gallon instead of the ton. Gas was turned off for much of the day, the dreaded 'Glimmer Men' making spot checks on houses to ensure compliance. Glimmer men cut off those consumers unfortunate enough to be caught indulging in the dangerous practice of using gas during the off periods.

Air raid shelters were built along the centre lines of most wide streets, great ugly mass concrete blockhouses with narrow entrances at each end. There were even two in Lower O'Connell Street, between the tram tracks still in use. Lethal tank traps, designed to slow down any invading army trying to enter the city, also appeared. They consisted of a series of boat-shaped concrete plinths connected by lengths of railway rail, with pointed sections of rail protruding so as to cause maximum damage to any vehicle running against them. Built in double banks a few yards apart, they were the full width of the road and had staggered entrances and exits just wide enough for buses to pass through, severely testing drivers' judgement and steering skills.

Tank traps were built on the principal bridges spanning the Tolka and Dodder. Because it was the only remaining river crossing carrying a tram service, Ballsbridge escaped having the tank traps. This too, was the era when air raid sirens were tested weekly, the alert and all-clear being sounded ten minutes apart at mid-day on Saturdays.

The motor trade went into almost complete hibernation. Imports of vehicles and parts stopped, effectively closing down both motor assembly and repairs. Increasingly scarce petrol supplies led first to rationing and later to a complete ban on private motoring, what was available being allocated to public transport, defence and emergency services. Doctors, veterinary surgeons and a few other essential professionals who needed them were allowed to keep their cars on the road.

Vehicles, Staff and Ingenuity

Except for the Defence Forces and essential public services, new commercial vehicles were unobtainable and in time the stock of spare parts ran out. The lack of materials caused severe problems for those employed in bus building, especially at Spa Road. In fact, several Spa Road craftsmen found employment at the Harkness Coachworks in Belfast, where a fleet of 88 AEC trolleybuses was being built for the Corporation Transport Department. Throughout the war, motor and engineering firms found the going progressively harder. As business decreased, they had to let go skilled staff for whom there was no work. There was a constant exodus of craftsmen to Britain where their skills were much appreciated. Because these men were exempt from conscription, employers were assured of their continued availability.

Some former DUTC personnel crossed the Irish Sea where they worked in many of the transport undertakings, while others joined the Defence Forces at home. Large numbers of the company's staff enrolled in voluntary organisations like the Red Cross, St John's Ambulance Brigade, Air Raid Precautions (ARP) Service, Local Defence Force (LDF, predecessor of to-day's FCA) or Local Security Force (LSF), set up to assist the Army and Guards, respectively.

Just when it could benefit most from the disappearance of private motoring, public transport suffered one blow after another. More and more people had to rely exclusively on public transport, which was frequently unable to cope. The need to conserve precious fuel and save wear and tear on vehicles led to successive reductions in services. These started later in the mornings, finished earlier in the evenings and were less frequent than heretofore on routes regularly shortened in further efforts at economies.

A number of serviceable buses were cannibalised to keep the remainder of the fleet working, although no double deckers were involved. For a time during the war, passengers using the remaining trams enjoyed longer hours of more intensive services than did those who had to depend on buses, which by 1943 ceased on most routes at 9.30pm. By contrast, the last tram from Nelson Pillar to Blackrock departed 15 minutes after midnight.

Shortages of vehicles, parts and fuel affected every part of the transport industry. Railway passenger and goods trains, long distance buses and road freight services all suffered increasingly. Under the Emergency Powers Act, numerous decrees affecting virtually every aspect of people's lives were issued regularly. Responding to the ever-worsening transport crisis, in 1943 a government Emergency Powers Order set up a powerful executive to co-ordinate available resources to the best possible advantage. Its chairman was A P Reynolds, the DUTC General Manager.

1944: A Year of Crisis

Overall, circumstances deteriorated drastically in 1944. Labour difficulties and growing public frustration with the ever-deteriorating transport situation were already making life increasingly difficult for politicians. A further complication was a drought, which severely curtailed the supply of electricity, at that time largely provided by the Shannon Scheme at Ardnacrusha. From 1st April last tram departures were put back to 9.30pm but worse was to follow just over two months later when electricity usage had to be so severely curtailed that the trams were taken off altogether. Double-deck buses were hastily filched from other services, some from as far away as Cork, to provide alternative transport.

In August, the DUTC's last four double deck buses, the non-standard Leyland Tiger 62-seaters R243 to R246, were placed on the Dalkey route, but they could at best be likened to a drop in the ocean. Regarded as large vehicles in their time, they seated 12 fewer passengers than a Bogie Luxury tram and had a standing capacity of eight against the tram's 20. Many people feared that this was the end of the trams but they did return, amid general satisfaction, on 22nd October.

Greater numbers of passengers trying to use a diminishing service made for longer waits and ever mounting dissatisfaction. People were also becoming disenchanted with the continuous flow of Emergency Powers Orders which they saw as more and more encroachments on their freedom. Understandably, these perceived intrusions changed tetchiness to anger, although some of the rules were very sensible. In 1943, for example, Regulation No 305 set out precisely how six or more people should queue at a tram or bus stop. The rules were set out in the DUTC timetables where the company asked citizens to enforce the Order, 'for the general good'.

Unlike other transport authorities, the DUTC, as previously noted, had never provided shelters for passengers, arguing that their duty was to provide a frequent and reliable service for which people would not have to wait. This view became increasingly at variance with public perception of an operator's responsibilities, especially when continually deteriorating services resulted in longer waits for trams and buses. In any event, the first of the company's shelters was provided in 1943 at Lansdowne Road. Their proliferation did not become universal until the post-tram era.

Formation of Coras Iompair Eireann

During the 1930s, there had been much official concern about the prospects facing public transport throughout the Irish Free State. The condition of the GSR was a particular worry and led to the establishment of a Tribunal of Inquiry on Public Transport in December 1938. The majority and minority findings of the Tribunal, published in August 1939, concurred favourably on the DUTC, their only real unease being over certain financial provisions.

No major organisational changes followed immediately after the 1939 Tribunal report, but it was clear that action could not be postponed indefinitely. Despite its problems with supplies, the DUTC seemed to fare better during this period than did the GSR. The railway company's severe pre-war difficulties had now reached major crisis proportions. Before the war, there had been a body of opinion in favour of nationalising transport, with all services coming under the control of a unified operating authority. Opposed were those who contended that the relative efficiency of the DUTC would be seriously eroded by its less competent partners in a countrywide public transport monopoly. They also feared that political patronage and interference would inevitably lead to ever more unsatisfactory services.

The ruling Fianna Fail party had decided, by 1944, to amalgamate the DUTC and the GSR. To do this, they introduced a Transport Bill but it was defeated and a very bitter general election campaign ensued. There were accusations of political and financial malpractice, but Fianna Fail secured their coveted overall majority. The Transport Bill was re-introduced and passed into law, providing for the setting up of Coras Iompair Eireann (Transport System of Ireland) to take over the operations of the DUTC and the GSR.

CIE came into being on 1st January 1945, with A P Reynolds as Chairman and Frank Lemass as General Manager. The loss of autonomy created something of a culture shock in middle management at the former DUTC head office in 59 Upper O'Connell Street, today occupied by Dublin Bus. The board and senior management were henceforth based at Kingsbridge (now Heuston) Station, headquarters of the former GSR. The erstwhile DUTC operation became CIE Dublin City Services, with a manager who reported to Kingsbridge, but 59 Upper O'Connell Street was for years afterwards referred to by ex-DUTC men as 'Head Office'. Despite having the new company's top management at Kingsbridge, ex-GSR personnel were seriously disgruntled at what they saw as a take-over by the DUTC.

The Dublin company had the reputation of being a most efficient organisation, the perception and hope in official quarters being that some of their expertise would rub off on the operations of the railways, the latter's image being inferior to that of the DUTC. Whether intentional or not, the sense that a take-over rather than a merger had been effected was heightened by memories of what had happened to the DUTC ten years earlier with the acquisition of the General Omnibus Company. Quite simply, some of the same people were again taking the top positions.

There was also some resentment at the adoption of the DUTC livery and symbol for all vehicles of the new company, the only change being that the words Iomchar Atha Cliath were dropped from the winged wheel which became the official CIE crest. On Dublin trams and buses, the legal or parliamentary lettering changed and the previously bilingual tickets were replaced by ones printed only in Gaelic. The names of the respective designated officers were dropped from the title, which simply read Coras Iompair Eireann, Staisiun Droichead an Riogh.

Most Dubliners believed that the absorption of the locally controlled DUTC into what they saw, somewhat inaccurately, as a remote and inherently inefficient state-owned organisation was an unmitigated disaster. However erroneous or exaggerated their opinions, they remained unconvinced of any possible benefits. This was in spite of CIE having a highly dedicated and professional public relations department. Unfortunately, this was often wrong-footed in its efforts to defend inept decisions, many of which originated from political sources. From the beginning, there was a general perception that profits from the Dublin services were subsidising rural ones and that the DUTC's proficiency was being inexorably diminished. There was much correspondence in the newspapers, many of the letters being worse than uncomplimentary to the politicians of the day.

Making Up for Material Deficits

Although the Second World War ended in 1945 it was some time before CIE experienced any relief from crippling shortages of rolling stock throughout its entire system. Except for the four 62 seaters of 1944, there had been no new deliveries of buses for several years and it was nothing short of a miracle that no double deckers had been cannibalised during the war period, unlike the single-deck fleet from which several vehicles had been sacrificed. The first new post-war double deck buses, six Daimlers and a solitary AEC, left Spa Road in May 1946, to be followed later that year and early in 1947 by 20 more Leylands. On the tramway system, things had been somewhat better, several of the single-truck cars reprieved in 1942 being surplus to requirements and thus available to provide spare parts.

As originally set up and financed, CIE managed to turn in satisfactory early results. In March 1946, the board decided to reduce fares. On 1st July, charges were slashed, all cross-city journeys being reduced to 3d. The fares to Dalkey and Terenure became 3d and 2d respectively, the 1872 fare to Terenure had been 3d! These reductions helped to allay Dubliners' fears that their fares were subsidising losses in other parts of the country. However, the optimism was short lived, because the company's affairs went into serious decline during the latter part of 1946. As a result, 1947 saw fares raised to around the levels at which they had been prior to the 1946 reductions.

If 1946 was disappointing, 1947 was a real disaster. During the early months of that year, the country suffered hardships probably worse than those of the war years. Everything was in short supply and to add to the misery, February brought the worst winter weather in living memory. Blizzards more terrible than those of 1933 swept the country causing severe and lengthy disruption to services. So bad were conditions on the tramways that the unvestibuled Water Lorry No 4, which usually doubled as a snowplough, needed backup. Tram No 328, reserved for the National Museum, was therefore fitted with ploughs and put to work keeping the lines clear. Fuel was in such short supply that the most stringent rationing was enforced. Electricity supplies were especially scarce, reduced tram services being introduced on 13th March. Under the new arrangements, last cars to Dalkey, Dartry and Terenure were to be at 11.00pm, up to an hour earlier than usual. Luckily, a thaw which began the next day sent great quantities of water down the Shannon, increasing output from Ardnacrusha generating station and enabling the full services to be restored on the 15th.

On 3rd September there began a bus and tram strike, which lasted until 2nd November, causing huge public disquiet and great hardship. This strike highlighted the least positive contribution made to the CIE organisation by the DUTC, spreading the company's bad industrial relations culture across the country. A minor dispute in any Dublin depot could now disrupt transport services in the most remote parts of the CIE network. The strike began over wages, hours and discipline in the Dublin City Services.

CIE managers encountering a DUTC-style dispute for the first time were shocked by its ferocity. Industrial action in pursuit of shorter hours and better pay they could understand, but they were unprepared for the industrial relations methods that came from the DUTC. By the time the strike ended with an ad-hoc settlement of the immediate causes, enough bad feeling remained to lay the foundations of the next dispute, a pattern discernible in almost every major Dublin transport strike. As during the 1935 strike, the government arranged for Army lorries to be deployed to mitigate the worst effects on the travelling public.

A Political Football

Because of its position vis-à-vis the state, CIE was seen, almost as soon as it was established, to be amenable to political influence. The company became embroiled in various public controversies, many of them not of its own making. In the sterile and nasty Civil War politics of the forties, the company became a whipping boy for public represen-

A favourite backdrop for photographers
was Rathgar Presbyterian Church, its
beauty obscured in this picture by trees.
No 17, a Standard Saloon that worked from
1925 to 1948, shares the relatively clear
road with three of the large American cars
that comprised most of Dublin's taxi fleet
for some years in the post war period.
F N T Lloyd Jones

tatives, whether crusading with chip-laden shoulders or simply disgruntled and mischievous, and, in most cases, hopelessly misinformed and prejudiced about the realities of the transport industry.

The company was regularly pilloried for every possible shortcoming, perceived or real. These ranged from simple service delays to failures in providing employment for the supporters of this or that politician. The problems caused by the 1947 weather and strike were placed ritually at CIE's door, greatly aggravating all the company's other difficulties. Personalities inevitably featured in political exchanges and Reynolds, already seen by the opposition, and many irritated trade unionists, as partisan, became their *bête noir*.

Following a general election in February 1948 a new Inter-Party or coalition government took over from the Fianna Fail administration. They quickly replaced Reynolds, an eminent civil engineer from the public service, T C Courtney, taking over as Chairman. The hopes of 1945 that DUTC efficiency would boost the former GSR component of CIE were by now well and truly dashed, with losses on the railways threatening the company's future. In what looked like desperation, Sir James Milne, an eminent British railway administrator, was commissioned to advise on the future of transport in Ireland. The Milne report made several radical suggestions but these found little favour with the authorities of the day.

Dublin transport, so long a great civic asset, had now become part of a national organisation with a host of worsening problems. In this context, the future prospects for the rump of a once great tramway system, which many people had hoped might be retained, could not have been gloomier. Moreover, contemporary attitudes, especially within the transport industry, were very anti-tram, the motorbus being seen as the panacea for every public transport problem.

Most of the press also favoured tramway abandonment, pro tram people being depicted as living in the past and opposing progress. The few environmentalists who spoke up or those who asked what might happen in the event of another fuel shortage, were dismissed as cranks. They were informed that all the pro tram arguments had already been dealt with comprehensively several years previously and this was now a closed subject. In any case, by this time the remaining tramway infrastructure was in need of reconstruction rather than maintenance and half the remaining fleet would have to be replaced, with the other half needing major overhauls.

A Hasty Introduction
George O'Callaghan recalled the lack of special training or even instruction given to conductors in the last years of the trams, although a few motormen were trained in the early post-war period. Then a conductor attached to Clontarf Garage, one fine summer Sunday morning he was sent to Blackrock depot where there was a staff shortage on what was going to be a very busy day. On arrival he found an impatient depot inspector and a motorman ready to take out a tram as soon as he had a conductor. The inspector assured George that conducting a tram was no different from being in charge of a bus and all he had to do was, 'put the trolley on the wire and mind the rope.'

He carried out the necessary moves to get the car out of the depot and placed the trolley on the running wire, departing empty for Nelson Pillar where queues were already forming. The tram took off smartly and all was well until they met a car coming in the opposite direction whereupon there was a flash. Both trams stopped dead and the trolley head crashed to the ground, followed by the running wire, thus bringing the section to a halt until the overhead repair crew arrived. He had, of course, innocently put

the trolley on the wrong wire, which a few short years earlier would have been a serious offence.

Rundown: Planning Final Closures
During this period plans to replace the remaining trams and improve the bus service were actively pursued. The permanent way yard at Donnybrook was cleared in preparation for the building of the new garage which became Donnybrook No 2, and all but essential repairs to track and overhead ceased. Tommy Thornton, who was a motorman on the Dalkey route at the time, recalls that the rundown, imperceptible at first, became more evident as time passed and it was generally accepted that the remaining trams would be taken off at the first possible opportunity.

Training of motormen also ceased at this time, a handful of qualified conductors being available in case of need. The beginning of the end was foreshadowed in the spring of 1948 with the announcement that a fleet of one hundred complete buses to Bolton specification was being bought from Leyland Motors. The first of these arrived at the end of April, going into service on 2nd May on the Clonskea route. Deliveries continued apace, but after July when about 45 Bolton buses had entered service, improving services all over the city, no more appeared for some time. In fact, new arrivals were being stockpiled in Donnybrook garage in preparation for replacement of the Terenure and Dartry trams.

The spring and summer months of 1948 were somewhat unreal for those working on the trams. While they knew the end was coming, there were some signs of normality. During this time, several of the long withdrawn Luxury trams at Terenure were sent to Ballsbridge, some initially to have one motor removed. They later returned to be totally eviscerated, being towed back to Terenure. One such was No 235, which is recorded as having one motor removed as early as August 1947, visiting Ballsbridge again in April 1948 for the second one to be taken out.

At that time, some optimists believed that these motors were being put back into stock to ensure continued tramway operation. A very hopeful sign was the overhaul and repainting, during the summer, of Luxury car No 153. On the day that car left Ballsbridge Charles Ross sounded quite upbeat about the future, but in retrospect it is obvious that he was simply whistling past the graveyard.

The Terenure Abandonment

In October, the long-expected change was announced and after the last departures on the night of Sunday 31st October, the Terenure and Dartry trams ceased to operate. Luxury car No 57, with Motorman Tom O'Brien and Conductor Tom O'Shaughnessy, left Nelson Pillar to mark the end of services on the 15 to Terenure, part of which had been Dublin's first tramway route in 1872. No 57 was followed into the depot by No 291, the last 14 from Nelson Pillar to Dartry; this was crewed by Motorman Tom Cahill with Conductor Paddy Butler who had to return to Rathmines from Dartry before making their way to Terenure.

While tramway funerals everywhere were accompanied by displays of high spirits, there was a somewhat worrying aspect on this particular occasion, aggressive souvenir hunters being much in evidence. An *Irish Times* picture taken at Nelson Pillar showed one of their more innocuous actions: the handing out of a cushion through an upper deck window of No 57 to someone below. The next morning, Bolton class buses R337 to R368 took up duty on the former tram routes and were joined by further new vehicles as they became available for service. The Dartry (14) service was extended to Classon's Bridge, while some of the Terenure (15) buses worked to Whitehall Road.

Extra for the Dalkey

The Terenure closure left just one tram route, the nine-mile Dalkey service, the Premier Line, the city's historic first electric tramway. It continued to operate efficiently, reflecting great credit on the staff who, although knowing the end was near, gave of their best in solving problems already aggravated by the lack of maintenance. Thirteen four-wheelers were transferred to the depots at Ballsbridge, Blackrock and Dalkey, initially as extras for Spring Show traffic or other important events.

The reprieved four-wheelers were also needed as replacements for any cars suffering major breakdowns, which at this stage would not warrant repair. This did in fact happen, one example being Windjammer No 70 which sustained a broken axle and was not put back in service. The 13 four-wheelers included five Standards, Nos 6, 129, 154, 193 and 246. The other eight were Luxury cars 31, 131, 132, 140, 176, 205, 266 and 268. It is interesting that the two vehicles on Brill trucks, Nos 266 and 268, survived, despite their alleged unpopularity. Except for No 205, already suitably equipped, all these cars had their B49 controllers changed to B13s for service on the Dalkey line.

A strange and long unexplained omission was the recently overhauled No 153. There was a curious but unconfirmed story that on its last night this car had to be taken out of service because of a sick passenger. It was said to have been replaced by Standard 154 and as the motorman was under orders to bring his car to Ballsbridge at the conclusion of his turn, No 154 outlived No 153. Years later, a more logical explanation of all the numbers that soldiered on was given by D McManus, at that time an apprentice at Ballsbridge. He said that the vehicles were chosen, all other things being equal, on the condition of their tyres.

Because all except essential tramway maintenance had long since ceased, the standard reply to every enquiry about the trams during their last months was that everything was worn out. In fact, the impression was given that there could be a serious accident if they were not scrapped. This led a correspondent to the *Evening Mail* of 14th January 1949 to point out that trams 6, 154, 266 and 268 had been put up for sale as scrap at the time of the Terenure closure but here they were, he said, still travelling the Dalkey line, and leading him to ask for an explanation. If he got one, it did not appear in the columns of the *Mail*.

Fare Increase

CIE, established in highly controversial political circumstances, was an unfortunate company. It had failed to achieve the impossible objectives set by its creators and its affairs seemed to go perpetually from bad to worse. By the early months of 1949, the state of its finances was a cause of massive anxiety. When in March 1949 fare increases took place, yet another spectre threw its venom into an already highly charged atmosphere. City bus fares in Cork, Limerick and Dublin were raised, leading inevitably to the old charges of urban passengers subsidising rural services.

The revisions were announced on Thursday 24th March, coming into force four days later on Monday 28th. Public opinion was outraged both at the scale of the increases and the short notice. Inevitably, the remaining trams had to take their share of the pain. The fare from Nelson Pillar to Dalkey rose from 5d to 7d, a 40% increase. On the full distance fare, logic was amazingly absent from the company's presentation. They failed to point out that a 5d fare was charged in 1935 with a cost of living index of 156 as against one of 307 in 1949.

Even if the case had been properly presented, its rationale would certainly have been lost in the storm of rage surrounding the new 2d minimum charge. Since 1884, Dublin had had a 1d fare, universally regarded by the citizens as sacrosanct. Explaining

Considerable numbers of horses could still be encountered on the streets of Dublin well after the last trams ran. This picture of No 102, held up on Terenure Road East, demonstrates how horse drawn commercial vehicles, in this case a slop merchant's float, could slow up other traffic. Slop merchants were entrepreneurs who collected waste and left over food from shops, hotels and other institutions. This material finished up in the numerous piggeries that existed at one time in the Dublin city area. Motormen had to practice extreme patience with carters who frequently obstructed the trams deliberately, though the small amount of room on either side of the tram tracks must be acknowledged. F N T Lloyd Jones

recent fare increases in February 1919, William Martin Murphy defended the retention of the 1d ticket. He pointed out that out of 71 million tickets sold in 1918, 41 million represented penny fares, 'which could not be increased.' A major psychological nuance recognised fully by Murphy was missed by his successors 30 years later. A shorter stage would certainly have averted much of the anger directed at CIE's hapless Public Relations Department.

There was an eerie similarity between the case made in an *Evening Mail* leading article on 25th March 1949 and the letters to the *Irish Times* on 14th June 1872 (see Chapter One). The *Mail's* argument posited that the average working passenger on a Dublin tram or bus paid 2d four times each day, Monday to Friday. At that time, most people travelled home at lunch hour and worked a half-day on Saturday. This resulted in a weekly expenditure of 3s 8d on 2d fares. An extra penny for each trip increased the weekly outlay by 1s 10d to 5s 6d. Leisure travel or journeys by other family members would have made further inroads into family finances. Pennies were very important in 1949, when many families had a total income of less than £4 per week.

The Final Months – Capacity Problems
For many years, the Dalkey trams had used the terminal tracks at the east (Clery's) side of O'Connell Street, the Terenure and Dartry cars working from the west (GPO) side. As soon as the last cars on Routes 14/15 had departed, however, the Dalkey services moved across to the west side. This move cut out the need for the half of the scissors crossover still in use behind the O'Connell Monument. This enabled some sets of points and a short section of overhead to be abandoned, but otherwise it was business as usual.

CIE's public position was that the trams would go as soon as possible but their departure date depended on the availability of new buses. In late 1948, there was a grave shortage of double deckers. Thirty five of the 120 new vehicles delivered during the year had been used to replace the Terenure and Dartry trams, 20 others enabling uneconomic and worn out petrol engined vehicles in Cork to be replaced. There was a crying need to restore severely curtailed routes and open up new ones, while hopelessly inadequate single deckers still serving busy and developing districts needed replacement. The Spa Road works was turning out double deckers as rapidly as possible, but also had to build new single deckers for country services.

An early closure of the Dalkey line seemed a little remote as 1948 ended. The shortage of buses and the daunting problem of matching the carrying capacity of the legendary trams working the route led many

people, rather unrealistically, to doubt that it would happen. Some protested spasmodically at the probability of final tramway closure but no notice whatever was taken of their viewpoint. Opponents of abandonment, depicted as anti-progress or living in the past, accused transport officials of selling out to vested interests and making our transport totally dependent on oil supplies. All the other familiar arguments, both pro and anti were paraded ad nauseam, the whole procedure being invested with a strong sense of deja vu.

The same arguments were fiercely conducted in many other cities where trams were threatened and, too often, summarily scrapped for doctrinaire political reasons. It is a great pity that, until recently, few participants in transport debates would concede that an integrated system, with trains, trams, buses and trolleybuses, each complementing rather than competing with the others, constitutes the optimum solution.

The End of the Dalkey Line
In the early months of 1949, CIE availed of an opportunity to buy a further 50 complete buses from Leyland, this time to Capetown specification. These vehicles, 21 of which (R391 to R411) were 8ft wide, the remainder (R412-R440) being to the older 7ft 6in width, were imported during the early summer and stockpiled at Donnybrook. As soon as delivery was complete, arrangements were made for the change-over but, as was usual in such circumstances, minimal public notice was given. This was probably intended to head off any possible protests and it was announced that the last Dalkey trams would run on Saturday, 2nd July. However, there was a hitch, relating mainly to operating terms for the staff involved, and a week's respite was given, the last day of tram services being the following Saturday, 9th July.

A formal ceremony was planned on this occasion, with the Irish Transport and General Workers' Union Band present at Nelson Pillar to play the last car out, but this was not to be. For more than an hour before midnight, huge crowds began to gather in O'Connell Street. The vast majority of these people came to attend the ceremony of cheering out the last tram, their only purpose being to take part in a unique and historic occasion when good humour would be tinged with sadness.

But there were others abroad on that night whose intentions were very different and spoiled things completely for everybody else, making it impossible for the band to play or indeed for the last trams to reach the Pillar. This would have been difficult enough in any event, because the crowds stretched as far as College Green and it was obvious that the Gardai had not expected such a large turnout. Taking advantage of the situation, gangs of what Dubliners call

gougers charged up and down the street, terrorising people and attacking the trams: they surged aboard, climbed out on to the roofs and cut the trolley ropes; it is a wonder that nobody was injured.

The last cars could not cross O'Connell Bridge, being turned in Westmoreland Street and Nassau Street. Eventually, Bogie Standard No 252 became the last tram, staggering out to Blackrock Depot with masses of people aboard, many of them bent on destruction. They were hanging from every part of the car, removing anything that could be dislodged – destination blinds, seats, handrails and other fittings, even the headlamp rims and reflectors. The sad remains managed to struggle into Blackrock Depot sometime after 1.00am on Sunday 10th July. Because the journey had started the previous day, the time of arrival has created confusion for some historians as to the exact date of the last Dublin tram. Besides No 252, several other trams were attacked on that memorable night, two others sustaining severe damage being Nos 117 and 314.

All the national newspapers carried stories about the night of shame, differing only in the words used by the various reporters and the people they interviewed. The report in the *Irish Press* of Monday 11th July headed **ONLY REMNANTS OF LAST DUBLIN TRAM LEFT BY CROWDS** began; 'Amid scenes of near-riot, the last trams to be operated by Coras Iompair Eireann limped home to their bases early yesterday morning under strong Garda escort. Since before eleven o'clock on Saturday night thousands had jammed in O'Connell Street to give them a big farewell. As they came in, the boarding parties got to work, and by the time they had finished, the trams looked as if they had been under artillery fire. The biggest damage was done after two o'clock yesterday morning. The very last tram – the 12.15am from Nelson Pillar to Blackrock – had been forced to start from the Ballast Office, as had a number of its immediate predecessors. But the mobs slowed its progress to a standstill, and when groups climbed on the roof there was grave danger that numbers of them would be electrocuted. The uproar was so severe that at this stage, however, that the appeals of the CIE officials could not be heard, and all attempts to restore an atmosphere of good humour was swamped in what one conductor described as 'the worst example of hooliganism I have seen in my life.'

'When the tram approached the Blackrock depot, every window smashed, every bulb missing, and every fitting stripped, it met fresh crowds. They milled around it, while Gardai and company officials – drivers, conductors and inspectors – strove to force a pathway. Eventually it lurched through the brick-red entrance for the last time – and then the officials had to use all their combined strength to shut the iron gates in the face of the crowd. Drivers and conductors kept their tempers in the face of the overwhelming odds. Expecting to find themselves faced with souvenir hunters, they saw masses of young men and women rip the woodwork away from the cars. On one car the upper side was broken away completely.

'One conductor – on the last tram to Dalkey – not only had his trolley [rope] slashed by penknife, and even his driving lights removed, but he lost his hand-brake as well. This meant driving the tram backwards, with the conductor up in front giving directions. He was an hour and a half late delivering up the shattered remains of the charge. The cheers of the crowds and the sounds of smashing glass were augmented by the reports of detonators attached to the tracks and the continuous hooting of motorists which could not get room to move on the roadway…When the last tram was finally corralled at Blackrock, company staff relaxed after three tough hours – and sang *Auld Lang Syne* to the wrecks.'

The *Irish Press* report was but one of several in similar vein, some papers adding editorial comment. The *Evening Herald* headed its strong editorial of 11th July 'DISGRACING THEIR CITY' and expressed wonderment that nobody was electrocuted. The paper said that, 'Great praise was due to the small force of Gardai taken completely by surprise….. and to the tramway officials who stuck to their posts so gamely to the bitter end.'

During the 1944 drought the streets had seemed strangely empty and silent without the trams, despite the presence of buses and other traffic. But everybody knew that the trams would be back, so there was an underlying sense of hope. This time it was different; when the buses took over the next day people realised that the streets could never be the same again. Indeed, as recently as his retirement in September 1993, the proprietor of Caffola's Ice Cream Parlour in O'Connell Street remarked that much of the atmosphere of the street disappeared with the trams.

One unusual but appropriate obituary appeared in the very first issue of *Buses Illustrated* magazine for November/December 1949. This was a frontispiece photograph taken from an upper window on the corner of Church Lane, and looking past Trinity College into College Street. At that time, trees had not yet been planted in College Green and so it was possible to see the solitary double-deck bus going towards Grafton Street. It was about to pass the statues of Henry Grattan, Edmund Burke and Oliver Goldsmith. This prompted the magazine's distinguished Editor, the late Charles Dunbar, to pick up Goldsmith's metre beautifully with his caption;

'Hail the conquering bus!' the statesman seems to say;
The last tram from Dalkey has gone its homeward way.'

According to the CIE accounts for 1949, the Dalkey trams earned £102,526 in fares during their last six months (plus one week) of operation, producing a net profit of £2,414. While it must be borne in mind that there was no provision for depreciation, it should also be recorded that unexplained 'other expenditure' of £28,453 was charged against the trams.

Comparisons and contrasts between the trams and buses were inevitably made at the time of the change-over. On 30th June 1949, the *Evening Mail*, mourning the imminent passing of the 'the stately vehicles' queried the reasons for change, making the points that, '…hardly anybody wanted change. These Dalkey trams, with tremendous passenger capacity in comparison with those on other lines, and pleasantly and comfortably furnished, were the pride of the late, much lamented, DUTC. They were showpieces and they certainly impressed visitors.'

Tourists and Comparisons
At the time of final closure, three generations of Dublin tram, Balcony (Windjammer), Standard and Luxury were working the Dalkey line. In its final months, this most impressive remnant of a once-mighty system attracted visitors who were interested in the line. Its rolling stock, old and new, its history and heritage, brought to Dublin people who would not otherwise have come. There were those whose interests were probably of a more general kind but who were also drawn by the reputation of the Dalkey trams. William Martin Murphy certainly got it right in 1907 when he spoke about people travelling on fine cars just for the pleasure of the experience.

Seating capacities of the trams working on the Dalkey line ranged from 60 (plus 12 standing) for the four-wheeled ex-Terenure Luxury cars to the 76 (plus 20) of the Bogie Luxury cars 326 and 327. The Bolton and Capetown buses seated 58 passengers, with eight allowed to stand but a few months later they were joined by the larger 66-seaters known as Spa Road Standards. The

capacity of the trams was almost reached in 1959 by the RA class 74-seater buses, but these fell short of the comfort offered by the Luxury cars.

Times allowed for the journey to Dalkey are also worth recording. The trams took 53 minutes to cover the nine miles from Nelson Pillar, the replacing buses being permitted 44 minutes. Both of these times contended with eight stops per mile, twice today's number. Asked about 1999 journey times, a Dublin Bus inspector was careful to differentiate between peak and valley times. Valley period running time is about the same as the 44 minutes of 1949, but at peak hours 60 minutes are needed. The inspector was also careful to point out that the slightest hitch can play havoc with the quoted times. Today's passenger might find it hard to believe that, every morning and evening, the Dalkey Expresses once ran more than four miles non-stop between Merrion Square and Blackrock.

The End of Terenure
Closure of the Terenure and Dartry services on 31st October 1948 saw the enactment of a procedure which, depressingly, was to be repeated following the Dalkey line closure nine months later. During the last weeks of operation on the 14/15 routes several unserviceable trams were sent to Terenure Depot. These included No 44, a Standard that had occupied the older portion of Blackrock depot with Water Lorry No 4 and Grinder No 73 for a long time. From Ballsbridge went Luxury four-wheeler No 242, its interior gutted by fire. Similarly damaged Bogie Luxury car No 295 from Dalkey, said to have gone on fire because of a carelessly discarded cigarette, would in other circumstances have been a noteworthy visitor to Terenure, which did not operate eight-wheelers.

From 1941, Terenure had nominally been home to all the remaining four-wheeled passenger trams, 28 Standards and 37 Luxury cars. A few Standards, including Nos 10 and 100, were withdrawn well

Four Luxury Saloons, single trucks 176 and 9 and bogies 93 and 282 are seen at Nelson Pillar. To the left is a Leyland TD5 Titan of the type that replaced 220 DUTC trams in 1938-41. Behind the cyclist on the right is a Leyland OPD1 Titan, one of 20 similar vehicles placed in service from October 1946 onwards and thus automatically giving the picture an authoritative earliest possible date. While No 9 was scrapped in 1948, the other three trams remained in service until July 1949. F N T Lloyd Jones

before 1948 and lay gathering dust in the depot with a larger number of Luxury cars. These included 12, 13, 22, 35, 43, 56, 78, 96, 104, 148, 196, 197 and 235. All had been liberally cannibalised, many being motorless following the procedures described elsewhere in this chapter. Just how long many of them had been out of service can be gleaned from the fact that they still displayed the DUTC garter belt instead of the winged wheel crest.

Selling off Everything

Unlike previous closures, as soon as the Terenure and Dartry trams ceased, advertisements appeared in the Dublin papers inviting offers for the redundant trams, 53 in number. As already noted, five Standards and eight Luxury cars had been transferred to the Dalkey line for further service, the vehicles for disposal being 23 Standards and 29 Luxury cars, plus the bogie car 295. The seats were taken out and sold separately, many ending up in community halls or public houses and the bodies were purchased for use as seaside homes, farm stores, outbuildings or similar purposes.

All electrical equipment was removed and sold to scrap merchants Sherlings of Dublin and Cork, who based staff at Terenure to cut up the tramcar trucks, sorting and removing all the material to their yard at Griffith Bridge, Rialto. During the process, traction current was maintained to the depot, enabling one tram, Standard No 291, the last Dartry car, to be used as a shunter, moving the other, already disabled, vehicles around. Following its last duty No 291 was also prepared for scrapping.

Buying and Moving Tram Bodies

Prices for tramcar bodies ranged from £15 to £30 plus delivery charges and there were two methods of moving them. CIE used a swan-neck trailer, which on earlier trips was hauled by a Chenard-Walcker drawbar tractor. Later journeys were made with an AEC Matador lorry temporarily adapted as an articulated tractor. Apart from Scammell Mechanical Horses, CIE, like many hauliers in these islands did not use articulated vehicles at that time and were awaiting delivery of their first modern purpose-built ballast tractors.

The second form of transport was more basic and belonged to the late Peter Morris of Ranelagh, who bought an ex-American Army GMC 6 x 6 chassis and cab. He fitted a vertical lifting frame to the rear of the chassis and assembled a special axle on which the tram body would rest between wide-spaced twin wheels. This axle was bolted under the tram about two thirds of the way from the front, the fender of the tram then being lifted and chained to the frame at the back of the tractor. Morris's outfit ranged all over the country, delivering tram bodies as

far away as Wexford, Clare, Galway and Donegal. Removals continued until the early summer of 1949 when Terenure depot was cleared, being offered for sale shortly afterwards.

Some items, ascending handles, interior lamp brackets and reflectors for example, were not removed from the tram bodies before sale. The platform steps, removed to facilitate lifting, were also thrown inside the body. Fares lists were left in situ, as were route number and destination scrolls. A spectacle to be encountered for years afterwards was that of a Dublin tram adjacent to a beach or in a remote farmyard still incongruously showing '15 Terenure' or some similar legend on its ends.

Repeat Performance: Insensitivity

Following the closure of the Dalkey line, repeated elements of the Terenure aftermath invested events with a strong sense of having been here before. When the last trams ran to Dalkey in the early hours of 10 July, instead of being shedded at Dalkey depot, they were immediately driven back to Blackrock. Any other cars which happened to be in Dalkey depot were also removed, the premises becoming an outstation for Donnybrook-based buses on early-morning Dalkey and Bray workings. With the trams concentrated at Ballsbridge and Blackrock, the Terenure procedures were repeated with the same dramatis personae.

On this occasion, the unwanted trams were 64 in number. They were mainly bogie vehicles, made up of 17 Balcony, eleven Standard and 19 Luxury cars. There were also the five Standard and eight Luxury four-wheelers from Terenure, plus the Directors' Car and three service vehicles: No 73 (the grinder), Stores Wagon 51 and the goods lorry (alias locomotive) 24. Nos 24 and 51 were simply broken up, all the others being offered for sale in the same way as the Terenure fleet nine months previously.

Like Terenure, Blackrock retained one tram in good order as shunter right up to the end, in this case it was Luxury four-wheeler No 31. Because current was turned on only when shunting was in progress, particular care was taken after each operation to ensure that no operational tram had a controller handle which might be carelessly left in the 'on' position.

A sad feature of both programmes was the employment of tramway personnel in breaking up the vehicles with which they had worked, many of them for all their lives. Several of these men were approaching retirement and there appears to have been a great lack of sensitivity in the way they were treated. Some, like Myles Byrne and John Browne were young enough to have served more years ahead of them with CIE but for Charles Ross who had served his apprenticeship and worked all his life in Balls-

bridge the departure of the last, sad tram, a mere shell, would be the end. Ballsbridge yard and depot was first to be cleared, by November 1949.

While current had been switched off from the overhead on the line, it was still available to operate the traverser for some months and because of the limited access, cars to be removed were placed inside the gate for lifting. The Directors' Car had been towed to Dalkey Depot where it remained until sold in 1950 to a resident of Barnhill Road in whose garden it stood for many years. By March of 1950 everything was gone from Blackrock, the last trams to leave being Nos 129, 132 and 328 sold for preservation but subsequently lost.

Recycling

Immediately after the trams were withdrawn, the tower wagons began removing overhead wires, the cross arms and decorative scrollwork disappearing from the traction poles shortly afterwards. Most of the poles continued in use by the public lighting authorities, many in their original positions, but several were transferred to other locations. These were invariably re-erected without their decorative bases, which were frequently used as litter bins or bollards in pedestrian areas. Several stretches of road still had former tramway poles as lamp standards in 1999, some notable stretches being on the former Dalkey route, Waterloo and Morehampton Roads and sections of the Lucan line. Shorter runs or individual poles were still to be found in other places.

One standard which remained in position until the creation of the boulevard in the centre of O'Connell Street was opposite Clery's and was used as a flagpole, with a telephone box at street level for use by taxi drivers. There was a strange symbolism in the survival of this pole in close proximity to the statue of James Larkin, behind whom one of its fellows can be seen in the best-known and most dramatic photograph of Larkin taken during the 1913 lockout.

Drivers and Motormen

From the beginning of tramway replacement in 1938 there was a programme to prepare motormen and conductors transferring to the buses. Those going as conductors adjusted easily but prospective drivers received intensive training for their new duties. The vast majority encountered no problems but some older men were given other duties. There were, inevitably, some borderline cases and John O'Byrne-Gregan, Superintendent at Donnybrook garage, recalled an incident arising from just one such situation. A nervous former tram motorman who became a bus driver damaged the side of a brand new bus during his first week of going through the narrow entrance to Dalkey Depot. Interviewed about the incident, he was suitably contrite but expressed amazement at what had happened, because in 25 years as a motorman he had never even scratched a tram at that gateway.

Transport staffs in all sectors of the industry felt great sympathy for the displaced and retired tramway workers. They knew at first hand of the sacrifices these men and their predecessors had made over the years in many good causes, great and small. They particularly remembered their colleagues' epic struggle for fair employment and human dignity, overlaid by a strong sense of public service. Their feelings found tangible expression two months after the Dalkey closure, when a large number of tramwaymen assembled to be honoured by their friends and colleagues.

An illuminated address was presented to the men on behalf of Dublin busmen and signed by representatives of all the garages. At the top of the parchment was the CIE winged wheel logo flanked by reproductions of the cap badges worn by DUTC motormen and conductors. Celtic designs down the sides were divided by garter belts based on those carried on the sides of DUTC vehicles, and at the bottom, surrounded by laurel wreaths, two miniature paintings depicted a horse tram and a Luxury car. Under the heading 'Address and Testimonial to the last of the Dublin tramwaymen assembled at the CIE Club on 3rd September 1949, the text is as follows; 'We bus workers of Dublin wish to place on record our keen sense of loss on your departure from our undertaking, consequent on the cessation of tramway services.

We speak not alone for ourselves but for all the citizens of Dublin when we say that your services to this city entitle you to a great and just pride. Your efficiency in all conditions and in all weathers, your cheerfulness and courtesy to passengers of all kinds in all circumstances, had become proverbial and had given our city an enviable reputation in Ireland and far abroad.

We who know you as fellow workers knew not only your zeal in the public service, but also your staunch spirit of loyalty to us and your resolute adherence at all times to the rights of workers generally which, from 1913 onward, contributed initially to Ireland's trade union movement We salute you as fellow citizens, as fellow transport men, whose memory will endure in the annals of this City and this Country.

We will remember you especially and those who went before you, on electric trams and on horse trams, as fellow workers who created a great tradition which it will be our privilege to endeavour to uphold'

Tidying up

The tramway tower wagons disappeared from the streets as soon as their last duties had been completed but the Commer, minus mechanical units, was used for many years afterwards to afford access to the roof lamps of Donnybrook Garage and later served the same purpose at Inchicore works. The last permanent way lorry, the Ford ZA 1717, was used to replace tram stop signs with those for buses in 1948-9. It then spent a few years carrying materials to repair street setts for which CIE was still responsible, before slipping away quietly in the early fifties. The official motor tax records show the last tramway maintenance vehicles Dennis Aces ZA 1589, 1664 and 1715, plus the Ford ZA 1717 as being officially scrapped on 5th June 1953.

Removal of the tram rails, which had a residual value, continued for several years, usually when road surfaces needed replacing. In 1955, CIE estimated that about seven miles of track remained. In the meantime, the sight of abandoned track inspired Samuel Beckett's observation '...straight up the high street and there not a wire to be seen only the old rails all rust.'

Following the withdrawal of the tower wagons, the redundant Marlboro' Street premises was incorporated into the Earl Place CIE Club, providing space for a ballroom. Rail removal and road reinstatement was undertaken extensively from 1950 onwards, but in several places the track was simply covered over, sometimes with concrete which raised the level of the roadway. From time to time, track is exposed when cuttings are made for access to underground services.

Revenants and Ringers

During Dublin's earlier tramless years there were several reminders of what had been, apart from trackwork and poles. Tram bodies could be encountered in the most unlikely locations and in some places groups of them were sited close together. During the building of the houses at Cappagh Road and Finglas West in 1949-51, Nos 174 and 243 served as site offices and materials stores. Among other resting places in the Dublin area was Blanchardstown which at one time had no fewer than six trams. The beaches at

Below left: **Shocked staff compose themselves on the upper deck of Bogie Standard No 314 at Blackrock depot after the orgy of destruction which accompanied the last tram journeys. No 314 was probably the least damaged of the last three cars.**

Below: **The scenes at Blackrock depot in the early hours of Sunday 10th July 1949 as Garda and CIE officials try to clear a path for the badly damaged No 252, Dublin's last tram, to enter the yard.** Both, Transport Museum Society of Ireland collection

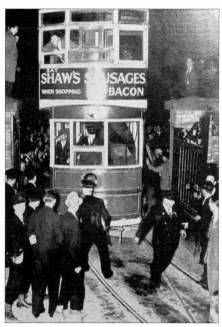

Donabate, Portrane and Rush also had their share, in the last mentioned location, two cars, Nos 185 and 326 were later incorporated into a seashore guesthouse. Another vehicle which survived for many years was a small open tramway wagon, bearing the lettering 'DUTCo' and the fleet number 68. This remained in the yard of the Spa Road bodyshops as a rubbish skip.

References have been made to ringers, trams which for one reason or another acquired the number of another vehicle. Tramway enthusiasts suspected that Dalkey Balcony Bogie car No 323, withdrawn for scrapping in 1944, might have been renumbered 113 and this indeed turned out to be the case. But it was not verified until some time after the car was acquired by the redoubtable Peter Morris of GMC tractor fame and placed in his yard at Woodstock Gardens, where the late William Birney established its true identity.

An even stranger ringer was one that nearly got away. In 1978, Transport Museum personnel were recovering parts from the body of No 46, a Standard that had been at Stratford-on-Slaney, Co Wicklow since 1949. On dismantling the body, which was in a state of near-collapse, it was found that the paint had worn off the dashes to reveal the number 10 beneath 46. Further investigation established that the vehicle was in fact No 10. A car numbered 10 had also been disposed of from Terenure but this unfortunately no longer existed and it is most likely that an examination of this would have established its original number as 46.

What Might Have Been

The late William Birney, who talked to as many former tramway staff as possible during the fifties, was intrigued on one occasion to be shown some sketches of a more advanced vehicle which was intended to follow the Luxury cars. The outline of this vehicle was recognisably a development of the previous design, but had a centre entrance and was to have been mounted on Maley and Taunton equal-wheel bogies. It seemed to owe more than a little of its overall concept to the celebrated 1934 Blackpool Balloon cars, most of which are still in service.

Unfortunately, the change of policy had killed off any ideas of building such trams and shortly after Bill Birney had seen the sketches most of the drawings which survived the end of the tramways simply disappeared. Some of these were destroyed and others are believed to have ended up in the United States of America. Beyond seeing the sketches, Bill Birney, an intrepid researcher with a passion for accuracy, could not get any further information about the proposed new trams. He believed, however, that the idea emanated from the former DUTC General Manager, G Marshal Harriss.

Urban Myths: Disrespect for the Past

Shortly after the final closure, people in reminiscent mood began to recount anecdotes about the tramways. One concerned a group of conductors who discovered that each of them had encountered a man who travelled regularly from a suburban terminus on the first tram and always had a pound which he offered for a twopenny fare. The conductors decided to stop this mean practice and so the next time the passenger offered his pound, he received a 2d ticket and all his change in pennies. This story sounded absolutely plausible until some time later, when it turned up in two other versions where the change was in cents and kopeks, it was an early example of an urban legend.

A CIE official told of hearing about a dog which had been observed sitting and looking forlornly through the gates of Blackrock depot before the trams there were disposed of. He was thought to have been looking for his master, a regular traveller he met every evening outside the depot but who died on the day the last trams ran. On making enquiries, the CIE man learned that this was yet another incident that had been reported from several other places where tramway systems had closed.

Vehicles of all types have been featured in stories of the paranormal, real or fictional, over the years. As originally written, the M R James chiller 'The Casting of the Runes', began on an Edwardian tramcar. There are also numerous other stories about haunted or phantom vehicles. The Dublin trams have not given rise to any ghost stories, although the trams and buses that ferry staff home at night have long been known as ghosts. There are several known instances from the tram era of inebriated citizens becoming very frightened as they made their unsteady homewards on foot. Invariably, their terror was induced by the grinder going about its nocturnal duties, and making spectacular displays of sparks as it did so. Visions of the devil coming for the sinner, as depicted by the clergy in former times, have always been part of this scenario, which harks back to the M R James theme.

The story about the eel that is said to have lived in the tank of Water Lorry No 4 probably lies halfway between myth and fact. A span of ten years has been mentioned, but exactly at what period of the car's existence is not certain. If this creature did in fact exist, it must have had a particularly bad time if its occupancy coincided with the 1947 freeze-up.

A persistent tale of the late 1940s featured a stranger to Dublin who wanted to drive his Austin Seven car to Dun Laoghaire. He had been told that if he followed closely behind a Dalkey tram he could not possibly go wrong. Because it was a very foggy morning he did exactly that, stopping behind the

tram at every stop until it reached Blackrock. Here it turned sharply to the right, the driver following it into the depot and bumping down into an inspection pit before he realised what had happened. The story goes that it proved impossible to open the doors while the car was in the pit and that depot staff had to recover the vehicle with the hapless motorist still inside. Whether true or false nobody now knows and the story seemed to be increasingly embroidered every time it was recounted.

In contrast to urban myths and phantom vehicles, there is one true story about children in virtually every city that had a tramway system. It is a simple tale of placing a halfpenny on the track as a tram approached in the hope that it would be flattened to the size of a penny. Countless damaged coins were the net result, but there are stories of elderly shopkeepers in dimly lit premises being conned into parting with a penny worth of sweets for coins that had received the tramway treatment.

For conductors, a much more serious danger lay in accepting counterfeit coins, the manufacture of which occupied some skilled petty criminals. The usual test of a suspect coin was to drop it on the ground, anything other than the appropriate ringing sound immediately giving the game away. The risk for conductors lay in not being able to get off the tram to carry out the test, most depots had a collection of dud pennies accepted by conductors. A collection of such coins is in the possession of the Civic Museum.

Regrettably, none of our folklore collectors has seen fit to gather material about the trams, or indeed about urban life generally. As a result, much has been lost, and there was a great danger of the trams receding entirely into the mists of the past without being properly commemorated. That the citizens of Dublin really appreciated their magnificent tramway system and regarded the cars almost as personal friends was put very eloquently by one old citizen who exclaimed, 'I remember the trams well, God be with them!'

A similar respect for a great system inspired a group of tramway staff and enthusiasts in their efforts to preserve three Dublin trams, Nos 129, 132 and 328, as museum pieces. They were defeated by vandalism, the elements and an apparent official desire to airbrush the Dublin trams from history. It looked at one stage as if the last line of AE's poetic observation meant that the Dublin trams did eventually 'wend to the great deep, the Holy Sepulchre.' All of them didn't, there are survivors. But that is another story.

Chapter Six

THE HILL OF HOWTH TRAMWAY

The Survivor

Following the closure of the Dalkey line in 1949, the childrens' column in the *Irish Press* ran a series of short essays on trams. The series ended with a picture of a Luxury car. Next day, however, there was a photograph of an open-topper with the caption:

'The Dalkey tram is finished,
Rathmines and Terenure
But daily on the Hill of Howth
Hard lines I still endure'

This tram was in a time warp. Its fleet number, 1, had not been seen in the streets of Dublin since before the Second World War and, except for works cars, open toppers had not worked in the city for more than ten years. This No 1 belonged to that last, proud bastion of electric traction in the Irish Republic, the Hill of Howth line already mentioned briefly in Chapter 2 and now legend. While not part of the DUTC system, though it did cross it at two points, its historical importance and the place it occupied in people's affections would make its omission from this volume unthinkable.

When and Why

Although Sutton and Howth stations, both on the northern shore of a peninsula, are less than two miles apart by rail there lies to the south and east the 563-foot high Hill of Howth. This area of exceptional amenity was seen to have great potential for both residential development and tourism when electric traction became a practical proposition in the mid-1890s. The GNR, whose Howth branch had been in operation for over half a century, obtained an Act in 1897 to construct a tramway connecting Sutton and Howth stations by a circuitous route of five and a quarter miles around the Hill. The line opened in two sections, the three and a quarter miles from Sutton station to the Summit on 7th June 1901 and the two miles from the Summit to Howth on 1st August.

A Brief Description of the Route

The Hill of Howth Tramway, laid to the 5ft 3in gauge, mostly with bullhead rail and sleepers, was single throughout with passing loops. Emerging from Sutton depot, which stood on the site of the new pumping station between the present Tramway Court and the railway, three tracks merged into one and curved to the right to run along the south side of Station Road behind a low wall. From a turnout in the depot forecourt the left-hand track of a passing loop crossed into the station yard, the first stage point. Leaving the station, it re-crossed the road to join the line from the depot and ran on to the next loop immediately before Sutton Cross. It then traversed the main road and the Dublin to Howth tramway on a diamond crossing. Hill of Howth cars travelling in either direction had right of way over trams coming from Dublin but had to yield to city-bound cars.

Beyond Sutton Cross, the tram ran along the south side of Greenfield Road on grooved rails in setts as far as Church Road, where there was a change to sleeper track. There were loops at Strand Road, Howth Demesne, St Fintan's and Barren Hill before the line left Carrickbrack Road at the Baily Post Office loop to run on private right-of-way along the line of the present main road.

Emerging again at the convent wall and crossing to the north side of the road which it followed to Stella Maris loop, it again took to the fields for the last section of the 365-foot climb to the Summit station. On the Howth side of the Hill the tramway ran in the fenced reservation which is now a footpath as far as Balglass. There were two passing loops, at Dungriffan Road and Island View, where it curved twice to ease the gradient which was somewhat sharper than 1 in 17 at its steepest. Crossing into Howth station by an overbridge, the abutments of which still exist, the line terminated beside the railway. Originally, there was a loop at the Howth terminus, but while this was later removed, a connection was made to the railway.

Power Supply and Signalling

Behind Sutton depot was the generating station, a brick structure of unmistakably GNR architectural style that now forms part of the Parsons paint factory. This was steam-powered, having three Lancashire boilers, each supplying a vertical compound engine direct-coupled to its generator. At the Summit there was a battery house charged from Sutton This ensured that cars running near the extremities of the feeder cables around the Summit did not encounter a drop in voltage, thus impairing their performance. It also powered late specials when Sutton generating station had closed down for the night.

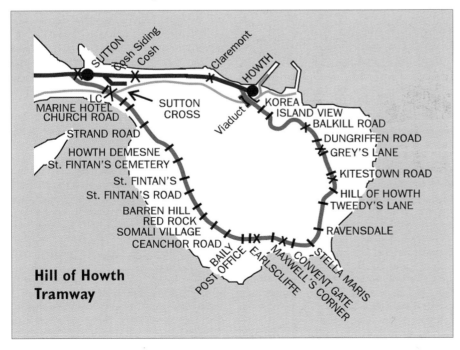

Hill of Howth Tramway

Brush cars Nos 1 and 3 outside Sutton depot. This three track building, capable of holding fifteen trams, was demolished in 1982. Tram No 3 was reserved for inclusion in a future transport museum, but succumbed to vandalism in 1965. Above the roof of the depot the chimney of the former power station can be seen. This building is still in use, its unambiguous GNR architectural style proclaiming its former ownership though its chimney has long since disappeared. Transport Museum Society of Ireland collection

The line was energised at 550 volts direct current and the GNR also supplied private customers in the area. Underground cables fed the line at the usual intervals, the Howth end being supplied from a cable laid along the railway, a shorter cable route with less loss of voltage. The overhead poles, about 295 in number, had side arms and brackets except at passing loops where they stood between the tracks and had double arms. They were unadorned apart from their pointed finials.

A simple and effective signalling system consisted of a box on a traction pole at every passing loop. Each box had a white bullseye lamp showing in each direction. An illuminated bullseye indicated a clear section ahead, a lamp out meant that the line was occupied. On entering a loop the motorman inserted a key in a rotary switch, turning off the light facing an oncoming car at the next loop, thus forbidding entry to the section until he cleared it. He also switched the light back on for the section he had just left unless another tram was following.

Up to four cars going in the same direction were allowed into a section at a time, all except the last displaying a large notice proclaiming 'Car to Follow'. The signalling suggests railway practice, and legally, the Hill of Howth line was an electric railway that happened to be worked with tramcars. As a result, the cars did not have carriage plates nor did the motormen and conductors require licences as those on the DUTC did.

Trams Nos 1 to 8

For the opening of the tramway, eight double deck open top bogie cars numbered 1 to 8 were supplied by Brush from the Falcon Car Works of Loughborough. These 67 seaters accommodated 30 passengers on longitudinal benches downstairs and 37 on reversible seats upstairs. All seats were slatted timber but there were strips of covering material on those downstairs. These trams, which had six windows between bulkheads, were mounted on Brill 22E maximum traction bogies, each car having two 30hp motors and BTH controllers. They had windscreens but were not fully vestibuled, being unglazed at the offside of the platforms.

In addition to the usual handbrake, Westinghouse air brakes were fitted, two large air tanks under the seats being replenished as necessary from a compressor in the depot. Some time after entering service these trams were fitted with cross-springs between the inner corners of the bogies; this improved their riding qualities and rendered them less prone to derailment. Owing to the proximity of poles and trees to the track, the original wire netting on the upper decks of the cars was raised shortly after the opening to prevent accidents to passengers.

Trams Nos 9 and 10

In 1902, two further trams, Nos 9 and 10, arrived. These were very different from the previous eight, being built by Milnes of Birkenhead, who had also supplied 37 motor cars and 30 trailers for the original Dublin fleet. Nos 9 and 10 were also open-top double deckers, but more massive than Nos 1 to 8, having nine windows on each side. They were designed with tourists in mind, having knifeboard or back to back seats for 16 passengers in the centre of the lower deck. An equal number was carried on four pairs of facing transverse double seats in each corner of the saloon. There were seats for 41 upstairs, giving a total capacity of 73.

Nos 9 and 10 had platform entrances at each side but those on the platform offsides were, in later years at least, permanently gated. These cars were on Peckham maximum traction bogies, their controllers and braking arrangements were similar to Nos 1 to 8.

As originally supplied Nos 9 and 10 had wire screens instead of glass in their side windows but they were subsequently glazed. The first livery of the entire fleet was crimson lake and ivory, elegantly lined out. Except for a brief, early programme involving platform and staircase steps, the cars never carried external advertising.

Because the depot was end-on to the running line at Sutton, the Hill of Howth trams always had the same end pointing towards Howth or Sutton. The ends were so designated in place of the 'No 1 End' and 'No 2 End' inscribed on DUTC cars. The trolley was on the sea or outer side of the cars with a single seat between it and the aisle. This contrasted with the DUTC cars which had their trolley standards adjacent to the aisle with the single seat to its outside.

No 11 – The Work Car

In the early days of the Hill of Howth Tramway, when overhead repairs had to be carried out a tower was erected on one of the cars, usually said to be No 3. In time, because of the need to carry materials up the line it was decided to provide a special vehicle and so No 11 was built. The origins of this car are very unclear, but it is believed to have been built at Dundalk in 1903. Not having its own running gear initially, it borrowed equipment from another car when its services were needed. In time it acquired Brill maximum traction trucks similar to those under Nos 1 to 8 and was a most versatile vehicle, used for many purposes.

The body of No 11 consisted of a cab at either end of a covered wagon body which had low hinged sides to allow for ease of loading and discharge. Removable panels in the backs and fronts of the cabs enabled long loads such as rails to be carried easily while a tower and ladder on the roof afforded access to the overhead. In later years, No 11 was fitted with a telephone, which could be connected into the wires along the line, enabling the crew to communicate with the depot.

Modifications and Livery Changes

Around the time of the Great War the crimson lake and ivory livery gave way to grained varnished mahogany, popularly known as the Teak livery. Nos 1 to 8 weathered very badly when so painted and by the late twenties looked the worse for wear. In 1929 when they began road motor services the GNR adopted a bus livery of blue and cream, which was applied to trams Nos 1 to 8 shortly afterwards. Oxford blue was the official name of the colour. About the time of the livery change, Nos 1 to 8 were also fully vestibuled and fitted with interior electric heating.

Because they saw very little service the teak paintwork on Nos 9 and 10 was in good condition and they never received the blue and cream livery. These cars were not popular with the crews, being open on both sides of the platform. This did not go down well with motormen while conductors found fare collection difficult because of the inside seating layout. As the absence of cross springs left them prone to derailment, they were allowed out only in the charge of certain motormen. Other complaints concerned their alleged heavy current consumption and the lack of interior heating. As a result, for many years they were rarely seen in service.

Enterprise Unrewarded
At the turn of the century there were high hopes of considerable residential development on and around the Hill of Howth but these expectations were premature. By the time any significant building took place most of the residents owned cars. While the Hill of Howth trams carried considerable summer traffic this unfortunately depended on the weather. Even in its best years the tramway always showed a loss and while the GNR frequently considered closing it down, it is to the company's eternal credit that it did not. The tourist potential of the Hill of Howth Tramway was never fully recognised and consequently remained unexploited, although its appeal was a rapidly appreciating asset in the fifties when it daily became more at odds with the world into which it had survived.

In the early years there were intervals of as little as 15 minutes between trams and there was one to connect with every train. Extra cars were provided to cater for large numbers of passengers on fine summer days. For a small system, this created the problem of striking a balance between the minimum and maximum number of men needed. The basic service called for only three or four crews per shift, but each additional car in service needed two extra trained staff who would at least have to be on notice that their services might be required. Allowances would also have to be made for reliefs.

At one time there were eight crews but this number was reduced in time and during its later existence the line depended at busy times on extra staff who were normally employed on other duties. Supervision was by the Depot Foreman and the Station Master at Sutton, the whole operation being run in an efficient but easygoing atmosphere. In 1933, however, as a result of a wage cut, a very bitter strike took place on the GNR from 30th January to 7th April. The tram service did not resume until 15th May, following government intervention.

ESB Power
Around 1930 when renewal of the power station plant was being considered enquiries were made about buying current from the ESB. This turned out to be a cheaper option than continued steam generation, so negotiations culminated in an agreement with the ESB in 1934. As a result the power station and battery house were closed and current was thenceforth supplied at 10kV by the ESB. A substation in an annexe at the side of the depot housed three mercury arc rectifiers putting out current at 550 volts dc for traction.

This arrangement continued up to the end of tramway operation, the only hiccup occurring during the fine summer of 1944 which, paradoxically, was a disaster for the tramway. The drought, which seriously curtailed the ESB's generating capacity and closed the remainder of the DUTC tramway system from June to October, also affected the Hill of Howth. Service was interrupted from June to September just when traffic would be at its maximum.

Surge and Decline in Fortunes
The Great Northern enjoyed a financial bonanza during the Second World War but, like all transport undertakings, was in serious trouble by the early fifties. On 1st October 1953 the company was taken over jointly by the governments of Northern Ireland and the Republic, each appointing five members to a Board to run the company. Savings were decreed where possible and it came as no great surprise when the tramway was threatened with closure from 31st March 1954.

Clearly taken aback at the ferocity of the opposition, the Board retreated. Indeed it looked for a time as if extra resources might be put into the line, which by this time was becoming busier. Because the Dublin trams had ceased in 1949 and Belfast's in 1954, travellers began arriving in growing numbers, probably out of nostalgia or curiosity or just to enjoy the scenery. There were also ever increasing groups of enthusiasts, many of them from abroad. However, local people, tramway staff and their supporters remained deeply sceptical.

The Tramway Staff – Selling The Service
The Hill of Howth Tramway staff enjoyed the respect of everybody in the area. In that intimate peninsular community, they were trusted friends who knew the needs of local people. They watched out for them, looked

Hill of Howth trams Nos 7 and 10 at the Summit in the mid-fifties. No 7 was one of the original Brush 67-seaters 1-8 of 1901, while No 10 was one of the Milnes pair supplied in 1902. Eight of the ten passenger cars lasted until the end of the tramway in May 1959. Two of the Brush cars, Nos 2 and 4, are preserved, as are both the Milnes vehicles. No 10 is in Britain's National Tramway Museum at Crich in Derbyshire and No 9, the last tram to run in public service in Ireland, is in Howth.
Transport Museum Society of Ireland Collection

after them and took very seriously their responsibility to unaccompanied children, always displaying excellent community spirit. In hard winter weather the tramway was a lifeline for people living on the Hill. Apart from the passenger service, goods were frequently transported to isolated houses along the line by the Work Car, as No 11 was known to the staff.

Hill of Howth tramwaymen made visitors welcome and happily looked after visiting transport enthusiasts. The two foremen in the years after the Second World War, Bob McAllister and his successor Norman Steele, probably did more for tourism than many highly paid publicists. Amazingly, nothing was done to exploit the tourist potential of the tramway, so diligently pushed by the staff at every opportunity.

Aside from being one of the few tramways to have its original rolling stock virtually unchanged since the beginning of the century, it was the last line anywhere exclusively worked by open-top vehicles. It also boasted the only authenticated instance of a decorated tram every Christmas, when Billy Rankin and Paddy Dowd proudly installed a tree, complete with coloured lights and decorations in 'their' tram, No 3.

Tickets

Hill of Howth tram tickets were of two types. Being an extension of the railway, through tickets were available to and from various stations and these, in their many variations, were of the Edmondson card type used by the GNR. Tickets issued for local travel were mostly of the Bell Punch type, the earliest ones being geographicals with the stage names printed on each value. The first ones, printed in landscape (horizontal) layout, were superseded by upright (portrait) versions.

Later issues had stage numbers similar to those on DUTC tickets but were specially printed, bearing the title of the tramway. For many years the reverse displayed advertisements for Nugget shoe polish. After the change of title from GNR (Ireland) to GNR Board in 1953 new tickets were printed showing the revised nomenclature. The highest value was 5d and it was not until a 6d fare was introduced that GNR bus tickets printed, like the tram tickets, by Williamsons, appeared. The tickets were cancelled with a hand punch or clippers, those issued on the Sutton side of the hill having an S-shaped excision, with 'H' on the Howth side.

The Beginning of the End, CIE Takes Over

In 1957 a thorough examination of Nos 1 to 8 was undertaken and as a result Nos 5 and 8 were withdrawn and slowly cannibalised. Their cross-springs were fitted to Nos 9 and 10, which had been enjoying a revival since about 1952 and now became regular performers. Their new-found ability to ride well and stay on the track made them firm favourites. It has been said that in their last seven years of service they did more work than in the previous 50.

The year 1957 turned out to be disastrous for the former GNR. At the end of that summer much of its system was closed down in pursuit of economies, especially in Northern Ireland where the government was implacably hostile to railways. There were also closures in the Republic with further ominous changes threatened by the Beddy Report on transport there.

When the 1953 inter-governmental agreement on the GNR ended in 1958 new arrangements were made, the fixed assets of the Board being vested in the nationalised

state transport authorities on either side of the border. In the Republic that was Coras Iompair Eireann, which took over on 1st October 1958, their acquisitions including the Hill of Howth Tramway. At that time, CIE was moving into a new phase of its existence, one of the objectives being the elimination of as many loss making enterprises as possible.

The Closure

The Hill of Howth Tramway was quickly identified as a loss maker and CIE let it be known that they intended to close it, although many responsible people tried to persuade them otherwise. Following months of uncertainty, it was announced on 14th May 1959 that the line would close two weeks later on Sunday 31st May. There were some rather feeble objections but most people seemed to sense the futility of opposition. In those days before people had learned how to protest effectively, the importance of heritage was still unrealised and authority was rarely challenged.

During the last days of operation the trams were frequently incapable of coping with the vast numbers of people who wanted to travel and all eight serviceable cars worked hard right up to the end. On the last day, seven crews were available and car No 2 was kept in reserve, not going out until the evening when it replaced No 10. Fearing a repetition of what had happened to the last Dublin trams ten years earlier, the CIE officials and Gardai kept final departure times secret until No 1, driven by Tom Redmond, the senior motorman, was actually on its way from the Summit to Howth just after 10 o'clock. On the return journey the St Lawrence's Pipe Band travelled on the upper deck. From the Summit No 1 was followed down by No 6.

Meanwhile No 9, driven by Christy Hanway and with Alf O'Reilly conducting, was struggling up towards the Summit from Sutton. This was to be the last tram from the Summit to Sutton and the number of people sitting, standing or simply hanging on has been put at well over a hundred. No 1 and No 6 passed down towards Sutton, but just beyond Stella Maris there was a red light marking an unbolted fishplate and so No 9 had to turn back. It has been suggested that this was done to prevent possible trouble at

Unprecedented crowds travelled on the Hill of Howth trams during the last weeks of operation and an enormous number of photographs were taken by professionals and amateurs alike. Here a late evening visitor gets his picture of No 1, to the lady's left are Paddy Dowd (in uniform) and off duty motorman Tom Redmond who has been honoured by having a housing development called after him.
Transport Museum Society of Ireland

the Summit, but it was more likely the work of vandals.

Followed by an enormous procession, No 9 made its way back to Sutton, the rain being ignored by the vast crowds who turned out to be part of a most significant piece of transport history. The tram eventually made its way back into the depot to sustained cheering, hooting horns and exploding fog signals. But behind the gaiety was a real aching sadness, because this was Ireland's last tram which Christy Hanway and Tom Redmond had just driven into history.

On Monday 1st June, three newly overhauled Leyland Titan 60 seaters commenced bus operation on the Hill of Howth. The new, separate 87 and 88 bus services worked on the Sutton and Howth sides of the peninsula respectively, it would be some time before the roads would be remotely capable of accommodating a through route. The buses which took over were Capetown class vehicles from the batch that had replaced the Dalkey trams in 1949. R438, 439 and 440 had their differential gear ratios changed to enable them to cope with the Howth gradients.

The former tramway personnel gave CIE several more years of faithful service in various roles. The platform staff were reassigned immediately after the tramway closed, initially going to Clontarf Garage as bus conductors. Among them were Peter Shiels, Paddy Dowd, Tom Whelan and John Montague. Colm Weafer afterwards became well known to forgetful passengers when he transferred to the Lost Property Office. Billy Rankin, sartorially elegant as ever, conducted on the Hill of Howth buses before going to Dublin Airport as a CIE supervisor. Tom Redmond also worked as a conductor until he took charge of Kilbarrack station, adjacent to his home.

The maintenance staff remained temporarily in Sutton Depot. Clearly in denial, they daily polished brass, cleaned glass and swept the cars, probably hoping for a miracle. For some time after closure the section as far as Sutton Cross enjoyed a sort of afterlife, occasional trips being made to facilitate photographers.

Journeys Melancholy and Triumphant
Within a few weeks, demolition commenced and No 11, in the capable hands of a heavy-hearted Christy Hanway, began the depressing task of bringing materials – cables, poles, overhead wire and rails back from the Hill. Starting at Howth station, successively shorter daily journeys were made as everything on the Howth side of the hill was removed. This operation took about five months until Baily Post Office was reached. Because road access was possible from there down to Sutton, motor lorries then took over, demolition work being finished early in 1960.

There was a greater appreciation of the Hill of Howth Tramway and its cars outside the Irish Republic than within it. Following closure there was world-wide interest in the cars as museum pieces. The cannibalised Nos 5 and 8 were broken up within a few months but all of the other nine trams were strong candidates for preservation.

Nos 2, 3, 4, 9, 10 and 11 were already earmarked for preservation, leaving Nos 1, 6 and 7 available. Norman Steele dealt with numerous enquiries about these cars, receiving several representatives of would-be purchasers. His efforts were, unfortunately, not successful and so these three trams were also broken up; Norman Steele felt especially sad about No 1, easily the best of the three and kept to the last in the hope that it might find a buyer. CIE deliberately set the purchase prices very low to give museums every chance of acquiring the trams.

The first of the trams to go was No 10, which departed for the Tramway Museum at Crich in Derbyshire in January 1960. Regauged, in 1985, No 10 was one of several historic trams that went into service in Blackpool to celebrate a century of electric tramway operation. It proved a most popular vehicle, remaining in the Lancashire seaside resort for some years before returning to Crich.

No 2 went to the Orange Empire Trolley Museum at Perris in California shortly afterwards, while in June No 4 left for the Belfast Transport Museum, being the first vehicle to arrive there. No 2 operates from time to time, while No 4 is now at the Ulster Folk and Transport Museum at Cultra, just outside Belfast. The bogies of No 6 were used in the restoration of Manchester tram No 765. Their work in Sutton finished, Norman Steele, Christy Hanway and Dick McGlew took up maintenance duties on the railway. Christy went to Amiens Street, Norman and Dick to the Fairview railcar depot.

Sutton depot, a catering repository for the 1960 Canada Cup Golf Tournament at Portmarnock, was later used for railway purposes. It was finally demolished in 1982, although the yard track fan, overgrown and forgotten, remained in position for several years. A solitary pole with its side arm and bracket also stood in Sutton station yard until recovered as a historic relic in the early eighties.

History and Legend
The Hill of Howth Tramway is now history. Like every well-loved institution, it is a rich repository of folklore and a source of many urban myths. Some stories are bizarre, frequently recounted events acquiring further embroidery every time they are recalled. One, which comes up regularly, concerns the speed of the trams, figures in excess of 40mph being quoted from time to time.

In fact on 31st May 1959, No 9, travelling flat out, was paced along Greenfield Road by a Ford Prefect car which recorded a sustained 24mph between Strand Road and Church Road. That would almost certainly have been the highest speed ever attained by a Hill of Howth tram. The car driver was the same Tommy Luccan who, years earlier, had paced a Dalkey Luxury tram at Booterstown at a speed over ten miles per hour greater than that of No 9.

There are innumerable stories of knocking-up, tramwaymen pounding their gongs to wake up people who had slept in, and as John Dunne observed in his *Ireland's Own* contribution, there were few places where houses had trams at the ends of their gardens. Carrying purchases from Sutton or Howth to sick or housebound residents are legion. This culture of care really comes to life in the story, probably the most appealing of all, about the Hill of Howth Tramway and told by a man who went to live near Baily Post Office in the fifties. From a rural area more than a hundred miles from Dublin where the sense of community was very strong, he was amazed by what he encountered in his first week on the Hill of Howth.

Each morning, this new resident caught a tram that connected with a train at Sutton, ensuring that he was in good time for work. On the Friday, however, the tram, more crowded than usual, stopped after travelling a short distance at the corner of a lane where it remained for no obvious reason. Getting worried, the neophyte asked the conductor why and was told, 'Friday is pension day so we're waiting for Mrs O'Neill'. Just then, a very old lady appeared in the lane and was helped aboard with many warm greetings. The new passenger then mentioned his fear of missing the train at Sutton, whereupon he was assured that the train driver also expected Mrs O'Neill and, sure enough, the train had waited.

Honouring the Past
Nothing could better illustrate the spirit of public service than the story of the tramwaymen and Mrs O'Neill. Acknowledging their work and their important place in history, a small housing estate at Sutton is known as Tramway Court while Tom Redmond has been honoured in the naming of Redmond Court near his home at Howth Junction.

In 1949, preservationists acquired former DUTC trams 129, 132 and 328 as museum pieces. When the Hill of Howth tramway closed Nos 3, 9 and 11 were set aside for inclusion in a possible future transport museum here. Now restored, No 9 is the sole survivor of that sextet, Ireland's last tram.

Appendix One

THE LINES SUMMARISED

To assist with quick identification of the various DUTC tram routes and the services that ran over them there follows, in route number order, a brief history and description of each.

Nelson Pillar to Sandymount (1, 2, 3)
This route was never served by horse trams. It operated via D'Olier Street and Pearse Street, passing the power station and Permanent Way yard at Ringsend Road. At Londonbridge Road it was joined by route 4. Route 1 terminated at Thomas Street, Ringsend, route 2 at Sandymount Green, 3 at Sandymount Tower. The Grand Canal Dock to Sandymount section opened on 4th July 1900, the complete line to Nelson Pillar on 18th March 1901. The route symbol was a green crescent. It closed in stages, the final section was abandoned on 26th March 1940. Cars were shedded at Gilford Road depot.

Nelson Pillar to Sandymount via Bath Avenue (4)
The Dublin Tramways Company's Nelson Pillar to Sandymount horse service opened on 1st October 1872. It ran via D'Olier Street, Westland Row, Merrion Square and Northumberland Road. Its depot was at Gilford Road. The truncated Beggar's Bush to Londonbridge Road section was the last horse line . The entire route was electrified from 14th January 1901. Henceforth it operated via Nassau Street and Westmoreland Street. This was the only route worked by single deck electric cars. It had no symbol. Trams were replaced by a bus service on 31st July 1932.

Dalkey (6, 7, 8)
Nelson Pillar - Merrion Square - Blackrock - Dun Laoghaire - Dalkey. The section to Haddington Road was originally part of the DTC Bath Avenue line via D'Olier Street and Westland Row. The Haddington Road

to Blackrock section was opened on 16th July 1879 by Dublin Southern District Tramways. The depot was at Shelbourne Road. The line from Blackrock to Dun Laoghaire was opened by the Blackrock & Kingstown Company in August 1885 along with a depot at Newtown Avenue. The section from Dun Laoghaire to Dalkey was opened by DSDT on 19th March 1879. This line's gauge was 4ft. There was a depot at Dalkey. The entire Haddington Road to Dalkey line was rebuilt by DSDT and opened as Dublin's first electric tramway on 16th May 1896. Bought by the DUTC in September 1896, electric operation was extended to the city centre via Westland Row on 12th July 1896. Trams began running via Nassau Street to Nelson Pillar from 12th October 1896. The route symbol was a green shamrock with a yellow 'K' superimposed for Dun Laoghaire trams. Route 6 ran to Blackrock, 7 to Dun Laoghaire and 8 to Dalkey. This was the last city line to close, on 9th July 1949.

Donnybrook to Phoenix Park (9, 10)
The DTC's Nelson Pillar to Donnybrook line via Nassau Street, Merrion Square, Waterloo

Road and Morehampton Road was operating by 14th March 1873 with a depot at Donnybrook. The line from Nelson Pillar to Phoenix Park was opened by NDST on 10th December 1876 and electrified on 22nd November 1898. The depot was at Phibsboro (Cabra). The Donnybrook section was electrified on 23rd January 1899, Donnybrook to Phoenix Park being the first cross-city electric service. An alternative route via Dawson Street and Baggot Street was opened on 14th May 1906. Symbols were a blue double diamond for cars via Merrion Square (route 10) and a blue double diamond with white bar for trams going via Dawson St (route 9). The southern section of route 9 and all of 10 was replaced by buses on 2nd June 1940, the northern section of route 9 closed four days later.

Clonskea to Whitehall (11)
Dublin Central Tramways horse cars began running from Ranelagh to Clonskea on 17th March 1879, the depot was at Clonskea. The NDST line to Drumcondra was working by early 1877. The DUTC constructed those sections not previously existing, electric cars starting to run from Clonskea via Appian Way and Leeson Street to Nelson Pillar on

The Hill of Howth Work Car, No 11, near Sutton Cross while the line was being dismantled. This multi-purpose vehicle dated from 1903 and boasted an early example of a mobile phone, an instrument was mounted in one of the cabs and could be plugged in anywhere along the line, enabling the crew to communicate with the depot. Howard Woods

1st December 1899. The Drumcondra line via North Frederick Street, electrified on 9th November 1899, was extended to Whitehall on 7th September 1903. Clonskea trams were running to Whitehall by 1930. The symbol was two overlapping yellow discs. The northern section was closed on 1st May 1939, the southern part of the line on 2nd July 1939.

Palmerston Park (12)
Opened on 3rd May 1879 by the DCT from College Green to Palmerston Road via Camden Street and Ranelagh, the route was extended to Nelson Pillar by the DUTC and electrified from 24th October 1899. The line's depot was Clonskea until 1905, thereafter Dartry. The symbol was a white circle, buses replaced trams on the route on 1st January 1939.

Dartry (14)
A line branching from the Terenure tracks at Rathmines, opened on 27th January 1905 using the new depot built at Dartry though Terenure depot was used in later years. Its symbol was a red triangle with a vertical white stripe. Route 14 trams ran through to Glasnevin during the 1930s. The line closed on 31st October 1948

Terenure (15)
Dublin's first line, opened by the Dublin Tramways Company on 1st February 1872. The depot was at Terenure. Electrified from 28th August 1899, the symbol was a red triangle, this line closed on 31st October 1948.

Rathfarnham to Drumcondra (16, 17)
The DCT opened a line via Harold's Cross to Terenure on 22nd June 1879 later extended to Rathfarnham. The NDST line from Nelson Pillar to Drumcondra was opened by 1877. The entire line from Rathfarnham to Drumcondra was electrified from 9th November 1899. Depots at Phibsboro and Terenure served the route whose symbol was a green Maltese cross. Buses replaced by trams on 1st May 1939.

Kenilworth Road to Lansdowne Road (18)
Horse trams began running between Rathmines and Ballsbridge on 22nd August 1898. The electric service from Kenilworth Road to Lansdowne Road commenced on 12th October 1899 using cars from Ballsbridge depot which bore the symbol of a white square. The line closed on 1st December 1940.

Rialto to Glasnevin (19, 20)
The NDST line from Nelson Pillar to Glasnevin opened on 10th December 1876 with cars from Phibsboro depot. The Dolphin's Barn line developed from the former DCT Rathfarnham route opened from Leonard's Corner in February 1896. Electrified from 4th December 1899, it was extended from

Botanic Avenue to Ballymun Road. The Rialto extension opened on 20th May 1905. The symbol was a brown lozenge. The Rialto extension closed in February 1938, the rest of the line following on 5th March 1939.

Inchicore (21)
This NDST line was in full operation by July 1878. Electrified from 4th September 1899, the line closed on 4th February 1940. Its symbol was a brown oval.

Kingsbridge to Hatch Street (22)
This DTC line opened on 3rd June 1872 and was electrified on 16th January 1900. The depot up to 1928 was Victoria Quay and afterwards Conyngham Road. The symbol was a white square. The early abandonment took place on 30th March 1929.

Parkgate Street to Ballybough (23)
The service from Parkgate Street ran over existing lines to the junction of Capel Street and Parnell Street, then over new line to Ballybough. Opened on 1st October 1900 and closed on 16th April 1938, Victoria Quay and latterly Conyngham Road depots provided the trams which carried the symbol of two red diamonds.

O'Connell Bridge to Parkgate Street (24)
A Dublin Tramways line which opened on 16th April 1874. Electrified from 18th October 1899 and closed on 16th April 1938, the route symbol was a white square, borne by cars from Victoria Quay and Conyngham Road depots.

O'Connell Bridge to Lucan (25, 26)
The 3ft gauge Dublin & Lucan Steam Tramway opened from Parkgate Street to Palmerstown in June 1881 and to Lucan on 17th February 1883. Electrified and regauged to 3ft 6in, as the Dublin & Lucan Electric Rail-

The four terminal and two through tracks at Nelson Pillar are apparent in this view from the top of the monument which also shows four of the five types still in use at the end of tramway operation in Dublin. No 112, on the left, was one of the four Bogie Balcony Standards built in 1924. Bogie Luxury Saloon No 299, next to it, was built in 1932. The two single truck vehicles to the right are Nos 17 of 1925 and Luxury Saloon No 176 of 1932. F N T Lloyd Jones

way it re-opened on 8th March 1900. Closed on 29th January 1925, the line was rebuilt to 5ft 3in gauge by the DUTC, opening to Chapelizod on 14th May 1928 and Lucan on 27th May. The line closed 12th April 1940.

College Green to Drumcondra via Capel Street
This NDST line was fully operational in 1877. Electrified from 5th January 1900, its trams came from Phibsboro depot. Abandoned on 21st March 1918, a partial service was briefly reinstated in 1922 possibly under the route number, 27. Its symbol was an inverted white ace of spades.

Nelson Pillar to Dollymount (13, 28, 29, 30)
A Dublin Tramways line from Clontarf to Amiens Street opened on 31st May 1873 and to Nelson Pillar by September of that year. The Dollymount to Annesley Bridge section was electrified on 11th November 1897, the remainder of the line to Nelson Pillar on 20th March 1898. Cars operated from Clontarf depot. The route symbol for the line which closed on 31st May 1938, was a green shield.

Howth (31)
The Clontarf & Hill of Howth Tramroad line from Dollymount to the East Pier at Howth opened on 26th July 1900. Operated as an extended part of the DUTC system, the route was abandoned on 29th March 1941.

Appendix Two

ROLLING STOCK CATALOGUE

Section One

ORIGINAL ELECTRIC FLEET
1896 - 1903

Thirty-seven Cars built by Milnes:
Nos 1-32 (1896) and **41-45** (1898) were 53-seaters (29/24). Nos 1-20 & 41-15 had four windows, 21-32 had five; Nos 21-32 were known as Clontarf cars. Nos 1-20 & 41-45 were ordered by DSDT. All were originally on Peckham trucks. Nos 2, 3, 20 and 24 later received DuPont trucks; 5, 6, 8, 16, 18, 29, 42 and 44 received DUTC trucks. No 18 also ran for a time on Brill bogies.

All except eight – Nos 1, 19, 22, 23, 25, 27, 28 and 30 – were later vestibuled, their upper deck (outside) seating being increased by four. In 1904 Nos 29 and 44 were fitted with top covers, the first Dublin cars to be so equipped. The first Milnes car replaced was No 3 (1912), the last, No 45 in 1933.

Five Cars built by London North Metropolitan
Nos 56-60 (1898), ordered by DSDT, were 54-seaters, originally on Peckham trucks; No 58 was briefly DuPont (1905). All except No 59 were later vestibuled, seating 58. First to be replaced was No 60 in 1918, the last No 57 in 1934.

Fifty Cars built in the United States of America
Nos 121-170 (1899) were on Peckham trucks, but Nos 121, 136 and 155 were later converted to DuPont. No 160 may have received a DUTC truck. 18 are recorded as being vestibuled: Nos 123, 129, 130, 133, 135, 138, 140, 141, 143, 148, 150, 153, 154, 155, 159, 160, 166 and 170. The first of these cars replaced was No 134 in 1918; the last in passenger service was No 140, renumbered 157 and top-covered, which lasted until c1939.

Table 1A:
Fifty-two Cars built by the DUTC

33	50	103	257	264	276	282	288
34	51	104	258	265	277	283	289
35	52	105	259	266	278	284	290
38	99	106	260	267	279	285	291
39	100	107	261	268	280	286	292
46	101	108	262	275	281	287	293
47	102	191	263				

Nos 33, 34 and 35 were built in 1897 and those in the following ranges in the years indicated. **1898** 38-52; **1899** 191; **1901** 257-280; and **1902** 281-293. Except No 46 (DuPont), all up to and including No 191 originally had Peckham trucks; No 47 received a DUTC c1915. Nos 257-268 and 275-293 originally had DuPont trucks. Nos 257-262, 288, 289, 291 and 292 later received DUTC trucks, some subsequently going on to Peckhams. No 262 ran experimentally on Brill bogies (1907), No 286 on a Barber radial six-wheeled truck (1912).

Cars numbered lower than 191 recorded as receiving vestibules are Nos 38, 46, 47, 103, 104 and 108. All the others were built with vestibules; Nos 257-262, 286 and 291-293 were fitted with DUTC top covers in 1905.

Nos 99-108 had five-window bodies, the others four. The first of these cars to be withdrawn were Nos 50 and 276 in 1918, the last was No 47, renumbered 138 in 1925 and replaced in 1932.

Table 1B:
Thirty-four Cars built by Browne of Brunswick Street:

61	88	94	173	177	200	204	271
62	89	95	174	178	201	205	272
63	90	171	175	179	202	269	273
86	92	172	176	180	203	270	274
87	93						

Nos 61-63 were delivered in 1898; Nos 86, 171-180, 200-205 and 269-275 in 1900; Nos 87-90 in 1902 and Nos 92-95 in 1903. All of these cars were on Peckham trucks. Nos 86, 93-95, 171, 176 and 178 are recorded as being vestibuled between 1911 and 1921; these cars had 54 seats when new, increasing to 58 when vestibuled. Nos 269-274 were built with vestibules and had 62 seats. The first of these cars to be replaced were Nos 63, 89 and 174 in 1918, the last was No 176, scrapped as No 276 in 1939. It was renumbered twice, being No 9 in 1932-33. (See Section 8)

Table 1C:
Eighty-six former DUTC horse trams
Original numbers and building dates were:

2	Jun 91	80	Mar 91	120	Oct 90	168	Nov 94
4	Dec 90	81	Jun 90	121	Dec 89	169	Nov 94
6	Sep 89	83	Nov 94	122	Mar 91	170	May 95
12	Oct 89	84	Jun 95	123	Mar 91	171	Apr 96
15	Dec 94	86	Jun 95	124	May 92	172	Jun 96
17	Apr 90	87	Jun 91	125	Dec 91	173	Jun 96
18	Dec 90	88	Apr 96	126	Dec 91	174	Jun 96
20	Oct 94	89	Jun 95	135	May 92	175	Jun 96
21	Jul 89	91	Jun 91	155	Dec 93	176	Aug 96
23	May 91	96	May 96	156	Dec 93	177	Sep 96
31	May 91	101	Apr 96	157	Feb 94	178	Sep 96
46	Dec 94	102	Aug 96	158	Mar 94	179	Nov 96
48	Nov 90	103	Dec 94	159	Mar 94	180	Nov 96
57	Jun 90	104	Jun 95	160	Apr 94	181	Dec 96
63	Dec 89	105	Oct 95	161	Apr 94	182	Dec 96
66	Jun 89	106	Dec 94	162	Jun 94	183	Dec 96
71	Dec 95	107	Nov 95	163	Jun 94	184	Dec 96
72	Apr 94	108	Dec 95	164	Jun 94	185	Apr 97
73	Dec 95	110	Dec 89	165	Jun 94	186	Apr 97
77	May 90	113	Oct 91	166	Jun 94	187	May 97
78	Dec 90	117	Jun 91	167	Oct 94	188	Jun 97
79	Jun 91	119	Jun 91				

No 171, originally No 95, was renumbered in May 1896. The new numbers of these cars as electrics is given in Table 1D.

Table 1D:
Eighty-six Horse Cars rebuilt as Electrics
(H = Horse No, E = Electric No):

E	H	E	H	E	H	E	H
36	126	78	48	119	174	228	117
37	21	79	57	120	71	230	180
40	6	80	161	181	169	231	101
48	31	81	2	182	123	234	188
49	66	82	163	183	72	235	46
53	87	83	77	184	165	236	107
54	158	84*	79	185	164	237	181
55	119	85	81	186	12	238	156
64	18	91	187	187	177	244	15
65	135	96	20	188	104	245	88
66	166	97	102	190	173	246	103
67	110	98	113	193	105	247	106
68	89	109	63	209	183	248	186
69	83	110	121	213	168	249	108
70	55	111	125	214	167	250	185
71	162	112	120	217	176	251	80
72	159	113	157	218	84	252 †	4
73	124	114	178	221	78	253 †	184
74	86	115	170	222	179	254 †	7
75	171	116	122	226	175	255	91
76	96	117	172	227	23	256	182
77	160	118	73				

* No 84 destroyed by fire 1899; number re-allocated to motorised trailer 34 (See table 1E); † denotes single-decker

Cars 36 and 37 were converted in 1897; unvestibuled former horse cars retained their original seating capacity of 46. Taking lowest and highest numbers for each batch, the balance were dealt with in the following years: 1898 – Nos 40-98 (32 cars); 1899 – Nos 109-193 (22 cars); 1900 – Nos 209-256 (30 cars). All up to No 228, plus 236, 237 and 238, were on Peckham trucks, the remainder on DuPont.

Nos 37, 40, 48 and 49 were later vestibuled. All former horse cars with numbers from 226 onwards, except 252-254, were vestibuled on conversion. Vestibuled ex-horse cars had 50 seats. In addition to cars 252-254, rebuilt directly from horse traction to electric 24-seat single-deckers, the following were later rebuilt as single-deckers: 49 (1904), 234 (1908) and 246 (by 1918). The first normal replacements for former horse cars appeared in 1910, the last in 1932 (No 245). No 72 was destroyed during Easter Week, 1916.

Table 1E:
Thirty motorised Milnes trailers
(E = Electric Car No, T = Trailer No):

E	T	E	T	E	T	E	T
84	34	199	54	216	40	232	35
189	23	206	28	219	52	233	48
192	33	207	37	220	31	239	36
194	24	208	30	223	49	240	32
195	51	210	38	224	53	241	46
196	21	211	22	225	25	242	27
197	55	212	29	229	26	243	50
198	39	215	47				

The twelve cars numbered between 84 and 208 emerged in 1899, the 18 numbered between 210 and 243 following in 1900. Nos 225, 240, 242 and 243 were on DuPont trucks, the remainder Peckham.

No 189 was vestibuled in 1923, No 208 by the 1920s and No 223 in 1915. The original seating capacity of these vehicles was 46, increased to 50 on those which were vestibuled; cars from 225 upwards were vestibuled on conversion. The first replacements for these trams appeared in 1918, the last in 1929 (No 243).

Table 1F:
Single-Deckers
There were eight four-wheeled single-deckers, all rebuilt from double-deck. All of these cars, except No 80, worked the Sandymount via Bath Avenue service and all except Nos 252-254 were vestibuled:

18 Rebuilt as single-decker Apr 1930, scrapped 1932
49 Rebuilt as single-decker July 1904, scrapped by 1926
80 Built 1926, using single-deck body of No 252; withdrawn by 1938
234 Rebuilt as single-decker Jan 1909, withdrawn by 1919
246 Rebuilt as single-decker by 1918, replaced by 1925
252 Ex horse car 4, Dec 1900, vestibuled 1904, scr by 1928
253 Ex horse car 184, Dec 1900, vestibuled1904, scr by 1928
254 Ex Horse car (17) Dec 1900, vestibuled 1905, body to 80, 1926

Summary:
The four-wheeled electric cars built up to 1903 comprised:
37 Milnes motor cars 34 Browne (CWW) 85 Ex Horse cars
30 Milnes Trailers 50 American Cars
5 London North Met 52 New DUTC cars **(Total 293 cars)**
Nos 301-312: Preston-built Open-top Howth cars, Peckham bogies – see Section 2, Bogie Cars.

Section Two

BOGIE CARS

Part 2A:
Single-deck
1922 294 **1926** 300 **1931** 320
1924 298 299 **1927** 324 **1932** 321
All seven were former double-deckers rebuilt for Sandymount via Bath Avenue (4) line. All except 324 (open top) were former Balcony cars; single deck seating capacity 33. After closure of Route 4 (July 1932), Nos 320, 321 and 324 were rebuilt as Open-top double-deckers for the Howth line. Nos 294, 298, 299 and 300 were scrapped, their numbers being taken by bogie Luxury cars.

Part 2B:
Open-top
1900 301 302 303 304 305 306 307 308
309 310 311 312
Clontarf & Hill of Howth 70-seaters built in Preston. All originally on reversed Peckham bogies; some later Mountain & Gibson or Hurst, Nelson bogies.
 All fitted with interior partitions 1907-1909.
 No 303 rebuilt following fire in 1902.
 No 307 had top deck glass surrounds 1913-1916.
 No 308 destroyed, North Earl St, Easter Week, 1916.

New DUTC vehicles replaced five of these cars as follows:
1920 307 308 **1923** 303 **1925** 302
1926 311

No 311 retained the roof of its predecessor. The remainder were rebuilt to the DUTC's Standard four-window pattern, retaining the original frames, in the following years:
1920 301 312 **1921** 306 **1922** 304 305
1924 309 **1925** 310

DUTC-built
1907 324 Brill 22E bogies; single-deck 1927-1932; rebuilt 1932 as open-top
1932 320 231 rebuilt from single-deckers, originally Balcony cars

Part 2C:
Balcony Cars
Preston-built cars, DUTC top covers
1906 294 295 298 299
1907 297 300 316 317
All originally on Peckham bogies without track brakes, some later altered to Hurst Nelson or Mountain & Gibson. 71seats

(40/31). Roof extended full length of car: 295 (1914), 296 (1922), 297 (1921). Rebuilt as single-deckers: 294 (1922), 298 (1924), 299 (1924), 300 (1926). All seven numbers taken by new Luxury cars 1931-1933 (See Part 2E)

Built by DUTC at Spa Road
1906 313 314 315
1907 318 319 320 321 322 323
1908 325 326 327 328 329 330
1910 79 81 83 85 183 231
1911 64 70 71 113 117 220
1912 3 91 185
1917 72
1918 221
Nos 313-315, 318-323 and 325-330 originally on Mountain & Gibson bogies, some later on Hurst Nelson. All others Hurst Nelson. Nos 79, 81, 313-315, 318-323, 325 originally had short Balcony roofs, extended to full length on 79 (1930), 81 (1929) 322 (1930) and 325 (1930). No 313 received a totally enclosed Standard Saloon top cover in 1929. No 314 replaced by Bogie Standard Saloon 1929. Rebuilt as single-deckers 320 (1931), 321 (1932). Both again later rebuilt as Open-toppers (See Part 2B). Replaced by Bogie Luxury Cars: 326, 327 (1936), 329, 330 (1934).

DUTC Standard Balcony Cars:
1924 82 112 214 228
All on Hurst Nelson bogies. 71-Seaters (40/31)

Part 2D:
DUTC Standard Saloons
1925 224 **1926** 218
1928 252 253 254 255 278 284 314
1929 181 184 313
All on Hurst Nelson bogies. Nos 218 and 224, described in the repair books as 76-seaters, had longitudinal seating on their lower decks. No 313 was the prototype 1906 Balcony bogie car with a new saloon top, and retained longitudinal seating downstairs. The other Bogie Standards had two and one seating downstairs, making them 46/28 (plus the moveable seat).

Part 2E:
Luxury Cars
1931 178 273 280 316
1932 295 297 298 299
1933 294 296 300
1934 93 108 159 317 329 330
1936 326 327
All on Hurst Nelson bogies. These cars were all 74 seaters (44/30) except 326 and 327 (76-seaters, 44/32). No 294 had high roof domes. Nos 326 and 327 had their destination and number scrolls recessed behind the upper deck windscreens.

Section Three

FOUR-WHEEL CARS BUILT 1918 - 1923

Tables listing 161 four-wheeled cars, with later modifications, built at Spa Road between 1918 and 1923

Table 3A:
Open-top Cars
1918	25	50	60	63	78	89	102	131
	134	163	174	191	194	272	276	282
1919	12	16	18	23	24	27	28	30
	32	33	34	35	42	51	52	53
	57	59	61	88	95	100	101	124
	125	126	128	132	136	137	144	145
	150	153	155	165	172	179	180	200
	201	234*	274	280				

1920	1	19	22	39	48*	87	90	92*
	105	107	122	127*	147	149	152	156
	157	161	164	170	173	177	202	203
	225*	230*	232*	236*	238*	239		
1921	62	92*	99	103*	110*	120*	139	141
	169	192*	205*	226*	233*	237*	241*	244*
	250*	251*	275*					
1922	96	133*	151	175*	187*	197*	235*	242
	248*	270						
1923	94*	142*						
Notes: No 25 retained five windows after rebuilding. Ninety of these cars incorporated parts from their predecessors, the 31 completely new vehicles being denoted by asterisks. All these Open-top trams are believed to have retained their original trucks except No 47 and 53 which were on Brill 21E.

Table 3B:
Thirty-three open cars received top covers from Standard Balcony cars (Section Four) later fitted with new saloon tops. The transfers were as follows, Ex denoting the car from which the top cover came.
	No	Ex	No	Ex	No	Ex	No	Ex
1927	48	222	107	74	142	209	151	168
	187	160	234*	198	238	118		
1928	94	29	110	219	133	44	225	259
	226	170	237	171	241	162	244	36
	248	67	250	7				
1929	39	53	95	129	120	217	122	90
	128	58	155	291	161	8	175	269
	232	116	236	279	275	260		
1930	42	265	134	100	137	124	156	54
	165	125	191	127				
* No 234 later received another top cover, from Car No 61, in November 1938.

Table 3C:
Fifteen open-top cars received new top covers
1925 166*
1929 16 141 251 270
1930 27 157 163 164 180
1931 50 61 150 177 230
Three Open-top cars received top covers from scrapped Balcony cars: 166 (ex 292) in 1925; 225 (ex 259) in 1928 and 271* (ex 293) in 1925. Cars marked * were rebuilt or renumbered – see Section 8.

Table 3D:
Forty Balcony Cars (1918-1922)
1918	63	257	259	266	268			
1919	55	68	84	98	216	288	290	
1920	66	69	76	115	207	210	256	267
	281							
1921	75	77	119	182	188	195	204	211
	212	213	227	258	261	262	286	289
1922	65	186	190					

Table 3E:
Twenty-seven Balcony cars had their route number plates replaced by roller blinds as follows:
39	Oct 36	137	Sep 36	187	Mar 37	238	Nov 34
50	Apr 37	151	Dec 38	190	Aug 36	241	Feb 37
77	Dec 36	155	Sep 36	211	Oct 36	244	Jun 37
120	Mar 37	156	Apr 36	213	May 37	261	Feb 37
122	Nov 36	164	Nov 33	216	Jul 37	262	Dec 36
128	Oct 36	180	Apr 37	226	Jan 38	288	May 37
134	May 36	182	Nov 36	227	Sep 38		
By the mid-1930s, all four-wheel Balcony cars were on Brill 21E trucks, except No 137 which retained its Peckham.

Section Four	Section Five	Section Six

SINGLE-TRUCK TOP COVERED CARS BUILT 1922 - 1936

Table 4A:

Thirty-Three Standard Balcony Cars Built 1922-4

1922	8						
1923	36	44	54	58	67	74	90	124
	129	160	162	198	265	269	291
1924	7	29	53	100	116	118	125	127
	168	170	171	209	217	219	222	260
	279

All these cars were on Brill 21E trucks. They were 58-seaters (34/24).

Table 4B:

The 33 cars in Table4A later received new saloon top covers as follows:

1927	74	118	160	168	198	209
1928	7	29	36	44	67	162	170	171
	219	222
1929	8	53	58	90	116	125	129	217
	260	269	279	291
1930	54	100	124	127	265

As rebuilt, they were 62-seaters (38/22)

Table 4C:

Fifty-Eight Standard Saloons Built 1924-1929

1924	111
1925	5	17	109	114	192	193	199	223
	229	246	277	292	293
1926	2	10	11	15	20	21	24	47
	49	59	97	144	146	154	174	247
	263	264	283	285
1927	6	14	37	38	40	46	60	73
	106	121	189	194	206	208	240	249
	287
1928	87	130	136
1929	158	215	243	259

All these cars were on Brill 21E trucks. Their seating capacity was 62 (38/24). Nos 10, 11 and 47 had two and one transverse seating on the lower deck.

Table 4D:

Thirty-Seven Luxury Cars Built 1931-1936

1931	26	35	41	131	153	196
1932	31	78	96	138	176	197	235	242
	245
1933	9	13	43	135	140	148
1934	45	56	104	123	266	268
1935	12	22	23	51	57	132
1936	102	103	167	205

All of these cars were on Maley and Taunton swing-link trucks except 266 and 268 which were Brill 21E. Nos 13, 43, 135, 140 and 148 had higher and more rounded domes then the other Luxury cars. Seating capacity of single-truck Luxury cars was 60 (38/22). No 13 was later converted to longitudinal seating on the lower deck.

COMPOSITION OF FINAL DUTC PASSENGER TRAMCAR FLEET c1937

Single-deck Storm Car (1)

80	Clontarf, for sea front service

Four-wheel Open-top Cars (39)

1	4	18	19	25	28	30	32	33
34	52	62	86	88	89	92	99	101
105	126	139	143	145	147	149	152	169
172	173	179	200	201	202	203	233	239
272	274	276

Bogie Open-top Cars (15)

301	302	303	304	305	306	307	308	309
310	311	312	320	321	324

Four-wheel Balcony Cars (87)

16	27	39	42	48	50	55	61	63
65	66	68	69	75	76	77	84	94
95	98	107	110	115	119	120	122	128
133	134	137	141	142	150	151	155	156
157	161	163	164	165	166	175	177	180
182	186	187	188	190	191	195	204	207
210	211	212	213	216	225	226	227	230
232	234	236	237	238	241	244	248	250
251	256	257	258	261	262	267	270	271
275	281	286	288	289	290

Bogie Balcony Cars (28)

3	64	70	71	72	79	81	82	83
85	91	112	113	117	183	185	214	220
221	228	231	315	318	319	322	323	325
328

Four-wheel Standards (91)

2	5	6	7	8	10	11	14	15
17	20	21	24	29	36	37	38	40
44	46	47	49	53	54	58	59	60
67	73	74	87	90	97	100	106	109
111	114	116	118	121	124	125	127	129
130	136	144	146	154	158	160	162	168
170	171	174	189	192	193	194	198	199
206	208	209	215	217	219	222	223	229
240	243	246	247	249	259	260	263	264
265	269	277	279	283	285	287	291	292
293

Bogie Standards (12)

181	184	218	224	252	253	254	255	278
284	313	314

Four-wheel Luxury Cars (37)

9	12	13	22	23	26	31	35	41
43	45	51	56	57	78	96	102	103
104	123	131	132	135	138	140	148	153
167	176	196	197	205	235	242	245	266
268

Bogie Luxury Cars (20)

93	108	159	178	273	282	282	294	295
296	297	298	299	300	316	317	326	327
329	330

Depots

Sandymount	Clonskea	Inchicore
Ballsbridge	Donnybrook	Conyngham Road
Blackrock	Dartry	Cabra
Dalkey	Terenure	Clontarf

WITHDRAWALS 1935 - 1945

1935	**Open-top Single Truck**	126		
	Balcony Single Truck	166		
1936	**Open-top Single Truck**	86	233	239
1937	**Open-top Single Truck**	25	30	32
	34	105		
	Balcony Single Truck	76		
1938	**Single-decker**	80		
	Open-top Single Truck	1	4	18	19
	28	33	52	88	89	92	99	101
	143	145	147	149	152	169	172	173
	179	200	203	272
	Balcony Single Truck	27	42	61	66
	98	107	137	156	204	210
	Balcony Bogie Cars	315	318	319	322
	325
1939	**Open-top Single Truck**	62	139	274	276
	Balcony Single Truck	39	48	50	55
	77	94	115	120	122	128	134	141
	142	150	155	163	164	175	177	180
	182	186	187	188	190	191	195	211
	213	216	225	230	232	236	237	238
	241	244	250	251	257	258	261	261
	267	271	275	281	286	288	290
1940	**Balcony Single Truck**	16	63	65	68
	69	75	84	95	110	119	133	151
	157	161	165	207	212	226	227	234
	248	256	270	289
	Standard Single Truck	2	5	7	11
	14	15	20	21	24	29	36	37
	38	40	47	53	58	59	67	74
	90	97	106	11	114	116	118	121
	124	125	127	130	136	144	146	158
	162	168	170	171	189	192	198	206
	208	217	219	222	223	229	240	247
	249	260	263	264	265	269	277	283
	285	292	293
	Bogie Open-top	320	324
1941	**Bogie Open-top**	301	302	303	304
	305	306	307	308	309	310	311	312
	321
1942	**Bogie Balcony Cars**	3	85	91	183
By 1942	**Single Truck Luxury Cars**	12	13	22
	35	43	45	56	103	196	235
1944	**Bogie Balcony Cars**	64	323
	Bogie Standard	313	

Notes:

No 313 was scrapped at Ballsbridge by 1945.

No 323 exchanged numbers with 113.

It is possible that some of the withdrawn Luxury Saloons may have returned briefly to service.

Trams were frequently left lying out of service for some time before being officially withdrawn.

Section Seven	Section Eight

119 TRAMS TAKEN OVER BY CIE IN 1945

CAR RENUMBERINGS AND TRUCK EXCHANGES

Four-wheeled Cars

Standards (28)

6*	8	10	17	44	46	49	54	60
73	87	100	109	129*	154*	160	174	193*
194	199	209	215	243	246*	259	279	287
291								

Luxury Cars (37)

9	12	13	22	23	26	31*	35	41
43	45	51	56	57	78	96	102	103
104	123	131*	132*	135	138	140*	148	153
167	176*	196	197	205*	235	242	245	266*
268*								

Bogie Cars

Balcony Trams (17)

70	71	72	79	81	82	83	112	113
117	185	214	220	221	228	231	327	

Standards (11)

181	184	218	224	252	253	254	255	278
284	314							

Luxury Cars (20)

93	108	159	178	273	280	282	294	295†
296	297	298	299	300	316	317	326	328
329	330							

Of the single-truck cars, 23 Standards and 29 Luxury cars were scrapped at Terenure following the closure of the Dartry and Terenure routes on 31st October 1948.

*These five Standard and eight Luxury single-truck cars were transferred to the Dalkey line and scrapped following closure of that service on 9th July 1949.

† Bogie Luxury car No 295 (fire damaged) was scrapped at Terenure in 1948. The other 47 bogie cars lasted until July 1949. Following final abandonment, scrapping was carried out at Ballsbridge and Blackrock.

Works Cars

Water Car 4	Haulage Wagon 24	Engineering Car 31
Stores Wagon 51	Grinder 73	Directors' Car

No 31 was scrapped following closure of the Permanent Way Yard at Donnybrook in 1947. Nos 24 and 51 were scrapped by 1949; No 73 was scrapped at Blackrock in 1949. The Directors' Car was sold complete to a Dalkey resident in 1950.

Table 8A:
Cars Renumbered:

No	Year	New No	Date	Notes
3	1896		1912	
7	1896	43	1924	A
9	1900	276	1933	B
10	1925	46		L
13	1896	201	1932	A, D
17	1896	158	1924	A
43	1896	18	1933	
45	1896	149	1933	
47	1898	138	1925	A, C
53	1919	93	1924	A
56	1898	272	1934	
59	1919	191	1926	A
78	1918	157	1926	A
81	1898	33	1909	A
90	1920	159	1922	A
100	1919	46	1923	A
124	1919	4	1922	
127	1899	239	1912	A
127	1920	166	1924	A, F
138	1898	134	1932	A, C, N
140	1899	157	1933	N
142	1899	143	1923	A
147	1920	188	1932	K
160	1899	38	1923	
170	1920	41	1924	A
176	1900	9	1932	A, B
188	1920	147	1932	A, K
192	1921	271	1925	A, E
204	1900	167	1921	A
232	1896	96	1920	
254	1900	80	1926	
259	1901	78	1918	G
272	1918	251	1933	A, H
287	1922	257	1926	A, J
125	1919	108	1923	A
323	1907	113	1944	M

Key:
No = Original Number, followed by year in which car was built; New Number is followed by year in which car was renumbered

Notes:
A Indicates body only transferred.
B No 176 was renumbered twice, first to 9, later became 276.
C No 47 was renumbered twice, first to 138, later became 134.
D Later became Stores Wagon No 51.
E Also received top cover from No 293.
F Received top cover from No 292 (of 1905) and truck from No 2 (of 1896), in 1925.
G Less top cover which went to No 225.
H Body of No 272 combined with truck and top cover of No 251.
J Body of No 287 combined with truck and top cover of No 257.
K A straight body exchange between Nos 147 and 188, the latter retaining the top cover.
L Exchanged identity with No 46 during 1940s: change discovered when body 46 dismantled in 1978.
M Renumbered when original No 113 scrapped in 1944
N Retained Top Cover.

Table 8B:
Truck Exchanges

Ex	Type	To	Year	Notes
2	DuPont	166	1925	
3	DuPont	155	1913	
12	Peckham	270	1903	
17	Peckham	90	1911	
18	Brill	11	1909	A
24	Peckham	260	1905	
32	Peckham	49	1912	
35	Peckham	231	1910	
44	Peckham	262	1908	
58	Peckham	218	1908	
69	Peckham	194	1913	
71	Peckham	206	1911	
72	Hurst Nelson	280	1930	B
78	Maley & Taunton	176	1948	
82	Peckham	120	1921	
84	Peckham	172	1919	
110	Brill	275	1939	
117	Peckham	18	1909	
127	Brill	154	1942	
128	Brill	234	1927	
142	Brill	128	1928	
154	Brill	127	1942	
155	Peckham	39	1910	
161	Peckham	48	1927	
176	Maley & Taunton	78	1948	
206	Peckham	59	1911	
218	Peckham	254	1905	
221	Peckham	167	1913	
231	DuPont	35	1910	
233	Peckham	238	1927	
238	Brill	233	1927	
254	DuPont	58	1905	
260	DuPont	24	1905	
262	DUTC	261	1906	C
262	DUTC	283	1914	C
262	DUTC	285	1914	C
270	Peckham	12	1903	
275	Brill	110	1939	
286	DuPont	20	1906	
286	Peckham	293	1911	
295	Peckham	294	1914	
307	Peckham	304	1912	
319	Mountain Gibson	315	1908	

Notes:
A The tram No 11 referred to was a Works Car.
B Bogies borrowed temporarily for tests.
C Car No 262 was used for several experiments; not all of its truck changes were fully recorded.

Section Nine

WORKS CARS

DUTC non-passenger trams – maintenance and freight vehicles – were never chronicled fully in the car repair books. Former passenger cars adapted for departmental work are especially difficult to identify; this list relies on surviving records and the memories of people who worked with or observed these vehicles. Following the cessation of goods haulage in 1927, much of the redundant rolling stock was probably scrapped. The Corporation locomotives and wagons are believed to have been scrapped around the same time.

Some conversions had comparatively short careers in their new roles, but their fleet numbers were often transferred to replacement cars. It is almost impossible to establish what works cars existed at any particular time, but a conscientious tester, A McAsey, identified the locomotives (and other support vehicles) working on various dates between October 1934 and July 1935.

The most practical method of cataloguing the vehicles of which details are available is by listing them in numerical order. It should be noted that the prestigious but un-numbered Directors' Tram which was, technically, a Works Car, is not listed here.

1 The first of three open motorised water tanks, referred to as lorries. In service by 1900. Used as a locomotive when required.
2 As No 1, similar remarks apply.
3 As No 1, similar remarks apply.
4 Tower wagon, recorded as having its controllers changed in June 1910.
4 Water lorry, had a cylindrical tank and a full length canopy mounted on a Brill truck. Scrapped 1949, body and tank to a farm at Mellifont Abbey, Co Louth (see photo on page 74).
5 Combined locomotive and site office, sometimes referred to as an attendance wagon. Was repaired in 1907 and 1915. Rebuilt, this loco may have been the one used by the Blessington Company at Terenure. Later renumbered 22 (See below).
6 Sanding wagon, working in 1907. Received a new main motor switch in September 1915.

7 Sanding wagon, recorded as being in service in 1907 and 1914. Peckham truck, B18 controllers.
8 A sanding wagon recorded as being repaired in 1908 and 1914. Peckham truck, B18 controllers.
9 Vacuum car, used to clean car interiors and seats. Recorded as having a BECC truck in 1908.
10 A motorless sand wagon on a BECC truck is recorded as being in service in 1908-1913.
11 Sand car or locomotive. Received Brill truck from car No 18, February 1909. Had also run on Brill bogies ex No 18. A locomotive numbered 11 existed in the mid-thirties.
12 Rail-grinder, motorless, coupled to No 73 in 1940s. Recorded as having a Peckham truck in 1909. Rotary machine for points and crossings.
20 Haulage wagon or locomotive. This vehicle was originally horsetram 101 which became electric car 231 in June 1900. It is recorded as having its interior and roof stripped on 22 September 1910 when it became haulage wagon 20. Its DuPont truck went to car 35 and it received the Peckham truck from car 81.
21 Referred to as ex-horse car. A locomotive bearing this number is on record in the 1930s. A rail grinder bearing this number is also known to have been in service in 1913.
22 Attendance wagon No 5 was renumbered 22. Locomotive. No 22 certainly existed 1933-35. This had a wagon body with a driving cab at each end.
23 Similar to No 22, earliest record is for October 1910 when it had a Peckham truck. Still working during the 1930s.
24 Haulage wagon or locomotive similar to No 22. Earliest reference is for January 1910. Shedded at Ballsbridge, scrapped 1949.
25 Haulage wagon 25 existed 1915. A locomotive numbered 25 and similar to 21-24 is recorded as working in 1933-35.
26 Ash wagon on bogies, referred to in 1914 repair records. This number was also carried by former passenger car 40, used as a stores wagon in the early 1920s. This vehicle may also have carried the number 52.
30S This 1919 Open-top tram, incorporating some parts from the 1896 car of the same number, had the letter S suffixed to its fleet number in the 1930s and served as a departmental vehicle at Conyngham Road.
31 1896 Milnes car, cut down to single-deck in the 30s and lettered 'Engineer's Dept' survived at Donnybrook until the Permanent Way yard was cleared in 1947.

50 Referred to as a new haulage locomotive and as Farmer's car, this vehicle received major repairs in 1914. It was mounted on a Peckham No 10 truck.
51 A stores wagon bearing this number existed in 1912. Incorporating parts from the 1900 Browne car of the same number, Open-top tram No 203 was renumbered 51 after 1933 and served as a stores wagon until 1948.
52 An ash wagon which existed in 1914. It received overhauled motors in 1915 and had its tank or body painted in 1916. See No 26 above.
64 Former horsecar 18 converted to electric traction in 1898 and replaced in 1911. Retained as a snowplough at Cabra depot, it was transferred to Donnybrook in May 1914. A subsequent entry records its truck as being of no value, its equipment being fitted to car 47.
70 Locomotive adapted from former passenger car 70 in 1911, still in use hauling cables c1938
71 Locomotive ex-passenger car 71, similar to No 70.
73 Three generations of works cars carried this number. The first reference is for November 1915, when permanent way wagon No 73 had its motors repaired. A stores wagon/works car numbered 73, received the body from car No 222 in 1924. During the thirties, this was replaced by the former passenger car 1 renumbered. Towed grinder 12, scrapped 1949
74 A locomotive recorded as in use 1933-35
75 Tower wagon, ex Dublin & Lucan, mounted on standard gauge truck by DUTC for use on Lucan line
76 Haulage wagon. Existed until c1940, shedded at Cabra depot c1938.
77 Former Open-topper used as stores wagon and breakdown car
78 Tower wagon, Howth line. Latterly mounted on BECC truck.
97 Former unvestibuled passenger car used from c1917 for transport of fish. Scrapped 1925.
98 Described as a Works Dept. car, this was formerly No 210, which was withdrawn from passenger service at an unknown date between 1912 and 1920. Top deck completely removed.
99 Former passenger car No 148, renumbered and used for miscellaneous engineering tasks after 1932. Upperworks removed.
113 Breakdown wagon adapted from the former horsecar 157 which was converted to electric traction and renumbered in 1899. It was shedded at Ballsbridge and underwent repairs in November 1914.

The DUTC had about seventy goods wagons, including flat, sided and tipping vehicles. There were also some cattle trucks. Wagon No 68 survived as a rubbish skip at Spa Road until the sixties.

Goods Wagons with numbers higher than 100 belonged to the Dublin & Blessington company.

This photograph shows one of the three original water lorries at O'Connell Bridge around the turn of the nineteenth century. Unusually for the driver of such a vehicle, the motorman is wearing full uniform. On the Ballast Office in the background, can be seen the time ball, electrically controlled from Greenwich, the dropping of which enabled Dubliners to synchronise their watches. Author's collection

Section Ten

ENGINEERING
MOTOR VEHICLES

The following table, compiled from various sources, lists all motor vehicles known to have been used by the DUTC for tramway maintenance. Starting with the Commer tower wagon No 1 of 1911, a separate fleet numbering system was used for several years, but by 1931 vehicles were often referred to simply by registration or, in the case of former buses, their original fleet numbers. Until the boundary changes of September 1930, more than half of the DUTC's depots lay outside the Dublin City area; at least one vehicle was therefore registered with Dublin County Council, the licensing authority for the Pembroke, Rathmines, Blackrock, Kingstown and Dalkey Urban Districts.

The DUTC's first motor tower wagon outside the Permanent Way yard in Ringsend Road around 1913. A Commer, it was one of the most highly regarded vehicles of its day, the marque being widely sold in Ireland by Thompson's who traded as the Dublin Motor Company. Solid tyres and chain drive were common on commercial vehicles for many years, pneumatics and shaft drive not becoming almost universal until after the Great War. Apart from the absence of a cab, note-worthy features include a second bench for the crew, a single headlamp and a bulb horn. The gate pier behind the wagon was still in position in 1999. Author's collection

ZI 2136, ZI 5826 and ZI 6558 were among nearly 80 buses acquired by the DUTC in 1934 but not renumbered or placed in service. They were adapted for tramway maintenance purposes as a temporary measure pending the availability of better vehicles.

ZA 243 remained in the Permanent Way Yard at Donnybrook until this was cleared in 1947.

At least one of the Dennis Aces was rebuilt as a tower wagon, the others were mobile welding plants.

ZA 1717 remained on tramway-related and Permanent Way duties for some time after the last tramway closure. Well cared for by its driver, it was known as 'Wally Murphy's Lorry'.

L1 and L2 were renumbered W1 and W2 in 1948. When no longer required for tramway work, they were employed as support vehicles in the Mechanical Engineer's Dept. (Road) and withdrawn in 1960.

DUTC buses were numbered in a straight series until 1936, when an alphanumerical system was adopted. New numbers (where allocated) are given opposite followed by original numbers in brackets. In relation to the vehicles shown as being scrapped in June 1953, it should be noted that scrapping often took place long before being officially recorded, and withdrawn stock routinely remained in the scrapyard for a long time after withdrawal.

No	Make	Regn	Year	Purpose	Notes
1	Commer	RI 2721		Tower Wagon	
2	Unknown				
3	Orwell	IK 2407		Tower Wagon	Battery-electric
		YI 2517			Battery-electric
	Ransomes	YI 5208			Battery-electric
	Commer	YI 7571		Tower Wagon	
	AEC 413	YI 7990	1926	Tower Wagon	32-s Bus C6 (406), converted 1936
	Morris-Commercial	ZI 2136	1928	Arc Welding	14-s Bus, new to SOS, acquired 1934
	Ford	ZI 5826	1931	Arc Welding	14-s Bus, ex Drumcondra OC, acqd 1934
	Chevrolet	ZI 6558	1933	Arc Welding	14-s Bus, ex General
	Dennis 'G'	ZA 243	1933		20-s Bus G13 (686), ex General
	Dennis 'G'	ZA 1125	1933		20-s Bus G14 (629) ex General. Scrapped 6 Feb 37
	Dennis 'Ace'	ZA 1589	1933		20-s Bus K3 (657) ex Dublin Bus Co Scr Jun 53
	Dennis 'Ace'	ZA 1664	1933		20-s Bus K1 (528) ex Savoy Scrapped Jun 53
	Dennis 'Ace'	ZA 1715	1933		20-s Bus K2 (667) ex Dublin Bus Co
	Dennis 'Ace'	ZA 1716	1933		20-s Bus K4 (667) ex Dublin Bus Co
	Ford	ZA 1717	1933	P. Way Lorry	20-s Bus 662, ex Dublin Bus Co Scrapped Jun 53
	Dennis 45-cwt	ZA 3779	1934	Tower wagon	Chassis Purchased New
L1	Leyland Lion LT5A	ZA 7553	1936	P. Way Lorry	Rebuilt from DUTC Bus N47 (524), 1943
L2	Leyland Lion LT5A	ZA 7551	1936	P. Way Lorry	Rebuilt from DUTC Bus N42 (521), 1944

Note: Following withdrawal, the chassis and tower of YI 7571 remained first at Donnybrook Garage and then at Inchicore Works for lamp maintenance until 1966.

Appendix Three

ROLLING STOCK ALBUM

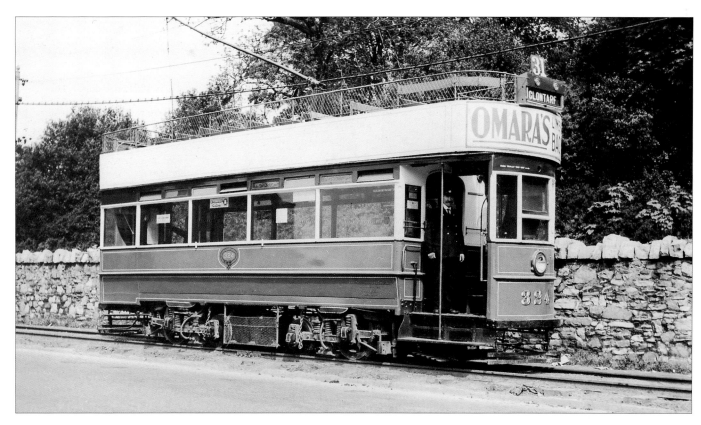

BOGIE TRAMS

Above: **No 324, built in 1907, was at the Dublin Exhibition from May to November in that year, entering service on 24th December. In April 1927, it became a single decker for the Bath Avenue line, on which it operated until that service was closed in July 1932. It was then rebuilt as an open-top 75-seater for the Howth line, returning to service in September 1932 and based at Clontarf depot until 1938 when it was transferred to Conyngham Road. To Dublin tramway staff No 324 was a source of pride, evident in the face of the motorman who posed for W. A. Camwell's photograph. With the other fourteen Howth open-toppers (301-312, 320, 321), this tram was broken up at Donnybrook in 1941.**

Left: **No 308 was a Howth line open-topper built in 1920 All of the original 1900 cars Nos 301-312 were replaced between that year and 1926. These cars, which were**

(continued from page 148)
joined in 1932 by Nos 320, 321 and 324, were all overhauled in the late thirties but withdrawn by 1940. All were scrapped shortly afterwards at Donnybrook, where this photograph was taken. C L Fry

Above left: **Windjammer No 185 was one of nine pre-World War One bogie cars still working in the last days of the Dalkey line. One of three similar cars built in 1912, this was one of the few trams painted in a variation of the DUTC green and cream livery. In this version, the cream of the lower deck window surrounds was carried up on to the cantrail, the decency panelling**

of the upper deck being finished in the olive green normally used for the band between decks. This photograph readily conjures up the powerful impression these vehicles would made when travelling at speed. D Coakham

Above right: **Dating from 1918, No 221 was the first Bogie Balcony car to have ventilation louvres instead of winding windows on the upper deck. This tram, seen here in Georges Street Dun Laoghaire, was one of the last five Dalkey Windjammers to be built, the four 1924 examples being even closer to Standard Saloons in general design.** A R Spencer

Below: **The original Luxury Saloon, No 280, emerging from Blackrock depot. The entrance to the original Blackrock and Kingstown horse tram premises, which remained in use up to 1949 and also housed the Blackrock electric substation, can be seen behind the traction pole. The imposing two bay, six track depot capable of housing up to 36 trams was one of two, the other was Dartry, with decorated gables, built by the DUTC in the first decade of the last century. Both are still in use and readily recognisable. Blackrock is occupied by a motor company and Dartry by a firm of consulting engineers.**
F N T Lloyd Jones

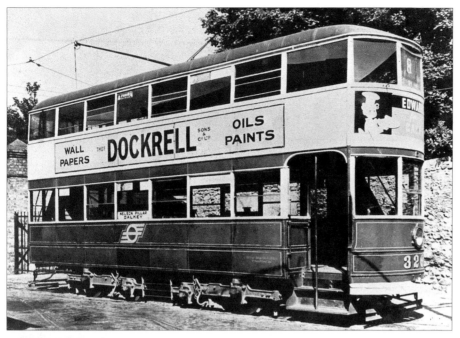

Left: **No 326 a 76 seat car seen in the yard of Blackrock depot, was the second last tram built at Spa Road, emerging on 3rd October 1936. Nos 326 and 327 were the only Bogie Luxury cars to have their destination and route number boxes behind the upper deck windscreens. Both vehicles were in service until the closure of the Dalkey line in 1949. The front advertisement is for Edwards, a once successful chain of cake shops.** CIE, Transport Museum Society of Ireland collection

Centre: **Bogie Luxury Saloon No 327, the last new tram to leave Spa Road works in October 1936, is seen at Nelson Pillar when still nearly new. The trolleys of two other trams, one of which is in the process of being turned, are visible behind it. No 327, which worked until July 1949, was the tram which ran away on Royal Marine Road in Dun Laoghaire in December 1938.** Camwell collection, National Tramway Museum

Bottom: **Bogie Standard No 254 built in 1928 stands in rural surroundings at the Lucan terminus in 1938. The building behind the tram was once a depot of the Dublin & Lucan Electric Railway, whose cars ran beyond this point to a terminus near the Spa Hotel. When the Lucan line closed in April 1940, the Bogie Standards were transferred to the Dalkey line.** Camwell collection, Tramway Museum Society

FOUR-WHEEL CARS

Photographs on opposite page:

Top: **This well-known picture by the famous tramway photographer W A Camwell, whose car is to the right of the picture, shows Standard Saloon No 24 at the Inchicore terminus in 1938. The Black Lion public house is to the left of the picture and around the corner to the right stood Inchicore depot and Spa Road works. An extended bus service replaced the Inchicore trams in February 1940.** Camwell collection, Tramway Museum Society

Bottom: **High domed Luxury Saloon No 148, built in 1933, was recorded in Rathmines in CIE days working on the 14 route to Dartry. This tram was withdrawn in October 1948.** F N T Lloyd Jones

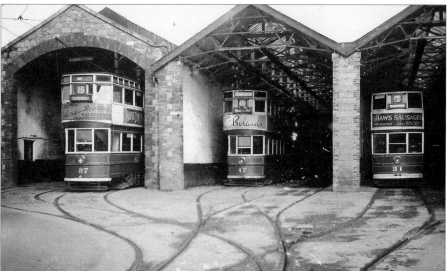

DEPOTS

Top: **Standard Saloon No 2 at Cabra (Phibsboro) depot in 1938, with haulage wagon No 76 and Balcony cars 157 and 142. Both the latter were built as open-toppers in 1920 and 1923, respectively. No 142 received its top cover from No 209 in 1927 when that car became a Standard Saloon. No 157, one of 15 open-top cars fitted with new top covers, left Spa Road as a Balcony tram in December 1930. The shallow traverser pit is visible in front of the trams.** Camwell collection, Tramway Museum Society

Centre: **Standard Saloons No 87 (1928) and No 17 (1925) are seen at Terenure depot along with Luxury Saloon No 31. This was one of the vehicles reprieved for further service on the Dalkey line in October 1948, ending its days as a scrapyard shunter at Blackrock.** A D Packer

Bottom: **Standard Saloon 44, Bogie Standard 284 and Haulage Wagon 24 in Dalkey depot. No 44, built as a Balcony car in 1923 and given a saloon top in 1928, was one of the cars withdrawn around 1942 and used as a source of spares until it was scrapped at Terenure in 1948. No 284 was one of the 1928 Lucan bogies and lasted until closure of the Dalkey line in 1949. Its body has been in store awaiting restoration since 1975. No 24, the last haulage wagon to survive, probably dated from 1910, and was allocated to Ballsbridge, where it was broken up in 1949.** F N T Lloyd Jones

Right: **Staircases removed and platforms sagging, No 33 awaits the end at Donnybrook in 1938, still in the grey livery carried between 1929 and 1935. Official withdrawal of the 39 remaining open-top four-wheelers began in 1935. None received the new green livery and all but four had gone by the end of 1938. No 33 dated from 1919 and incorporated parts from its 1897 Spa Road-built predecessor.** Fayle collection, Irish Railway Record Society

Centre: **Engineering tram No 73, formerly passenger car No 1, the second vehicle to carry this number in the service fleet, was photographed at Donnybrook attached to its grinder, No 12. To the right of the picture can be seen the front of a Dennis tower wagon.** Author's collection

Bottom: **The two three track sheds at Dalkey depot illustrate the differing widths allocated to horse trams and the larger electrics operated by the DUTC. Conditions in a planning permission granted in 2000 required the developer of the property to retain the yard track fan as an historic monument. It is a great pity that no such official importance was attached to the vehicles seen here in the depot when they were withdrawn from service more than 50 years ago.** Author's collection

NELSON PILLAR

Photographs overleaf:

Top: **We conclude this brief photographic section with two fine views taken at Nelson Pillar, the hub of Dublin's tramway system. At Nelson Pillar terminus in 1938, No 111 (The Sergeant), the 1924 prototype Standard Saloon, lays over with its trolley apparently tied down, a frequent sight at the Pillar. Beside it No 21, built in 1926, is ready to go to Clonskea, while Luxury Saloon No 43 is Sandymount bound. On the right, unmistakable with its non-standard livery is the 1912 Dalkey Windjammer No 185. This car ran for 37 years until 1949, while Nos 21 and 111 were both withdrawn in 1940. No 43 had the shortest innings of the four, from 1933 to 1941. Between Nos 21 and 43, one of the Leyland Titans that replaced the Dollymount trams on 1st June 1938 can be seen turning into North Earl Street.** Camwell collection, Tramway Museum Society

Bottom: **Bogie Luxury Saloon No 108 built in 1934 worked the Dalkey route for 15 years. Seen here at Nelson Pillar in 1948, the body of this vehicle stood beside a sports field at Blackrock until 1990. By that time it had suffered from exposure to the elements and vandalism and moreover was land-locked by housing developments. It was destroyed finally by being set on fire.** G S Hearse

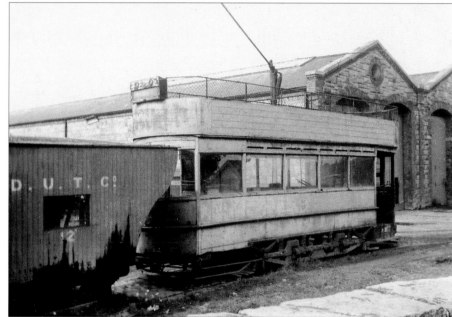

Appendix Four

DUBLIN TRAMWAY TICKETS

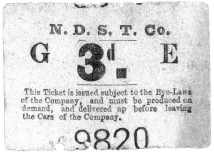

A selection of tickets reproduced at 95% of the original size.

Appendix Five

EPILOGUE AND PROLOGUE

For several years after the 1949 tramway abandonment, the degeneration from which Dublin had been suffering since the early1800s continued apace. The agrarian ethos that dominated official thinking for decades following independence hardly recognised Dublin as part of the much-vaunted Irish nation. It also failed to distinguish the infrastructure and culture of a large city from that of the smallest village. However, not everything was negative; for example, slum clearance continued, but was not completed until the late 1960s.

The new suburban social housing estates, and the even more numerous private ones, were largely reached by extensions of bus routes that had replaced former tram services. Public transport usage increased during the fifties, but an exclusively bus-based system was incapable of coping. And, as in so many other places, the unending spiral of inflation, dearer fares and increasing car ownership in time set the bus on its course to becoming the transport of last resort. At the same time, the inner city slid further into decay: whole streets were abandoned to dereliction or greedy and selective speculators.

In 1954 Ireland's last urban trams, those in Belfast, finally expired after a run-down period of sixteen years. Five years later, the demise of the island's last electric tramway – on the Hill of Howth Tramway – further illustrated the inability of the authorities to identify and improve valuable transport assets. 1968 saw the end of Belfast's splendid trolleybus network, leaving public municipal transport throughout the island of Ireland totally dependent on the bus.

The fifties and early sixties also saw eight of the nine remaining British municipal tramway bastions fall. Five of these had placed fleets of new trams in service in the post war years, but only the truncated Blackpool system survived. But in Europe and further afield, progressive administrators retained and updated their tramway systems. It was becoming apparent already that it was inevitable that in time their re-introduction in places that had banished them would constitute an attractive alternative to the car and a powerful weapon against pollution. This did indeed happen, Manchester being the first city in these islands to welcome back the tram.

For over thirty years in the Irish Republic, peaks of modest prosperity alternated with troughs of deep depression but even during times of relative plenty, successive governments resisted every proposal to invest in transport infrastructure. Campaigners for better public transport were disregarded until increasing traffic congestion reached crisis levels. The development of the electrified DART service between Howth and Bray was a major achievement by those in CIE who persisted in the face of antipathetic vested interests. DART effectively filled the gap left by the closure of the tramways to Howth and Dalkey, and criticism of its worsening overcrowding is in fact due to its success.

Tramway plans for Manchester and other cities inevitably led to fresh thinking in Dublin. A shortlived City Streets Commission, killed off by a singularly uncaring administration in 1987, intended to reintroduce trams to the city centre, a line between Parnell Square and St. Stephen's Green being envisaged initially. 1987 was also the year that saw CIE reconstituted as a holding company with three operating subsidiaries; Dublin Bus enjoying more autonomy than its monolithic predecessor, was able to identify more closely with the city and its needs. The company has invested in quality vehicles, turned out in colourful liveries. It has also tried to sort out a multitude of inherited problems, while simultaneously improving services within prevailing financial and political constraints.

Celebration of Dublin's millennium in 1988, various incentives to encourage urban renewal and a firm resolution to deal with ever worsening traffic congestion led to the decision to reintroduce trams to the city; the scheme was unveiled in February 1993. Transport preservationists derived particular pleasure from this event, DUTC Bogie Standard No 253 from Howth Museum being the vehicle on which the plans were announced, thus bridging the gap between the old and new tramway systems. Carried on a special trailer, No 253 and preserved Bolton class Leyland bus R389 – which had run over the former Terenure (15) tram route for many years – were used very successfully for a several days as part of a high profile public awareness campaign.

As Dublin's traffic problems became ever worse, the Dublin Transportation Initiative was set up. This examined every facet of transport in the Dublin area and in its final report, published in 1995, put forward comprehensive proposals, both immediate and long term, to cope with the traffic and transport crisis. Among the projects suggested was the construction of a light rail or tramway system with three lines: City Centre to Tallaght via Heuston Station, Inchicore and Naas Road, initially known as Line A; City Centre to Cabinteely via South

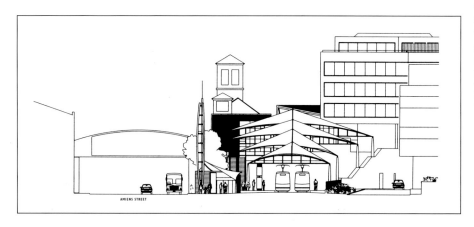

The familiar outline of the Italianate tower at Connolly station in Amiens Street, looms over this drawing of the proposed tram terminus at the station. Trams have not served this location since the early 1940s.
LUAS

Great George's Street, Ranelagh and Dundrum, initially called Line B; and City Centre to Ballymun via Drumcondra. The Tallaght and Cabinteely lines were to be complete by 2000, no date being given for the Ballymun route, and this will probably materialise as part of a proposed new metro system. Changes were made in the routeing of the Tallaght line, relocated between James's Street and Blackhorse Bridge to run via the Grand Canal to Blackhorse Bridge instead of via Emmet Road and Tyrconnel Road, which ran into opposition from local traders. The City Centre-Cabinteely line's original route was altered to run from St. Stephen's Green via Harcourt Street, instead of South Great George's Street to Ranelagh.

Until the 1970s, Tallaght, the outer terminus of Line A, was a small village surrounded by some new private development. Until closure in 1932 it was served by the Dublin & Blessington Steam Tramway, and after that by various bus routes. Dublin Corporation built thousands of houses around Tallaght from around 1970 and plans for better public transport access, including a dedicated busway, were under discussion for several years until the Luas Tramway scheme was put forward.

Sandyford was little more than a hamlet on the road from Dundrum but huge developments, both residential and industrial, began in the 1980s and gathered pace in the following decade. Like Tallaght, the area needed improved public transport and there were several proposals to re-open the Harcourt Street to Bray railway which closed in 1958. Again, the idea of bringing trams back into the Dublin transport was the one that inspired the Luas line to Sandyford.

Late in 1995, a ministerial order established the Dublin Transportation Office to plan, oversee and coordinate transport schemes for the Dublin area. CIE set up the Light Rail Project Office to expedite the tramway scheme. This took some time to get into its stride, its progress frequently delayed by fractious and frivolous objectors. Neither were matters helped by ministerial portfolio changes, opposing political ideologies and partisan lobbying.

Overcoming several obstacles, the Transport (Dublin Light Rail) Act went on the Statute Book in 1996. This set out the procedures to be complied with in planning, constructing and operating tramways. A public inquiry was mandatory and a Light Railway Order had to be obtained from a government department; at first this was the Department of Public Enterprise but following a reallocation of responsibilities it is now a function of the Minister for Transport.

The Light Rail Project Office, which carried a heavy burden in advancing its programme, was subsumed into the Railway Procurement Agency, established by the Transport (Railway Infrastructure) Act of 2001. The project name adopted for the tramway scheme was Luas, the Irish word for speed, and this quickly became as widely recognised and used as DART had become some years earlier. A splendid illustrated history and description of the entire Luas project, written by Stephen Hirsch, was published by the Irish Railway Record Society in May 2005.

Following many setbacks, those charged with reintroducing trams to Dublin eventually saw work getting under way in April 2001. Ansaldo was the main contractor, with sub-contractor Ballast Nedam, while Sinclair Knight Merz was responsible for track and infrastructure. Work included the realignment of public utilities, building new bridges and reconstructing existing ones, erecting two depots, and many ancillary works. Both lines were opened in 2004.

The present city terminus of the Green Line, originally called Line B, is at St. Stephen's Green. It goes along the west side of the Green and through Harcourt Street, at the end of which it turns left and then right to reach the alignment of the former Harcourt Street to Bray railway line. It follows this to beyond Dundrum and currently terminates adjacent to the depot at Sandyford 9km (5.6 miles) from the city centre.

There are four noteworthy structures along the Green Line. First is the viaduct that carries the line over the River Dodder at Milltown. This attractive masonry bridge, known as the Nine Arches, lay disused from December 1958 when the Harcourt Street railway closed.

At Dundrum a bridge was needed to span an extensive and complicated road junction. The design adopted has provided the Green Line with a spectacular cable-stayed bridge, which is now a noted landmark. It has been named, appropriately, after William Dargan, the great engineer, railway contractor and philanthropist, who lived nearby. Immediately on the southern side of this bridge the former Dundrum station building, a protected structure, has survived in good condition. Finally, a little further on, the line passes under Upper Kilmacud Road, which has the only extant road bridge over the route. The Green line opened on 30th June 2004.

There are 13 stops on the Green Line: St. Stephen's Green, Harcourt, Charlemont, Anelaghg, Beechwood, Cowper, Milltown, Windy Arbour, Dundrum, Balally, Kilmacud, Stillorgan and Sandyford. There are park-and-ride facilities at Sandyford, and a 7km extension to Cherrywood is expected to open in 2010.

What was formerly called Line A, which runs for more than 14.5km (9.2 miles) from Connolly Station to Tallaght, is now the Red Line. Its city terminus is on the site of the former ramp at Connolly Station, the concourse of which is reached by escalators. The site of the terminus is on what was formerly a long ramp or roadway leading up to platform level at the station. The removal of this ramp and the demolition of the high wall that separated it from Amiens Street has created a pleasant urban open space.

On leaving Connolly, the line runs through Store Street and on under the Loop Line railway viaduct to Abbey Street. It then continues through a series of streets parallel to the North Quays, serving the Four Courts, Smithfield (a redeveloped urban square and the scene of many public events) and the National Museum (Collins Barracks) before turning across what was formerly Kingsbridge to serve Heuston Station. Red Line trams next run up Steeven's Lane, past St. James Hospital and along the line of a long-closed branch of the Grand Canal, the active main channel of which it follows from

The two Luas lines. Courtesy of LUAS: www.luas.ie

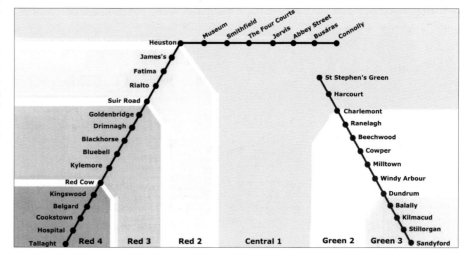

Top: **As yet unnumbered 3000 series car at Red Cow depot, 28th November 2002. Unvestibuled car No 224 from the Transport Museum in background.** Author

Centre: **Green Line car No 4010 at St.Stephen's Green terminus on opening day, 30th June 2004.** Author

Bottom: **Interior view of a Green Line Luas tram.** Author

Suir Bridge to the Naas Road. A length of street track and a central reservation bring the line to the notorious Red Cow junction where the M50 motorway around Dublin connects with the main road to Cork and Limerick.

A dedicated tramway bridge carries the Red Line across the M50, alongside which are the Red Cow Depot and park-and-ride site. The tramway runs beside the M50 to Kingswood where it turns west as far as Cookstown Reservoir. Finally it turns south-eastwards along Cookstown Road and past Tallaght Hospital to its terminus at The Square, adjacent to the eponymous shopping complex and the offices of South Dublin County Council. The Red Line opened on 28th September 2004.

The stops along the Red Line, 23 in number, are: Connolly, Busaras, Lower Abbey Street, Jervis, The Four Courts, Smithfield, Museum, Heuston, James's, Fatima, Rialto, Suir Road, Goldenbridge, Drimnagh, Blackhorse, Bluebell, Kylemore, Red Cow, Kingswood, Belgard, Cookstown, Hospital and Tallaght. A proposed branch of the Red Line will serve the City West complex, located near the Naas Road west of Red Cow.

East of the Red Line's Connolly terminus lies the extensive North Wall area, developed as docks, warehousing, industry and railway yards in the 18th and 19th centuries. Since 1987, this very run-down area has been extensively redeveloped in a similar way to that which has taken place in London and other cities. An extension of the Red Line, expected to open in 2010, will run through this district along Mayor Street, which is parallel to the North Wall Quay. The extension, 1.5km (0.93 miles) will terminate at The Point, a large theatre built in 1878 as a railway depot. It will also run adjacent to the new Docklands railway station.

Construction of a metro that will serve northern and western suburbs as well as the airport and the north Dublin town of Swords is to begin shortly. It will have a close relationship with the Luas system, which will be further enlarged under the government's Transport 21 programme. Work on extending the Green Line to O'Connell Street, expected to begin by 2010, will affect

city's most commercially vital, environ-
lly sensitive and historic core. Mean-
the success of the existing Luas
is very similar to that of the DART –
popular support and a constant strug-
o cope with continually growing num-
of passengers. The tram gongs
nstantly ring out this cheerful rebuke to
he negativity of the Jeremiahs.

The Luas tramways are 1,435mm (4' 8½")
gauge and double track throughout. Current is taken at 10kv ac from the National
Grid to 13 substations. It is then stepped
down through rectifiers to 750v dc and fed
to the overhead, which is supported by
poles with side arms or span wires. Where
possible in the city centre, the span wires are
fixed to buildings.

In February 2008 the Luas fleet consisted
of 40 Alstom SA Citadis articulated trams, 14
on the Green Line and 26 on the Red Line;
all are partially low-floor. The Green Line
cars are 40 metres long, with two end and
three intermediate sections, allowing for 80
seated and 276 standing passengers. The
end sections are 12.5m long with a 11m
intermediate section consisting of two sections, a 4.57m centre vehicle and 6.5m suspended section. The low-floor bogie under
the second centre car has two 120kw motors
and the suspended car is supported by the
centre cars in front of and behind it. The
Green Line trams are numbered 4001-4014.

Twenty-six 30-metre double-articulated cars
were delivered for the Tallaght (Red) Line.
They consisted of two end sections, each
12.5m long with a 4.57m-long centre section.
These trams were mounted on three two-axle
bogies with two 140kw motors. Until 2007,
all these three-section vehicles had 56 seats,
with provision for 190 standees, and were
numbered 3001-3026. During 2007, a programme to lengthen the Red Line trams to
40m was undertaken, converted cars retaining their 30xx fleet numbers.

All the Luas trams run at a maximum
speed of 70kph (43mph) on reserved or seg-
regated track, but are restricted to 50kph
(30mph) for street running. In accordance
with the government's programme for Pub-
lic-Private Partnerships (PPPs), operation of
the Luas system was awarded to Veolia (formerly Connex) for five years, with maintenance entrusted to Alstom for 15 years.

Services on both lines operate from 5.30am
to 12.30am Monday-Friday; first runs are at
6.30am on Saturdays and 7.00am on Sundays. Headways are 5-6 minutes at peak
times, the maximum being 15 minutes late at
night. There are three fare zones on the
Green Line and four on the Red Line. Tickets
are available from vending machines at the
stops or from shops acting as ticket agents.
The variety of season tickets available in 2007
will be expanded with the introduction of a
proposed integrated system covering all
transport modes – buses, trams and trains.

INDEX